THE ECONOMICS OF PUBLIC UTILITY REGULATION

MIT Press Series on the Regulation of Economic Activity
General Editor
Richard Schmalensee, MIT Sloan School of Management

1 *Freight Transport Regulation*, Ann F. Friedlaender and Richard H. Spady, 1981

2 The SEC and the Public Interest, Susan M. Phillips and J. Richard Zecher, 1981

3 *The Economics and Politics of Oil Price Regulation*, Joseph P. Kalt, 1981

4 *Studies in Public Regulation*, Gray Fromm, editor, 1981

5 *Incentives for Environmental Protection*, Thomas C. Schelling, editor, 1983

6 *United States Oil Pipeline Markets: Structure, Pricing, and Public Policy*, John A. Hansen, 1983

7 *Folded, Spindled, and Mutilated: Economic Analysis and U.S. v. IBM*, Franklin M. Fisher, John J. McGowan, and Joen E. Greenwood, 1983

8 *Targeting Economic Incentives for Environmental Protection*, Albert L. Nichols, 1984

9 *Deregulation and the New Airline Entrepreneurs*, John R. Meyer and Clinton V. Oster, Jr., with Marni Clippinger, Andrew McKey, Don H. Pickrell, John Strong, and C. Kurt Zorn, 1984

10 *Deregulating the Airlines*, Elizabeth E. Bailey, David R. Graham, and Daniel P. Kaplan, 1985

11 *The Gathering Crisis in Federal Deposit Insurance*, Edward J. Kane, 1985

12 *Perspectives on Safe & Sound Banking Past, Present, and Future*, George J. Benston, Robert A. Eisenbeis, Paul M. Horvitz, Edward J. Kane, George G. Kaufman, 1986

13 *The Economics of Public Utility Regulation*, Michael A. Crew and Paul R. Kleindorfer, 1987

THE ECONOMICS OF PUBLIC UTILITY REGULATION

M. A. Crew
P. R. Kleindorfer

The MIT Press
Cambridge, Massachusetts

First MIT Press edition, 1986

Printed and bound in Great Britain

Library of Congress Cataloging-in-Publication Data

Crew, Michael A.
  The economics of public utility regulation.

  (MIT Press series on the regulation of economic
activity; 13)
  Bibliography: p.
  Includes index.
  1. Public utilities. 2. Public utilities—Government
policy—United States. 3. Public utilities—Law and
legislation.—United States. I. Kleindorfer, Paul R.
II. Title. III. Series.
  HD2763.C68 1987 338.4′73636′0973   86–10417
  ISBN 0–262–03127–2

Contents

Preface and Acknowledgements   vii

PART I   WELFARE ECONOMIC FOUNDATIONS

1 Background   3
2 Efficiency and Equity Aspects   10

PART II   SURVEY OF THE THEORY OF PEAK-LOAD
          PRICING

3 Deterministic Models of Peak-load Pricing   33
4 Stochastic Models of Peak-load Pricing   56

PART III   PRINCIPLES AND PRACTICE OF
           REGULATION

5 Origin and Operation of Regulation in the USA   93
6 Models of Monopoly Regulation   120
7 Alternative Governance Structures for Natural
    Monopoly   146

PART IV   REGULATED INDUSTRIES

8 Electricity   169
9 Telecommunications   210
10 Gas   235
11 Water Supply   245
12 Implications for Future Research and Policy   263

Notes   268

Appendix   282

References   285

Index   297

Preface and Acknowledgements

The ideas for this book arose out of the work on public utility regulation, public choice and the new institutional economics that we have undertaken jointly and severally since publication of our *Public Utility Economics* in 1979. The period since 1979 has been one of turmoil for public utilities and their regulators. Electric utilities have been plagued with problems of nuclear power with the historic Three Mile Island nuclear accident occuring in March 1979. Since then the electric utility industry has never been the same for regulators and managers. In 1 January, 1984 the greatest corporate divestiture of all time took place as American Telephone and Telegraph (AT&T) divested its local operating companies. In addition, on 1 January, 1984, well-head prices of natural gas were significantly decontrolled. While this pales somewhat compared to the AT&T divesture, it is still a major event with significant implications for the industry. Meanwhile airline rates were completely deregulated when the Civil Aeronautics Board was abolished on 1 January, 1985. The problems associated with nuclear power occurred at the same time as an old technology, cogeneration, was entering something of a revival. This provided a credible alternative, if only on a small scale, to central-station genera-tion. These events all have major implications for the operation and regulation of utilities that were not captured in our earlier book. Such major changes, together with the heightened interest in deregulation, particularly by governments in the USA and the UK, have provided the motivation and background for the present book.

We have been greatly assisted in our research on this book. The Rutgers University Advanced Workshop in Public Utility Economics and Regulations has been useful in providing stimulating ideas for this book. So also have the Annual Rutgers Research Seminars which provided opportunities for us to present our work to persons from disciplines other than economics. Thanks are due to participants and sponsors of these activities. Former Dean of the Rutgers Graduate School of Management, Horace J. De Podwin's interest and encoura-gement, especially in the early stages of these projects, was particularly valuable in providing an excellent climate for such activities to develop.

We have been greatly assisted by our colleagues and coauthors.

Keith Crocker has been especially helpful in his painstaking reading and helpful suggestions on several drafts of the book. His comments have saved us from making some errors and have resulted in new insights and far greater clarity of exposition. Charles Rowley has been a stimulating source of ideas relating public choice and regulation. Comments and discussions with John Dura, Miles Bidwell, Cary Giese, John Kling, Clifford Mastrangelo, Don Schlenger, Gary Davis and Howard Kunreuther have been valuable to us.

We would like to thank Linda Brennan for typing and research assistance, and Lorraine Kenny for typing assistance.

As with our previous book our wives contributed greatly by their support and interest in this endeavour.

MICHAEL A. CREW
PAUL R. KLEINDORFER

Part I

Welfare Economic Foundations

1 Background

In this book we examine some of the important issues of theory and policy in the economics of public utility regulation. Our aim is to employ economic theory to provide an analytical basis for policy evaluation. In this chapter we start by examining briefly the nature of public utility economics and regulation and sketching the contents of the rest of the book.

Public utilities are easily recognised. Gas, electricity, telephone and water are the traditional examples, followed more recently by cable television and waste treatment facilities. The question of whether a company is a public utility is essentially technical, though there is a body of legal and historical precedent to support the view that an industry must be of some public or social significance to be considered a public utility. The technical features defining a public utility are those giving rise to economies of scale in public utilities and their resulting 'natural monopoly' position. The point is intuitively obvious. There are definite cost savings in having only one water main in the street, and similarly with the other utilities. Such economies of scale give rise to the fundamental problem of public utility economics: how to establish institutional arrangements which will take advantage of these economies of scale, but will not involve monopolistic excesses. This problem is not typically left to the operation of unregulated markets, although several innovative proposals have been made for at least partially deregulating public utilities. For example, Demsetz's (1968) suggestion to allow franchise bidding is apparently a means of allowing markets to operate without using regulation. However, for the traditional public utilities, this proposal runs up against the problem of asset specificity. When it comes to rebid for a franchise, because of fixed plant, such as that buried in the streets, replacement is not feasible. In such cases the valuation of these facilities is subject to real problems arising from information asymmetries and opportunistic behaviour. For such reasons, as we will see later, solutions to the natural monopoly problem are typically addressed by some kind of government regulation, rate-of-return regulation and public enterprise being just two of the principal solutions. This book is ultimately concerned with evaluating various solutions to regulating natural monopolies. The proper starting point for this is the definition of natural monopoly.

The traditional approach to defining monopoly was concerned with a single-product industry, and assumed that all that was required for natural monopoly was that the average cost curve was everywhere decreasing, or equivalently that

$$C(\lambda x) < \lambda C(x), \qquad \lambda > 1 \tag{1.1}$$

for any $x \neq 0$, where $C(x)$ is the total cost of producing x. However, recent work by Baumol (1977) has shown that the problem of defining natural monopoly is more complex. To assist in defining natural monopoly, Baumol uses the notion of subadditivity, which enables him to examine issues of multiple products. Indeed, most utilities are multiproduct. For example, telephone companies sell various services, and electric utilities sell peak and off peak power. Cable television (CATV) companies offer many different products and may even get into other areas like providing local telephone service and data services. Among utilities, gas and water companies are the closest to being single product.

Strict subadditivity of the cost function means that 'the cost of a sum of any m output vectors is less than the sum of the costs of producing them separately', Baumol (1977, p. 809). More formally *strict global subadditivity of costs* occurs for the multiproduct cost function $C(x)$ in the set of products $N = \{1, \ldots n\}$, if for any m output vectors $\mathbf{x}^1, \ldots, \mathbf{x}^m$ of the goods in N we have:

$$C(\mathbf{x}^1 + \ldots + \mathbf{x}^m) < C(\mathbf{x}^1) + \ldots + C(\mathbf{x}^m), \tag{1.2}$$

where $\mathbf{x}^i = (x_1^i, \ldots, x_n^i)$ is the ith output vector. Baumol argues that subadditivity should be the proper criterion for defining natural monopoly, since it implies that every output combination is always produced more cheaply by a single firm. This is the essence of natural monopoly. If we interpret (1.1) in a multiproduct sense (i.e. assume $\mathbf{x}$ in (1.1) is a vector), then one might conjecture that (1.1) and (1.2) are equivalent. This is, however, not the case. In a multiproduct world, scale economies as defined by (1.1) are neither necessary nor sufficient for subadditivity, i.e. for monopoly to be the least costly form of productive organisation for all output combinations.

This extension of the study of natural monopoly to include multiproduct considerations has also spawned additional developments, in the areas of economies of scope and sustainability. These have an important role in what follows, in examining such issues as cross-subsidy and regulation. Economies of scope are an extension of the notion of joint production and a particular case of the more general concept of subadditivity discussed above. They are concerned with sharing of facilities implicit in the peak-load problem. Economies of scope are said to occur when it is possible to produce two or more products by a single firm more cheaply than it is possible to produce them by more than one firm.[2] Economies of scope may be said to exist in the case of two products x_1 and x_2, when for any two output vectors $(\mathbf{x}_1, \mathbf{x}_2)$

$$C(x_1, x_2) < C(x_1, 0) + C(0, x_2), \tag{1.3}$$

i.e. joint production is cheaper than separate production.[1] An example of a cost function satisfying both (1.2) and (1.3) for two products is

$$C(x_1, x_2) = F + C_1 x_1 + C_2 x_2,$$

where F is a fixed (joint) cost and C_1, C_2 are per unit variable costs.

The existence of economies of scope, implied by joint resources, is in itself not sufficient for the existence of a natural monopoly. The issue also hinges on the transactions costs of sharing joint production facilities. As noted by Teece (1980, p. 226), the ease 'with which a common input or services can be traded across markets will determine whether economies of scope will require the enterprise to be multiproduct in its scope'. In the case of peak loads, peak and off-peak demands are supplied jointly by the same firm because the costs of alternative arrangements are overwhelmingly high. However, in other instances it may be that the costs for contracting for use of the shared input may be sufficiently low to justify a non-monopoly arrangement. For example, while there might exist economies of scope in having a single firm supply both local and long-distance service, it may be that the costs of a number of long-distance carriers contracting with a separate local telephone company may be relatively low compared to the benefits available from competition between carriers.

Multiproduct issues and economies of scope are especially important in understanding the long-run sustainability of monopoly if entry is allowed into the monopoly sector. In a single-product world, if a natural monopoly is truly 'natural', it is the dominant form of organisation and its scale economies are such that competitors cannot undercut it. Its price would be sustainable against entry.[2] As long as the competitor's costs exceed the monopoly price given by P_m in Figure 1.1, the monopoly is sustainable against entry by competitors. Attempts by regulators to lower the price below P_m will make the industry even less attractive to potential entrants. This is the traditional single-product case where sustainability of the natural monopoly is not the issue.

Contrast this with the multiproduct monopoly where subadditivity and/or economies of scope exist. Here prices may be set, we assume by the regulators, such that entry to some markets becomes attractive. In this case the monopoly would not be sustainable against entry.

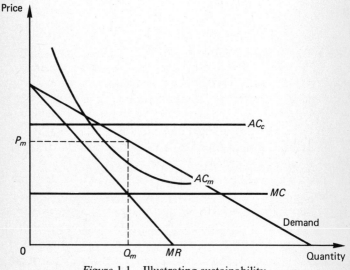

Figure 1.1　Illustrating sustainability

Sometimes the reason for entry is obvious, namely that some prices are set too high in order to subsidise other prices. Cross-subsidisation, however, is not the only reason why prices are not sustainable, as Faulhaber (1975) has pointed out. An example will illustrate this. Assume that there are three services and the costs of supplying them are given in Table 1.1. This cost structure is subadditive. It is cheaper to supply any combination of services jointly rather than separately. It is cheapest of all to supply all three services jointly. In achieving this socially optimal result, however, this cost structure may not be feasible without regulation. For example, take the case where prices are such that each service generates $25 in revenue. This is not sustainable, because the users of, say, services 1 and 2 would be able, by excluding service 3, to cut their costs to a total of $49. If they announced that they

Table 1.1 Sustainability of a multi-product firm

Service	Separately	Any two together, e.g. 1 and 2 together, 3 separate	All three together
1	30	49	—
2	30		—
3	30	30	—
Total	90	79	75

would only stay in if they are charged $49, they would leave service 3 paying $26. Service 3 combined with either 1 or 2 would then pay a total of $26 + $49/2 = $50.5, which exceeds the stand-alone cost of $49. However, the $75 overall revenue requirement is apportioned, it will be the case that two services are always contributing in excess of $49, and thus there is always an incentive to make a new deal. In this case the multiproduct monopoly is subadditive and therefore socially optimal. However, it is not sustainable against entry. Clearly the extent to which this kind of problem occurs is important because it implies, in a more complicated way, the kind of trade-offs that exist with single-product natural monopoly. There the tradeoff is between the scale economies foregone and market power. With the multiproduct monopolist, similar tradeoffs exist. It is a choice between enforcing the monopoly or allowing entry. If entry is allowed, costs are higher. If monopoly is enforced by means of entry barriers and regulation, incentives for efficient resource allocation may be attenuated.

We will now briefly sketch some of the issues in employing regulation in the natural monopoly problem. Originally, with single-product natural monopoly, the objective of such regulation was just a matter of allocative efficiency, the idea being to promote the maximisation of net benefit as expressed by

$$\text{Net benefit} = \text{total consumer and producer benefits, less} \atop \text{total production costs} \qquad (1.4)$$

To the extent that there is concern with equity, (1.4) might be modified by introducing equity constraints. In its simple form shown in (1.4), regulation involves controlling allocative inefficiency and reaping the scale economies. Traditionally, the efficiency issues of interest involved only pricing. However, the nature of efficiency concerns has become broader, involving such considerations as X-efficiency and transaction costs.

X-efficiency was originated by Leibenstein (1966) when he argued that in the absence of competition there was no compelling reason why cost would be minimised. With market power, if the firm did not minimise cost, it would not be driven out of business by competition in the product market. The competition in the capital market, operating through the market for corporate control, was perceived as less direct and less immediately compelling, leaving the potential for product inefficiency (Williamson 1970). Regulation was perceived as blunting further the incentive for X-efficiency (Williamson 1967).

X-efficiency, as an all-embracing term, is useful when broad notions of welfare losses from monopoly and regulation are being discussed. However, institutional design requires that we be more specific about the nature and source of these inefficiencies. Here transactions costs enter the picture through the new institutional economics pioneered by Williamson (1975). Production costs are seen as one aspect of the total costs of performing a set of transactions.[3] The broader study of transactions involves comparison of all of the costs associated with the transaction, including contracting, administration and regulatory costs. The thrust of the new institutional economics is the comparison of alternative governance structures (the contractual and technological arrangements for performing the relevant set of transactions) as to their relative efficiency, including all relevant transaction costs. Governance mode A may have high production costs and low transactions costs. Mode B may have high transactions costs and low production costs. The total is what is relevant. Thus, X-inefficiency, when precisely measured, would refer to the excess of production and transactions costs of a particular governance structure over and above the optimal governance mode.[4]

Efficiency in a dynamic sense is also important when examining governance modes. To be an efficient governance mode requires not only the satisfaction of the static efficiency requirements discussed above, but also the provision of incentives for growth and technological change.

These considerations all suggest a more sophisticated version of the net benefits measure in (1.4). This is achieved by incorporating transactions costs, and possible equity, in the net benefits maximisation across alternative regulatory institutions and policies, i.e.

Net benefits = total consumer and producer benefit less production cost less transactions costs subject to equity
constraints   (1.5)

The objectives embodied in (1.5) will provide the basis of our analysis
of natural monopoly regulation, with the main emphasis being on the
operation of control mechanisms, that is, of governance structures. In
Chapter 2 we will introduce the basic welfare foundations, starting with
the neoclassical treatment of efficiency and equity. We then develop the
principles of the new institutional economics which will be employed
later in this analysis. These two analytical methods are then employed
in turn to examine the problems of natural monopoly and regulation.

In Part II we provide a fairly comprehensive statement of welfare-
optimal pricing, with special emphasis on the peak-load pricing problem. The peak-load problem in utilities is pervasive as we will see in our
study of the individual industries in Part IV. To provide background
for this we summarise the major results derived in our earlier book,
Public Utility Economics, Crew and Kleindorfer (1979a). We examine
deterministic models in Chapter 3 and stochastic models in Chapter 4.

Part III is concerned with developing a basic analytical framework
for evaluating governance structures for natural monopoly. The emphasis will be on the US systems of monopoly regulation. Chapter 5
will examine the origins and practice of monopoly regulation in the
USA. Chapter 6 develops several models appropriate for the examination of the USA system of privately owned regulated monopolies. We
study rate of return regulation (RoR), the predominant governance
structure in the USA, in detail. Chapter 7 brings together the results of
Chapters 5 and 6 with a 'comparative institutional assessment' to
analyse governance structures for natural monopoly, including comparison with systems such as public enterprise.

Part IV is concerned with the effect of regulation on utilities in the
USA. Although transactions costs consideration are involved, the main
topics examined are pricing and efficiency. The industries covered are
the traditional ones: telephone, electric, gas, and water.

In Part V we summarise the main strands of the book and offer our
assessment of promising areas for future research.

2 Efficiency and Equity Aspects

As we are concerned with providing a normative basis for natural monopoly regulation, we now examine the welfare economic foundations of public policy decisions. A vast literature[1] in welfare economics and cost-benefit analysis underlies these issues. We restrict attention here to a brief overview of the traditional welfare analysis and the 'new institutional' approach to public utility problems. The traditional view, examined in Section 2.1, holds efficiency paramount in defining the net social worth of a particular policy. This net social worth is traditionally defined as the sum of consumers' and producers' surpluses generated by the policy in question, i.e. the excess of consumers' total 'willingness to pay', net of the actual price paid, plus producers' profits. This traditional economic approach is described analytically in Section 2.1.

Historically, the use of consumers' and producers' surplus as a measure of welfare was apparently first proposed by Jules Dupuit (1844) in connection with the evaluation of public works projects. Alfred Marshall (1890) developed and extended the concept, and Hotelling (1932 and 1938) used it as a basis for his proposals on public utility pricing. Although there have been detractors, the use of consumers' and producers' surplus is now broadly accepted as appropriate for welfare analysis in public utility economics. Maximising net benefit as measured by this traditional welfare function leads to the efficient outcome that price should equal to marginal cost. This result, under certain conditions, leads to under-recovery of costs and is subject to all the caveats of second-best policy. These issues are discussed in Section 2.2 and further amplified in Section 2.3 where the sustainability issue is addressed.

According to Zajac (1978 and 1982), efficiency objectives are not the sole focus of the actual practice of regulation. He contends that regulation of natural monopoly is principally concerned with equity rather than efficiency. Accordingly we will review equity aspects of the natural monopoly problem in Section 2.4. Section 2.5 will be concerned with developing the foundations of the new institutional economics necessary for the development which follows.

2.1 THE SOCIAL WELFARE FUNCTION

As indicated above, the traditional measure of welfare employed in evaluating public utility policies has been the following:

$$W = TR + S - TC, \tag{2.1}$$

where W = net social benefit, TR = total revenue, S = consumers' surplus and TC = total costs.

In the case of a single product, the net benefits of (2.1) accruing at a given output level x may be expressed as:[2]

$$W = \int_0^x P(y)dy - C(x), \tag{2.2}$$

where $P(x)$ is the (inverse) demand function and $C(x)$ is the total cost function. The integral (2.2), which we refer to as 'gross surplus', encompasses both total revenue, $TR(x) = P(x) \cdot x$, as well as consumers' surplus S. In this case S is just the area of the Marshallian triangle (i.e. the shaded area in Figure 2.1):

$$S(x) = \int_0^x [P(y) - P(x)]dy. \tag{2.3}$$

$TR - TC$ includes any profit (or loss) by the producer. Note that benefits to the producer $(TR - TC)$ and the consumer(s) are valued equally in the social welfare function (2.1). The reader can easily compute from (2.2) that $dW/dx = 0$ implies $P(x) = dC/dx$, i.e. maximising W in (2.2) leads to price = marginal cost.

In the case where the price of more than one commodity changes, the definition of gross surplus is somewhat more complicated.[3] Let a typical commodity bundle be represented by $\mathbf{x} = (x_1, \ldots x_n)$. (We use bold-face type to denote vectors and vector functions.) Let $\mathbf{X}(\mathbf{p}) = (X_1(\mathbf{p}), \ldots, X_n(\mathbf{p}))$ be the n demand functions for x, and let $\mathbf{P}(x) = (P_1(\mathbf{x}), \ldots, P_n(\mathbf{x}))$ be the inverse demand function for these commodities, i.e. $\mathbf{P}(\mathbf{X}(\mathbf{p})) = \mathbf{p}$ for all price vectors $\mathbf{p}$. When, for each commodity, $P_i(\mathbf{x}) = P_i(x_i)$ – i.e. the demand for commodity i is unaffected by price changes of other commodities – we have the case of independent demands. In this case the natural extension of (2.2) to encompass the multiproduct case would simply sum the gross surpluses of each of the n commodities. The resulting net social benefits at the vector of outputs $\mathbf{x} = (x_1, \ldots, x_n)$ would be:

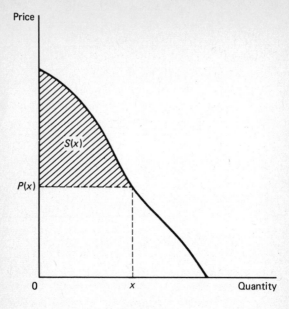

Figure 2.1

$$W = \sum_{i=1}^{n} \int_0^{x_i} P_i(y_i) dy_i - C(x). \tag{2.4}$$

In general, of course, since products may be complements or substitutes in consumption, one would expect P_i to depend on the entire output vector **x** and not just on x_i. In this general case Hotelling (1932) suggested that the appropriate analogue to (2.2) and (2.3) should be:

$$W = \int_{F(0, \mathbf{x})} (\sum_{i=1}^{n} P_i(\mathbf{y}) dy_i) - C(\mathbf{x}), \tag{2.5}$$

where gross surplus is represented as a line integral[4] along some curve $F(0,\mathbf{x})$ connecting the origin (of n-space) and the vector **x**. Thus gross surplus in (2.5) is measured, just as in (2.2), as the total willingness to pay, integrated along some adjustment curve from **0** to **x**. As it turns out, the line integral in (2.5) will generally depend on the particular path $F(0,\mathbf{x})$ along this gross surplus is measured. However, as shown in, for example, Crew and Kleindorfer (1979), W in (2.5) will depend only on **x** and not on the path $F(0,\mathbf{x})$ provided that:

$$\frac{\partial P_i}{\partial x_j} = \frac{\partial P_j}{\partial x_i} \text{ for all } i,j, \tag{2.6}$$

or equivalently

$$\frac{\partial X_i}{\partial p_j} = \frac{\partial X_j}{\partial p_i} \text{ for all } i,j, \tag{2.7}$$

Conditions (2.6)–(2.7) are called 'integrability conditions'. When they hold, W in (2.5) is well defined and may be written, independent of $F(\mathbf{0},\mathbf{x})$, as:

$$W = \oint_0^{\mathbf{x}} (\sum_{i=1}^n P_i(\mathbf{y})dy_i) - C(x), \tag{2.8}$$

a function of $\mathbf{x}$ alone. Moreover, if (2.7) holds, the partial derivatives of gross surplus exist and satisfy:

$$\frac{\partial}{\partial x_i} \oint_0^{\mathbf{x}} (\sum_{i=1}^n P_i(\mathbf{y})dy_i) = P_i(\mathbf{x}), \tag{2.9}$$

so that the first-order conditions, $\partial W/\partial x_i = 0$, for maximising W in (2.8) again here lead to marginal-cost pricing.

We will generally assume the integrability conditions (2.6) or (2.7) to hold whenever we use the traditional function W. These conditions clearly hold when $P_i(x) = P_i(x_i)$, the independent demand case, since for this case $\partial P_i/\partial x_j = 0$ whenever $i \neq j$. Hotelling (1932 and 1935) also showed that the integrability conditions hold if each consumer, in determining his joint demand for the commodities $x_1, \ldots, x_n$, assumes that his budget constraint need not be met exactly.[5] This and other economic rationale for (2.6)–(2.7) are discussed further in Pressman (1970).

The use of the consumer's surplus to measure benefit has not been without its detractors.[6] However, its use is widespread in applied welfare economics, for example Mishan (1971 and 1981). Further justification for its use has been provided by Willig (1976) who demonstrated, under conditions quite reasonable for the utility sector, that consumer's surplus closely approximates the consumers benefit in money terms.[7] Accordingly we will continue the tradition of using consumer surplus as a measure of benefit.

2.2 SECOND BEST AND THE NATURAL MONOPOLY PROBLEM

Maximising the traditional net social benefit function leads to marginal-cost pricing. This is reassuring since marginal-cost pricing is one of the cornerstones of economic efficiency. The general theory of marginal-cost pricing holds that under perfectly competitive conditions setting the price of every commodity equal to its marginal cost is required for (Pareto) efficiency. The familiar logic of this requirement is that if the price of some commodity is not equal to its marginal cost, then this price would not reflect accurately the cost of producing the additional unit and would thus fail to give the appropriate signal to purchase the optimal quantity. If, for example, price were above marginal cost, some consumers would not consume something for which they would have gladly paid the cost of production.

While marginal-cost pricing has strong arguments in its favour, there are also significant problems with it. First, if any of the various conditions for a competitive equilibrium are immutably violated elsewhere in the economy, the price-marginal-cost equality may be violated in these other sectors. Such departures from marginal-cost pricing then raise the question of the optimality of marginal-cost pricing in the remaining sectors. Problems of this sort resulting from a breakdown of price-marginal-cost equality are termed 'second-best-problems'; if first-best (Pareto optimality) is not attainable, we do the next best thing. Some of the early contributors on second-best, Lipsey and Lancaster (1956) for example, argue that there are just no general rules for optimality in second-best situations. Each case has its own peculiar second-best solution. Later developments, however, have been more positive. Farrell (1958) argued that the second-best optimum is likely to be close to the first-best optimum, implying that price should be set at least equal to marginal cost, and in the case of substitutes, above marginal cost. Davis and Whinston (1965) indicate that where there is little or no interdependence between sectors, enforcing competitive prices in the competitive sector may be appropriate. Textbooks on industrial organisation, like Scherer (1970) and Sherman (1974), also reflect a more positive attitude towards second-best problems. When faced with the impossibility of having an economy operate on quasi-competitive lines (maintaining the price-marginal-cost equality in all sectors) there still may be a presumption in favour of competition, as Scherer (1970, p. 26) argues: 'On the positive side, if we have absolutely no prior information concerning the direction in which second-best solutions lie, eliminating avoidable monopoly power is as likely statistically to improve welfare as to reduce it.'

Lancaster (1979) has recently summarised the problem of second best in the context of the electric utility industry. Because of the small size of individual regulated industries in relation to the whole economy, to achieve any significant counterbalance to the distortions of the whole economy would require a very large manipulation of the individual small sectors. This, Lancaster argues, 'may simply result in drastic changes in output and/or prices in the regulated sector for little increase in overall welfare' (p. 92). If all regulated industries were under a common control, then it might be worthwhile investing in second-best policies. However, that not being the case, the alternative seems to be to optimise in individual sectors or as Lancaster (1979, p. 93) puts it: 'Unless a simultaneous second best solution is determined for the complete regulated sector, therefore, it would seem that the next best thing (the 'third best?') is to ignore second best elements in pricing policy at the decentralized level.' This constitutes a reasonable argument for marginal-cost pricing in the utility sector.

Other arguments may be put forward in support of competitive solutions in second-best situations. The previously mentioned 'X-efficiency' hypotheses, originated by Harvey Leibenstein (1966), offers support for such solutions. Leibenstein argued that another inefficiency, likely to be at least as great as the allocative inefficiency which results from a price-marginal-cost divergence, is the inefficiency which arises from a failure to combine resources effectively in production. This he calls 'X-inefficiency' and is, he argues, more likely to arise under monopolistic situations. In a competitive product market, firms that fail to achieve X-efficiency are unlikely to obtain sufficient return to stay in business. However, a monopoly, with the cushion of monopoly profits, does not need to minimise costs to survive. For a monopoly there is only the discipline of the capital market operating externally to make it X-efficient. Thus there may be an additional welfare loss from monopoly arising from X-efficiency,[8] and considerations of X-efficiency may well strengthen the presumption in favour of competitive solutions, like the marginal-cost pricing solutions discussed here.

Suppose for the moment that we lean in the direction of marginal-cost pricing for public utilities. Even if costless regulation could enforce such a pricing policy, there would remain the critical problem of decreasing costs.[9] If, as in the traditional view of most public utilities, average costs are declining, then they are necessarily greater than marginal costs.[10] Thus declining average costs lead to deficits under marginal-cost pricing, presenting a number of problems. Although these deficits may be covered by tax revenues, significant allocative distortions may be caused by the tax levies themselves, perhaps more severe than the distortions which would be caused by pricing the public utility's output at average cost in the first place. There are also serious managerial incentive problems with allowing a utility to operate at a deficit while guaranteeing that its losses will be covered. There may also be political problems in asking taxpayers to subsidise a privately-owned utility. If public utilities must compete for investment resources in a capital market, these problems become further complicated with stockholder liability and ownership issues.

Two alternatives which have served as the focus for discussing the issue of decreasing costs have been fair rate-of-return regulation and welfare optimal break-even pricing. Let us consider these two approaches briefly.

Consider first a profit-maximising monopolist producing the two commodities $\mathbf{x} = (x_1, x_2)$, with total cost $C(\mathbf{x})$ and faced with 'willingness to pay' (i.e. inverse demand) functions $P_1(\mathbf{x})$, $P_2(\mathbf{x})$. Such a monopolist would set price and output so as to:

$$\text{Max}_{\mathbf{x} \geqslant 0} \sum_{i=1}^{2} x_i P_i(\mathbf{x}) - C(\mathbf{x}). \tag{2.10}$$

This leads to the familiar solution that marginal revenue is equated to marginal to marginal cost, i.e. $\partial R(\mathbf{x})/\partial x_i = \partial C(\mathbf{x})/\partial x_i$, where $R(\mathbf{x}) = \Sigma x_i P_i(\mathbf{x})$, or from (2.10):

$$x_i \frac{\partial P_i}{\partial x_i} + x_j \frac{\partial P_j}{\partial x_i} + P_i(\mathbf{x}) = \frac{\partial C(\mathbf{x})}{\partial x_i}, \tag{2.11}$$

where $j \neq i$; $i, j = 1, 2$. Depending on the sign of $\partial P_j/\partial x_i$ various possibilities result, but the usual presumption is that own effects dominate cross effects so that the first term in (2.11), which is negative since $\partial P_i/\partial x_i < 0$, dominates the second, leading to higher prices $P_i(\mathbf{x})$ and lower output $\mathbf{x}$ than would obtain under marginal-cost pricing.

In order to limit these welfare losses due to monopoly pricing we might attempt to regulate the level of profits to some 'fair' level, say high enough to pay competitive rates to the various factor used in producing $\mathbf{x}$, including capital. This approach presumes that some form of regulatory commission will be set up to adjudicate what the competitive rates for various productive factors are and also to monitor how much of each regulated factor is used in the production process. As we show in detail in Chapter 6, welfare gains can materialise from such a system which is administered properly, though there are many complications. The critical difficulty with this approach is that it creates an incentive for the profit-maximiser to inflate his use of, or claimed use of, those productive factors which are regulated in an attempt to understate profits.

A second approach, which owes much to Ramsey (1927), Boiteux (1956) and the recent synthesis by Baumol and Bradford (1970), is to deal directly with the problem of deficits by allowing departures from marginal-cost pricing in order to break even and avoid a deficit. The best departure from marginal-cost pricing can be found by optimising some welfare function subject to an explicit break-even constraint. If all goods in the economy are brought under the umbrella of this welfare optimisation, the Lipsey–Lancaster second-best formulation (discussed earlier) results. If only some goods are brought under the optimisation umbrella (e.g. those in a particular economic sector), we still speak of a second-best solution, and we refer to this as a 'piecemeal' solution. The discussion above on marginal-cost pricing, break-even constraints and managerial and political incentives leads to the conclusion that public utility pricing should be second best, at least in a piecemeal sense, while breaking even in the utility sector. For the case at hand where the sector produces $\mathbf{x} = (x_1, x_2)$, this piecemeal second-best problem can be stated as follows (compare with (2.10)):

$$\text{Max}_{\mathbf{x} \geqslant 0} \; W(\mathbf{x}) = \oint_0^x \sum_{i=1}^{2} P_i(\mathbf{y}) dy_i - C(\mathbf{x}), \tag{2.12}$$

subject to:

$$\Pi(\mathbf{x}) = \sum_{i=1}^{2} x_i P_i(\mathbf{x}) - C(\mathbf{x}) \geqslant \Pi_0, \tag{2.13}$$

where Π_0 is the required profit level. Associating the Lagrange multiplier μ with (2.13), we form the Lagrangian:

$$L(\mathbf{x},\mu) = W(\mathbf{x}) + \mu(\sum_{i=1}^{2} x_i P_i(\mathbf{x}) - C(\mathbf{x}) - \Pi_0), \tag{2.14}$$

and consider the first-order conditions $\partial L/\partial x_i = 0$ (assuming $x_i > 0$) and $\partial L/\partial \mu = 0$ (assuming (2.13) holds as an equality at optimum). This yields $\Pi(x) = \Pi_0$ and:

$$P_i(\mathbf{x}) - MC_i(\mathbf{x}) + \mu(MR_i(\mathbf{x}) - MC_i(\mathbf{x})) = 0, \quad i = 1,2, \tag{2.15}$$

where $MR_i = \partial R/\partial x_i$, $MC_i = \partial C/\partial x_i$. From (2.15), then, deviations $(p_i - MC_i)$ of price from marginal cost should be proportional to the difference between marginal revenue and marginal cost. In the case of independent demands $P_i(\mathbf{x}) = P_i(x_i)$ so that (2.15) may be rewritten as:

$$\frac{P_i(x_i) - \mathrm{MC}_i(\mathbf{x})}{P_i(x_i)} = -\frac{\mu}{(1+\mu)} \frac{1}{\eta_i}, \quad i = 1, 2, \tag{2.16}$$

where $\eta_i = [(P_i(x_i)/x_i)(1/P'_i(x_i))]$ is the price elasticity of demand and where $\mu/(1 + \mu)$ is the 'Ramsey Number', which when equal to unity results in the profit-maximising solution. This last is the so-called *inverse elasticity rule*; it says that the percentage deviation of price from marginal cost should be inversely proportional to elasticity. The intuitive rationale for this rule is that in achieving a required level of profit in a welfare optimal fashion those prices ought to be raised the most which will least distort the resulting output pattern from the socially efficient pattern obtainable through marginal-cost pricing.[11] This suggests that contributions toward covering the deficit should be extracted more from products with inelastic demands than from those which are more price sensitive.

This intuitive and important result holds as long as the demand for each product is independent. Where demands are interdependent, some modifications are required in this rule. In view of the importance of interdependent demands in natural monopolies, we now examine the problem of Ramsey pricing with interdependent demands in more detail. We also wish to illustrate here the relationship between the traditional welfare analysis (based on (2.1)) and a more direct approach to welfare analysis based on consumer preferences. To this end, we assume consumers are of various types $t \varepsilon T$, where $f(t)$ is the number of consumer type t. The preferences of consumers are assumed to be of the separable form

$$U(\mathbf{x}, m, t) = V(\mathbf{x}, t) + m, \quad t \varepsilon T, \tag{2.17}$$

where $\mathbf{x} = (x_1, \ldots, x_n)$ is the vector of goods supplied by the regulated sector and m is a numeraire commodity. Let the prices for $\mathbf{x}$ be denoted $\mathbf{p} = (p_1, \ldots, p_n)$, so that consumer t's demand vector, $\mathbf{x}(p, t)$ is the solution to

$$\underset{x \geqslant 0}{\mathrm{Max}} \; [V(\mathbf{x}, t) + M(t) - \sum_N p_i x_i], \tag{2.18}$$

where $M(t)$ is initial wealth of consumer t and $N = \{1, \ldots, n\}$. Assuming that purchases of $\mathbf{x}$ do not exhaust the consumer's budget, $M(t)$, implying that he gets utility from holdings of m, it follows from (2.18) that an interior solution obtains where $\partial V / \partial x_i = p_i$ and $\partial X_i(\mathbf{p}, t) / \partial p_j = \partial X_j(p, t) / \partial p_i$, for all i, j, t.

Suppose the products **X** are jointly supplied by a monopolist with cost function $C(\mathbf{X})$, where $\mathbf{X} = (X_1, \ldots, X_n)$ is total demand, i.e.

$$X_i(\mathbf{p}) = \int_T x_i(\mathbf{p},t) f(t) \mathrm{d}t. \quad i \varepsilon N \tag{2.19}$$

The Ramsey problem can then be stated as

$$\underset{p \geqslant 0}{\mathrm{Max}}\, W(\mathbf{p}) = [\int_T (V(\mathbf{x}(\mathbf{p},t),t) - \underset{N}{\Sigma} p_i x_i(p,t)) f(t) \mathrm{d}t + \Pi(p)] \tag{2.20}$$

subject to:

$$\Pi(\mathbf{p}) = \underset{N}{\Sigma} p_i X_i(\mathbf{p}) - C(\mathbf{X}) \geqslant \Pi_0, \tag{2.21}$$

where $\Pi(\mathbf{p})$ is profit and Π_0 some desired profit level (e.g. 0).

Comparing (2.20) and (2.4) or (2.12), we see that the term

$$S = \int_T (V(\mathbf{x}(\mathbf{p},t),t) - \underset{N}{\Sigma} p_i x_i(\mathbf{p},t)) f(t) \mathrm{d}t$$

corresponds to consumer surplus, the excess of willingness to pay $V(\mathbf{x},t)$ over actual payments $\Sigma\, p_i x_i$, summed across all consumers. Thus, (2.20)–(2.21) is a direct analogue of the 'demand function' form of the Ramsey problem (2.12)–(2.13).

When coupled with appropriate lump-sum transfers among consumers and the firm, the Ramsey solution to (2.20)–(2.21) can Pareto dominate every other price schedule and lump-sum transfer schedule satisfying (2.21). This efficiency property depends on the quasi-linearity of preferences (2.17). For more general preferences, the same result can be argued to hold approximately when the regulated sector is small (i.e. $\Sigma p_i x_i(\mathbf{p},t) \ll M(t)$, for all $t \varepsilon T$), as Willig (1976) has shown.

The Ramsey solution is obtained from the first-order conditions for the Lagrangian $L(\mathbf{p}) = W(\mathbf{p}) + \mu \Pi(\mathbf{p})$, corresponding to (2.20)–(2.21), i.e.

$$\frac{\partial L}{\partial p_i} = \int_T \left(\sum_{j \varepsilon N} \left[-x_i(\mathbf{p},t) + \left(\frac{\partial V(\mathbf{x},t)}{\partial x_j} - p_j \right) \frac{\partial x_j(\mathbf{p},t)}{\partial p_i} \right] \right) f(t) dt$$

$$+ (1 + \mu) \left(X_i(\mathbf{p}) + \sum_{j \varepsilon N} (p_j - C_j) \frac{\partial X_j}{\partial p_i} \right), \quad i \varepsilon N, \tag{2.22}$$

where $\mu \geqslant 0$ and $C_j = \partial C_j / X_j$. Using $p_i = \partial V / \partial x_i$ and (2.19), and assuming an interior solution ($p_i > 0$, $i \varepsilon N$), setting $\partial L / \partial p_i = 0$ in (2.22) yields

$$\sum_{j \in N} \frac{(p_j - C_j)}{X_i} \frac{\partial X_i}{\partial p_i} = -\frac{\mu}{1 + \mu}, \qquad i \varepsilon N \tag{2.23}$$

which we rewrite in the form[12]

$$\sum_{j \in N} \frac{R_j}{R_i} \frac{(p_j - C_j)}{p_j} \eta_{ji} = -k, \qquad i \varepsilon N \tag{2.24}$$

where $\eta_{ji} = (\partial X_j/\partial p_i)(p_i/X_j)$ is (cross-)elasticity, $R_i = p_i X_i$ is revenue from product i, and where $k = \mu/(1 + \mu) \geqslant 0$ is the so-called Ramsey number which is positive except at the welfare optimum (where (2.21) is not binding) where $k = 0$. The conditions for the profit-maximising solution are identical to (2.24) with $k = 1$.

As noted by Phillips and Roberts (1985), the conditions $\partial x_i(\mathbf{p}, t)/\partial p_i = \partial x_i(\mathbf{p}, t)/\partial p_j$, for all i, j, t, imply by (2.19) that $\partial X_j/\partial p_i = \partial X_i/\partial p_j$ so that (2.23) can also be written as

$$\sum_{j \in N} \frac{(p_j - C_j)}{p_j} \eta_{ij} = -k \qquad i \varepsilon N \tag{2.25}$$

When there are only two products in the regulated sector, we can solve (2.24)–(2.25) explicitly to obtain

$$\frac{p_i - C_i}{p_i} = \frac{-k}{\Delta} (\eta_{jj} - \frac{R_j}{R_i} \eta_{ji}), \quad i = 1, 2, \quad j > i, \tag{2.26}$$

where $\Delta = \eta_{11} \eta_{22} - \eta_{12} \eta_{21}$. If own-price effects dominate ($|\eta_{ii}| > |\eta_{ji}|$ for $i \neq j$) then $\Delta > 0$. We note that (2.26) reduces to the standard inverse elasticity rule in (2.16) when $\eta_{ji} = 0$ for all $j \neq i$ and that (for both the Ramsey problem and the profit-maximising problem):

1. If products 1 and 2 are substitutes ($\eta_{ij} > 0$ for $i \neq j$), then $P_i \geqslant C_i$, $i = 1, 2$, with $p_i > C_i$, $i = 1, 2$, except at the unconstrained welfare optimum.
2. If products 1 and 2 are complements ($\eta_{ij} < 0$ for all i, j), then $p_i < C_i$ is possible at optimum for one of the two products.

We note in passing that the above results easily generalise to n products if one assumes the stronger dominance relation $|\partial X_i/\partial p_i| > \Sigma_{j \neq 1} |\partial X_j/\partial p_i|$, $i \varepsilon N$. In particular, substitutes should never be priced below marginal cost. Whether complements are priced below marginal cost depends on the relative magnitudes of η_{ij} and R_i.

Returning to the two-product case, given the assumption that $\Delta > 0$ in (2.26), it is possible that $|\eta_{11}| > |\eta_{22}|$ and yet $(p_1 - C_1)/p_1 > (p_2 - C_2)/p_2$, which is contrary to the simple inverse elasticity rule of (2.16) which would imply prices always greater than or equal to marginal cost. If the product of R_1/R_2 and η_{12} were sufficiently large, this could easily happen. Thus the combination of X_1 providing a large share of the total revenue and being a strong complement with X_2 would imply a significant divergence from the simple inverse elasticity rule. Product 2, in this case, could actually be subsidised (sold below marginal cost) because of the beneficial effects it had on sales of product 1. However, as interdependencies in demand are reduced, optimal pricing approaches the simple inverse elasticity rule (2.16). These results may be illustrated by means of a simple example.

Example: Suppose consumers have homogeneous preferences, with resulting demand functions

$$X_i(\mathbf{p}) = a_{i0} - a_{i1}p_1 - a_{i2}p_2, \qquad i = 1,2 \tag{2.27}$$

where $a_{ij} > 0$, for all i,j, and where we also assume the following regularity conditions

$$\frac{\partial X_1}{\partial p_2} = a_{12} = a_{21} = \frac{\partial X_2}{\partial p_1} ; \frac{\partial X_i}{\partial p_j} = a_{ij} < a_{ii} = \frac{\partial X_i}{\partial p_i} , \; i \neq j. \tag{2.28}$$

For this example, one readily computes that the conditions (2.25) may be written as

$$\sum_j a_{ji} (p_j - C_j) = kX_i(p), \qquad i = 1,2, \tag{2.29}$$

which can be solved as in (2.26) to yield

$$p_i = \frac{k}{1+k} \frac{[a_{jj}a_{i0} - a_{ij}a_{j0}]}{a_{11}a_{22} - a_{12}a_{21}} + \frac{1}{1+k} C_i, \; i = 1,2, \; j \neq i. \tag{2.30}$$

Since $k > 0$ and, from (12), $\Delta = a_{11}a_{22} - a_{12}a_{21} > 0$, it is clear that $p_i < C_i$ occurs whenever $a_{jj}a_{i0} - a_{ij}a_{j0} \leqslant 0$, e.g. $p_1 < C_1$ when $a_{22}a_{10} \leqslant a_{12}a_{20}$, which is possible for many plausible cases. We will return to considerations of interdependent demand in relation to the individual industries in Part III.

In concluding this discussion of second-best pricing, we should note that an alternative to the break-even pricing rules formulated above is the use of two-part or other non-linear tariffs (e.g. Oi (1971)). The simplest such tariff would collect a fixed cost C for service and a per unit charge p for each unit consumed. Thus, for a single product x, the consumer's bill under such a two-part tariff would be

$$B(x) = \begin{cases} 0, & \text{if } x = 0 \\ C + px, & \text{if } x > 0 \end{cases} \qquad (2.31)$$

Clearly, one way of dealing with the deficit problem is to set $p = MC$, while setting C just high enough to transfer revenues to the firm to cover its deficit. This otherwise efficient approach may run into problems if the required C (at least for certain consumers) is higher than their surplus at price $p = MC$. Such consumers would clearly consume nothing. We return to these issues in the next chapter. Here we only note the complexities which are raised by the joint objective of breakeven *and* efficient pricing.

2.3 SUSTAINABILITY OF NATURAL MONOPOLY

A natural monopoly is called sustainable if there is some break-even price vector which will not attract entry from a competitor using the same production technology as the monopolist. Sustainability is a central concept in understanding when entry restrictions are required in order to garner scale and scope economies associated with a natural monopoly. As discussed in Chapter 1, this is especially important for multiproduct firms which use common inputs. It can very well be the case that every allocation of common costs leads to some subset of products paying more than the cost of producing the given subset independently. In such a case, there would clearly be incentives for competitive entry, and the monopoly in question would not be sustainable. As noted by Baumol, Bailey and Willig (1977), this does not mean that the monopoly could not ward off entry by adjusting its price-output configuration. Unsustainability of a given price vector simply means that the price in question will attract entry. If there is no sustainable price vector, there is arguably a case for entry restrictions.

Interest in sustainability issues has gained momentum with recent deregulation moves, especially in telecommunications, which have been directed at encouraging dynamic efficiency and productivity by allowing competitive entry into some of the markets of the multiproduct monopolist. The theoretical framework for analysing sustainability grew out of early work by Faulhaber (1975) on cross-subsidisation, and later work by Panzar and Willig (1977) and Baumol, Bailey and Willig (1977). Let us first consider an example, based on Panzar (1980).

Consider the following cost function $C(X_1,X_2)$ for a 2-product firm:

$$C(X_1,X_2) = F + c_1 X_1 + c_2 X_2, \tag{2.32}$$

which exhibits both economics of scale and scope, as discussed in Chapter 1. Suppose demand for the two products is independent, i.e. $X_i(\mathbf{p}) = X_i(p_i)$, $i = 1,2$. We represent in Figure 2.2 the locus of zero-profit points $\mathbf{p} = (p_1,p_2)$ such that

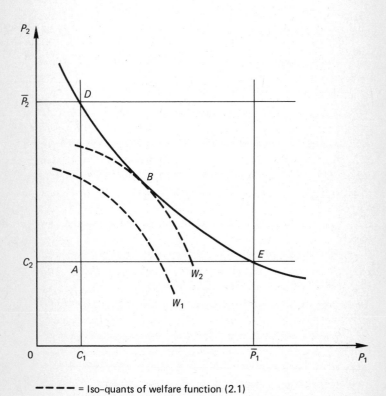

$----$ = Iso–quants of welfare function (2.1)

Figure 2.2   Illustrating sustainability (based on Panzar, 1980, p. 174).

$$\Pi(\mathbf{p}) = \sum_{i=1}^{2} (p_i - c_i)X_i(p_i) - F = 0 \tag{2.33}$$

Similarly, let $\bar{p}_i$ represent the lowest price at which a stand-alone firm (using the same technology (2.32)) could break even, i.e.

$$\bar{p}_i = \text{Min } \{p_i \geqslant 0 \mid (p_i - c_i)X_i(p_i) = F\}, \ i = 1,2 \tag{2.34}$$

From Figure 2.2 it is clear that the only break-even price vectors which could be sustainable lie on the locus DE. In fact every price p^m on DE is sustainable since (we assume) an entrant must set prices $p^e \leqslant p^m$ to attract any demand. However, any such price vector would clearly allow the entrant only to make losses. Moreover, any price vector to the right of $\bar{p}_1$ (respectively, above $\bar{p}_2$) could easily be challenged by a stand-alone firm marketing only product 1 (respectively, only product 2). Thus, the locus DE is the set of all sustainable prices for this example. For reasons discussed below, we are particularly interested in whether the Ramsey optimal prices $p^* = (p_1^*, p_2^*)$ are sustainable (point B in Figure 2.2). From (2.16), it is clear that $p_i^* > c_i$, $i = 1,2$, so that the Ramsey solution clearly lies on the locus of DE. Thus, in this case, the Ramsey solution is sustainable.

As it turns out, a somewhat stronger property holds, even under more general cost conditions. Baumol, Bailey and Willig (1977) point out that for a monopolist to ascertain that price-output vectors other than the Ramsey solution are sustainable may require 'global information about demand and cost function for its products' (p. 351). Thus, when the Ramsey solution is sustainable, it may be the only safe bet for the monopolist to thwart competitive entry, if such is allowed. In this sense, one may think of entry threat to a monopoly as a 'weak invisible hand' (Baumol, Bailey and Willig) inducing efficient (Ramsey) pricing.

Given the just noted importance of sustainability of Ramsey prices, it is interesting to inquire more generally when Ramsey prices are sustainable. Thus, consider the case where there are n products with joint demand function $\mathbf{X}(\mathbf{p}) = (X_1(\mathbf{p}), \ldots, X(\mathbf{p}))$ and cost function $C(\mathbf{X})$. Baumol, Bailey and Willig show for this general case that Ramsey prices are sustainable when the following two conditions are satisfied:

c1. The products are weak gross substitutes, i.e. $\partial X_i / \partial p_j \geqslant 0$ for all i,j such that $i \neq j$.

c2. The cost function $C(\mathbf{X})$ exhibits both economics of scale and scope, in the sense that C has *strictly decreasing ray average costs* (scale economies), i.e.,

$$C(\lambda \mathbf{X}) < \lambda C(\mathbf{X}) \text{ for all } \lambda > (2.35) \ \mathbf{X} \neq 0, \tag{2.35}$$

and C is *transray convex*, (scope economies), i.e.,

$$C(\alpha \mathbf{X} + (1 - \alpha)\mathbf{Y}) \leqslant \alpha C(\mathbf{X}) + (1 - \alpha)C(\mathbf{Y}) \text{ for } 0 \leqslant \alpha \leqslant 1, \tag{2.36}$$

where $\mathbf{X}$, $\mathbf{Y}$ are arbitrary nonnegative output vectors.

Note that assumptions c1 and c2 are satisfied by the above two-product example, since independent demands imply c1 and (2.32) clearly satisfies c2. Figure 2.3 illustrates the implications of (2.35)–(2.36), namely that expansions of scale will decrease average costs and that 'mixtures' give rise to joint economies.[13]

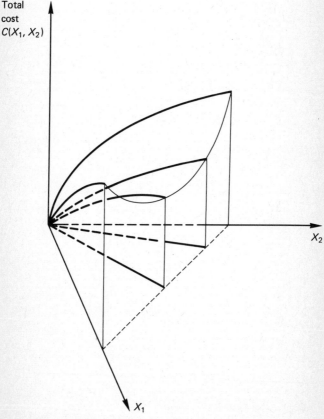

Figure 2.3   Scale and scope economies

We have only discussed here when Ramsey pricing is sustainable. One might also inquire when the efficient two-part pricing policy of the previous section is sustainable. For the two-product example examined above, this efficient two-part tariff would set $p_i = c_i$ (achieving the welfare optimum A in Figure 2.2) and would recover fixed costs F through lump-sum levies on consumers (which again are assumed not to be so high as to drive these consumers out of the market). This tariff would be sustainable if no potential entrant could entice some group of consumers away from the incumbent by offering a more favourable tariff, which could cover the entrant's production costs. The sustainability of two-part and non-linear tariffs, however, has received little attention to date.[14]

Other important discussions of sustainability conditions are due to Baumol, Panzar and Willig (1982, 1984) and Phillips (1980). These works point out the difficulty of determining *ex ante* whether or not a given demand and cost structure represents a sustainable monopoly. Baumol and his co-authors' book also discusses the fragility of sustainability over time when economies of scale are strongly related to sunk investment costs (which is the norm for the traditional utilities).[15] Existing results on sustainability also do not cover non-linear tariffs or complementary goods, which are common in some monopoly sectors (e.g. telecommunications). For these reasons, relaxing entry restrictions in the monopoly sector can be at the regulator's and the public's peril, in that significant instability and destructive competition could develop *ex post* if the monopoly is not sustainable.

2.4 EQUITY ASPECTS IN NATURAL MONOPOLY REGULATION

Among economists efficiency is generally held to be the appropriate objective of control for natural monopoly (e.g. Schmalensee (1979), and Kahn (1970 and 1971)). Equity and distribution issues are either suppressed or purposefully ignored. Williamson (1966) for example, has argued that macroeconomic policy instruments, like subsidies and taxes, are more effective in bringing about distributive justice than microeconomic policy instruments such as public utility prices. However, this efficiency orientation does not appear to be shared by regulatory bodies in practice. Zajac (1982, p. 1) asks 'Why does the public find it so hard to accept principles that are so obvious to trained economists?' Indeed, according to Zajac not only would the economist's goal of efficiency be an overwhelmingly minority view among utility regulators, but it would also appear to have precedent against it. Rather, equity, fairness and 'economic justice' appear to be paramount concerns of the public and of regulators.

In explaining the nature of economic justice, Okun (1975) developed the concept of 'economic' rights similar to civil rights. Typically, however, economic rights, like public education, use up more resources than civil rights but have public good characteristics similar to civil rights. Because of this, Okun argues that basic economic rights should be kept out of the market, the market having the role of promoting efficient allocation *after* basic needs (and rights) have been taken care of, or put quite memorably, 'the market needs a place, and the market needs to be kept in its place' (p. 119).

Perhaps the best known recent contributions on economic justice are due to Rawls (1971 and 1974b). He argued that there are two basic principles of justice:

1. Each person has an equal right to the most extensive scheme of equal basic liberties compatible with a similar scheme of liberties for all.
2. Social and economic inequalities are to meet two conditions: they must be (a) to the greatest expected benefit of the least advantaged (the maximin criteria); and (b) attached to offices and positions open to all under conditions of fair equality of opportunity. (p. 639)

While Rawls' principles do not seem to be formally incorporated into the regulatory process, regulation is arguably motivated by notions of equity and fairness. This is apparent from the early history of the regulation of economic activity in England, where the doctrine of *justum pretium* or 'just price' originated. The price, in some sense, had to be fair. Fairness was concerned with such issues as preventing 'perceived' exploitation by rising food prices in time of famine.[16] The notion of just price became incorporated in the legal system, which was used to enforce the regulation of such 'just' prices irrespective of the efficiency consequences. This system was an early forerunner to the system of price regulation currently used to regulate monopoly. Moreover, the legal system as the adjudicatory system for regulation is deeply imbued with due process, equal access to information, and other considerations tightly linked to justice and fairness. Thus, the intellectual heritage of the legal system on economic issues, and therefore the regulatory apparatus, owes almost everything to notions of justness or fairness and almost nothing to notions of efficiency.

It is these issues of fairness which give rise to various forms of average cost pricing embodied in regulation by commission is the USA. The basic idea behind this, as we review in detail in Chapter 5, is that $P = AC$ would seem to remunerate the producer just the right amount, i.e. no excess returns would be earned. Moreover, if joint costs across consumer groups are apportioned according to 'cost causation' principles, each consumer group can also be argued to be paying its fair share.

The problems with this scenario are several, however. Quite aside from issues of efficient pricing discussed earlier, producers may not be X-efficient if they are assured that all costs can be passed through to the consumer. Regulators can, of course, devote additional resources to controlling X-inefficiency. Such controls may be expected to be countered by various tactics of the regulated firm. In the resulting spiral of administration and adjudication, significant costs may be incurred in search of meagre benefits. Balancing the costs and benefits of regulation thus extends beyond the normal purview of neoclassical economics into micro-institutional issues of control costs, incentives and information acquisition. For these reasons, the new institutional economics (Williamson 1979) will be important in our comparative analysis of alternative regulatory institutions.

2.5 THE NEW INSTITUTIONAL ECONOMICS

The new institutional economics was formalised in Williamson (1975). The 'old' institutional economics is best illustrated by the work of Commons (1934) who held that the transaction was the ultimate unit of economic investigation. He examined issues such as legal control, contracting and cooperation. Coase (1937) pioneered the development of an analytical framework for transactions costs which was a crucial antecedent to the new institutional economics. Coase examined the issue of whether a given set of transactions would best be performed within a single economic organisation (a firm) or by several economic agents interacting through the market. The new institutional economics also draws on Hayak's (1945) institutional analysis of markets; on the market failure literature concerning risk, as in Arrow (1971); public goods, as in Samuelson (1954); information asymmetries, as in Akerlof

(1970); and the contractarian approach to the theory of the firm, as in Alchian and Demsetz (1972).

These foundations were synthesised by Williamson (1975 and 1979) into the transactions cost framework for comparative institutional design, which has become the bulwark of the new institutional economics. Central to Williamson's analysis are the notions of bounded rationality and opportunities. Bounded rationality originated with Simon (1961, p. *XXIV*) who used bounded rationality to refer to human behaviour that is 'intendedly rational but only *limitedly* so'. In other words, there are definite limits on the ability of the human mind to process information and to reason logically. These are seen as a constraint or decision-makers. Opportunism refers to 'self-interest seeking with guile' (Williamson 1975, p. 26). In small numbers situations where information asymmetries exist (one party has information not available to the other party) the first party has an incentive to behave opportunistically. As a result, information may be impacted, i.e. not made available completely to the second party. These problems may be overcome through markets when large-numbers interaction is possible. In other contexts, a hierarchy (e.g. a firm) may be the more efficient institution to mediate the transactions in question.

It is precisely this question of efficient institutional design (e.g. markets versus hierarchies) which has become the central issue in the new institutional economics. This issue is normally referred to as the comparative analysis of governance structures, where a governance structure is simply the institutional framework in which transactions take place.[17] An efficient governance structure would be one that economises on bounded rationality and attenuates opportunism. Hierarchical governance rather than market governance will be preferred when contingent claims contracting or frequent recontracting is not feasible and where divergent expectations, small numbers and the potential for opportunism exist. Williamson (1979) developed a framework for examining the efficiency of alternative governance structures, depending on the characteristics of the transactions which these structures are intended to mediate or control. Characteristics of interest include:

1. *Extent of transaction-specificity of investment.* When highly specific or idiosyncratic investments have to be made to perform a set of transactions, safeguards must be provided for the protection of the investor, because of the low resale value which arises from the limited alternative use possibilities of these specific investments.

An example of a highly specific investment is a concrete driveway.
2. *Frequency of transactions.* Occasional transactions presumably provide greater possibilities for opportunism since reputation effects and learning are likely to be weak relative to recurrent transactions. An example of an infrequent transaction is having a driveway paved, while a recurrent transaction is the purchase of food.

Williamson argues that idiosyncratic investment combined with recurrent transactions will lead at one extreme to unified governance (or a hierarchy) while at the other extreme of non-specific investment market governance would be the efficient and expected outcome. The presence of idiosyncratic investment and recurrent transactions to a high degree in the natural monopoly or public utility sector suggests that the efficient governance structure for natural monopoly is hierarchical. Given the need to achieve efficiency and equity goals as outlined above, this result is further strengthened. Indeed the analysis leads us to the social welfare function stated in Chapter 1 as (1.5), i.e. to the problem of determining a governance structure which maximises benefits, net of transaction costs. We return to this problem in Chapter 7, where we evaluate the principal governance structures for natural monopolies. Meanwhile we will continue to use the traditional social welfare function (2.1), which neglects costs and equity, welfare-optimal pricing and investment policies in Part II. The main justification for neglecting these (i.e. using (2.1)) in the interim is to determine efficiency benchmarks, against which policies concerned with transactions costs and fairness can be judged.[18] For example, two inefficient policies can be compared in terms of their net benefits. They can also be compared with the net benefits of the efficient solution derived from maximising net benefit. In this way the 'costs' of various notions of fairness can be evaluated. Traditional inefficiencies associated with monopoly can be evaluated by the same approach. Thus, our initial approach will be to analyse various solutions to the natural monopoly problem using traditional neoclassical techniques. This appears to be a necessary prerequisite before proceeding to the more complete new institutional economics framework in Chapter 7 and Parts IV and V.

Part II

Survey of the Theory of Peak-load Pricing

3 Deterministic Models of Peak-load Pricing

Our purpose in this chapter is to set out the basic peak-load model as originated by Boiteux (1949) and Steiner (1957), and developed by Hirshleifer (1958) and Williamson (1966). Such problems arise when a utility's product is economically non-storable and demand fluctuates over time. Under these circumstances non-uniform utilisation of capacity can result. Thus using a 'peak-load pricing' policy to discourage consumption in peak periods and encourage off-peak consumption can improve such utilisation. The evaluation of the trade-off between utilisation gains and consumer welfare is the central issue of peak-load pricing theory. We will not provide rigorous proofs for most of these results but simply sketch their development. (Rigorous proofs may be obtained in Crew and Kleindorfer (1979a), which is referenced in detail throughout.) In Section 3.1 we present the Boiteux–Steiner–Hirshleifer contributions for the simplest cases of equal-length periods and independent demands. In Sections 3.2 through 3.4 we examine the problems of diverse technology, interdependent and time-varying demand. Section 3.5 concerns profit maximisation, second-best and other issues.

3.1 THE BOITEUX–STEINER MODEL

Boiteux (1949) and Steiner (1957) arrived at solutions to the peak-load problem independently, and their approach has become the basis for further work in the area. Boiteux's contribution, published in French, had little impact on the Anglo-American literature until Steiner had published his own contribution, which set off a growing literature in the Anglo-American journals. By contrast Boiteux's impact in France, and especially in the *Electricité de France*, was substantial.

Steiner (1957) adopted the conventional welfare maximising approach discussed in Chapter 2, namely setting prices to achieve 'the maximisation of the excess of expressed consumer satisfaction over the cost of resources devoted to production' (p. 485). He assumes a typical 'day' divided into two equal-length periods, each governed by its own independent demand curve, denoted $D_1(p)$ and $D_2(p)$. The peak-load problem in Steiner results from the assumption that one of these two demand curves lies everywhere above the other. The demands are independent in the sense that the price charged in one period has no effect on the quantity demanded in the other period. Costs are assumed to be linear: b is operating cost per unit per period; β is the per-day cost providing a unit of capacity. Thus a unit demanded in a period will cost b if the capacity already exists to supply it, and b plus β if additional capacity has to be installed. Once a unit of capacity is installed (at a cost β) it is available for meeting demands in both periods. It is assumed in Steiner's analysis that sufficient capacity will be installed to meet demand.

The solution to the two-period problem is given in Figure 3.1, in

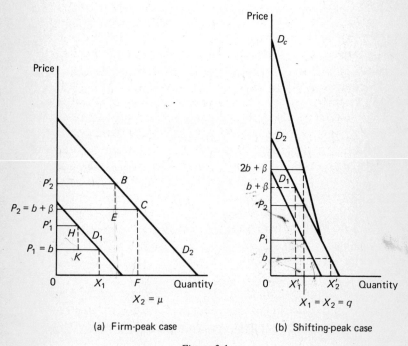

Figure 3.1

which the demand curves D_1 and D_2 are drawn. Figure 3.1a illustrates the 'firm-peak case' and involves pricing at $p_2 = b + \beta$ and $p_1 = b$, with period outputs $x_2 > x_1$ as indicated and with capacity $q = x_2$.

To illustrate why this solution is optimal, consider prices p_2' and p_1'

supplier surplus

slightly higher than the given p_2, p_1. We will sum and compare the areas of net revenue and consumers' surplus for each case. For the peak period, net revenue corresponding to p_2' will be increased by $p_2'BEp_2$, but consumers' surplus will be reduced by $p_2'BCEp_2$, a net loss in welfare of BEC. Similarly, under p_1' a welfare loss of HJK results. For other perturbations of p_1, p_2, similar losses in welfare occur. Optimal capacity will be $q = \max(x_1, x_2)$ because of the fact that at the optimal prices quantity demanded cannot exceed capacity.

Note that in the firm-peak case, the peak-period revenue (p_2, x_2) covers the clearly identifiable peak-period costs, both capacity (βq) and running costs (bx_1); and the off-peak period revenue (p_1x_1) only covers running costs. Since it follows directly from our welfare function that no price less than b nor greater than $b + \beta$ is warranted, charging the highest feasible price in the peak period and the lowest feasible price in the off-peak period is something of a polar case. Steiner's analysis shows that as long as these prices can be charged while still leaving spare capacity $q - x_1 > 0$ in the off-peak period, such prices are in fact optimal.

By contrast if the prices $(b + \beta, b)$ are charged in the 'shifting-peak case', shown in Figure 3.1b, quantities $x_2' < x_1'$ would result. The peak would apparently 'shift' in that what was the off-peak demand (x_1) would become the larger quantity demanded, and thus the determinant of the amount of capacity required. This solution appears odd and, in fact, fails to maximise welfare. The correct solution is obtained by adding vertically the two demand curves D_1 and D_2 to get D_c. (The reader may verify this solution by an analogous argument, comparing areas, to that which we just employed for the firm-peak case.) Where D_c cuts the horizontal line drawn at $2b + \beta$ gives optimal capacity q, allowing prices to be read off as p_1 and p_2, which, as in the firm-peak case, satisfy $p_1 + p_2 = 2b + \beta$.

Note, in the shifting-peak case, that peak users pay a higher price than off-peak users even though the quantity supplied is identical in both periods. This supplies some of the rationale of Steiner's (1957) contention that welfare-optimal peak-load pricing may involve price discrimination.

In the shifting peak case both demands contribute to capacity cost (β), and capacity is fully utilised in both periods. Note that there is no precise rule for allocating capacity costs between peak and off-peak; it depends on the relative strength of these demands. Thus, if peak demand increases relative to off-peak demand, optimality would require that the peak demand pays relatively more of the capacity cost of β. It is not just the relationship between the demands that determine whether it is a firm or a shifting peak; the size of capacity costs relative to demands is also important. Thus in Figure 3.1b, if β were to fall, this case would become a firm peak; and if β were to rise in Figure 3.1a, this would become a shifting peak.[1] Intuitively it is apparent why this happens. If capacity costs are relatively large, any failure (as in firm-peak case) to utilise capacity fully is expensive, and encourages better utilisation of a switch-over to shifting peak. Note that in both the shifting-peak and the firm-peak case profit equals zero, a consequence of our welfare function and the assumed constant returns to scale.

Before completing our analysis of the two-period case we would like to note an interesting graphical device employed by Steiner to summarise both the firm-peak and shifting-peak cases on the same diagram. In Figure 3.2 we have redrawn the demand curves of Figure 3.1; this time however, using $(0,b)$ as the origin of the diagram instead of $(0,0)$. However, the capacity costs on the price scale continue to be measured in absolute terms so that the distance $b\beta$ in Figure 3.2 equals β, i.e. the point β represents the price $b+\beta$. Then the above discussion may be seen to imply the following for Figure 3.2. If capacity costs are greater than $\hat{\beta}$, a shifting peak occurs; otherwise a firm peak obtains. In the former case (e.g. β') period outputs and prices may be read along the vertical line drawn at $D_c(\beta')$ (e.g. $x_1' = x_2' = q'$, as shown). In the firm peak case (e.g. β) prices are $p_2 = b + \beta$, $p_1 = b$, with corresponding quantities.

This device is particularly valuable when it comes to extending the peak-load geometry to more than two periods, in that it makes simple addition of the demand curves possible, as in Figure 3.3, where we illustrate a three-period case.[2] By changing the level of capacity cost we can note the three possibilities:

shifting peak in all three periods;
shifting peak in periods 1 and 2; and
firm peak in period 1.

The three regions of capacity cost corresponding to these possibilities are labelled (i), (ii), (iii) in the diagram. The capacity cost β is in region (i), and this implies a shifting peak in all periods with $q = x_1 = x_2 = x_3$, and corresponding prices. For β' a shifting peak in periods 1 and 2 obtains with resulting prices p_2' and capacity q', as shown. Finally, if capacity cost is β'', period 1 is a firm peak and $q'' = x_3 > x_2 > x_1$, with prices $p_3'' = b + \beta''$, $p_2'' = b$. In all cases it can be verified that $p_1 + p_2 + p_3 = 3b + \beta$, and that profits equal zero. The case where only periods 2 and 3 present a shifting-peak situation (in the sense that their

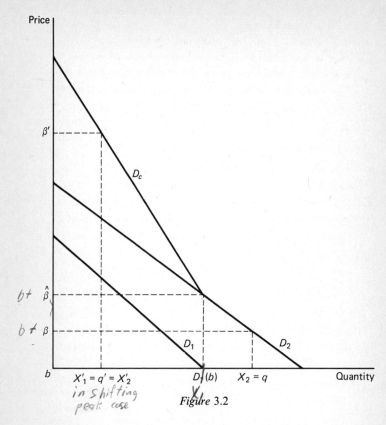

Figure 3.2

period outputs are equal at optimum) never arises as long as their demand curves are non-intersecting, so that the above three cases are exhaustive. Of course, if the assumption that demand curves do not intersect is abandoned, other possibilities may arise.

The extension to n periods is analogous, and there too we find the sum of the n-period prices equals $nb + \beta$ and that there are exactly n possibilities, each of which corresponds to the case where, for some $j \leqslant n$, periods $1, \ldots, j$ all have output equal to capacity, with remaining periods all priced at marginal running costs (b).

3.2 INTRODUCTION TO PROBLEMS OF DIVERSE TECHNOLOGY

The classical models of peak-load pricing analysed in Section 3.1 embody strong simplifying assumptions concerning demand and tech-

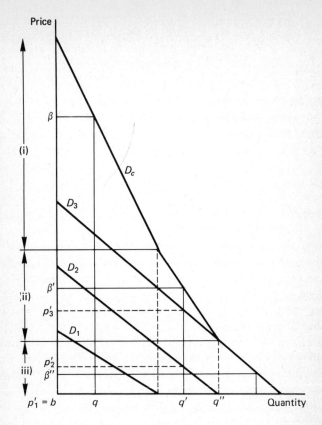

Figure 3.3

nology. In this section we begin our inquiry into the implications of relaxing one or other of the assumptions of the traditional theory. We continue to maintain the assumption that demand curves are known with certainty. Since a number of generalisations of the traditional theory have been presented during the past decade for this deterministic demand case, a brief historical sketch of these developments may be useful at the start.

The first major extension to the traditional model was presented by Pressman (1970), who synthesized earlier works by Hotelling and the marginal-cost pricing schools[3] in providing a model of peak-load pricing incorporating demands with time interdependencies (e.g. the peak-period price affects off-peak demand) as well as a more general specification of technology. This contrasts sharply with the traditional models which assume proportional costs and time-independent demands.

A further theoretical generalisation appeared in the present authors' papers, starting with Crew and Kleindorfer (1971), which investigated the implications for pricing and capacity decisions of a diverse technology where more than one type of 'plant' is available to meet demand.[4] Such cases are typical for public utilities and present interesting new trade-offs. For example, in the firm-peak case discussed in Section 3.1 it may be economical to employ an additional plant type to help meet peak-period demand. Such a 'peaking plant' would typically have lower construction costs and higher operating costs relative to existing plants, thus offering cost advantages in meeting a peak demand of short duration.

Returning to our historical sketch, two additional recent developments deserve attention. Panzar (1976) presented a reformulation of the peak-load problem in which technology is specified through a neoclassical production function. Dansby (1975) used the same technology specifications as Crew and Kleindorfer (1975a,b) but allowed demand to vary continuously with time, while still maintaining only a finite number of pricing periods. Thus, within each pricing period, demand was allowed to vary with time. Bös (1986) and Chao (1983) review other recent advances in the theory of peak-load pricing.

The above approaches share many common features, and it is important to understand these, inasmuch as we shall analyse only the Crew and Kleindorfer model in detail. To illustrate the similarities in these approaches, consider first the following n-period peak-load pricing problem, similar to Pressman (1970);

$$\text{Max } W = \int_0^{\mathbf{x}} \{ \sum_{i=1}^n P_i(\mathbf{y}) dy_i \} - C(\mathbf{x},z)$$

subject to $x_i \leqslant z$, $x_i \geqslant 0$, $z \geqslant 0$, $i = 1, \ldots, n$, $\qquad (3.1)$

where $\mathbf{x} = (x_1, \ldots, x_n)$, x_i is demand in period i, $P_i(\mathbf{x})$ is the inverse demand function, z is installed capacity, and $C(\mathbf{x},z)$ represents total costs. Notice that demands are allowed to be interdependent ($P_i(\mathbf{x}) = P_i(x_{1,x2}, \ldots, x_n)$), so that a line-integral formulation of gross surplus is used in (3.1), and the integrability conditions (2.6) are assumed as usual.

For comparison consider the n-period model from Crew and Kleindorfer (1975a), where technology is specified explicitly through m types of capacity, indexed $l = 1, \ldots, m$, having constant marginal operating cost b_l and marginal capacity cost β_l. With this specification of technology the corresponding problem to (3.1) is:

$$\text{Max } W = \int_0^{\mathbf{x}} \{ \sum_{i=1}^{n} P_i(\mathbf{y}) dy_i \} - \sum_{i=1}^{n} \sum_{l=1}^{m} b_l q_{li} - \sum_{l=1}^{m} \beta_l q_l \qquad (3.2)$$

subject to:

$$\sum_{l=1}^{m} q_{li} = x_i, \text{ for all } i \qquad (3.3)$$

$$q_l - q_{li} \geq 0, \text{ for all } i,l \qquad (3.4)$$

$$x_i \geq 0, \, q_l \geq 0, \, q_{li} \geq 0, \text{ for all } i,l, \qquad (3.5)$$

where x_i is demand in period i, q_l is capacity of type (or plant) l, and q_{li} is output from plant l *in period* i. Constraint (3.3) specifies that demand be met in each period, while (3.4) requires output from plant l in each period not exceed capacity of plant l. Similarly, the first term in W is gross surplus, the second term represents total operating costs, and the third represents capacity costs. It is assumed at the start that different prices ($P_i(x)$) may be charged in each of the n sub-periods comprising the basic cycle of interest. This assumption is relaxed below (Section 3.4). Equal-length periods are assumed with corresponding units for demand and capacity, as discussed in Chapter 3. Note, in particular, that the marginal capacity cost is a unit cost for the entire cycle (no matter into how many periods it may be subdivided, i.e. regardless of n).[5]

Now the above two formulations are closely related. Indeed, starting with (3.2) one could define the cost function in (3.1) as:

$$C(\mathbf{x},z) = \text{Min } [\sum_{i=1}^{n} \sum_{l=1}^{m} b_l q_{li} - \sum_{l=1}^{m} \beta_l q_l], \qquad (3.6)$$

subject to:

$$\sum_{l=1}^{m} q_{li} = x_i, \text{ for all } i \qquad (3.7)$$

$$\sum_{l=1}^{m} q_l = z; \, q_{li}, \, q_l \geq 0, \text{ for all } l,i, \qquad (3.8)$$

where $\mathbf{x}$, z in (3.6)–(3.8) are given. Thus $C(\mathbf{x}, z)$ in (3.6) is the minimal cost of providing period outputs $\mathbf{x} = (x_1, \ldots, x_n)$ and total capacity z when available technology is specified as in (3.2)–(3.5). The reader should be convinced that the solutions to (3.1) with $C(\mathbf{x}, z)$ as defined in (3.6), will be precisely the same solution as the solutions to (3.2)–(3.5). This equivalence amounts simply to the assertion that the welfare maximisation (3.2) implies the cost minimisation (3.6) at the optimal output levels of x_i. A similar transformation would of course work if more general (non-proportional) cost functions were assumed for the m available capacity types. Thus the main difference between (3.1) and (3.2)–(3.5) is that the latter treat technology choice explicitly.

Similarly the use of a neoclassical production function to express technological possibilities, as in Panzar (1976) and Marino (1978), can be viewed as an alternative representation of (3.1) or (3.2)–(3.5). Just as in (3.1)–(3.5) the welfare-optimal solution here would involve cost minimisation, i.e. minimising factor costs at the optimal output levels. Thus, given the familiar conditions for optimal factor substitution, the neoclassical specification of technology leads to essentially the same insights as (3.1) or (3.2)–(3.5).

The thrust of the above discussion is that the major recent reformulations of the peak-load pricing problem may be viewed as close substitutes for one another in a welfare-maximising framework.[6] For this reason, and in order to present a unified discussion of technology choice and pricing policy, we shall concentrate on the more detailed representation (3.2)–(3.5).

3.3 MULTI-PERIOD PRICING WITH A DIVERSE TECHNOLOGY

We start our analysis with the problem represented by (3.2)–(3.5) which assumes that different prices can be charged in each of the equal-length supply periods $i = 1, \ldots, n$. Our first task in solving the problem will be to derive first-order conditions using the Kuhn–Tucker theorem. First form the Lagrangian, L:

$$L = W + \sum_{i=1}^{n} \lambda_i \left(\sum_{l=1}^{m} q_{li} - x_i \right) + \sum_{i=1}^{n} \sum_{l=1}^{m} \mu_{li}(q_l - q_{li}) \tag{3.9}$$

Assuming strictly positive output, i.e. $x_i > 0$, at the optimal solution, the Kuhn–Tucker conditions for (3.2)–(3.5) are then:

$$P_i(\mathbf{x}) = \lambda_i, \qquad \text{for all } i \tag{3.10}$$

$$\sum_{i=1}^{n} \mu_{li} \leqslant \beta^l, q_l \left(\sum_{i=1}^{n} \mu_{li} - \beta_l \right) = 0, \qquad \text{for all } l \tag{3.11}$$

$$\lambda_i - \mu_{li} \leqslant b_l, \ q_{li} (\lambda_i - \mu_{li} - b_l) = 0, \qquad \text{for all } l,i \tag{3.12}$$

$$\mu_{li} \geqslant 0, \ \mu_{li}(q_l - q_{li}) = 0, \qquad \text{for all } l,i. \tag{3.13}$$

Before proceeding to an analysis of the general case we solve (3.10)–(3.13) for the case of two independent demands, first for one plant and then for two plants. We assume that the demands satisfy $D_1(p) < D_2(p)$ for all p so that period 2 is the peak period. For these cases the analysis is simplifed considerably because of the fact that for *independent* demands, (3.9) is strictly concave and the conditions (3.10)–(3.13) are necessary and sufficient for optimality.

For the one-plant case $m = 1, n = 2$, the reader may verify the Steiner (firm-peak) result, i.e. assuming $D_1(b_1) < D_2(b_1 + \beta_1)$, so that a firm peak obtains, the following solves (3.9)–(3.13):

$$p_1 = b_1 = \lambda_1; \ \mu_{11} = 0 \tag{3.14}$$

$$p_2 = b_1 + \beta_1 = \lambda_2; \ \mu_{12} = \beta_1, \tag{3.15}$$

where $q_1 = q_{12} = x_2 > x_1 = q_{11}$.

For the two-plant case $m = 2 = n$, ahead of detailed considerations of optimal plant mix follow in this section, we assume plant 1 has the cheaper marginal running cost ($b_1 < b_2$) and that both plants will be used at the optimum. Then, by a simple process of elimination, while assuming $x_1, x_2, q_1, q_2 > 0$, we obtain the following solution to (3.9)–(3.13) (again for the firm-peak case, where at optimum $x_2 < x_1$):

$$p_1 = 2b_1 + \beta_1 - (b_2 + \beta_2) = \lambda_1; \ \mu_{11} = \lambda_1 - b_1, \ \mu_{21} = 0 \tag{3.16}$$

$$p_2 = b_2 + \beta_2 = \lambda_2; \ \mu_{12} = \lambda_2 - b_1, \ \mu_{22} = \beta_2 \tag{3.17}$$

$$q_1 = q_{11} = q_{12} = x_1 > 0, \ q_{21} = 0, \ q_2 = q_{22} = x_2 - x_1 > 0. \tag{3.18}$$

Let us explain (3.16)–(3.18) intuitively. Given $b_1 < b_2$, we must also have $\beta_1 > \beta_2$ if both types of capacity are to be used at optimum (otherwise, if $\beta_1 < \beta_2$ plant 2 would be both more expensive to build and to operate). Now, from (3.18), we see that $q_{11} = x_1$, so that off-peak demand is met by plant 1, which is more expensive to construct but cheaper to operate than plant 2. Note that plant 1 continues to supply $q_{12} = x_1$ units in the peak period, the additional peak requirements $x_2 - x_1 = q_{22}$ being met by plant 2. The use of the cheaper operating-cost plant in both periods is as expected, with the more expensive operating-cost plant used only to meet peak demand.

Since plant 2 is only used in the peak period at optimum, we must have:[7]

$$b_1 + \beta_1 > b_2 + \beta_2, \tag{3.19}$$

which states that the marginal cost of supplying a unit of peak demand using type 2 capacity should be less than that of meeting this marginal unit with type 1 capacity. Similarly, since plant 1 is used to capacity in both periods, the cost of the marginal unit supplied by plant 1 is $2b_1 + \beta_1$, and the following must hold:

$$2b_1 + \beta_1 < 2b_2 + \beta_2, \tag{3.20}$$

since otherwise plant 1 would not be needed.

Regarding the optimal prices, a close look at (3.16)–(3.17) reveals the expected result that prices are set at marginal cost. For example, given (3.20) and the above discussion, the minimum cost of meeting an additional unit of demand in period 1 is to increase plant 1 capacity by 1 unit and decrease plant 2 capacity by 1 unit, while maintaining the operating regime (3.18). The increased costs of meeting the additional unit of demand in period 1 are $b_1 + (\beta_1 - \beta_2)$, but note that the additional unit of plant 1 installed will also be used in period 2, since $b_1 < b_2$, with net savings in operating costs of $b_2 - b_1$. The total incremental cost of meeting the additional unit of demand in period 1 is therefore $b_1 + (\beta_1 - \beta_2) - (b_2 - b_1) = p_1$, as given in (3.16). A similar discussion serves to show that p_2 in (3.17) is the long-run marginal cost of meeting an additional unit of demand in period 2. Finally, it is interesting to note from (3.16) and (3.19)–(3.20) that $b_1 < p_1 < b_2$. Thus (3.16)–(3.20) imply the following bounds:

$$b_1 < P_1 < b_2 < b_2 + \beta_2 = P_2 < b_1 + \beta_1 \tag{3.21}$$

Note from (3.14)–(3.15) that the introduction of a more diverse technology leads to lower peak-period prices and higher off-peak prices. The reader may verify, however, that costs are exactly covered

at the optimal prices (3.16)–(3.17) just as they are in the one-plant case
with prices (3.14)–(3.15).

Summarising the two-period, two-plant case, the cost conditions
(3.19)–(3.20) must hold if both types of capacity are to be used at
optimum. Given this and the fact that (once installed) plants with
cheaper operating cost will always be used first, the usual rule of pricing
at marginal cost emerges. Net profits are zero at optimum. We will see
below that analogous cost conditions and pricing results obtain more
generally.

Optimal plant mix

Before considering more general cases, we have to consider some of the
features of the optimal plant mix. We only briefly sketch the principal
results, which are rigorously demonstrated in Crew and Kleindorfer
(1979a). Before going any further, we can state one obvious category of
plants that is not used, namely, any plant type l whose b_l and β_l are both
higher than some other available plant type. Thus, without loss of
generality, we can assume that the m available technologies have been
numbered so that the following cost conditions hold:

$$\beta_1 > \ldots > \beta_m > 0; \quad 0 < b_1 \ldots < b_m. \tag{3.22}$$

Next we note that whatever (optimal) output vector $(x_1, \ldots, x_n)$
obtains, the optimal q_l, q_{li} must be solutions to the following capacity
planning problem:

Problem CP: For $\{x_i \leqslant 0 \mid 1 \leqslant i \leqslant n\}$ given,

$$\text{Min } CQ = \sum_{i=1}^{n} \sum_{l=1}^{m} b_l q_{li} + \sum_{l=1}^{m} \beta_l q_l \tag{3.23}$$

subject to:

$$\sum_{l=1}^{m} q_{li} = x_i, \text{ for all } i \tag{3.24}$$

$$0 \leqslant q_{li} \leqslant q_l, \text{ for all } i, l, \tag{3.25}$$

where $Q = (q_{11}, q_{12}, \ldots, q_{1n}, q_{21}, \ldots, q_{m1}, \ldots, q_{mn}, q_1, \ldots, q_m)$ and where
C is the corresponding cost vector in (3.23). The next step in solving the
cost-minimisation problem CP is to provide a means of narrowing

down the choice of plants beyond (3.22). This involves the following Lemma which we state without proof.

Lemma: For all plant types k and $\hat{k}$ for which $k < \hat{k}$, the following must hold if both plants are to be used in the optimal solution:

$$\frac{\beta_k - \beta_{\hat{k}}}{n} < b_{\hat{k}} - b_k < \beta_k - \beta_{\hat{k}} \tag{3.26}$$

If the left-hand (respectively, right-hand) inequality in (3.26) is violated, only plant $\hat{k}$ (respectively, plant k) need be used in any optimal solution.

For two periods and two plants the reader may easily reconcile (3.19)–(3.20) with the Lemma setting $n = 2$. While the Lemma indicates which plants are used it does not indicate the amounts of capacity q_l, and amounts produced by each plant in each period, q_{li}. To derive this is complicated and calls for a lengthy proposition which we do not state here (see Crew and Kleindorfer 1979a, pp. 42–50, 63–5). We will, however, state the following important results which are of general interest regarding optimal plant mix.

Result A: The efficient technological frontier is downward-sloping and convex in (b, β) space (as shown in Figure 3.4).

Result B: Assuming (3.22) and (3.26) are satisfied, capacity is installed and operated in order of increasing operating cost. In particular plant 1, is used in every period ($q_{li} > 0$ for all i).

We can now proceed to examine some issues in optimal pricing. Our treatment will be *illustrative* using examples.

Optimal practice

Let us first note that equation (3.10) indicates that price is to be set to λ_i, the Lagrangian multiplier associated with constraint (3.3) at period i. This is none other than the long-run incremental cost of meeting an additional unit of demand in period i, i.e. $\lambda_i = LMRC_i$. (To establish this simply note from the theory of linear programming that the optimal solution to the dual linear programme to Problem *CP* is characterised by (3.11)–(3.13), and we may interpret λ_i as the shadow price of constraint (3.24) at optimum. Clearly, the shadow price of (3.24) at optimum is the per unit incremental cost of marginally

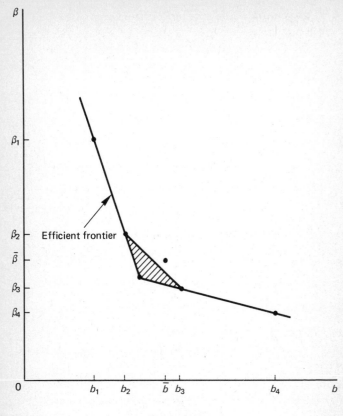

Figure 3.4

increasing x_i. Thus $\lambda_i = LRMC$.) Given this meaning for λ_i, we may begin a more specific analysis of optimal pricing.

From the just stated result that $q_{1i} > 0$ for all i, we see from (3.12) that $\lambda_i - \mu_{1i} = b_1$ for all i. Since plant 1 capacity q_1 is positive, (3.11) implies:

$$\sum_{i=1}^{n} \mu_{1i} = \beta_1 \tag{3.27}$$

so that from $\lambda_i = \mu_{1i} + b$ and (3.10):

$$\sum_{i=1}^{n} p_i = nb_1 + \beta_1. \tag{3.28}$$

From (3.11) and $\mu_{li} \geqslant 0$ we obtain $\mu_{li} \leqslant \beta_l$ for all i,l. Thus from (3.10) and (3.12):

$$\lambda_i = p_i \leqslant b_l + \mu_{li} \leqslant b_l + \beta_l, \text{ for all } i,l \tag{3.29}$$

To obtain more stringent bounds on the optimal prices requires additional detail, as in Crew and Kleindorfer (1979a). We state the main result here without proof:

$$b_1 \leqslant \lambda_i = p_i \leqslant b_m + \beta_m, \qquad i = 1, \ldots, n. \tag{3.30}$$

If only plant 1 were available, (3.28) would still hold. Note, however, that the addition of further plant types has reduced the possible peak price from $b_1 + \beta_1$ to $b_m + \beta_m$. Equation (3.30) is the general analogue to the two-period, two-plant result (3.21).

We now state some specific cases, starting with the case $m = n = 2$ and the previously given results (3.16)–(3.18), this time for the inter-dependent demand case. Simply note that if (3.19)–(3.20) hold and $x_2 > x_1$ at optimum (the firm-peak case), then coupling (3.18) with the Kuhn–Tucker necessary conditions (3.10)–(3.13), we obtain (3.16)–(3.17) as the unique solution.

For the shifting-peak case and $m = n = 2$, where $x_1 = x_2 = x$ at optimum, we note from (3.28) that:

$$p_1 + p_2 = p_1(x) + p_2(x) = 2b_1 + \beta_1 \tag{3.31}$$

must obtain, where $x = (x,x)$. This is then used to solve for x (and therefore also p_1, p_2). Note that only plant 1 is used in the two-period case where $x_1 = x_2 = x$, so that a less diverse optimal technology obtains under a shifting-peak case.

Mild regularity conditions assure that the shifting- and firm-peak cases are mutually exclusive and that the p_1, p_2 solving (3.31) satisfy $p_1 < p_2$. Thus, to solve the $m = n = 2$ case, one checks whether the prices (3.16)–(3.17) lead to $x_2 \geqslant x_1$. If so, a firm-peak solution obtains; otherwise the shifting peak solution determined through (3.31) obtains. We see that the case $m = n = 2$ is solved completely.

For the case $n = 3$ we note that there are many possibilities (twelve, in fact) for ordering the outputs x_1, x_2, x_3 according to magnitude. Assuming, given our usual notation, that demand intensities go from low to high in going from period 1 to period 3, we need only consider the cases: $x_3 > x_2 > x_1$; $x_3 = x_2 > x_1$; $x_3 > x_2 = x_1$; and $x_3 = x_2 = x_1$. For each such assumed ordering, we would in theory have to solve the Kuhn–Tucker conditions (3.10)–(3.13) for p_1, p_2, p_3 and then check at the prices so obtained the assumed initial ordering was valid. For example, in the firm-peak case $(x_3 > x_2 > x_1)$, the optimal prices are as follows:

$$p_1 = 3b_1 + \beta_1 - (2b_2 + \beta_2) \tag{3.32}$$

$$p_2 = 2b_2 + \beta_2 - (b_3 + \beta_3) \tag{3.33}$$

$$p_3 = b_3 + \beta_3 \tag{3.34}$$

We must check that at these prices the assumed ordering $x_3 > x_2 > x_1$ holds. If so, a solution is at hand. The reader should note that with prices determined by (3.32)–(3.34), $p_1 < p_2 < p_3$ will always hold.

The shifting peak result for the case where at optimum $x_1 > x_2 = x_3$ (which case arises when the prices (3.32)–(3.34) lead to $x_1 < x_3 < x_2$) is given by:

$$p_1 = (3b_1 + \beta_1) - (2b_2 + \beta_2) \tag{3.35}$$

$$p_2 + p_3 = 2b_2 + \beta_2 \tag{3.36}$$

$$q_1 = x_1 = q_{li}, \text{ for all } i; \; q_2 = x_2 - x_1 = q_{22} = q_{23}; \; q_{21} = 0 \tag{3.37}$$

where only plants 1 and 2 are now used. (Thus, just as in the case $m = n = 2$, so also here the shifting-peak case leads to a less diverse optimal technology as compared with the firm-peak case $x_3 > x_2 > x_1$.) Note that (3.36) is to be solved together with the requirement $x_2 = x_3$ here. Obviously this could be somewhat tricky in practice, with highly interdependent demands.

Other sub-cases of the three-period and n-period cases can be analysed in a similar way. The important point to realise is the strong interaction between optimal technology, and optimal pricing. Basically, the more variable demand is between the periods $1, \ldots, n$, the more diverse will be the optimal technology, though optimal diversity interacts strongly with cost parameters as well. Looking at the same thing from the pricing side, the more diverse the available technology, the less will be the tendency to flatten demand through peak-load pricing, i.e. the flatter the optimal price schedule will be.

3.4 TIME-VARYING DEMAND AND UNEQUAL-LENGTH PERIODS

We have assumed up to this point that the pricing periods ($i = 1, 2, \ldots, n$ above) are of equal length and that within each such pricing period demand is constant over time. In this section, following Dansby (1975), we relax both assumptions. We assume the cycle of n periods is divided into a set of off-peak periods N_0 and a set of peak periods N_p, where $N_0 \bigcup N_p = \{1, 2, \ldots, n\}$, and where the prices p_0 and p_p must prevail uniformly throughout the respective off-peak and peak periods. The following problem emerges:

$$\text{Max } W = \oint_0^x \{\sum_{i=1}^n P_i(\mathbf{y})dy_i\} - \sum_{i=1}^n \sum_{l=1}^m b_l q_{li} - \sum_{l=1}^m \beta_l q_l, \qquad (3.38)$$

subject to:

$$\sum_{l=1}^m q_{li} = x_i, \text{ for all } i \qquad (3.39)$$

$$q_l - q_{li} \geq 0, \text{ for all } i, l \qquad (3.40)$$

$$P_i(x) = p_0, \ i\varepsilon N_0; \ P_i(x) = p_p, \qquad i\varepsilon N_p \qquad (3.41)$$

$$x_i \geq 0, \ q_i \geq 0, \ q_{li} \geq 0, \ p_0, \ \geq 0, \text{ for all } i, l, \qquad (3.42)$$

where all variables other than p_0, p_p are as in (3.2)–(3.5). Note that the problem (3.38)–(3.42) is obtained from (3.2)–(3.5) by adding the constraints (3.41). The new problem formulation now allows for unequal-length periods and time-varying and interdependent demand.

To derive first-order conditions for (3.38)–(3.42) we associate multipliers ζ_i with constraints (3.4) and, differentiating the resulting Lagrangian as in (3.9), we obtain the following analogues to (3.10)–(3.13):

$$P_i(x) = \lambda_i + \zeta_i \sum_{j\varepsilon N_0} \frac{\partial P_j}{\partial x_i} = p_0, \ i\varepsilon N_0 \qquad (3.43)$$

$$P_i(x) = \lambda_i + \zeta_i \sum_{j\varepsilon N_p} \frac{\partial P_j}{\partial x_i} = p_p, \ i\varepsilon N_\mathrm{p} \qquad (3.44)$$

$$\sum_{i\varepsilon N_0} \zeta_i = \sum_{j\varepsilon N_p} \zeta_j = 0 \qquad (3.45)$$

$$\sum_{i=1}^n \mu_{li} \leq \beta_l, \ q_l \left(\sum_{i=1}^n \mu_{li} - \beta_l\right) = 0, \text{ for all } l \qquad (3.46)$$

$$\lambda_i - \mu_{li} \leq b_l, \ q_{li}(\lambda_i - \mu_{li} - b_l) = 0, \text{ for all } i, l \qquad (3.47)$$

$$\mu_{li} \geq 0, \ \mu_{li}(q_l - q_{li}) = 0, \text{ for all } i, l. \qquad (3.48)$$

Notice that (3.46)–(3.48) are the same as (3.11)–(3.13). This allows similar solution techniques to be applied here. In particular the multipliers λ_i and μ_{li} have the same meaning here as in (3.10)–(3.13), namely λ_i is the long-run incremental cost of meeting an additional unit of demand in period i. We will concentrate on the independent demand case where $\partial P_i/\partial x_j = 0$, $i \neq j$. In solving for optimal prices for this case note from (3.43)–(3.45) that:

$$\sum_{i\varepsilon N_0} \frac{P_0 - \lambda_i}{\partial P_i/\partial x_i} = \sum_{i\varepsilon N_0} \zeta_i = 0 = \sum_{i\varepsilon N_p} \zeta_i = \sum_{i\varepsilon N_p} \frac{P_p - \lambda_i}{\partial P_i/\partial x_i} \tag{3.49}$$

so that solving for p_0, p_p in (3.49) yields the following optimal prices when demands are independent:

$$P_0 = \sum_{i\varepsilon N_0} \alpha_i \lambda_i, \ \alpha_i = \frac{1}{\partial P_i \partial x_i} \bigg/ \left(\sum_{j\varepsilon N_0} \frac{1}{\partial P_j/\partial x_j} \right) \tag{3.50}$$

$$P_0 = \sum_{i\varepsilon N_p} \alpha_i \lambda_i, \ \alpha_i = \frac{1}{\partial P_i/\partial x_i} \bigg/ \left(\sum_{j\varepsilon N_p} \frac{1}{\partial P_j/\partial x_j} \right) \tag{3.51}$$

Since clearly

$$\alpha_i \geqslant 0 \quad \text{and} \quad \sum_N \alpha_i = \sum_{N_p} \alpha_j = 1,$$

we see that P_0 and P_p are convex combinations of period long-run marginal costs in the respective off-peak and peak pricing periods. Thus, when a different price can be charged in each period, we have price $= \lambda = LRMC$, and when the constraints (3.41) are imposed, a weighted average of period-specific $LRMCs$ results, with period weights determined by the slope of the period demand curve relative to the slope of other period demands in the pricing period, where the slopes are evaluated at the optimal output x.

To illustrate, consider the case $m = 1$ and assume a firm peak where, for some period $k \ \varepsilon \ N_p$, $q_{1k} = q_1 > 0$ and where $0 < q_{1i} < q_1$ for all $i \neq k$. Then from (3.46) and (3.48) we have $\mu_{1k} = \beta_1$ and $\mu_{1i} = 0$ for $i \neq k$. From (3.47) $\lambda_i = \mu_{1i} + b_1$ so that $\lambda_k = b_1 + \beta_1$ and $\lambda_i = b_i$ for $i \neq k$. Thus from (3.50), (3.51) we have:

$$p_0 = b_1 \tag{3.52}$$

$$p_p = b_1 + \alpha_k \beta_1 \leqslant b_1 + \beta_1 \tag{3.53}$$

where α_k is given in (3.51). Thus we see that p_p never exceeds $b_1 + \beta_1$, which is the optimal price to charge in period k if different prices could be charged in each period i. The above result reflects a trade-off between suppressing peak demand in period k and resulting welfare losses from pricing above b_1 in periods ($i \varepsilon N_p$) other than k. From the definition of α_k in (3.51) the greater the slope of demand in period k relative to other demands $i \varepsilon N_p$, the smaller will be the factor α_k and therefore the lower the price p_p.

To investigate the shifting peak where $m = 1$, suppose $x_i = q_{1i} = q_i$ for $i \varepsilon \bar{N}$ and $q_{1i} < q_1$ for $i \notin \bar{N}$. Then, from (3.46)–(3.47), $\lambda_i = b_1 + \mu_{1i}$ for all i with $\mu_{1i} = i \ \varepsilon \ \bar{N}$, and:

$$\sum \mu_{1i} = \beta_1 \tag{3.54}$$

Substituting the just-given λ_i in (3.50)–(3.51), we obtain the following prices:

$$p_0 = b_1 + \sum_{\bar{N} \cap N_0} \alpha_i \mu_{1i} \tag{3.55}$$

$$p_p = b_1 + \sum_{\bar{N} \cap N_p} \alpha_i \mu_{1i} \tag{3.56}$$

where the μ_{1i} *in* (3.55)–(3.56) *are determined from* (3.54) *and the shifting-peak requirement that, at the prices* (3.55)–(3.56), $x_i = q_1$ *for all* $i \varepsilon N$.

Two examples may serve to illustrate the shifting-peak case. In the first, assume that $\bar{N} \subset N_p$ and that $\partial P_i / \partial x_i = \partial P_j / \partial x_j$ for all $i, j \varepsilon \bar{N}$. Then $p_0 = b_1$ and, $P_p = b_1 + \beta_1 / n_p$, where n_p is the number of periods in N_p. Only when the peak is flat (i.e. $\bar{N} = N_p$) will capacity costs be completely recovered.

As a second example, consider the case where $\bar{N} = (j, k)$, with $j \varepsilon N_0$ and $k \varepsilon \bar{N}_p$. Then (3.55)–(3.56) imply:

$$p_0 = b_1 + \alpha_j \mu_j \qquad p_p = b_1 + \alpha_k \mu_k \tag{3.57}$$

where μ_j and μ_k are determined through the requirements that $\mu_j + \mu_k = \beta_1$ and $x_j = x_k$ (at the prices (3.57)).

3.5 PROFIT MAXIMISATION AND SECOND-BEST RESULTS

It is interesting to compare the above welfare-optimal results with those of a proft-maximising monopolist. As a change of pace we will investigate this issue using the Pressman formulation (3.1) instead of (3.2)–(3.5). We restrict attention to the two-period, firm-peak case (where at optimum $x_2 > x_1$) throughout this section. We first note that the solution to (3.1) for this case is easily found from Kuhn–Tucker theory to be:

$$P_1(\mathbf{x}) = \partial C(\mathbf{x},z)/\partial x_1, \ P_2(\mathbf{x}) = \partial C(\mathbf{x},z)/\partial x_2 + \partial C(\mathbf{x},z)/\partial z \qquad (3.58)$$

i.e. long-run marginal-cost pricing as expected. We may reformulate (3.1) as follows for the proft-maximising case:

$$\text{Max } \Pi = \sum_{i=1}^{2} x_i P_i(\mathbf{x}) - C(\mathbf{x},z) \qquad (3.59)$$

subject to $x_i \leqslant z$, $x_i \geqslant 0$, $z \geqslant 0$, $i = 1,2$.

Forming the Lagrangian for (3.59) and taking first-order conditions, we obtain:

$$\partial R(\mathbf{x})/\partial x_i = \partial C(\mathbf{x},z)/\partial x_i + \mu_i, \ i = 1,2 \qquad (3.60)$$

$$\partial C(\mathbf{x},z)/\partial z = \mu_1 + \mu_2 \qquad (3.61)$$

$$\mu_i \geqslant 0, \ \mu_i(z - x_i) = 0, \ i = 1,2, \qquad (3.62)$$

where $R(\mathbf{x}) = $ total revenue $= \Sigma x_i P_i(\mathbf{x})$ and μ_i is the multiplier associated with the constraint $x_i \leqslant z$. Since $x_1 > x_2$, we obtain the following profit-maximising result:

$$\partial R/\partial x_1 = \partial C/\partial x_1, \ \partial R/\partial x_2 = \partial C/\partial x_2 + \partial C/\partial z, \qquad (3.63)$$

which differs from (3.58) only in that marginal revenue, instead of price, is equated to marginal cost. This result would obtain if profit maximisation were carried out in (3.2)–(3.5) in place of welfare maximisation; the corresponding results for the profit-maximising case throughout the preceding analysis are then obtained by equating marginal revenue in period i to $LRMC_i = \lambda_i$. Under mild regularity conditions this leads to higher prices and lower outputs under monopoly pricing, as we now illustrate for the case where $C(\mathbf{x},z)$ is given by

(3.6)–(3.8) with $m=n=2$. For this case we obtain the optimal solution by substituting $\partial R/\partial x_i$ for p_i in (3.16)–(3.17), that is:

$$\partial R/\partial x_1 = 2b_1 + \beta_1 - (b_2 + \beta_2), \quad \partial R/\partial x_2 = b_2 + \beta_2 \tag{3.64}$$

Since $\partial R/\partial x_i = P_i(\mathbf{x}) + x_i \partial P_i/\partial x_i + x_j \partial P_j/\partial x_i$ $(j \neq i)$, we see that if cross-effects are not too large (so that $x_i \partial P_i/\partial x_i + x_j \partial P_j/\partial x_i < 0$), then $\partial R/\partial x_i < P_i(\mathbf{x})$ for $i=1,2$. Thus comparing (3.64) with (3.16)–(3.17) we see that, normally, prices will be everywhere higher and output everywhere lower under profit-maximising behaviour than under the corresponding welfare-optimal solution.

When demands are independent, $\partial R/\partial x_i = P_i(x_i) + x_i dP_i/dx_i$, and we may write (3.63) as:

$$p_1 = \partial C/\partial x_1/(1 + 1/\eta_1), \; p_2 = [\partial C/\partial x_2 + \partial C/\partial z]/(1 + 1/\eta_1), \tag{3.65}$$

where $\eta_i =$ elasticity in period $i = P_i(x_i)/(x_i dP_i/dx_i)$. Thus the more elastic demand is in period i, the lower will be the price in period i. In fact, as Bailey and White (1974) have pointed out, if η_1 is sufficiently small compared with η_2, then the peak-price may actually be lower than the off-peak price with profit maximisation.

The above analysis indicates that the transaction and comparison of welfare-maximising and profit-maximising solutions is straightforward. The deleterious welfare consequences of the pure profit-maximising solution are evident here and have provided the rationale for state intervention and regulation of utilities. As we indicated in Chapter 2, and as we discuss more fully in Part III, a critical issue for evaluating such public control is an understanding of second-best solutions which maximise welfare while providing a specified level of profit. Such a profit-constrained, welfare-maximising approach is especially important under increasing returns to scale ($\partial C^2/\partial^2 z < 0$ above) where deficits occur under marginal-cost pricing, the first-best solution. Two approaches have been suggested for dealing with this problem: (a) the determination of second-best prices by appending a minimum profit constraint to (3.1); and (b) the use of multipart tariffs. Let us consider each of these briefly.

Consider the first problem of maximising (3.1) subject to $\Pi \geqslant \Pi_0$, where Π is as in (3.59) and Π_0 is a pre-specified minimum profit level. Taking first-order conditions (while still assuming $n=2$ and $x_2 > x_1$) we obtain the following:

$$P_1(x) + \zeta \partial R/\partial x_1 = \partial C/\partial x_1 \, (1+\zeta) \tag{3.66}$$

$$P_2(x) + \zeta \partial R/\partial x_2 = (\partial C/\partial x_2 + \partial C/\partial z) \, (1+\zeta) \tag{3.67}$$

$$\zeta \geqslant 0, \quad \zeta(\Pi - \Pi_0) = 0, \tag{3.68}$$

where ζ is the multiplier associated with the constraint $\Pi \geqslant \Pi_0$. Again restricting attention to the case of independent demands, (3.66)–(3.67) may be written:

$$p_1 = P_1(x_1) = [(1+\zeta) \, \partial C/\partial x_1]/[1 + \zeta(1 + 1/\eta_1)] \tag{3.69}$$

$$p_2 = P_2(x_2) = [(1+\zeta) \, (\partial C/\partial x_2 + \partial C/\partial z)]/[1 + \zeta(1 + 1/\eta_2)] \tag{3.70}$$

where ζ is determined from (3.68). Since $\zeta > 0$ when the constraint $\Pi \geqslant \Pi_0$ is binding (i.e. when the unconstrained welfare-maximising solution yields $\Pi < \Pi_0$), we see that the second-best prices (3.69)–(3.70) are both higher, with relative price increases proportional to demand elasticity as with the inverse elasticity rule discussed in Chapter 2.

Following Bailey and White (1974) we summarise the above discussion in Table 3.1, which provides comparative results for the profit-maximising, welfare-maximising and second-best solutions for the case of a simple two-period, one-plant technology with costs b and β.

Table 3.1

Objective	Peak price	Off-peak price
Maximise welfare	$b + \beta$	b
Maximise profits	$\dfrac{b + \beta}{1 + \dfrac{1}{\eta_1}}$	$\dfrac{b}{1 + \dfrac{1}{\eta_2}}$
Maximise welfare subject to $\Pi \geqslant \Pi_0$ (ζ determined by (3.68))	$\dfrac{(1+\zeta)(b+\beta)}{1 + \zeta(1+1/\eta_2)}$	$\dfrac{(1+\zeta)b}{1 + \zeta(1+1/\eta_2)}$

The second approach to second-best pricing is the use of multipart tariffs, as explained by Oi (1971), Ng and Weisser (1974), and Leland

and Meyer (1976). In the simplest case[8] a two-part tariff obtains where customers are first charged a licence fee (or connect charge) F. After paying the licence fee consumers may purchase additional units in period i at price p_i as usual.

Consider the case of a single period ($n = 1$). For a single consumer at a given price (p) consumer's surplus (S) is defined straightforwardly as previously. Now if F exceeds S, clearly the consumer will consume nothing at price p (since he would have to first pay F to do so, with the result that net surplus at price p would be negative). If $S \geqslant F$, of course, then the price pair (F,p) could be levied, and demand would be x for this consumer.

Turning to the problem of welfare-maximising (F,p) pairs, we may note that, neglecting income effects, the optimal solution is easily seen to be price equals marginal cost, providing that this allows a licence fee F to be collected at this price sufficiently high to satisfy $\Pi \geqslant \Pi_0$, and sufficiently low so that no consumer disconnects (because $F > S$). The problem of solving for optimal (F,p) pairs when marginal cost is not feasible is difficult since it must consider explicitly the set of subscribers implied by each (F,p) combination. For any given subset $\bar{V} \subset V$ of the total consumer population V, one can solve for second-best (F,p) pairs by appending to the problem ((3.1), subject to $\Pi \geqslant \Pi_0$) the additional constraint that only pairs (F,p) are considered for which the surplus at p exceeds F for every consumer in $\bar{V}$. By then considering all possible subsets of V which allow for the profit constraint to be met, the welfare-optimal subscriber set $\bar{V}*$ and corresponding prices ($F*,p*$) can be obtained. Not surprisingly, distributional matters may play a role here in determining (through F) the subscriber subset. Also not surprisingly, Pareto improvements over simple tariffs may be effected through the use of the more flexible two-part tariffs as a policy instrument in meeting budget constraints. Such two-part tariffs are also frequently encountered in practice, as we discuss in Part IV.

The above discussion underlines some of the difficulties one may encounter in attempting to interpret and implement marginal-cost pricing in practice. The important thing to bear in mind is the central position of long-run marginal-cost pricing as the basis for understanding the trade-offs which practical necessity may force on the policy-making process.

4 Stochastic Models of Peak-load Pricing

So far, in setting out the classic peak-load model and its extensions, we have retained the assumption of that model that demand is deterministic. Many public utilities face demands that have not only the strong periodic element of the peak-load model, but also an important random element. Stochastic demand creates various complications which typically are not considered in the deterministic case. It is necessary to decide whether demand is to be met, and what happens, by way of rationing, when demand is not met.[1] The analysis which follows is directed at answering these questions. In Section 4.1 we describe briefly some of the main contributions to the literature on peak-load pricing under uncertainty. In Section 4.2 we provide a general framework for analysing the problems of stochastic demand, comparing the results with the deterministic solutions derived in Chapter 3. Section 4.3 is concerned with examining some major issues of the stochastic problem, namely dealing with excess demand and rationing, Section 4.4 presents illustrative examples and Section 4.5 is a brief summary of stochastic peak-load pricing.

We consider the analysis of this chapter of particular importance to the issues of public utility regulation. For this reason, and our desire to make its implications clear, we continue with its development by means of illustrative numerical results in Section 4.5. The reader may in fact just wish to skim the Sections 4.1–4.4 first, and then go on to Section 4.5 for concrete illustrations of the theory presented here.

4.1 PROBLEMS OF STOCHASTIC DEMAND

The interest in stochastic demand in public utility economics is rather recent. After the contributions of French economists discussed by Drèze (1964), Brown and Johnson (1969) re-emphasised its importance. Their articles initiated a controversy, confined mainly to the *American Economic Review*, as to the effects of stochastic demand on public utility pricing. Brown and Johnson made the familiar cost assumptions of the Boiteux–Steiner–Williamson peak-load model, but they replaced the periodic demands of the peak-load model by a one-period stochastic-demand model. Like the deterministic case they assumed that the utility was welfare-maximising, or more precisely expected welfare-maximising to take into account the effect of stochastic demand. Immediately a discrepancy was apparent between their results and previous results. Their solution to the one-period stochastic model was simply $p = b$, in stark contrast to the corresponding one-period deterministic solution[2] of $p = b + \beta$. This difference was paradoxical, and the more so since their solution was apparently to hold no matter how small the level of uncertainty. Thus, as the long-accepted optimal solution for deterministic demand was $p = b + \beta$, their solution of $p = b$ implied an unexplained and counter-intuitive discontinuity in the optimal stochastic solution as the degree of uncertainty approached zero.

Aside from this odd behaviour of Brown and Johnson's optimal price, another unusual aspect of their development was the possibility of frequently occurring excess demand at their indicated solution. This low level of reliability at optimum was criticised by Turvey (1970) as implausible (e.g. if gas supplies are unreliable, explosions might occur as the gas comes on and off in premises temporarily unoccupied). Taking up this point, Meyer (1975a) reformulated the Brown and Johnson model by adding reliability constraints to it. This raised the issue of how the optimum levels of such constraints were to be determined. This issue has since been addressed by Carlton (1977) and Crew and Kleindorfer (1978) but there are still a number of problems unresolved here, as we discuss in Section 4.3 below.

Another criticism of Brown and Johnson's paper, voiced clearly by Visscher (1973), concerned their assumptions as to how demand was rationed in the event of demand exceeding capacity. Brown and Johnson assumed that in this event consumers were serviced by means of a costless rationing process in accordance with their willingness to pay. This assumption turns out to have a crucial effect in their analysis, as we will demonstrate in Section 4.3. Intuitively their assumption appears highly implausible at first sight because it implies that one of the major benefits of pricing, namely rationing according to marginal willingness to pay, is available without having to worry about the actual price charged!

To summarise, the Brown and Johnson paper has been seminal in focusing recent discussion on stochastic peak-loading problems. In particular, this discussion has underlined the importance of reliability and rationing in dealing with welfare-optimal pricing under uncertainty. Accordingly we analyse in the next section a simple model of pricing under uncertainty with special attention to these matters and to their interaction with technology choice. Thereafter, additional aspects of the recent literature on rationing are taken up.

4.2 A SIMPLE MODEL OF PRICING UNDER UNCERTAINTY[3]

In this section we extend our analysis of Chapter 3 on optimal pricing under a diverse technology to cover problems with stochastic demand. In doing so we have made a number of simplifying assumptions which must be underlined at the very beginning. First, demand uncertainty is quite simply characterised (through additive or multiplicative perturbation of a mean demand function). Second, demands are assumed independent across periods, except for possible correlation in the random components of demand. Third, we will use the expected value of the traditional welfare function, net of rationing costs, as our welfare measure.

The use of the traditional welfare function is doubtless the most serious of the simplifications undertaken here. The first implication of this is our willingness to assume risk neutrality and negligible income effects in consumer preference. Quite aside from considerations of risk-aversion on the purely monetary side, there is a presumption in using this welfare measure that consumer preferences as regards reliability may be represented adequately through expected willingness to pay as represented by a given (reliability-independent) demand curve. However, if reliability is viewed as an aspect of product quality, then it is clear that demand curves may shift as reliability shifts.[4] We neglect such issues here, with the partial justification that in many public utilities only a very narrow band of (high) reliability is *a priori* reasonable. In such cases demand shifts due to reliability changes in this band would also be small, so that the traditional welfare measure would continue to be reasonable for such cases.

We now spell out the assumptions of our model. When not otherwise indicated, notation and assumptions of Chapter 3 are retained.

Demand

Unless stated otherwise, demand in each period i is assumed independent of other period demands and is represented in additive form[5] as:

$$D_i(p_i, \tilde{u}_i) = X_i(p_i) + \tilde{u}_i, \tag{4.1}$$

where $X_i(p_i)$ represents mean demand in period i and u_i is a disturbance term with expected value $E(\tilde{u}_i) = 0$. We assume X_i to be continuously differentiable and to possess an inverse denoted by p_i. X_i and P_i are assumed to satisfy the following regularity conditions:

$$-A \leqslant \frac{dP_i}{dx_i} < 0; \frac{dX_i}{dp_i} < 0. \tag{4.2}$$

where $A > 0$ is some fixed constant.

Letting $u = (u_1, \ldots, u_n)$, we assume that u is a continuous random variable, i.e. denoting by F and F_i the cumulative distribution functions of u and u_i respectively, we assume that F and $F_i, i = 1, \ldots n$, are continuous. The random variables u_i need not be stochastically independent.

Production costs

We retain the same conventions regarding ordering, capacity costs and running costs of the n-plant model discussed in Chapter 3. In particular we exclude dominated plant types, assuming simply that:

$$0 < b_1 < b_2 \ldots < b_m, \quad \beta_1 > \beta_2 \ldots > \beta_m > 0. \tag{4.3}$$

In Chapter 3 we noted that the optimal short-run allocation of demand to capacity is achieved by using first the plant with lowest operating costs. For emphasis we repeat the mathematical expression for the optimal amount of output of plant l in period i below:

$$q_{li}(x_i, q) = \text{Min } [x_i - \sum_{k=1}^{l-1} q_{ki}(x_i, q), q_l]. \tag{4.4}$$

As previously, total production costs can be derived straightforwardly using (4.4) and substituting for x_i from (4.1) as:

$$\text{Total production costs} = \sum_{l=1}^{m} \sum_{i=1}^{n} b_l q_{li} [D_i(p_i, u_i), q] + \sum_{l=1}^{m} \beta_l q_l. \tag{4.5}$$

Rationing costs

The presence of stochastic demand means that a situation may occur where quantity demanded exceeds capacity. Thus in terms of Figure

4.1, when price is given by p_i and demand by $D_i(p_i,u_i)$, optimal output is simply x_i. However, where demand is given by $D_i(p_i,u_i')$ output can only be z. There is an excess demand of $x_i'-z$. This creates a rationing problem, which can be resolved in a number of ways. One might simply serve consumers in random order until capacity is exhausted; or when consumers must queue up for service, those with the lowest willingness to pay may be willing to stand in line the longest, leading to rationing in order of lowest willingness to pay; as a final example, the utility might determine the marginal valuations of individual consumers and then ration according to these, i.e. in order of marginal willingness to pay.

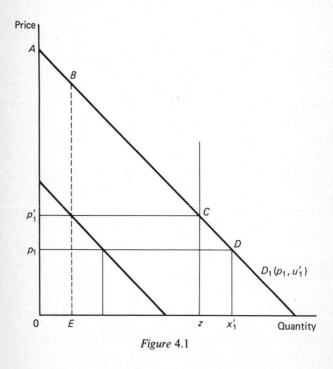

Figure 4.1

It should be clear that different rationing schemes may yield different consumers' surplus in the event of excess demand. Considering Figure 4.1, for example, and assuming the demand curve $D_i(p_i,u_i')$ obtains, rationing in order of willingness to pay leads to gross surplus $OACz$, whereas rationing in order of lowest willingness to pay yields a surplus of $EBDx_i'$, where $E=x_i'-z$ is the excess demand for p_i, z, u_i' as shown. Of course, rationing according to (highest) willingness to pay will always lead to higher gross surplus than other rationing schemes and in this case, indeed, $OACz > EBDx_i'$.

Besides the differential effects of rationing on consumers' surplus, different rationing schemes may also have different costs of administering them. In representing the total welfare impact, we need to consider both surplus losses and administrative costs. Our approach will be to take as a base case the (perfect) rationing scheme proposed originally by Brown and Johnson (1969) which assumes costless rationing according to willingness to pay. For a specific rationing scheme r, we then define (incremental) rationing costs R_r (or just R when r is clear) to be any surplus losses and administrative costs over and above those incurred under the Brown and Johnson scheme. Alternatively, the reader may think of r as rationing according to willingness to pay and of R_r as the cost of implementing this scheme.

In general one may expect R_r to depend on price, output and capacity in complex ways. We restrict attention in this section, however, to rationing costs which depend only on the level of excess demand. Specifically, we assume that R_r is of the form:

$$\text{Total rationing costs} = R = \sum_{i=1}^{n} r_i(D_i(p_i, \tilde{u}_i) - z), \tag{4.6}$$

where $z = q_1 + q_2 + \ldots + q_m$ is total capacity, and where rationing costs in period i are just $r_i(D_i - z)$, where r_i is assumed non-negative, convex and continuously differentiable and such that $dr_i(y)/dy = 0$ when $y \leqslant 0$.

The social-welfare function

As announced earlier, we will use the expected value of the traditional welfare function as our measure of net benefit. To obtain a formal expression for this requires some care, however.

Let us first consider the problem of measuring gross benefits using Figure 4.1. In case of $D_i(p_i, u_i)$ total revenue plus consumers' surplus is given in exactly the same way as in the deterministic case by the area under the curve to z, provided we make our base-case assumption that rationing takes place according to marginal willingness to pay. In this case, therefore, gross surplus is the integral under the (inverse) demand curve up to the actual amount supplied. We can incorporate these considerations mathematically as follows. For any given value of the disturbance term, $u = (u_1, \ldots, u_n)$, and for given price and capacity vectors $\mathbf{p}$ and $\mathbf{q}$, the actual output in any period is:

$$S_i(p_i,u_i,z) = \text{Min} \{D_i(p_i,u_i), z\}. \tag{4.7}$$

Using (4.7) we see that, for given u, p and q, consumers' surplus under rationing according to willingness to pay is therefore (note: $z = q_1 + q_2 + \ldots q_m$);

$$CS(\mathbf{u},\mathbf{p},\mathbf{q}) = \sum_{i=1}^{n} \int_0^{S_i(p_i,u_i,z)} P_i(x_i - u_i)dx_i, \tag{4.8}$$

since, from (4.1), the inverse demand curve for given u_i is $X_i^{-1}(x_i - u_i) = P_i(x_i - u_i)$.

Now using (4.8) and recalling our definition of rationing cost as being relative to Brown and Johnson rationing, we obtain the following measure of welfare returns

$W_r(\mathbf{u},\mathbf{p},\mathbf{q})$ for any given rationing scheme r and fixed u, p, q:

$$W(\mathbf{u},\mathbf{p},\mathbf{q}) = \sum_{i=1}^{n} \int_0^{S_i(p_i,u_i,z)} P_i(x_i - u_i)dx_i - \sum_{i=1}^{n}\sum_{l=1}^{m} b_l q_{li}(D_i(p_i,u_i), q) -$$
$$\sum_{l=1}^{m} f_l q_{li} - \sum_{i=1}^{n} r_i(D_i(p_i,u_i) - z). \tag{4.9}$$

Taking expected values, the desired welfare function may now be expressed as:

$$\bar{W}_r(\mathbf{p},\mathbf{q}) = E_u\{W_r(\tilde{u},\mathbf{p},\mathbf{q})\}. \tag{4.10}$$

The problem of interest is to maximise W over the set of feasible rationing schemes and non-negative price and capacity vectors. In this section we will assume a fixed rationing scheme r, and we write simply $W(\mathbf{p},\mathbf{q})$ for welfare returns. We return to comparative rationing results in the next section. We also assume that the random variable $\tilde{u}$ is such that $W(\mathbf{p},\mathbf{q})$ exists for all feasible price and capacity vectors.[6]

Optimality conditions[7]

As the derivation of the optimality conditions is rather technical, we have placed it in the appendix to this chapter. After giving below the optimality conditions, we proceed to derive first some results concerning optimal capacity and efficient technology, and second some implications for price:[8]

$$\frac{\partial \bar{W}}{\partial p_i} = p_i X_i'(p_i) F_i(z - X_i(p_i))$$

$$- \sum_{l=1}^{m} b_l X_i'(p_i)[F_i(Q_l - X_i(p_i)) - F_i(Q_{l-1} - X_i(p_i))]$$

$$- X_i'(p_i) E_{\tilde{u}_i}\{r_i'(X_i(p_i) + \tilde{u}_i - z)\}, \qquad i = 1, \ldots, n. \qquad (4.11)$$

$$\frac{\partial \bar{W}}{\partial q_k} = \sum_{i=1}^{n} \{ \int z - X_i(p_i) P_i(z - u_i) dF_i(u_i)$$

$$- b_k[1 - F_i(Q_k - X_i(p_i))]\} + \sum_{l=k+1}^{m} b_l [F_i(Q_l - X_i(p_i))$$

$$- F_i(Q_{l-1} - X_i(p_i))] + E_{\tilde{u}_i}\{r_i'(X_i(p_i) + \tilde{u}_i - z)\} - \beta_k,$$

$$k = 1, \ldots, m \qquad (4.12)$$

In the above expression prime denotes derivative and capacity through plant l is denoted by Q_l, so that:

$$Q_l = \sum_{k=1}^{l} q_k, \qquad l = 1, \ldots, m, \qquad (4.13)$$

where we continue to use z for total capacity so that $z = Q_m$. Also, since F_i is the cumulative distribution function (*CDF*) of u_i, note that $F_i(Q_l - X_i(p_i))$ is just the probability $Pr\{u_i \leqslant Q_k - X_i(p_i)\} = Pr\{X_i(p_i) + \tilde{u}_i \leqslant Q_l\}$, i.e. the probability that demand does not exceed capacity (Q_l) of the first l types.

The above expressions were obtained essentially by a marginal argument and can be best understood intuitively in this light. Regarding (4.11), for example, if we use the just stated meaning of $F_i(Q_1 - X_i(p_i))$ and set $\partial \bar{W}/\partial p_i = 0$, we obtain the following condition which the optimal prices must satisfy:

$$p_i X_i'(p_i) Pr\{D_i(p_i, \tilde{u}) \leqslant z\} = \sum_{l=1}^{m} b_l X_i'(p_i) Pr\{Q_{l-1} \leqslant D_i(p_i, \tilde{u}_i) \leqslant Q_l\}$$

$$+ X_i'(p_i) E_{\tilde{u}_i}\{r_i'(D_i(P_i, \tilde{u}_i) - z)\}. \qquad (4.14)$$

Now when demand is greater than capacity z, increasing the price slightly will leave the sum of revenue and consumers' surplus unchanged. On the other hand, if demand is less than z, a slight increase in price will clearly decrease consumers' surplus plus revenue by an amount equal to the prevailing price times the resulting decrease in demand. Thus the left-hand side of (4.14) represents the expected marginal benefits in the form of revenue and consumers' surplus at price p_i. Similarly, the right-hand side is seen to be the sum of expected marginal operating and rationing costs. To see that the first term represents expected marginal operating costs, simply note that plants are operated in the order 1 through m; so if demand falls between Q_{l-1} and Q_l, then plant l is the last plant in use and small changes in price therefore yield marginal operating-cost changes equal to $b_l X_i'(p_i)$.

A similar argument to the above leads to an understanding of (4.12) in terms of expected marginal costs and benefits of capacity increases. We delay this discussion until we have recast the conditions (4.12) in a more convenient form, but the interested reader may refer to Brown and Johnson (1969) for a discussion of the single-plant, single-period case. Note, in particular, that (4.11) and (4.12) reduce to their first-order conditions when $m = n = 1$ and when rationing costs are zero.

Before proceeding some notational conventions will be useful. Since F_i is the *CDF* of u_i it follows that $F_i(u_i) = P_r\{\tilde{u}_i \leqslant u_i\}$ for any $u_i \varepsilon R$. Using this fact we define the quantities:

$$F_i^l = F_i(Q_l - X_i(p_i)) = Pr\{D_i(p_i, \tilde{u}_i) \leqslant Q_l\}, \quad \text{for all } i, l. \tag{4.15}$$

Note that since $z = Q_m$, $F_i^m = F_i(z - X_i(p_i))$. Now using the property of any cumulative distribution function that $x \leqslant y$ implies $0 \leqslant F_i(x) \leqslant F_i(y) \leqslant 1$, we have:

$$0 = F_i^0 \leqslant F_i^1 \leqslant \ldots \leqslant F_i^m \leqslant 1, \quad i = 1, \ldots, n, \tag{4.16}$$

We can now restate the first-order conditions (4.11) (or (4.14)) for price by cancelling $X_i'(p_i)$ from all terms and dividing by F_i^m (assuming, of course, that $F_i^m > 0$, so that demand in period i does not always exceed capacity):[9]

$$p_i = \sum_{l=1}^{m} \gamma_{li} b_l + E\{r_i'(X_i(p_i) + \tilde{u}_i - z\}/F_i^m, \quad i = 1, \ldots, m, \tag{4.17}$$

where $0 \leqslant \gamma_{li} \leqslant 1$ is given by:

$$\gamma_{li} = (F_i^l - F_i^{l-1})/F_i^m = Pr\{Q_{l-1} \leqslant D_i(p_i, \tilde{u}_i) \leqslant Q_l \mid D_i(p_i, \tilde{u}_i) \leqslant z\}, \tag{4.18}$$

We note that (4.17) and (4.18) imply that p_i is between b_i and b_m in the absence of rationing costs, and increased by an appropriate amount when rationing costs are present. From (4.18) we can see that γ_{li} is the probability that plant l will be the last plant to be used, conditional on the event that there is sufficient capacity to meet demand. Thus price in each period must equal the conditional expected marginal operating plus rationing costs.

Optimal capacity and efficient technology

The conditions characterising optimal technology and order of operation are similar for the stochastic case to those derived in Chapter 3 for the deterministic case. We therefore only summarise these results. The reader wishing to see full-blown proofs of these results should consult Crew and Kleindorfer (1976).

Result 1: For each $k \in \{1, \ldots m\}$, the following must hold if plant k is to be used in any optimal solution:

$$n(b_{\hat{k}} - b_k) > \beta_k - \beta_{\hat{k}}, \qquad \text{for all } \hat{k} > k. \tag{4.19}$$

Notice that Result 1 is just the left half of Lemma (3.26) of Chapter 3. The right half of Lemma (3.26) need not hold in the stochastic case.

Result 2: Assuming (4.19) holds for $k = 1$, plant type 1 will always be used (unless no capacity whatsoever is installed).

As noted in Chapter 3, this result applies in the deterministic case. It applies for stochastic demand for similar reasons. Since plant type 1 is the one with minimum operating costs and maximum capacity costs, Result 2 simply states that this should be the base-load plant type. The only requirement is, of course, that (4.19) hold, so that, for all other plant types k, $nb_1 + \beta_1 < nb_k + \beta_k$, i.e. the marginal cost of installing and operating the base-load plant over the entire cycle should be less than that of any other available plant type.

Result 3: The efficient technological frontier in the (b, β) plane is downward-sloping and convex. In particular, together with (4.4) and (4.19), the relations:

$$\frac{\beta_l - \beta_{l+1}}{b_{l+1} - b_l} < \frac{\beta_{l-1} - \beta_l}{b_l - b_{l-1}} < n, \quad \text{for } l = 2 \ldots m-1, \tag{4.20}$$

must hold if the plant mix $\{1, \ldots, m\}$ is to be used.

The rationale behind Result 3 is as follows. Suppose two plants with cost characteristics (b_1, β_1) and (b_2, β_2) were available. Then every convex combination of these cost characteristics is also available as a plant type by simply operating plants 1 and 2 the appropriate proportions of time. Given the above, it is clear that any plant lying above the line segment joining any two plants in the (b, β) plane cannot be efficient since an appropriate fictitious plant can be achieved on this line segment which would have both a lower b and a lower β.

Result 4: Assuming (4.20), if $q_k > 0$ for some $k \in \{2, \ldots, m\}$, then in any optimal solution $q_l > 0$ for every $l \in \{1, \ldots, k-1\}$. Thus every optimal plant mix consists of contiguous plant types arranged in order of increasing operating costs.

Result 4 can be understood by reversing the above argument for Result 3. If a plant type on the technological frontier is skipped, then some fraction of the two plants adjacent to the skipped plant could be thought of as equivalent to a fictitious plant which would be dominated by the skipped plant. This result contrasts somewhat with the deterministic case where the optimal plant mix may consist of non-contiguous plant types. The deterministic case is explicitly ruled out here by our assumptions, which preclude non-continuous random variables which, for example, arise from deterministic demand where $P_r\{\tilde{u}=0\}=1$.

Let us now summarise succinctly the above results. We first note that $\partial \bar{W}/\partial q_k$ in (4.12) contains the following common term M for each $k = 1, 2, \ldots, m$:

$$M = \sum_{i=1}^{n} \int_{z-X_{i(pi)}}^{\infty} P_i(z-u_i)dF_i(u_i) + E\{r_i'(X_i(p_i)+\tilde{u}-z)\}. \quad (4.21)$$

In view of the above results the optimal plant mix is of the form $\{1, \ldots, \hat{m}\}$ where $\hat{m} \in \{1, \ldots, m\}$ is the number of the last plant used in the optimal solution. Now using $\partial \bar{W}/\partial q_1 = 0$ if $q_1 > 0$, and successively eliminating M from $\partial \bar{W}/\partial ql + 1 - \partial \bar{W}/\partial ql = 0$ for $l = 1, \ldots, m-1$, yields from (4.11) and (4.12) the following $\hat{m}+n$ necessary conditions for the $\hat{m}+n$ variables $(p_1, \ldots, p_n)$, $(q_1, \ldots, q_{\hat{m}})$:

$$p_i F_i^{\hat{m}} = \sum_{l=1}^{\hat{m}} b^l(F_i^l - F_i^{l-1}) + E\{r_i'(X_i(p_i)+\tilde{u}_i-z)\}, \quad i=1, \ldots, n \quad (4.22)$$

$$n - \frac{\beta_l - \beta_{l+1}}{b_{l+1} - b_l} = \sum_{i=1}^{n} F_i^l, \quad l=1, \ldots, \hat{m}-1 \quad (4.23)$$

$$\sum_{i=1}^{n} \int_{z-X_{i(pi)}}^{\infty} [P^i(z-u_i) - b_{\hat{m}} + r_i'(X_i(p_i)+u_i-z)]dF_i(u_i) = \beta_{\hat{m}}. \quad (4.24)$$

We may rewrite (4.23) as:

$$\beta_l - \beta_{l-1} = (b_{l+1} - b_l) \sum_{i=1}^{n} (1 - F_i^l) = \sum_{i=1}^{n} (b_{l+1} - b_l) Pr\{D_i(p_i, \tilde{u}_i) \geqslant Q_l\},$$
$$(4.25)$$

which implies that the marginal capacity cost of using additional units of plant l to replace units of $l+1$ should equal the expected marginal operating cost savings of making the incremental change to plant l. Notice that (4.24) is precisely the condition that would be obtained if only one plant type, namely $\hat{m}$, were available.

Efficient prices

Our main results concern bounds on the optimal prices and a demonstration that peak-load pricing is efficient.

Result 5: The following bounds obtain for the optimal prices p_i:

$$b_1 \leqslant b_1 + R_i \leqslant p_i \leqslant b_m + R_i, \quad \text{for all } i, \tag{4.26}$$

and

$$nb_1 \leqslant \sum_{i=1}^{n} p_i \leqslant nb_1 + \beta_1, \tag{4.27}$$

where $R_i (= E\{r_i'/F_i^m\})$ represents expected marginal rationing costs in period i.

The bounds in (4.26) have already been indicated in connection with (4.17) and follow simply from the observation that p_i is to be set equal to the sum of conditional expected marginal running and rationing costs. Given this, the left-hand inequality in (4.27) follows immediately, since marginal running costs are always at least b_1. As for the right-hand inequality in (4.27), suppose for the moment that the sum of all prices exceeded $nb_1 + \beta_1$. We would then simultaneously increase capacity of type 1 by, say, ε units and decrease each price slightly, still maintaining their sum greater than $nb_1 + \beta_1$ so as to generate ε units of expected additional demand. Rationing costs will not have changed, but these changes would lead to an increment of more than $(nb_1 + \beta_1)\varepsilon$ in expected revenue alone (i.e. neglecting the additional consumers' surplus). Moreover, the increase in expected costs from these changes is only $(nb_1 + \beta_1)\varepsilon$, the cost of installing and operating the additional units of type 1 capacity over the entire cycle. Thus the original situation could not have been optimal.

Note that (4.26)–(4.27) imply that p_i actually lies between b_1 and $b_1 + \beta_1$, as in the deterministic case.[10] Also the right-hand inequality in

(4.27) holds as an equality in the deterministic case, whether the technology is diverse or not. This is not so in the stochastic case, as we show by example below.

We now examine the pricing implications of peak-load effects. As a simple example, we may rewrite (4.7) when $m = 1$ as follows:

$$p_i = b_1 + E\{r_i'(X_i(p_i) + \tilde{u}_i - z)\}/F_m^1. \tag{4.28}$$

Now, if $r_i \equiv r_j$, $X_i(p) > X_j(p)$, for all p, and if $\tilde{u}_i, \tilde{u}_j$ are identically distributed, then it is readily seen from (4.28) that $p_i \geqslant p_j \geqslant b_1$, this result following directly from the increasing nature of marginal rationing costs. Accordingly, when rationing costs and peak loads are present, it follows that a peak-load pricing policy is optimal.

It is interesting to illustrate the effects of rationing costs by specialising (4.28) to the case where r_i is of the linear form $r_i(y) = cy$ $(y \geqslant 0)$ and $r_i(y) = 0$, $y \leqslant 0$, where $c > 0$ is the unit cost of excess demand (above costless rationing, according to willingness to pay). In this case (4.28) becomes:

$$p_i = b_1 + (1 - F_i^1)c/F_i^1 \tag{4.29}$$

Concentrating on the two-period case, and assuming $F_i^1 = 1$, perfect reliability in the off-peak period, (4.29) yields the following optimal prices:

$$p_1 = b_1, \quad p_2 = b_1 + (1 - F_2^1)c/F_2^1. \tag{4.30}$$

Thus peak-load pricing is optimal here as long as $c > 0$. The reader should also note that Result 5 implies that z will be adjusted so that always $p_2 \leqslant b_1 + \beta_1$. In particular non-positive profits always obtain in this case.

Even in the absence of rationing costs peak-load pricing can be shown to be efficient. The essential rationale for this is that prices are to be set equal to conditional expected marginal operating costs. These costs, in turn are monotonically increasing with output, which thus implies a peak-load pricing policy. We summarise these remarks informally in Result 6.

Result 6: If rationing costs in periods i and j are functionally identical $(r_i \equiv r_j)$ and if mean demand is higher in period i than in period j $(X_i(p) > X_j(p)$ for all $p)$, then, under mild regularity assumptions, price in period i should be higher than in period j $(p_i > p_j \geqslant b_i)$.

The 'mild regularity conditions' referred to above amount to conditions which ensure that, for any fixed price $p_i = p_j = p$, the conditional (on demand not exceeding capacity) distribution of demand in period i is to the right of the corresponding distribution for period j. When this is so, then charging the same or higher price in period j as in period i would lead to a (stochastically) larger conditional demand in period i than in period j. Since marginal operating and rationing costs are increasing, their conditional expected value would then be higher in period i than in period j. As noted, however, price is to be set equal to this expected value so it must be that $p_i > p_j \geqslant b_1$.

An example of when the regularity condition in question holds is the case where period i is a strong peak relative to period j, in the sense that $P_i\{D_i(p,\tilde{u}_i) \geqslant D_j(p,\tilde{u}_j)\} = 1$ for any (reasonable) price p (i.e. for $b_1 \leqslant p \leqslant b_1 + \beta_1$). Another example is when $\tilde{u}_j$ are identically distributed according to a normal, exponential, or uniform distribution. The interested reader should consult the Crew and Kleindorfer (1979a, p. 96) for technical details on these matters.

Summarising the above discussion and results, an upward-sloping system-wide marginal operating-cost curve (which is a natural consequence of a diverse technology), when coupled with marginal-cost pricing, implies the efficiency of peak-load pricing under uncertainty. Departures from perfect, costless rationing also contribute to the optimality of peak-load pricing. In fact the more inefficient the rationing scheme is, the more pronounced will be the price differential between peak and off-peak prices.

Before continuing it is interesting to note a few straightforward extensions of the above analysis to cover multiplicative demand uncertainty and other specifications of technology. The case of multiplicative uncertainty is obtained by replacing (4.1) with the following specification:

$$D_i(p_i, \tilde{v}_i) = \tilde{v}_i \, X_i(p_i), \tag{4.31}$$

where $\tilde{v}_i$ is a non-negative random variable with expected value $E\{\tilde{v}_i\} = 1$. Leaving all else as above, one easily derives optimality conditions for this case which are exactly analogous to (4.11)–(4.12). From this all the above results carry over to the demand specification (4.31).

A second extension of the above analysis concerns replacing the technology specification embodied in (4.5) by a more aggregate specification (see also Section 4.3 for similar results for the deterministic case) as follows:

$$\text{Total production costs} = \sum_{i=1}^{n} C_0\,(S_i,z) + C_1(z), \tag{4.32}$$

where $S_i = S_i(p_i, u_i, z)$ is the output in period i as given in (4.7). The technology specifications (4.32) leads to the same pricing and total capacity rules as did the earlier diverse technology specification. In particular price is to be set to the sum of conditional expected marginal operating and rationing costs.

From the extensions we see that the results derived thus far are fairly robust to changing assumptions on demand and technology specification. We next investigate the effects of alternative rationing policies in more detail.

4.3   RATIONING, RELIABILITY AND PROFITS

In the previous section we outline the problem of maximising a welfare function of the form:

$$\bar{W}_r(\mathbf{p},\mathbf{q}) = E\{W_{BJ}(\tilde{u},\mathbf{p},\mathbf{q}) + \sum r_i(D_i(p_i,\tilde{u}_i),z)\}, \tag{4.33}$$

where W_{BJ} represents welfare returns under Brown and Johnson perfect rationing (costless rationing according to willingness to pay) and where Σr_i represents additional surplus losses and administrative costs associated with the rationing scheme in actual use. We have thus far only concerned ourselves with a given, fixed rationing scheme, and then only under the assumption that r_i in (4.33) is of the form $r_i(D_i - z)$, depending only on excess demand. In this section we relax these assumptions and study the effect of alternative rationing schemes on optimal reliability and profitability of the welfare-maximising monopoly. We restrict attention throughout to the case $m = n = 1$, where plant type 1 has cost parameters b and β.[11] We first reconsider our results of the previous section and then turn our attention to other rationing schemes (whose costs Σr_i in (4.33) need not be expressed in terms of excess demand as we have assumed to this point).

Rationing with costs proportional to excess demand

Let us reconsider the results of the previous section (for additively perturbed demand (4.1)) when $m = n = 1$ and $r_i(y) = c\,\text{Max}(y,0)$, i.e. costs beyond perfect rationing are proportional to excess demand. The welfare function (4.9)–(4.10) then becomes (suppressing the subscript $i = 1$):

$$\bar{W}(p,z) = E\{\int_0^{S(p,\tilde{u},z)} [P(x - \tilde{u}) - b]dx - \beta z - c\,\text{Max}[D(p,\tilde{u}) - z, 0]. \quad (4.34)$$

The first-order conditions for optimal price and capacity are (4.22) and (4.24), which we may rewrite as follows when $\hat{m} = 1$:

$$(p - b)F(z - X(p)) = c(1 - F(z - X(p))) \quad (4.35)$$

$$\int_{z - X(p)}^{\infty} (P(z - u) - b + c)dF(u)) = \beta, \quad (4.36)$$

where $F(u) = Pr\{\tilde{u} \leqslant u\}$ is the *CDF* of the disturbance term in (4.1). We deal with two cases below, $c = 0$ and $c > 0$.

The Brown–Johnson case ($c = 0$): We first recall the Brown–Johnson results, which were obtained for the case $c = 0$. For this case, Brown and Johnson cancelled the term $F(z - X(p))$ in (4.35) to obtain $p = b$. This clearly assumes that $F(z - X(p)) = Pr\{X(p) + \tilde{u} \leqslant z\} = $ reliability is non-zero at optimum, an assumption which we now show need not hold. To see when zero reliability is optimal, note that if $Pr\{X(p) + u \leqslant z\} = 0$, then the lower limit of integration in (4.36) becomes effectively $-\infty$ and (4.36) reduces to:

$$E\{P(z - \tilde{u})\} = b + \beta, \quad (4.37)$$

a condition on z alone. Thus any price yielding $F(z - X(p)) = 0$, with z as in (4.37), is optimal.[12] Clearly if p is such a price, then so is any price $p' \leqslant p$ (although we will typically only consider prices which at least recover operating expenses). Also, satisfying (4.37) and $F(z - X(p)) = 0$ is easiest when the range of the disturbance term u goes to zero, (5.37) converges[13] to $P(z) = b + \beta$, i.e. optimal capacity converges the deterministic optimal capacity $z_d = X(b + \beta)$. As the range $\tilde{u}$ increases, one may expect the range of prices satisfying $F(z - X(p)) = 0$ to behave as illustrated in Figure 4.2.[14] There we plot optimal prices versus the variance of $\tilde{u}$. Up until $\hat{V}$ it is seen that a (decreasing) range of optimal prices obtains. Thereafter, only the Brown–Johnson solution is optimal. When there are multiple optima, each such optimal solution yields the same expected welfare, but with different revenue effects. Considering the point V in Figure 4.2, for example, revenue and profits increase in going from the Brown–Johnson, $P = b$, solution to the maximal optimal solution $P = p$, while expected surplus decreases correspondingly. Note that since output can never exceed z and since price always satisfies $p < b + \beta$ (see also Result 5), welfare-optimal solutions to the Brown–Johnson problem all entail strictly negative profits, except in the deterministic case.

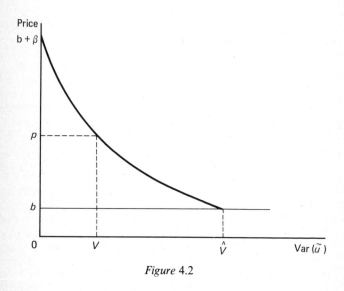

Figure 4.2

Considering the deterministic case in Figure 4.2, it is interesting to note that $P = b$ is indicated to be optimal. The fact that this solution has not generally been recognised as optimal stems from the fact that previous derivations for the deterministic case have only considered solutions satisfying the constraint that sufficient capacity be installed to meet peak demand. In the absence of such a (reliability) constraint, it may easily be verified that the Brown–Johnson solution is indeed 'optimal' for the familiar welfare criterion which does not discriminate between producers' and consumers' surplus. It is in fact the optimal solution which provides minimum profit, minimum revenue and maximum consumers' surplus and excess demand.

As a final point on the Brown–Johnson case, the reader should note that when demands are linear the left-hand side of (4.36) is exactly $P(z)$, since $E\{\tilde{u}\} = 0$. Thus, when demands are linear, there is a range of levels of sufficiently low uncertainty over which the optimal capacity decision is precisely z_d. Corresponding optimal prices are simply those satisfying

$F(z_d - X(p)) = 0$. When demands are not linear, optimal capacity may be greater than, or less than, deterministic optimal capacity when uncertainty is small, depending on the concavity or convexity of the demand curve. That is, $E\{P(z - \tilde{u})\}$ may be less than, or greater than, $P(z - E\{\tilde{u}\}) = P(z_d)$.

The Case $c > 0$: We now return to the case $c > 0$ in (4.35)–(4.36). It is clear in this case that $F(z - X(p)) > 0$, i.e. reliability will be positive at optimum. From this and the fact that $P(z - u) < P(X(p)) = p$ for almost all u in the integral in (4.36), we have from (4.36):

$$\int_{z - X(p)}^{\infty} (p - b + c)dF(u) < \beta. \tag{4.38}$$

Rewriting the integral in (4.38) as $(p - b + c)(1 - F(z - X(p)))$, we see from (4.35) that this implies $p < b + \beta$. In particular profits are strictly negative at the welfare-optimal solution.

Comparative statistics easily establishes, under mild regularity conditions, that as c increases, i.e. as rationing gets more inefficient, capacity, price and reliability all increase. From this it also follows that profits, gross of rationing costs, also increase as c increases. The rationale for this behaviour is clear. As non-price rationing (in the event of excess demand) becomes more inefficient, more reliance must be placed on price rationing and increased capacity to decrease excess demand.

An interesting footnote to this analysis is the behaviour of the optimal solution as c approaches infinity. In this case, as the reader may verify from (4.35)–(4.36), price approaches $b + \beta$ and reliability approaches unity, i.e. capacity approaches $X(b + \beta) + u^*$, where $Pr\{\tilde{u} > u^*\} = 0$. Thus, for rationing schemes whose costs above perfect rationing depend only on excess demand, reasonably high rationing costs lead to the deterministic price as the welfare-optimal solution. This, and the fact that $p \leqslant b + \beta$ no matter what c is, stem from the symmetrical way in which z and $X(p)$ enter rationing costs here. The flavour of these results changes when other forms of rationing-cost functions are assumed in (4.33), as we now demonstrate.

Random and other rationing schemes

Visscher (1973) and Carlton (1977) have studied other forms of rationing than those we have been concerned with so far. We first summarise their results, discuss them briefly in relation to the above analysis, and then examine one case, random rationing, in somewhat more detail.

Table 4.1 summarises the Visscher–Carlton results. The rationing schemes listed are as follows:

Brown–Johnson = Costless rationing according to willingness to pay.

CED = Rationing whose costs above Brown–Johnson rationing depend only on excess demand (as we have dealt with to this point).

RAN = Random rationing: consumers are served randomly in the event of excess demand, until capacity is exhausted.

LWP = Rationing in order of lowest willingness to pay until capacity is exhausted.

Gross profit refers to expected revenues minus expected operating and capacity costs and excludes any rationing costs or surplus losses.[15] The additive and multiplicative disturbance specifications are those given by (4.1) and (4.31) respectively.

Table 4.1   Comparing various rationing schemes

Rationing scheme	Additive disturbance		Multiplicative disturbance	
	Price	Gross profit	Price	Gross profit
Brown–Johnson (B–J)	$b \leqslant p < b+\beta$	Negative	$b \leqslant p < b+\beta$	Negative
$CED(c > 0)$	$b < p < b+\beta$	Negative($>$ B–J)	$b < p < b+\beta$	Negative($>$ B–J)
RAN	$b < p < b+\beta$	Negative	$p > b+\beta$	Zero
LWP	$b+\beta$	Negative	$p > b+\beta$	Positive
Deterministic	$b+\beta$	Zero	$b+\beta$	Zero

The results on RAN and LWP are due to Visscher (additive disturbance) and Carlton (multiplicative disturbance). The results on Brown–Johnson and *CED* rationing are derived pp. 85–9. A detailed discussion of the additive case is also contained in Sherman Visscher (1978).

If we think of rationing inefficiency as increasing in the order Brown–Johnson, RAN, LWP, then we see reflected in Table 4.1 the following conclusion which we derived earlier for the class of *CED* rationing schemes. As rationing becomes less efficient, the welfare-optimal solution entails increased prices, capacity, reliability, (gross) profit, and, of course, decreasing welfare.

In order to give some further substance to the principles just noted, let us consider the case of random rationing with multiplicative demand in more detail. We follow the development of Carlton (1977).

Suppose demand is given by $D(p,\tilde{v}) = \tilde{v}X(p)$. Then, if in the event of excess demand, a service is distributed randomly among those willing to pay the quoted price, welfare returns are given for any fixed v by:

$$W_R(v,p,z) = \begin{cases} \int_0^{vX(p)} (P(x/v) - b)dx - \beta z, & \text{if } vX(p) \leqslant z \\[2mm] \dfrac{z}{X(p)} \int_0^{vX(p)} (P(x/v) - b)dx - \beta z, & \text{else.} \end{cases} \quad (4.39)$$

Taking expected values in (4.39) over $\tilde{v}$, we obtain the following expected welfare returns under random rationing:

$$\bar{W}_R(p,z) = \int_0^{z/X(p)} \int_0^{vX(p)} (P(x/v) - b)dx \, dF(v)$$

$$+ \int_{z/X(p)}^{\infty} \frac{z}{X(p)} \int_0^{vX(p)} (P(x/v) - b) \, dx \, dF(v) - \beta z. \quad (4.40)$$

We will in fact generalise (4.40) to the form:

$$\bar{W}_R(p,z) = \int_0^{z/X(p)} \int_0^{vX(p)} (P(x/v) - b)dx \, dF(v)$$

$$+ \int_{z/X(p)}^{\infty} \frac{ez}{X(p)} \int_0^{vX(p)} (P(x/v) - b)dx \, dF(v) - \beta z. \quad (4.41)$$

where $e > 0$ will be varied to allow a comparison across a class of rationing schemes 'centred' on random rationing (where $e = 1$). Clearly, the greater is e, the more efficient is the rationing process.

Now define $s = z/X(p)$ and change variables in the inner integrals in (4.41) to obtain $\bar{W}$ in terms of the decision variables p, s as follows:

$$\bar{W}(p,s) = \int_0^s v \int_0^{X(p)} (P(x) - b)dx \, dF(v)$$

$$+ \int_0^{\infty} es \int_0^{X(p)} (P(x) - b)dx \, dF(v) - \beta s X(p). \quad (4.42)$$

Setting $\partial \bar{W}/\partial p = \partial \bar{W}/\partial s = 0$, we obtain the following first-order conditions for maximising $\bar{W}$:

$$(p-b)[\int_0^s v\,dF(v) + e\int_s^\infty s\,dF(v)] - \beta s = 0 \tag{4.43}$$

$$[\int_0^{X(p)}(P(x)-b)dx]\,[(1-e)sf(s) + e(1-F(s))] - \beta X(p) = 0, \tag{4.44}$$

where $f(s) = dF(s)/ds$. Denote by $I(e,s)$ the quantity:

$$I(e,s) = \frac{1}{s}\,[\int_0^s v\,dF(v) + es\int_s^\infty dF(v)]$$

$$= \frac{1}{s}\,[\int_0^s (v-es)dF(v) + es] < e. \tag{4.45}$$

Then, from (4.43), optimal price is:

$$p = b + \frac{\beta}{I(e,s)}, \tag{4.46}$$

so that for sufficiently inefficient rationing (e.g. for any $e \leqslant 1$), price exceeds $b + \beta$.

Expected profits (excluding any rationing costs) are:

$$\bar{\Pi} = (p-b)X(p)\int_0^s v\,dF(v) + (p-b)sX(p)\int_s^\infty dF(v) - \beta sX(p). \tag{4.47}$$

Multiplying (4.43) by $X(p)$ and comparing with (4.47) yields:

$$\Pi = (p-b)sX(p)(1-e)\,(1-F(s)). \tag{4.48}$$

From this and (4.46) we see that profits are negative, zero, or positive as $e > 1$, $= 1$, or < 1 respectively.

The above provides further confirmation of the general principle enunciated earlier that the more inefficient the rationing scheme, the more reliance will have to be placed on normal price rationing to clear the market, i.e. the higher will be the welfare-optimal price and profits. In addition it is interesting to note that welfare-optimal prices (and profits) are higher under multiplicative demand uncertainty than under additive uncertainty. This is doubtless because under multiplicative uncertainty, price and uncertainty interact, with the consequence that random outcomes on the high side are magnified by price effects, lending even greater importance to the rationing effects of price in avoiding excess demand.

The rather different consequences of the above alternative demand uncertainty specifications will hardly be greeted with pleasure outside of economic circles. Nonetheless they indicate the strong interaction of price, uncertainty and rationing methods and the need to deal with these issues within a unified framework.

Second-best pricing

Let us now briefly consider how the above results might change if a minimum profit constraint were imposed.[16] To analyse this we return to our assumption that demand is of the form (4.1) and rationing costs are proportional to excess demand. We consider the following problem:

$$
\text{Max } \bar{W}(p,z) = \int_0^{z-X(p)} \int_0^{X(p)+u} (P(z-u)-b)dx \, dF(u)
$$

$$
+ \int_{z-X(p)}^{\infty} \int_0^{z} (P(z-u)-b)dx \, dF(u)
$$

$$
- \int_{z-X(p)}^{\infty} c(X(p)+u-z)dF(u) - \beta z, \tag{4.49}
$$

subject to:

$$
\bar{\Pi}(p,z) = \int_0^{z-X(p)} (p-b)(X(p)+u)dF(u)
$$

$$
+ \int_{z-X(p)}^{\infty} (p-b)z \, dF(u) - \beta z \geqslant \Pi_0. \tag{4.50}
$$

Note that the objective function in (4.49) is just (4.34) and the constraint (4.50) is a minimum profit constraint.

Forming the Lagrangian for (4.49)–(4.50) we have:

$$
\text{L} = W(p,z) + \theta(\Pi(p,z) - \Pi_0). \tag{4.51}
$$

The first-order conditions for solving (4.49)–(4.50) are $\partial L/\partial p = \partial L/\partial z = 0$ and $\theta \geqslant 0$. After simplification these yield the following:

$$
(p-b)X'(p)F(z-X(p))(1+\theta) - cX'(p)(1-F(z-X(p)))
$$

$$
+ \theta[X(p) - \int_{z-X(p)}^{\infty} (X(p)+u-z)dF(u)] = 0 \tag{4.52}
$$

$$\int_{z-X(p)}^{\infty} [P(z-u)-b+c+\theta(p-b)]dF(u)-(1+\theta)\beta=0 \qquad (4.53)$$

From (4.52) we have:

$$\frac{p-b}{p}=\frac{\theta}{1+\theta}\frac{E\{S(p,z_l,\tilde{u})\}}{pX'(p)F(z-X(p))}+\frac{1}{1+\theta}\frac{c(1-F(z-Z(p))}{pF(z-X(p))} \qquad (4.54)$$

where $S(p,z,\tilde{u})$ is output as in (4.7). We may rewrite (4.54), as in Sherman and Visscher (1978):

$$\frac{p-b}{p}=\frac{\theta}{1+\theta}\frac{1}{\eta F(z-X(p))}\left[1-\frac{E\{\tilde{e}\tilde{d}\}}{X(p)}\right]$$

$$+\frac{1}{1+\theta}\frac{c(1-F(z-X(p))}{pF(z-X(p))}, \qquad (4.55)$$

where η is (mean) demand elasticity and $E\{\tilde{e}\tilde{d}\}$ is expected excess demand.

To understand (4.54)–(4.55) better, let us note, taking derivatives in (4.50), that the profit margin for the expected profit-maximiser is given by:

$$\frac{p-b}{p}=\frac{1}{\eta F(z-X(p))}\left[1-\frac{E\{\tilde{e}\tilde{d}\}}{X(p)}\right]. \qquad (4.56)$$

When $c=0$ we see that (4.55) and (4.56) produce a result analogous to the deterministic case (see Section 3.5) whereby the rules for setting profit margins for the welfare-maximiser and the profit-maximiser differ only by a constant ($\theta/1+\theta$ above). As Sherman and Visscher have noted, this similarity is not surprising when perfect rationing obtains, since then both the profit- and the welfare-maximiser can ignore rationing in their pricing policies and concentrate on raising revenue.

Returning to the general case $c\geqslant0$, we see that welfare-optimal profit margins are increased when rationing is inefficient. As c approaches infinity, it may be verified from (4.52)–(4.53) that $F(z-X(p))$ tends to unity, and that $c(1-F(z-X(p))$ tends to $(1+\theta)\beta$, so that the pricing rule (4.54) reduces to:

$$\frac{p-b}{p}=\frac{\theta}{1+\theta}\frac{1}{\eta}+\frac{\beta}{p}, \qquad (4.57)$$

which, as the reader may verify from Chapter 3, is the deterministic second-best optimal profit margin (when θ is determined so as to satisfy (4.50)).

Note that as the constraint (4.50) becomes more stringent, θ increases, and the pricing rule (4.55) becomes more like the profit-maximising rule (4.56). This last statement depends, of course, on our definition of profit as excluding any rationing costs. If some portion of these costs were included in the monopolist profit function,[17] then less divergence would emerge between the profit- and welfare-maximising solutions.

As regards optimal capacity, we may rewrite (4.57) as:

$$\frac{1}{1+\theta} \left[\int_{z-X(p)}^{\infty} (P(z-u)-b+c)dF(u)-\beta \right]$$
$$+ \frac{\theta}{1+\theta} \left[\int_{z-X(p)}^{\infty} (p-b)dF(u)-\beta \right] = 0. \qquad (4.58)$$

The first term in (4.58) (set to zero) is the first-order condition an expected welfare-maximiser must satisfy and the second is the corresponding condition for an expected profit-maximiser. Again, the multiplier θ measures the tautness of the constraint (4.50). As θ increases, (4.58) becomes more like the profit maximising condition. As the constraint (4.50) becomes more stringent, capacity would therefore tend to decrease to the expected profit-maximising level, while price and profits would tend to increase.

Concluding this brief discussion of second best, it can be seen that something like an inverse elasticity rule continues to obtain for the optimal price, though now excess demand and rationing compound the problem of raising revenues in the least distorting way. We noted though that here again pricing rules approaching the deterministic case emerge when reliability is high at optimum. We consider the intuitive rationale for this immediately below.

Rationing costs and reliability constraints

We continue to assume that rationing costs depend only on excess demand. We are interested in comparing the welfare-optimal procedures described above with the approach suggested by Meyer (1975a) of adding explicit reliability constraints to the Brown–Johnson problem formulation. To do so we reconsider our original problem of maximising (4.10), now omitting rationing costs and instead constraining reliability. Thus we are interested in the following problem:

$$\text{Max } \bar{W}'(p,q) = E\{W'(p,q,\tilde{u})\}, \tag{4.59}$$

subject to:

$$F_i[z - X_i) \, (p_i)] \geqslant \varepsilon_i, \ i = 1,2, \tag{4.60}$$

where ε_i $(0 \leqslant \varepsilon_i \leqslant 1)$ is a specified reliability level for period i and where the welfare function $\bar{W}'$ in (4.59) is defined through (4.9) by assuming $r_i \equiv 0$, $i = 1, \ldots, n$, i.e. by omitting rationing costs from the welfare function.

Now suppose the reliability levels ε_i in (4.60) are set to $\varepsilon_i = \hat{\varepsilon}_i = F_i[\hat{z} - D_i(\hat{p}_i)]$, with $(\hat{p}, \hat{q})$ an optimal solution to our original problem of maximising the expected value $\bar{W} = \bar{W}' - \Sigma \, E\{r_i\}$ in (4.10). Since rationing costs are increasing monotonically and are convex in excess demand, it is clear that the higher the required reliability levels ε_i in (4.60), the lower will be the expected rationing costs at optimum. Therefore, (4.60) may be regarded as a constraint on expected rationing costs, and if the reliability levels ε_i are (optimally) specified as $\varepsilon_i = \hat{\varepsilon}_i$, then the solution $(\hat{p}, \hat{q})$ to maximising $\bar{W}$ also solves the reliability constrained problem (4.59)–(4.60).

Thus reliability constraints may be thought of as a surrogate for rationing costs, provided of course that they are specified optimally. In particular, this equivalence between rationing costs and reliability constraints (when rationing costs are of the form (4.6) explains why essentially deterministic pricing behaviour occurs when rationing becomes inefficient (as we have noted on several occasions). This is so because highly inefficient rationing requires very high reliability at optimum and the original problem then reduces to an equivalent deterministic problem with demand specified by taking the appropriate (very high) fractile of the original, given, stochastic demand distribution.

4.4 SOME NUMERICAL ILLUSTRATIONS

The purpose of this section is to illustrate by means of numerical examples the theory set out earlier. This should help to clarify some of our earlier analysis, as well as illustrate a number of extensions not otherwise obvious. We restrict attention to a simple example with linear demands and additive random disturbances. Given these assumptions a number of interesting insights emerge to support our theoretical discussion of the preceding sections. We illustrate, in particular, that deterministic solutions are good approximations of stochastic optimal solutions when the optimal reliability level is required to be high.

Basic data and deterministic solutions

We are concerned with a case where there are two periods ($n=2$) with linear demands given by $D_i(p_i,\tilde{u}_i)=X_i(p_i)+\tilde{u}_i$, where:

$$X_1(p_1)=40-1/7\,p_1 \tag{4.61}$$

$$X_2(p_2)=80-5/7\,p_2. \tag{4.62}$$

We assume that the disturbance terms $\tilde{u}_i$ are uniformly distributed on $[-\gamma,\gamma]$, where γ is a positive constant.

We continue to assume that surplus losses and administrative costs of rationing, beyond those incurred under costless rationing according to marginal willingness to pay, depend only on the level of excess demand. Accordingly, we define rationing costs as:

$$r_i(y)= \begin{cases} 0 \text{ if } y\leqslant 0 \\ \alpha y^2 \text{ if } y>0, \end{cases} \tag{4.63}$$

where $\gamma>0$, and y is, of course, the excess of demand over capacity as defined in equation (4.7).

For purposes of our examples, we have three plant types whose cost characteristics are given in Table 4.2. Let us consider the following combinations of the above:

Table 4.2

	b	β
Plant 1	1	15
Plant 2	3	12
Plant 3	5	10

$$\text{Mix } A = \{1\}; \text{ Mix } B = \{1,2\}; \text{ Mix } C = \{1,2,3\}; \text{ Mix } D = \{3\}. \qquad (4.64)$$

Let us begin our comparison by noting some results for the deterministic case. These are given in Table 4.3. Note, in particular, that the results (3.26) of Chapter 3 imply that only plants 1,2 are used in Mix C.

Table 4.3

Mix	Period 1 price (p_1)	Period 2 price (p_2)	Total capacity (z)
A	$p_1 = b_1 = 1$	$p_2 = b_1 + \beta_1 = 16$	68.57
B	$p_1 = 2b_1 + \beta_1 - (b_2 + \beta_2) = 2$	$p_2 = b_2 + \beta_2 = 15$	69.29
C	$p_1 = 2b_1 + \beta_1 - (b_2 + \beta_2) = 2$	$p_2 = b_2 + \beta_2 = 15$	69.29
D	$p_1 = b_3 = 5$	$p_2 = b_3 + \beta_3 = 15$	69.29

Solutions for the stochastic case

We first examine the case of stochastic demand and finite rationing costs. The effects of rationing costs are in line with intuition. In Figure 4.3 we consider the case where $\gamma = 10$ and Mix B is used. As a result of the stochastic demand, we have a rationing problem. By varying rationing costs $0 \leqslant a < \infty$ we alter the magnitude of the rationing problem. We see clearly the effect of changing rationing costs in Figure 4.3. When rationing costs are zero irrespective of the level of excess demand, we have a Brown–Johnson type solution of $p_1 = 2$ and $p_2 = 3$. However, as rationing becomes more expensive, pricing becomes more attractive, and price increases, eventually converging to the deterministic optimum. Similarly, Figure 4.4 illustrates, for the case $a = 0.01$ and Mixes A and B, that the optimal solution converges to the deterministic solution as the range of the disturbance term decreases.

The effects described above are very much along the lines of intuition. As a becomes large, a very high level of reliability is optimal, so that the public utility is faced with the essentially deterministic problem of planning to meet a very high of the demand distribution. This leads to the optimality of the deterministic prices. Of course, as γ becomes small, a nearly deterministic problem also results. Although not shown, the reader will also find it intuitively obvious that total capacity installed at optimum approaches the

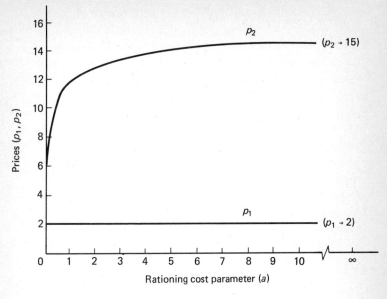

Figure 4.3

upper fractile of the peak-period demand distribution as either α gets large or γ gets small.

Some light is thrown on the Brown–Johnson solution as well as the problem of stochastic demand by means of an example where rationing costs are zero ($\alpha=0$) and where the strength of the randomness in demand is allowed to vary. Figure 4.5 illustrates the case for Mix D, with optimal prices for any value of the random disturbance. At $\gamma=0$ (the deterministic case) any price between 5 and 15 is optimal.[18] As γ increases, the range of optimal prices decreases until at a little over $\gamma=7$ it converges to zero, with the Brown–Johnson solution of $p_1=p_2=b_3=5$ as the unique optimal solution. As we discussed in the previous sections, the existence of multiple optima when γ is small arises from the fact that the traditional welfare function, as interpreted by Brown and Johnson, does not distinguish between consumers' and producers' surplus. Thus the effect of the assumption of costless rationing according to willingness to pay ($\alpha=0$) is for the deterministic price to be just one of an infinity of prices within the range described above for the case of deterministic demand, this range shrinking as demand becomes 'more random'. Intuitively, in Figure 4.5 the curve AB is the locus of

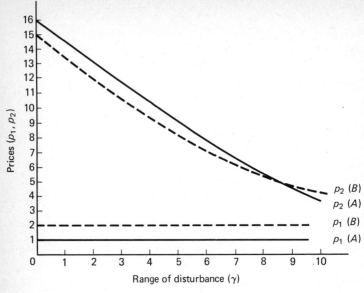

Figure 4.4

points for which peak-period reliability is just equal to zero. Thus as γ approaches zero the range of peak-period excess demand along AB (i.e. $\alpha\gamma$) shrinks to zero and deterministic pricing emerges.

In Figure 4.6 we explore these relationships between optimal prices and reliability in more detail for Mix D and two values of the random disturbance term $\gamma = 5$ and $\gamma = 15$. In this case, however, we impose an explicit reliability constraint $P_r\{D_i(p_i,\tilde{u}) \leqslant z\} > \varepsilon$, $i = 1,2$, in place of the rationing costs (4.63). As expected, similar behaviour is observed at optimum for these explicit reliability constraints to that which we just now discussed for the case of rationing costs. In particular prices converge to the deterministic optima as required reliability is increased to one. These results are further summarised in Table 4.4. Results for the expected profit-maximising case are also shown for comparative purposes. In Figure 4.7 we show (for Mix D) the interaction between reliability and optimal capacity. Here it is assumed that price is adjusted optimally (according to Figure 4.6) to maintain the desired reliability level. As more reliability is required, more capacity is also required. The trade-off is simple. If more reliability is desired, it can be achieved by either increasing price or capacity, and optimality in the

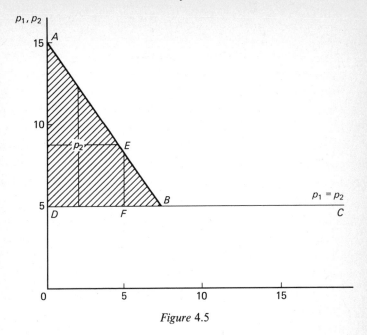

Figure 4.5

sense of maximising expected welfare can be achieved by some (optimal) combination of both of these.

We also examined some effects of technology through cost changes on optimality in the stochastic case. We show (for Mix B) in Figure 4.8 the effects of a change in the value of b_2 on optimal prices for $\gamma = 10$ and $\alpha = 0$. As b_2 rises, p_2 rises with a kink at A, where $p_2 = 4.05$ and p_2 drops sharply. Similarly, p_1 increase until B and then decreases sharply. The kinks at B and A arise from the fact that along CB only plant 2 is used; along BA both plants 1 and 2 are used; and along ADE only plant 1 is used. For Mix B we show in Figure 4.9 the corresponding effects of changes in b_2 upon capacity. As b_2 rises, total capacity decreases until at a price of 4.05 plant 2 ceases to be used and therefore total capacity ($z = q_1 = 68.56$) is no longer affected in any way by further increases in b_2.

These numerical examples illustrate a number of important points about the relationship between deterministic and stochastic demand, in particular the extent to which the deterministic solution approximates the stochastic solution when randomness is small or optimal reliability is high. We also illustrated the fact that rationing costs and explicit

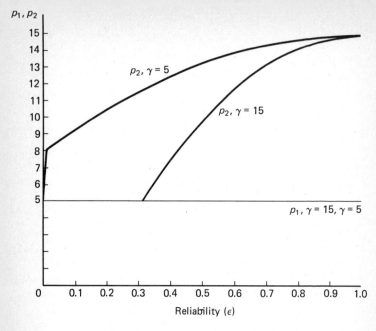

Figure 4.6

reliability constraints are symmetrical in their effects on optimal pricing and capacity. Finally, we examined the impact of alternative technologies and illustrated the sensitivity of optimal prices to available technology.

4.5 CONCLUSIONS

The results of this chapter might be summarised briefly by saying that welfare-optimal pricing under uncertainty entails marginal-cost pricing rules similar to those obtaining under certainty. However, determining and quantifying the appropriate marginal costs here requires that rationing and excess-demand conditions be considered explicitly. We may summarise the essence of the various welfare-optimal policies derived as follows. Optimal capacity should be set so that losses in consumer's surplus net of operating costs (as determined by the rationing scheme in use) are just equal to the *LRMC* of increasing capacity, all of this to take place at optimal prices. The optimal prices

Table 4.4   Optimal solutions for the example

		Welfare-maximising case			Profit-maximising case		
		$\gamma=0^*$	$\gamma=5$	$\gamma=15$	$\gamma=0^*$	$\gamma=5$	$\gamma=15$
$\varepsilon=0\dagger$	p_1	5.00	5.00	5.00	142.50	142.50	142.50
	p_2	5.00–15.0	5.00–8.0	5.00	63.50	63.39	63.19
	Q	69.29	69.69	70.73	34.65	38.00	44.71
$\varepsilon=0.5$	p_1	5.00	5.00	5.00	142.50	142.50	142.50
	p_2	15.00	13.24	9.74	63.50	63.39	63.19
	Q	69.29	70.54	73.04	34.65	38.00	44.71
$\varepsilon=0.9$	p_1	5.00	5.00	5.00	142.50	142.50	142.50
	p_2	15.00	14.92	14.77	63.50	63.45	63.40
	Q	69.29	73.34	81.44	34.65	38.67	46.76
$\varepsilon=0.98$	p_1	5.00	5.00	5.00	142.50	142.50	142.50
	p_2	15.00	14.99	14.98	63.50	63.49	63.49
	Q	69.29	74.09	83.70	34.65	39.45	49.05
$\varepsilon=1.0$	p_1	5.00	5.00	5.00	142.50	142.50	142.50
	p_2	15.00	15.00	15.00	63.50	63.50	63.50
	Q	69.29	74.29	84.29	34.65	39.65	49.65

Range of the disturbance term (γ)

Reliability level required

* The deterministic case.
† The Brown–Johnson case.

are complicated (although typically they may be expected to be close to deterministic optimal prices when reliability is high); but essentially they are obtained by equating expected benefits from the actual marginal unit of demand met to the expected *SRMC*. Given the above capacity rule, this amounts to determining price by maximising expected consumers' surplus (given the rationing scheme or load-shedding procedure used) subject to optimal reliability levels.

An issue which we have not addressed, but which is clear in principle, is the selection of an optimal rationing scheme. This would simply proceed by comparing the optimal welfare returns and costs of implementation associated with each such scheme. A further issue which we have ignored is that of redistributing the social costs of excess demand. It should at least be clear, however, that an unregulated

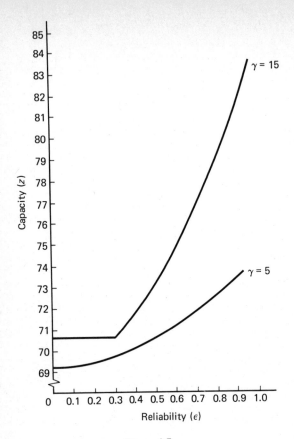

Figure 4.7

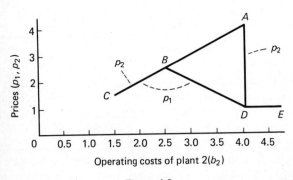

Figure 4.8

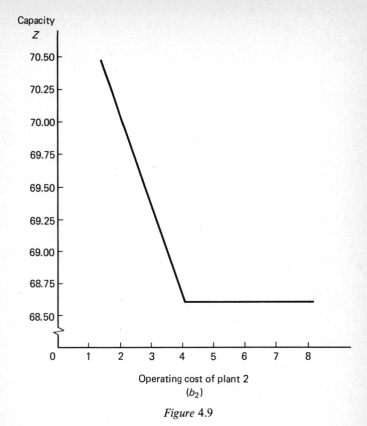

Figure 4.9

monopolist will take a fairly callous view of these costs unless he has to bear a portion of them.

We may expect some additional complications on the reliability problem in dealing with the regulated firm. These are dealt with in Part III.

Part III

Principles and Practice of Regulation

5 Origin and Operation of Regulation in the USA

Our approach to this point has been primarily to consider the nature of welfare optimal behaviour for natural monopoly. Henceforth we deal with the operation of various governance structures for natural monopoly. In this chapter, and in Chapter 6, we will be concerned with regulation of privately-owned natural monopoly. This is mainly a US phenomenon. However, in view of the interest in privatisation, for example, the sale of half of the stock of British Telecom to the public, the efficiency consequences of US regulation may be of interest outside the USA. In view of this we have attempted to compare the efficiency properties of various governance structure for natural monopoly, including rate-of-return regulation and public enterprise, by means of comparative institutional assessment in Chapter 7.

In this chapter we will be concerned with examining the origins and operation of regulation in the USA. Such institutional details are important for development of the analysis of Chapters 6 and 7 as well as the subsequent chapters on the individual industries. Section 1 will discuss the background and origins of monopoly regulation. Section 2 will examine selected theories purporting to explain the motivation and driving forces behind regulation. Section 3 will examine some theories about the operation and incentives of regulatory systems. Section 4 will introduce some notions of the new institutional economics intended to analyse the transactions cost properties of the regulatory process. Section 5 provides some conclusions and motivation for the rest of the book.

5.1 ORIGINS OF MONOPOLY REGULATION

Once the notion of overwhelming scale economies and therefore natural monopoly is accepted, a seemingly clear explanation and justification of monopoly regulation appears to be readily available in terms of simple neoclassical analysis. In this case a simple tradeoff results between market power and scale economies along the lines of Williamson (1968). If a monopoly in Figure 5.1, by means of scale economies, is able to supply at the lower average cost AC_m than a competitive – or more realistically duopoly or oligopoly industry – with average costs given by AC_c, then as long as the cost savings, given by the rectangle P_cBFE, exceed the loss in consumer surplus from the monopoly price (P_m), given by the triangle ABC, there will be a welfare gain from the monopoly organisation of the industry. If, by means of regulation, a price lower than the monopoly price can be achieved, then there would appear to be an equity gain as well as the efficiency gain from regulating the natural monopoly.

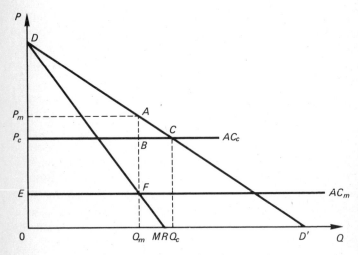

Figure 5.1   The benefits of monopoly

Some of the early motivation for regulation reflected this intent to obtain the scale economies inherent in natural monopoly. For example, Theodore Vail's comments in the 1910 Annual Report of AT&T reflected this intent.

> It is believed that the telephone system should be universal, interdependent and interconnecting, affording opportunity for any subscriber in any exchange to communicate with any other subscriber of another exchange ... It is believed that some sort of connection with the telephone system should be within reach of all ... It is not believed that this can be accomplished by separately

controlled or distinct systems nor that there can be competition in the accepted sense of competition.

Previously Vail, in AT&T's 1907 annual report, had recognised that the monopoly implied by his vision of a fully integrated system would require some government control mechanism or regulation:

> It is contended that if there is to be no competition there should be public control. It is not believed that there is any serious objection to that control . . . provided that capital is entitled to its fair rate of return . . . and enterprise its just reward.

Compare and contrast this with developments on the other side of the Atlantic as illustrated by Joseph Chamberlain's (1894) arguments in the UK for public ownership of utilities through the municipality.

> The supply of gas and of water, electric lighting and the establishment of tramways must be confined to very few contractors. They involve interference with the street, and with the rights and privileges of individuals. They cannot, therefore be thrown open to free competition, but must be committed, under stringent conditions and regulations, to the fewest hands. As it is difficult . . . satisfactorily to reconcile the rights and interests of the public with the claims of an individual, or a company seeking, as its natural and legitimate object, the largest attainable private gain, it is most desirable that, in all these cases, the municipality should control the supply, in order that the general interest of the whole population may be the only object pursued.

While Chamberlain's view might be regarded as reflecting a utopian view, it also shows a healthy scepticism as to the benefits of regulation, which events seem to indicate, was justified. Regulation in practice seems not to have been concerned with efficiency. Moreover, once the regulatory apparatus has been set up it tends to take on a 'life of its own' with consequences different from what had been originally intended. Tullock (1975, p. 672) put this point more colourfully:

> Even in those cases where the government regulation was fairly clearly motivated by a desire to help some particular group, it usually turns out that at least some features are not to the

advantage of the benefited group. Apparently government moves in mysterious ways its wonders to perform, and is not completely controlled by even the best organized pressure group.

While the original intent of regulation seems to have been concerned with efficiency to some extent, the actual practice of regulation did not develop in this way. Its prime concern seems to have been equity. This is not surprising in view of the fact that the legal system, through which regulation of industry has been accomplished, makes some claims of being concerned with fairness. Some support for this notion of fairness and equity is found in the early history of regulation. Martin G. Glaeser (1957, p. 196) argues this very point:

> Regulation of private industry has been attempted by government from the earliest times. All attempts at such regulation owed much to a very ancient ideal of social justice, which, as applied to economic life by the early Church Fathers, became their very famous doctrine of *justum pretium* or 'just price.' They opposed this idea to the contemporaneous doctrine of *verum pretium* i.e., 'natural price' which the Roman law had derived from Stoic philosophy.

The doctrine of *verum pretium* would presumably encompass both competitively determined prices and monopoly prices. Its concern was only with contracts between buyers and sellers that were willingly undertaken. So strong was the notion of just price that early attempts at regulation were concerned with regulating competitive markets. Glaeser refers to food price regulation in time of famine. As such markets were typically competitive, regulation would have the effect of decreasing efficiency. However, the apparent desire to prevent undue enrichment of food producers and merchants and protect consumers from the effects of high prices led to attempts at regulation. This overrode the efficiency considerations. This same motivation to prevent undue enrichment and to protect the consumer can be traced in the development of regulation over the past hundred years.

The origins of modern US regulation are usually traced back to the case of *Munn* v. *Illinois*.[1] The Supreme Court ruled: 'When, therefore, one devotes his property to a use in which the public has an interest, he in effect grants to the public an interest in that use, and must submit to be controlled by the public for the common good.' The principle thus established confirmed the right of government to regulate privately-owned business that it deemed used its property in the public interest. The situation was summarised in a later case by Justice Bradley who, referring to *Munn*, stated: 'we held that when an employment or business becomes a matter of such public interest and importance as to create a common charge or burden upon the citizens; in other words, *when it becomes a practical monopoly, to which the citizen is compelled to resort*, [emphasis added] and by means of which a tribute can be exacted from the community, it is subject to regulation by the legislative power.'[2] Note the emphasis on the need to protect the public from monopoly exploitation. The concern is not with allocative inefficiency in the sense of the divergence of price and marginal cost but with pure and simple exploitation, or the divergence of price and average costs. Implicit in these legal decisions has been the notion that price should reflect average costs both to protect the consumer as well as to ensure that the firm did not make losses.

The legal basis for regulating private property was further clarified in *Budd* v. *New York* where three limitations on the use of private property were recognised:

> First, that he shall not use it to his neighbor's injury, and that does not mean that he must use it for his neighbor's benefit; second, that if he devotes it to a public use, he gives to the public a right to control that use; and third, that whenever the public needs require, the public may take it upon payment of due compensation.[3]

In a further historic case, *Nebbia* v. *New York*, the Supreme Court held that an industry need not have monopolistic structure to be regulated. The *Nebbia* case involved the sale of milk at discount prices rather than public utilities. Nebbia argued that his business was competitive rather than monopolistic and that a state's fixing the price of milk was against the US Constitution. The Supreme Court found otherwise. It argued that as long as the requirements of due process were met 'a state is free to adopt whatever economic policy may reasonably be deemed to promote public welfare'.[4] To the extent that promoting the public welfare is an equitable concern, this decision reiterates the concern for equity.

While the courts required that regulated industries (utilities) provide their property for use by the public, they attempted to be even handed in requiring that utilities got a 'fair' rate of return on their investment. The notion of 'fair' rate of return is summarised in the *Hope* case. The term 'reasonable' is the word most frequently used by the courts and various commentators to describe what regulators should aim for in rates.[5] Justice Douglas stated

> the fixing of 'just and reasonable' rates involves a balancing of the investor and the consumer interests ... From the investor or company point of view it is important that there be enough revenue not only for operating expenses but also for the capital costs of the business ... [T]he return to the equity owner should be commensurate with returns on investments in other enterprises having corresponding risks.[6]

However, fairness in regulation does not extend to a *guarantee* by the regulators that the utility will earn a fair rate of return. In other words, while being protected against arbitrary acts by regulators, they are not protected from the operation of economic forces. The *Market Railway Company* case states the position.

> The due process clause of the Fourteenth Amendment ... does not assure to public utilities the right under all circumstances to have a return upon the value of the property so used. The use of, or the failure to obtain, patronage, due to competition, does not justify the imposition of charges that are exorbitant and unjust to the public.[7]

The operational implications of the *Hope* case can best be illustrated by means of the simple formula used in rate of return (RoR) regulation, which the *Hope* case legitimated. As will be clear presently, RoR regulation is based on the concept of cost-plus, which is commonly employed in sectors of the economy, like defence, where government is the main customer. Regulators determined the revenue required to give the utility a fair rate of return and then set prices so as to recover this revenue. This can be stated by means of the following cost-plus formula.

$$R = O + s(V - D) \qquad (5.1)$$

where R = revenue requirements
           O = operating expenses, including current depreciation
           s = allowed rate of return
           V = gross value of utility's property (i.e. rate base)
           D = accumulated depreciation

The regulator is concerned with all of items on the right-hand side of (5.1). Operating costs include all wages, managerial salaries, fuel costs, taxes, and the many other items that add up to the cost of doing business. The allowed rate of return is fixed by the regulator in line with the precedents mentioned above. The value of the rate base is dependent upon whether the regulator uses original costs, which is the typical approach, or replacement costs. It also depends on what property the regulator allows in the rate base. If a regulator does not consider an item of plant 'used and useful', it may not be allowed in the rate base. The amount of accrued depreciation is also determined by the regulator based upon schedules specified by the regulator. Commonly utility plant is considered to be long-lived and regulators require it to be depreciated over a long period. If regulators allowed accelerated depreciation this would have the effect of increasing operating expenses while reducing the rate base.

When there are several identifiable classes of consumer (e.g. residential and business), there is typically an attempt to apportion total operating and capital costs in (5.1) to each consumer class on the basis of cost causation principles. This apportionment gives rise to separate revenue requirements and rates for each consumer class designed to recover the apportioned costs for that class.

Summarising, the general principles underlying RoR regulation are that the firm should recover its costs (i.e. price $= AC$) and consumers should pay a fair price, with fairness argued on the basis of cost causation and apportionment procedures. Neither efficient pricing nor X-efficiency (i.e. efficient production) seem to be directly addressed by RoR regulation in its traditional form. Of course, there is nothing to preclude RoR regulation, and state or federal regulators, from addressing such price or production-efficiency issues.

Concerning pricing efficiency, the regulatory commission could direct that prices charged to different consumer groups (e.g. for different products) should be Ramsey optimal. This would entail some difficult information problems, of course, in ascertaining demand elasticities and marginal costs, but the regulatory commission could be at least 'intendedly Ramsey'. Concerning X-efficiency, various productivity incentives can be incorporated in the framework of RoR (or other) regulation. The essence of these, as we discuss in Chapter 6, is to share productivity gains with the firm in the form of increased profits, thus providing efficiency incentives. At the least, the regulator can attempt to control the size of all the variables on the right-hand side of (5.1), disallowing certain items if they are excessive.

The power of state and federal regulators to implement (5.1) was established in the *Hope* decision, which explicitly confirmed the independence of regulatory commissions from the Courts. As Phillips (1984, p. 163) put it, 'Freed from court domination, the federal and state commissions, acting within broad legislative provisions, have the responsibility for establishing their own criteria to determine both the rate level and the rate structure. And as long as the "end result" is just and reasonable the courts (at least the Supreme Court) will not intervene.'

All this emphasis on 'fair and reasonable' rates seems to be much more closely related to equity than it does to efficiency. It seems to be the deviation between price and average cost that occurs as a result of monopoly that is of concern to regulators rather than the price-marginal cost divergence, that is the concern in economics. This provides some basis for Zajac's (1978, 1982) argument that regulation's prime concern is with 'economic justice'.

As he notes, attempts by regulators and the courts to operationalise this concept have rarely involved considerations of economic efficiency. Zajac in stating the principles of economic justice clearly states another principle of justice that pervades the legal system, and this is the concern for the status quo.[8] The law takes very seriously the rights of individuals to the status quo. Indeed the common law's primary concern seems to be with the rights of the status quo to the extent that it emphasises precedent and the notion of *stare decisis*. Regulation, with its strong legal foundations, has much of the same concern for the status quo. This is apparent in the institutional resistance to change, even where change may benefit more people than it harms. This was particularly evident, for example, in some decisions of regulators following the AT&T divestiture where they have refused to allow reforms such as local measured service.

The stated intent of monopoly regulation was to be fair, equitable, and reasonable. The intent is similar to that of the legal system. For example, where one party feels another has damaged him or exploited him the legal system would seek to adjudicate. Whether the end result is fair or equitable is a different matter but the ostensible reason for bringing the court into the matter was the need to provide a neutral third party, who uses procedures that, if not generally accepted as fair, at least aim to treat both parties equally. Similarly the regulatory process, modelled as it is on the legal system, ostensibly provides the same neutrality, on the one hand aiming to protect the consumer from the evils of monopoly power and on the other attempting to see that the utility's property is not confiscated. While we consider this the undoubted objective based upon the case law and practice, the end results may not have worked out exactly in this way. Indeed, the consumer may not have been well protected and the producer may not have earned a monopoly return.

While regulation does not seem to be very concerned with promoting efficiency, either in a traditional static sense or in the sense of providing incentives for research and development, it does achieve a stable basis for operations which has, for the most part, resulted in companies being prepared to make the investments required. It has, in addition, provided the form if arguably not the substance of consumer protection. The reasons for this are difficult to find within the narrow confines of neoclassical economics. However, the insights provided in the public choice literature on rent seeking do indeed seem to offer the basis for an explanation. According to Buchanan, Tollison and Tullock (1980, p. ix) rent seeking 'is meant to describe the resource-wasting activities of individuals in seeking transfers of wealth through the aegis of the state'. It concerns the expenditure of resources to cut up the cake rather than make it larger.

In an attempt to clarify the nature of rent seeking in monopolies we will develop an example in detail. Consider the case of grants of a monopoly franchise for the sale of salt. If an individual can costlessly persuade the sovereign to grant him the monopoly in the sale of salt, he will be able to charge a price such that marginal cost equals marginal revenue and make super normal profits. This affects distribution and efficiency in that the monopolist enriches himself to the extent of $ACGB$ and a welfare loss of CGF in Figure 5.2 occurs from the divergence of marginal cost and price. For this simple case these are the only effects of monopoly. Let us consider some variations on this theme.

Our assumption that the monopolist was able costlessly to influence the sovereign and was able to retain his monopoly in perpetuity are strong to say the least, and without them the simple framework of Figure 5.2 begins to fall apart. Let us accordingly relax these assumptions in turn.

Let us assume that the sovereign when he sees the rents that our monopolist is making, apparently in perpetuity, decides that he wants a piece of the action and tells the monopolist that he wants a lump sum payment each year of $ACGB$. This has no effect on efficiency but changes distribution. The sovereign now takes the rents himself. Note that this assumes that the monopolist decides to make no investment in attempting to get the sovereign to change his mind.

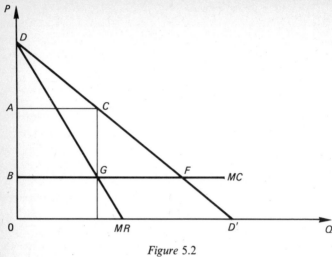

Figure 5.2

What happens if the sovereign is not concerned about the monopoly rents being earned but that others are? Some are concerned that it is inequitable for him to make this profit. Other courtiers would like the monopoly profits for themselves. Let us assume that these courtiers start to expend resources to convince the sovereign that they should have the monopoly. If the expenditure of resources takes the form simply of making gifts to the sovereign and very little else, the welfare consequences are still the same. However, if they take the form in part of expending resources to convince the sovereign to spread these rents around, then the results are different. Those resources used to convince the sovereign must be deducted from *ACGB* and constitute an additional welfare loss. This is then our primitive example of rent seeking; those resources used, but not transferred, to bring about a change in distribution. In this simple case note that this may not be the only example of rent seeking. We mentioned that consumers were upset at the high price they had to pay for salt. Some of them complained to the sovereign either directly or through their masters or through the courts the sovereign had made available. This involved travelling to Londinium, and other expenses to put the case. The salt monopolist, however, is not going to take these kinds of attacks on his monopoly lying down. He will find it optimal to invest resources to defend himself against such attacks. Where he prevails quickly and with small investment of resources, the welfare and distributional effects are very little different from the original case. However, if the opposing forces and he are pretty well equally matched, then both sides may expend resources until the whole of the area $ACGB$ is dissipated.

Rent seeking then in this simple example can be seen to take three forms: (a) expenditure of resources up front to obtain the monopoly franchise, (b) on-going expenditures to defend the monopoly against intruders, (c) expenditures by others to attack the monopoly. The consequences of (a) and (b) are both welfare reducing, as Tullock (1967) has shown. However, in terms of the gains that may be achieved from ending rent seeking in a particular instance, the difference between the two is crucial. Suppose the sovereign refused to discuss the salt monopoly further. If on pain of death no one was allowed to mention the salt monopoly again, rent seeking would be ended. Those people who had invested resources in trying to wrest away the monopoly from the salt monopolist would lose the resources they had expended. As these are bygones, this would not have any further welfare consequences. However, the resources continually expended by the monopolist and any future expenditures by rent seekers trying to take over his monopoly would be saved. Thus, at the limit, the edict by the sovereign would result in savings of $ACGB$ of resources otherwise wasted on on-going rent seeking.

The important point here is that rents are created by an artificial shortage – in particular a government or regulatory induced shortage. Rent seekers will therefore expend resources attempting to persuade government or regulators to allow them access to these artificial rents. Hopefully relatively few resources would be devoted to rent seeking. However, we will see that this is not necessarily the case. Indeed, in public utility regulation, there appear to be considerable incentives for rent seeking, as we now discuss.

RoR regulation's ostensible aims are to protect the consumer and at the same time provide the firm with a 'fair' rate of return. These aims of regulation are overseen and interpreted by the legal system. This means that conspiracy is made more difficult as is enrichment by the principals since the legal system provides a barrier, at a high cost, to these. To see how rent seeking can nonetheless occur under RoR regulation, let us consider in a bit more detail how the regulatory process functions. Before a public utility is allowed to change its prices it has to seek approval of its state regulatory commission. It must file its case and then be prepared to be examined on it. While the procedure varies in different states, the example of New Jersey will suffice for our purposes. Following the filing by the company, intervenors have the opportunity to object to the company's case. Intervenors, principally the state-appointed Rate Counsel, then file their own testimony criticising the company's case. The options then are for the two sides either to discuss their differences and agree to a 'stipulation' which has to be approved by the regulators, or to litigate the case before an administrative law judge. The litigation, if such occurs, involves almost all the features of normal court proceedings, such as cross examination, rebuttal and the like. The judge then prepares his report which goes to the commission (in New Jersey, the Board of Public Utilities) for a final decision. The board reaches its decision on the amount of money it is going to allow the company (the target revenue R in equation (5.1)). It then passes the case to the board staff who work out rates they consider will be just sufficient to raise the desired sum of money.

When all of the figures in (5.1) are agreed by the board and corresponding rates derived, an order is issued which allows the company to charge these rates. If the company believes that the order treats it grossly unfairly in the sense that it believes it can show failure of due process it may appeal to the appellate court, the state supreme court and even to the United States Supreme Court if federal law is involved. More likely, however, it will begin working on preparing for another rate case to enable it to expedite filing. In any event, the company will continue working on a day-to-day basis with the regulators. This continuing contact is important in establishing what regulators are likely to accept and also for behind the scenes lobbying for positions the company wishes to institute in the future.

The process described above can be costly, involving considerable expenditure of resources by the company, the regulators and the intervenor. Moreover, given the quasi-judicial nature of the process the company has little control over the outcome. The process described also appears to provide little incentive toward economising scarce resources, because of the cost-plus nature of the process, and it generates a considerable potential for rent-seeking activities:

1. rent seeking by managers to indulge their preferences for certain expenses – the notion of expense preference developed by Williamson (1967);
2. rent seeking by hourly paid workers through the activities of their unions;
3. rent seeking by intervenors;
4. rent seeking by commissioners;
5. rent seeking by expert witnesses;

6. rent seeking by certain customers and suppliers of the utility;
7. rent seeking by stockholders.

One may interpret the several theories of regulation that have been developed as an attempt to explain the causes and effects of the above forms of rent seeking on the structure and operation of regulation. This will also be our basic theme in the remainder of this chapter as we review these theories.

5.2 THEORIES ON THE ORIGINS AND PURPOSE OF REGULATION

In this section, we review several theories concerning the origins and intended purpose of regulation. The following section is concerned with the operation and incentives of regulatory systems. Since our concern is solely with monopoly regulation, we will continue our attention to those theories that seem to be most relevant to this problem. We will examine three classes of theories: public-interest theories, capture theories, and other theories. The final category of 'other' theories is concerned with equity aspects primarily.

The public-interest theories of regulation stem from the notion that regulation aims to discharge and does discharge the 'public interest'. The problem is that the term public interest is itself vague. Another problem with the theory is that it 'is more often assumed than articulated'.[9] It views regulation as a response to demands by the public to correct inequitable or inefficient practices that arise in unregulated markets. It is an attempt to correct the problems brought about by market failures. For the economist this might mean using regulation to perform the function of competition by inducing the monopolist to act like a perfect competitor. This now looks like a vain hope for regulation. In the 1960s there were great hopes for the role of government in correcting market failures. These turned out to be misplaced because of the fundamentally flawed assumptions underlying this aspiration. These were stated by Posner (1974, p. 336) as follows: 'One assumption was that economic markets are extremely fragile and apt to operate very inefficiently (or inequitably) if left alone; the other was that government regulation is virtually costless.'

In place of the public-interest theories, several 'private-interest' theories have been proposed to explain the origins of regulation through rent-seeking activities of those who see themselves *ex ante* as beneficiaries of regulation. The best known of these are the 'capture' theories. These, according to Posner (1974, p. 343) can be divided into two classes, the 'economic theory of regulation' and the 'political scientist's' formulation. We are concerned with the economic theory since we agree with Posner's view that while the political scientist's formulation draws attention to the role of pressure groups in capturing the regulatory process, it is predictively weak. Regulation is viewed as a product in that it provides services such as cartel management. In its most sophisticated form as stated by Peltzman (1976) the theory has both a demand side and a supply side. The demand side is the industries desiring the cartel management that regulation can provide and that cannot be provided by more direct means because of anti-trust laws. It is another instance of the tar baby effect where the attempt to regulate through anti-trust results in adjustments being made elsewhere. Proponents of the theory would cite examples of how industries have lobbied to be regulated. At first sight this might look like powerful evidence in support of the demand side of the theory, but it ignores the alternatives. If public ownership were the alternative to regulation, it is not inconceivable that utility managements might choose regulation just to avoid state takeover. It may not be a matter of seeing regulation as an opportunity for more effective cartel management.[10] Other problems perceived with the theory include numerous instances where regulation is clearly not perceived to be operating in the regulated companies' interests. Examples of this are available in the decisions of many state regulatory bodies, like rates that do not permit the companies to earn even the low rates of return allowed, disallowance of certain items in the cost service or in the rate base, and excessively long periods over which capital may be recovered. Part of the problem may be explained in terms of the supply side of the theory which Peltzman argues derives from politicians' and agencies' desire to maximise vote margins by using regulation as a redistributive device. This may explain in part why some of the results of regulation may not be consistent with the original goals of the companies which 'captured' the regulatory process.

There are other reasons why the capture theory may not apply to on-going public utility regulation. The argument is that the implied conspiracy of capture theory would be unlikely to operate in on-going RoR regulation given the quasi-judicial nature of the process, the way regulatory proceedings are conducted in the public arena, and the manifest failure of some utilities to achieve more than a normal return in the long run. In order to preserve the independence of the regulatory commission and to reduce the risk of conspiracy, in many jurisdictions public advocates or rate counsels have been charged with representing consumers' interests or the public interest at rate proceedings. As a result the utilities face an adversary who is in the same situation as the 'other side's' lawyer, a relationship where conspiracy is made difficult to say the least.

While we may argue that the nature of the regulatory apparatus does not support conspiracy, the end result, in economic efficiency terms, may be just as bad or even worse. Basically Posner's (1975, p. 819) scathing attack on regulation providing the important insight that 'the costs of regulation probably exceed the costs of private monopoly' may well describe the effects of current RoR regulation judged entirely in efficiency terms.

In terms of the 'other theories' we will examine briefly Niskanen (1971, 1973), Goldberg (1976) and Owen and Braeutigam (1978). Niskanen would argue that regulation can be understood in terms of the behaviour of bureaucracies. He defines a bureau as being an organisation that derives its budget from sources other than the sale of its output and where the bureaucrat's compensation, or more particularly, the chief bureaucrat's compensation does not depend upon the success of the organisation, say as defined in terms of surplus of revenue over cost. He argues that they will then try to maximise the total budget of the bureau, and exchange a specific output for a specific budget. Lindsay (1976) argues that because bureaus will be compensated based upon the ouput that is measurable this may affect the output they produce. Thus a bureaucratic theory implies regulatory behaviour to serve the ends of the bureaucrat which may not be consistent with the original intentions behind the creation of the regulatory apparatus.

Goldberg (1976) sees regulation as a means of solving the transaction-specific investment problem. To provide service a utility must undertake certain investments that are specific to the transaction of supplying the customer. Goldberg argues that without a grant of monopoly a utility may face a hold-up problem and would not have sufficient incentive to provide the transactions-specific investment required. He thus views regulation as a contract, administered by the regulator to protect the consumer from being exploited and to provide a means of resolving disputes and differences that may arise in situations where the capital is long-lived and where all contingencies cannot be specified in advance in the form of a long-term contract.

In our view, Goldberg's 'administered Contract' framework is a reasonable description of the operation of RoR regulation in the monopoly sector. We explore further issues in this spirit in the next two sections. For the moment, let us simply note the fundamental issue raised by this perspective, namely to what extent are the transactions cost of governance for administering this contract worth the (equity and efficiency) benefits achievable thereby?

Owen and Braeutigam's (1978) theory is a blending of parts of the theories discussed above. It sees regulation as being provided at the demand of the public a means of attenuating the risks associated with the operation of market forces. For example, regulation can slow down the rate of technological change thereby reducing the risks of windfall gains and losses that may befall individuals. Stability is considered to be an important goal and regulation provides individuals the chance to adjust to changes occurring. Owen and Braeutigam's theory then is similar to Zajac's theory in emphasising equity, in particular, the rights of the status quo, as opposed to efficiency.

The above theories point to various rent seekers at various stages of regulation. At first inception, industry in a turbulent environment might seek regulation as a system of cartel management. As the industry matures, regulators as bureaucrats might emerge as budget-maximising public servants. Depending on the visibility of the industry and its importance as a percentage of consumer budgets, consumerism and public interest arguments could well hold sway. In all of this, one can imagine the ready support of the legal profession and other experts in supporting the various contenders for power and rents in the evolving administered contract which regulation embodied. To understand the manner in which rents accrue to these and other rent seekers, it is essential that we consider the operation of regulation in more detail.

5.3 THEORIES CONCERNING THE OPERATION AND INCENTIVES OF REGULATORY SYSTEMS

We first develop a simple principal–agent model of the regulatory process to provide a preliminary basis for understanding regulation. There are a number of ways the principal–agent may be structured in the case of public utilities. The simplest form is where the consumers and the regulatory commission are seen as the principal and the utility as the agent. This is depicted in Figure 5.3. The principal is the regulatory commission representing the consumers. The regulatory commission attempts to achieve the desired vector of public utility services (right-hand box) by a number of regulatory instruments (vertical arrow) like rate-of-return and price regulation, moral suasion, threats and appeal to the public through the media. The public utility responds to these signals according to its motivation (e.g. whether or not it aims to maximise profit) with a set of behavioural rules and a resulting vector of prices, quantities, quality and profit. The commission attempts to see what effect its instruments are having on the public utility by monitoring and enforcement. The effect of this is that these get changed as they move through the monitoring and enforcement arrangements (see box and arrows on left). Information on prices, etc., also comes back directly (on the right-hand side of the diagram) from the actual vector of services made available for consumption. In addition there is exogenous pressure at work, shown in the top right-hand corner. This can come from a number of sources. A regulatory commission might find itself under pressure from the federal or state governments.

Pressures like the ones described above may be one reason for believing that a different representation of the principal–agent problem may be more accurate in describing the regulation of public utilities. In particular it may make more sense to consider the consumers as principal and the regulatory commission as the agent who contracts with a further agent, the utility to supply the vector of public utility services. Such extended agency relationships are common. For example a consumer might hire a lawyer or a physician as his agent. The lawyer may act as his advocate and purchasing agent, while the physician acts as his purchasing agent. The lawyer may then, as the consumer's agent hire other lawyers and expert witnesses to present his client's case. In the English legal system such extended agencies are institutionalised. The client may not hire a barrister himself. In addition a client does not meet with his barrister except in the presence of his solicitor. The institutionalisation of such extended agency relationships indicates that there are other interests to be served in this situation than the objectives of the client alone. For example the lawyers are clearly interested in their own compensation, and in protecting themselves from legal action by the client. As for each winner there is normally a loser, lawyers on average have half of their clients who are losers. While it is true that the legal system provides considerable protection for the lawyer, the solicitor-barrister example is a further illustration of how extended agency can be used to further the interests of the lawyers and not just the client. That the process survives may be explained not just in terms of the benefits it gives to the lawyers but also to benefits it provides to clients. By hiring a barrister the solicitor presumably gets the services of

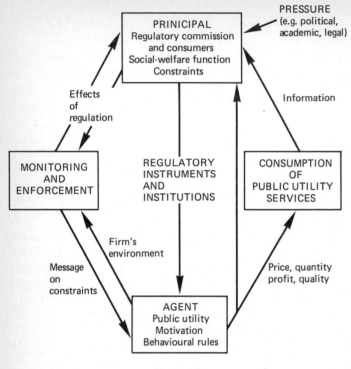

Figure 5.3

a better advocate than if the client hired him or if the solicitor played the role of advocate himself. Similarly he is better informed about fees than the client and may be in a better position to prevent hold-up of the desperate client, to the extent that barristers rely upon solicitors to hire them in the future. On the other hand, the process may be wasteful of labour. It might be considered an institutionalised means of capturing rents by the legal profession which is less blatant than some other alternatives.

In a similar manner, the regulatory commission does not supply utility services directly to the consumer. It contracts with the utility to do this. Just as the relationship between the English barrister and client cannot take place independently of his solicitor or the consumer cannot contract with the utility except on terms set out by the regulator. Because of the extended agency nature of the provision of natural monopoly or utility services it is possible, and indeed likely, that regulatory commissions will have interests other than those of the principal. Similarly the utility will have its own interests which will not coincide completely with those of the regulators or the consumers. The regulators may wish, along the lines of Williamson (1964) and Niskanen (1971), to expand their own budgets to enable them to have larger staffs and perquisites. Bös, Tillmann and Zimmermann (1983) have developed the bureaucratic theories to include the situation of a public enterprise that receives part of its revenues from its customers and part from subsidy. They provide an empirical example of London Transport. While their model may reflect the situation facing many public enterprises in Europe it has lesser direct relevance to the US regulation. However, such models of bureaucracy, especially those employing the principal–agent framework, seem to us to offer fruitful opportunities to explain regulatory behaviour not present in current theories. Indeed they might be part of a more complete theory which takes into account considerations of bounded rationality, equity and constrained efficiency, driven by rent seeking and subject to transactions costs. While we do not develop such a complete theory here, we will be concerned in the next section with some of the considerations involved in the transactions costs of existing regulatory governance structures.

5.4 THE PRACTICE OF RATE-OF-RETURN REGULATION

We might summarise the above theories as saying that, for the case of natural monopolies, the prospect of appropriating rents generates considerable interest in setting up and controlling a monopoly franchise. Given that the legal system is ultimately responsible for adjudicating the allocation of such rents, notions of due process (see Mashaw (1985)), and fairness slowly permeate the regulatory institutions set up to protect/control/oversee the monopoly franchise. These institutions may be viewed in steady state as an institutional embodiment of the equilibrium of the various contenders for available rents. Given the nature and importance of public utilities, these institutions must also be able to legitimate the outcomes of the on-going administered contract between regulators, firms and consumers. This legitimation process induces transactions costs which may be large enough to make the net benefits of regulation negative.

We now consider the transactions costs of regulation in more detail. First, at a general level, one might ask whether regulation would be allowed to continue if its net efficiency impact is negative. There are a number of explanations provided for this in the public choice literature, which we will briefly sketch. They arise from the notion of rent seeking originated by Tullock (1967) and described earlier. Because of the competitive nature of the process, acquiring a grant of monopoly is costly. The successful applicant has to expend up-front resources to obtain the grant monopoly. Once obtained, he may have to expend further resources to maintain the monopoly from attack. In either case such expenditures are inefficient, creating welfare losses and may help to explain the obstacles in the path of deregulation. In the case of full up-front capitalisation of the rents, there may be little incentive to deregulate because there are few gains from it as argued by McCormick, Shughart and Tollison (1984). In the case of continuous dissipation of rents to maintain a monopoly, considerable welfare losses result. For example, suppose in Figure 5.2 that all the monopoly rents are dissipated on a continuous basis. The welfare losses in this case are not just the Marshallian triangle *CGF* but in addition the rectangle *ACGB*. Thus, rent-seeking can result in a greater loss than unregulated monopoly. Although this case has the opposite welfare implication to the McCormick, Shugard and Tollison case, it also results in a similar attenuation of incentives for deregulation. As long as some of the current rent seekers can capture some rents[12] – i.e. earn in excess of their transfer earnings, which would occur as long as competition amongst rent seekers is not perfect – they will have an incentive to retain the regulatory process even though the original recipient of the monopoly grant is getting no monopoly return. The idea is that the beneficiaries of the process gain considerably, but the costs of the process are very thinly spread. Thus the losers have little incentive to do anything about it, particularly because of the free-ridership problems that would arise for anyone wishing to introduce reform.

As we will argue below, there is evidence to support the notion that RoR regulation has institutionalised on-going rent seeking. If this is the case, it is important to determine whether the losses from such rent seeking exceed the gains from the regulatory process. Otherwise RoR regulation may have us locked into a situation where two protagonists compete for the rents available before a quasi-judicial body, the regulatory commission. As in some civil proceedings, there are few limits on the expenses the parties incur, because so much is at stake, and most of the costs are already sunk. Indeed, there seems little to prevent the costs increasing until all the rents are spent. However, given that parties to the regulatory process, unlike litigants in civil cases which are normally one-of-a-kind occurrences, meet frequently in proceedings, it is possible that incentives for cooperation along the lines of Axelrod (1984) may develop which limit the losses that each side finds it rational to inflict upon each other. Cooperation of this kind is akin to a restriction of competition or cartel management in duopoly. However, in the case of rent seeking, cooperation results in a net gain to society, because it means that all the rents will not be completely dissipated. This leaves a residual which might be shared between the company and the consumers. In the case of lawyers, there may be an incentive not to dissipate all the rents because the effects on their reputation of doing so may be bad, which may be important to them in view of the long-run recurrent nature of their client relations.

In our 1985 paper we examined both of the above issues and we found that in terms of the net-benefit approach, at least in the case of water in New Jersey, little seemed to be gained from the regulatory process because the visible transactions costs, to say nothing of the invisible transactions costs, exceeded the benefits of price control provided by regulation. We also found that there was some evidence to suggest that both the companies and the Rate Counsel did, however, cooperate on occasions in an attempt to mitigate each side's, and therefore rate payers' losses. This might imply that the limits are adaptively set to the rents that are remaining.

We now present our (1985) model and summarise our empirical results.

We expand the definition of the traditional social welfare function:

$$W = TR + S - C - (G_1 + G_2) \qquad (5.2)$$

where $W =$ net benefit

$TR =$ total revenue

$S =$ consumer's surplus

$C =$ total cost, excluding the transactions costs of governance

$G_1 =$ the firm's regulatory transactions costs

$G_1 =$ the consumers' representative's regulatory transaction costs

The aim of the actors in rate proceedings is for the firm to get as high a price as it can (subject to an assured maximum of the monopoly price), and for the consumers' representative to keep the price increase as low as possible.

In Figure 5.4, P^0 is the price before the company begins rate proceedings. P^1 is the price awarded as a result of the rate case. The firm's gain is given by the shaded area $P^1AFP^0 + DEFB$. The consumers' loss is given by P^1AEP^0. Thus, if we ignore transactions costs, $ABC < CDE$, implies that the firm's gain exceeds the consumers' loss and the price increase will result in a net benefit. The first thing to note is that the net gains, ABC and CDE, are rather small in relation to the loss by consumers.

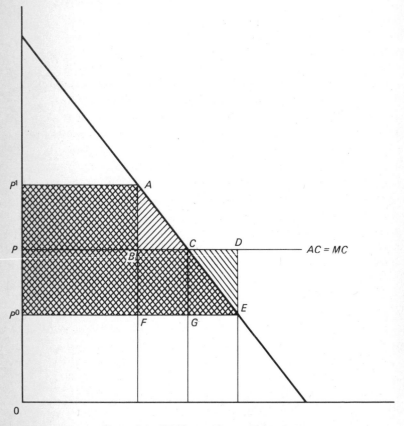

Figure 5.4   Welfare and transactions costs

This may be illustrated by means of a simple example. We assume a linear cost function $C(Q) = cQ$ and constant elasticity demand function $Q = AP^{-\eta}$. Let total regulatory transactions costs be denoted $G = G_1 + G_2$. Then, if G is expended to arrive at a price P, total welfare at the pair (P,G) is[13]

$$W(P,G) = \int^{Q(P)} (x/A)^{-1/\eta} \, dx - cQ(P) - G$$

$$= [\eta P/(\eta - 1) - c]Q(P) - G \tag{5.3}$$

We now use (5.3) to illustrate the impact of regulatory transactions costs.

First, let us compare the (P,G) pairs $[kc, 0]$ and $[(1 + t)c, G]$, where $0 \leqslant k < 1$ and $t = [G/(cQ(1 + t)c)]$. The pair $(P,G) = [kc, 0]$ corresponds to a firm operating at a loss recovering only the fraction k of it costs. The firm can either continue at this price level (with lump-sum subsidies) or it can achieve a price increase through a rate proceeding. Suppose the total transactions costs of the proceeding are G and the resulting price P is just sufficient to recover total cost $cQ(P)$ plus G, i.e. $P = c + G/Q(P) = c(1 + G/cQ(P)) = c(1 + t(c,G,P))$. Comparing the welfare resulting from these two cases, one computes for the present example that $W((1 + t)c, G) = W(kc, 0)$ when

$$t = k[(1 - (1 - k)\eta) \, / \, k]^{1/(1 - \eta)} - 1. \tag{5.4}$$

Table 5.1 shows illustrative values of η, k, and t for which (5.4) holds. If t (i.e., G) is larger than that achieving equality in (5.4), then welfare losses will be incurred by instituting the rate proceeding.

Table 5.1   Welfare effects of transactions costs

	$\eta \cong 1$*	$\eta = 0.5$
$k = 0.9$	0.56%	0.28%
$k = 0.95$	0.14%	0.07%

Transactions costs $t = G/cQ$ as a percentage of total costs (cQ) sufficient to make the welfare effects of a break-even price change equal to zero at selected values of k and η.
*Note that (5.3) is not defined for $\eta = 1$, but it has the limit indicated as η approaches 1.

The results in Table 5.1 suggest that only small expenditures of regulatory transactions costs are justified, because any increase in transactions costs above these levels will make net benefits (W) in (5.2) negative. Thus, such regulatory expenses, at least with this simple measure of efficiency, quickly eat up the benefits associated here with them.

In view of the way even small transactions costs offset the benefits arising from the regulatory process we will now briefly examine how transactions costs arise in the process. The adversary process results in the utility's attorney's facing usually a publicly appointed intervenor which we will call the public advocate. The situation they face at first sight is akin to that of the prisoner's dilemma. Each party would be better off if they were able to cooperate to the extent that each side's transactions costs would be reduced and the point C in Figure 5.4 that maximised net gain, W, would be achieved. However, to the extent that the process may be characterised as a prisoner's dilemma, the two parties may have incentives not to cooperate. We will now illustrate how this may happen with the aid of Table 5.2. The firm's strategies are shown in the far left column and intervenor's strategies in the top row.

Table 5.2   Prisoner's dilemma model

Firm's strategy	Intervenor's strategy	
	Cooperate	*Max independently*
Cooperate	$U(P) - g_1, S(P) - g_2$	$U(P - \Delta) - g_1, S(P - \Delta) - G_2$
Max Independently	$U(P + \Delta) - G_1, S(P + \Delta) - g_2$	$U(P + \delta) - G_1, S(P + \delta) - G_2$

Where Δ, G_1, G_2 are large and where $\Delta \gg |\delta|$, $G_1 \gg g_1$, and $G_2 \gg g_2$.

We denote the firm's profits by $U(P) - G_1 = TR - C_1 - G_1$ and consumer surplus by $S(P) - G_2$, where P is price resulting from the regulatory process and G_1, G_2 are the transactions costs paid by the firm and intervenor in negotiating P. We assume that the firm and public intervenor attempt to maximise $U(P) - G_1$, and $S(P) - G_2$ respectively. If both parties cooperate, total welfare is maximised with $W = U(P) - g^1 + S(P) - g_2$. This is greater than the situation where each agent independently maximises with $W = U(P \pm \delta) - G_1 + S(P \pm \delta) - G_2$. This is because where both cooperate each incurs lower transactions costs of g_1 for the firm and g_2 for the intervenor and the price would likely be set close to the optimal P in Figure 5.4. Where each independently maximises his respective objective function the resulting P might lie anywhere between $P+\delta$ and $P-\delta$, where δ is small in absolute value, and where G_1 and G_1 are assumed large relative to g_1 and g_2. If, however, one party cooperates and the other does not, gains arise for the non-cooperating party. In the case of the firm it results in the higher price $U(P+\Delta)$ less the transactions cost G_1, while the intervenor loses with $S(P+\Delta-g_2)$, saving only on transactions costs. Similarly when the intervenor maximises and the firm cooperates, the firm loses with $U(P-\Delta)-g_1$ and the intervenor gains with $S_2(P-\Delta)-G_2$. If each follows the minimax solution – as expected – both are worse off as shown in the bottom right cell. Each therefore has, in this application of the classic prisoner's dilemma, an incentive not to cooperate although both would lose if both do not cooperate (i.e. if the rate-case is litigated).

It is conceivable that the prisoner's dilemma may not apply in the simple form as outlined above. In view of the fact that, in practice, frequent interaction may and does occur between companies and the advocate, it is arguable that some modified form of the prisoner's dilemma, such as the 'repeated Prisoner's Dilemma' as examined by Axelrod and Hamilton (1981) and Axelrod (1984), applies. Here other strategies rather than simple cooperation or cheating may arise, and may even dominate. One such strategy is TIT-FOR-TAT, which in Axelrod and Hamilton's experiments was a very robust strategy. TIT-FOR-TAT involves 'cooperating on the first move and then doing whatever the other player did on the preceding move'. (Axelrod and Hamilton 1981, p. 1393) Whether TIT-FOR-TAT is efficient and stable depends upon the probability of further interaction between the parties, the higher the probability the more likely TIT-FOR-TAT is to be efficient and stable. In the case of utilities and a permanent public advocate, the chance of meeting again would presumably be large implying that TIT-FOR-TAT is a (Pareto efficient) Nash equilibrium in the repeated prisoners' dilemma game. With other intervenors the probability would be lower and the non-cooperative strategy may be the only Nash strategy in the repeated game.

The empirical results of Crew and Kleindorfer (1985), which examined rate case activity on the part of water utilities in New Jersey, provided some evidence suggestive of behaviour consistent with the repeated prisoner's dilemma paradigm. This was particularly evident in the case of large companies who seemed to be quite skilled in framing requests for rate relief. Similarly litigation on the part of large companies tended to occur only when cooperation broke down and the public advocate made a stand which required them to litigate to obtain what they perceived as their legitimate entitlement. Small companies, which had less frequent contact with the public advocate, were less well versed in matters such as the size of the rate request. Here cooperation was less in evidence and behaviour more akin to the classic prisoner's dilemma seemed to be observed.

Lest we give a too negative picture of regulation in practice, we should point out the following plausible explanation for the New Jersey-water-company findings summarised above. Namely, there may simply be economies of scale in the form of fixed costs of obtaining regulatory expertise. Large companies can afford these; small companies cannot. Once these fixed costs are paid, the regulatory process functions reasonably efficiently in the sense of the administered contract approach of Goldberg (1976). The extent to which this scenario is valid remains to be seen in empirical research. The above simple analysis shows, however, that transactions do not have to be very significant before they wipe out any hoped for gains in allocative or X-efficiency which regulation might provide. At the least this would suggest increasing the efficiency benefits of regulation or decreasing its transactions costs.

5.5 CONCLUSIONS

There are two competing views on the net benefits of regulation. The traditional view is that economies of scale or scope imply the desirability of protected monopoly, with regulation a necessary evil to safeguard consumers against monopoly exploitation. The presumption in the traditional view is that the costs of the regulatory process are small relative to surplus gains achieved through regulation. A contrasting view, which has been gaining prominence, is that the costs of regulation exceed its benefits. This view rests primarily on the transaction costs, rent seeking and other inefficiencies induced by regulation. As we have seen in this chapter, the origins and legal history of regulation, at least in the USA, have been unconcerned with these efficiency arguments. Rather the origins, on-going justification and structure of regulation have been much more concerned with fairness than with efficiency. Because of its judicial nature it attempts to achieve fairness, possibly at the cost of efficiency. It is not clear, however, that the benefits from fairness exceed the costs by way of inefficiencies induced by the regulatory process. Our research on New Jersey water companies suggests that the costs of the process may exceed the benefits, especially when small utilities are involved. If this is indeed the case, the existence of regulation presents a problem. If there are many losers from the process and a few major gainers, how is it that the process continues? Of course in some areas, for example airlines, regulation has been abolished giving some support to the notion that the benefits were perceived as less than the costs. In others such as telecommunications, the industry has been restructured apparently to allow deregulation, but regulation still survives.[14] Its continued survival may be explained by a number of factors, such as a high value placed on fairness, risk aversion by all parties, any residual benefits derived by rent seekers, and the lack of interest and understanding of the effects of the process generally. Fairness may be highly valued partially since it is a commodity whose cost each member of society is not bearing directly. This combined with the risk that the consumer would be exploited by a monopoly without regulation make the prospect of deregulation of utilities not very attractive unless the costs of the regulation are perceived to be huge. As many of the costs are hidden, this perception is unlikely. Moreover, rent seekers have something to gain from the process and may take steps to influence legislators for its continuance. As Tullock (1975) has argued, some of the gains from regulation may have been capitalised, as for example in the case of taxi medallions, which would mean that windfall losses would occur as a result of deregulation. Thus given the protection given by the legal system in general to the status quo, to say nothing of how regulation itself preserves such rights, it is not surprising that regulation remains.

In the rest of this book we are going to examine in detail some of the efficiency consequences of the regulatory process. In Chapter 6 we will examine in general the efficiency consequences of RoR regulation. In Chapter 7 we will develop a comparative institutional assessment of various governance modes for natural monopoly. Chapters 8–12 will examine the problems of the various public utilities. Some of the issues discovered in this chapter will surface again in the course of these chapters.

6 Models of Monopoly Regulation

This chapter is concerned with examining some simple models of regulation. These take several forms, corresponding to the general concerns of monopoly regulation. They include models of:

1. *Profit or price level regulation*, including rate-of-return regulation,
2. *Price structure regulation*, concerned with the structure of tariffs (e.g. mandated peak-load or two-part tariffs),
3. *Productivity and incentive regulation* concerned with inducing X-efficiency.

Naturally, the scope of regulation is considerably broader than the above three areas of concern here, e.g. including health, safety and environmental regulation, which we neglect. Our concern will be to briefly describe the major theoretical contributions developed to address the above three areas of regulation and for understanding the costs and benefits of applying such regulation to the monopoly problem.

In Chapter 5 we discussed some of the hypotheses intended to explain the origin of regulation. In this chapter, we examine in neoclassical terms several theories of price and productivity regulation. We begin with an analysis of rate-of-return (RoR) regulation, based on the research tradition pioneered by Averch and Johnson (1962) In Section 6.1 we set out the basic Averch–Johnson model. Sections 6.2 and 6.3 examine the applications of extensions of this model to the peak-load problem under deterministic and stochastic conditions. Section 6.4 discusses the problem of welfare-optimal rate-of-return for the RoR regulated monopoly.

In Section 6.5 we consider one example of price structure regulation under the heading of appropriate rules for distributing fixed costs across multiple products provided by a regulated monopolist. Our earlier analysis indicates that the optimal solution to this problem is to use the Ramsey inverse elasticity rule. The problem we address in Section 6.5 is how best to approximate this rule when the regulator is uninformed of the demand functions and can only rely on simple data such as that available from accounting records.

In Section 6.6 we consider several alternative forms of regulation which were proposed to address the problems of allocative and X-inefficiency which arise in the Averch–Johnson theory. We discuss various forms of incentive regulation, by which the regulated firm is purportedly induced (e.g. through subsidies or productivity incentives) to improve its efficiency. We also review recent theories for the related problem of designing optimal incentives to regulate a monopolist whose cost and demand conditions are either unknown or incompletely known. Section 6.7 concludes with a summary of results and concerns of the neoclassical analysis of regulation and sets the stage for the comparative institutional analysis of Chapter 7 in the new institutional economics framework.

6.1 THE BASIC AVERCH–JOHNSON RESULT

In this section we will examine one of the major issues in the economic theory of regulation, namely the Averch–Johnson effect. We confine our attention to the single-product case with two factors of production.

The Averch–Johnson effect has received more attention in the recent literature on the economic theory of regulation than any other topic.[1]

We employ the following notation:

Π = profit.

x = output (measured in physical units).

K = capital.

L = labour.

r = firm's cost of capital.

w = unit cost of labour (wage rate).

$s\ (>r)$ = rate of return allowed by regulatory commission.

x = $F(K,L)$, where F is a quasi-concave neoclassical production function with positive marginal products and for which $F(0,L)=F(K,0)=0$ for all K,L.

P = $P(x)$ = inverse demand function.

R = Px = revenue.

h = cost of physical unit of capital; henceforth we assume $h=1$.

β = rh.

The firm is assumed to maximise profit subject to the regulatory constraint. That its rate of return does not exceed the allowed rate s, that is:

$$\text{Max } \Pi = P(F(K,L))F(K,L) - rK - wL, \tag{6.1}$$

Subject to:

$$\frac{PF(K,L) - wL}{K} \leqslant s. \tag{6.2}$$

Assuming $s > r$, rewriting (6.1) and (6.2) and setting up a Lagrangian we have:

$$\Lambda = R - rK - wL - \lambda(PF(K,L) - wL - sK). \tag{6.3}$$

Denoting MR = marginal revenue, the first-order conditions are:

$$\frac{\partial \Lambda}{\partial K} = (1-\lambda)MR\frac{\partial F}{\partial K} - (1-\lambda)r - \lambda(r - s) = 0 \tag{6.4}$$

$$\frac{\partial \Lambda}{\partial L} = (1-\lambda)MR\frac{\partial F}{\partial L} - (1-\lambda)w = 0. \tag{6.5}$$

Thus (6.4)–(6.5) represent a solution to the problem of maximising profit subject to a regulatory constraint. Such a solution differs from the profit-maximising solution since, as we show directly, it is not a cost-minimising solution for the achieved level of output $x = F(K,L)$. Cost minimisation would require:

$$\frac{F_K}{F_L} = \frac{r}{w}. \tag{6.6}$$

where $F_K = \partial F/\partial K$, $F_L = \partial F/\partial L$, the marginal products of K and L respectively. Readers may prove (6.6) for themselves.

To see the difference between the regulated solution and a cost-minimising solution divide (6.4) by (6.5) to obtain:

$$-\frac{dL}{dK} = \frac{F_K}{F_L} = \frac{r}{w} - \frac{\lambda(s-r)}{(1-\lambda)w} < \frac{r}{w}. \tag{6.7}$$

If the regulatory constraint is binding, then $\lambda > 0$,[2] implying that the cost-minimising conditions (6.6) do not hold so that a regulated profit-maximising firm will not minimise costs. From (6.7) we see that the marginal rate of technical substitution ($-dL/dK$) of capital for labour is lower for the regulated firm than for a cost minimiser. Given the assumed convex shape of production isoquants (recall that F is assumed quasi-concave), it follows immediately that under regulation capital is over-utilised and labour under-utilised relative to any cost-minimising solution. This is called the Averch–Johnson effect.

The Averch–Johnson effect is robust for other models of firm behaviour. For example, as Crew and Kleindorfer (1979a and 1979b) have shown, it applies to expense preference models of the firm along the lines of Williamson (1964). Where a regulated firm maximises a utility function containing profits and staff expenditures, we show that an Averch–Johnson effect remains, although it is attenuated compared to the case of the profit-maximising firm. The robustness of the effect to alternative assumptions is not so strongly supported empirically, however. Studies by Courville (1974), Hayashi and Trapani (1976), Peterson (1975) and Spann (1974) provide support for the hypothesis. However, the Boyes (1976) and Smithson (1978) tests for the Averch–Johnson effect were not significant. The ambivalence of these findings suggests that more complex models of firm behaviour and the institutional environments are required in understanding the effect of rate-of-return on efficiency.

If the Averch–Johnson effect were, *ceteris paribus*, the only result of RoR regulation, then regulation would be an unambiguous disaster. However, as shown in Section 6.4, regulation can increase output and reduce price sufficiently so that, even though costs are not minimised, there is a welfare gain from regulation. Nonetheless, it is not possible to say in general that output or capital intensity of the regulated firm will exceed that of pure monopoly.[3]

The Averch–Johnson result is important because it shows how rate-of-return regulation (RoR) introduces an inefficiency in the capital-labour ratio. RoR, as we argued in Chapter 5, the primary concern is with the equity aspects of monopoly, preventing the monopolist from exploiting consumers. This is in part achieved, but at the cost of introducing another inefficiency. This phenomenon was first articulated by McKie (1970, p. 9) as, 'Extension of control in response to perpetually escaping effects of earlier regulation may be called "the tar baby effect", since it usually enmeshes the regulatory authority in a control effort of increasing complexity with little gain in efficiency but a growing feeling of frustration.' Thus there is little prospect that any benefit will be derived by getting rid of the effect by further regulation.

As we show in Sections 6.2 and 6.3, the manifestation of Averch–Johnson effects in the peak-load problem add further complexities of their own, so that the benefits of additional regulation may be illusory.

6.2 THE PEAK-LOAD PROBLEM AND REGULATION[4]

We employ the framework developed in Chapter 3 for an RoR firm. Demand for a homogeneous, economically non-storable commodity fluctuates over an interval of n equal-length periods and may be met by means of any combination of available types of plant. These plants have the familiar cost structure employed in Chapter 3. The operating cost per unit of output of plant l is given by b_l. The firm must incur cost per unit of capacity β_l for plant l. An efficient firm will only employ plants whose cost parameters satisfy the following conditions:

$$0 < b_1 < b_2 < \ldots < b_m; \ \beta_1 > \beta_2 > \ldots > \beta_m > 0. \tag{6.8}$$

We first state the unregulated problem (6.9)–(6.12):

$$\text{Maximise } \Pi = \sum_{i=1}^{n} x_i P_i(x) - \sum_{i=1}^{n} \sum_{l=1}^{m} q_{li} - \sum_{l=!}^{m} \beta_l q_l \tag{6.9}$$

subject to:

$$\sum_{i=1}^{m} q_{li} = x_i, \quad \text{for all } i; \tag{6.10}$$

$$q_l - q_{li} \geqslant 0, \quad \text{for all } i, l; \tag{6.11}$$

$$x_i \geqslant 0, \ q_l \geqslant 0, \ q_{li} \geqslant 0, \quad \text{for all } i, l. \tag{6.12}$$

To derive the regulated problem, we simply add to problem (6.9)–(6.12) the regulatory constraint:[5]

$$\Pi \leqslant (s/r - 1) \sum_{l=1}^{m} \beta_l q_l, \tag{6.13}$$

where we use the following notation:

Π = profit
x = $(x_1, \ldots, x_n)$ = vector of quantities demanded in (equal-length) periods $i = 1, \ldots, n$

r = the firm's cost of capital

h_l = cost of a physical unit of capital of plant type l

β_l = rh_l = capacity cost of plant l

$s(>r)$ = allowed rate of return

$P_i(x)$ = inverse demand function ($= P_i(x_i)$ if demands are independent)

q_l = capacity of plant l

q_{li} = output produced by plant l in period i

From (6.9)–(6.13) we set up a Lagrangian with multipliers η_i, μ_{li}, and λ associated with the constraints (6.10), (6.11), (6.13) respectively.

$$L = (1-\lambda)\Pi + \lambda(s/r - 1)\sum_{l=1}^{m}\beta_l q_l + \sum_{i=1}^{n}\eta_i\left(\sum_{l=1}^{m}q_{li} - x_i\right) +$$

$$\sum_{i=1}^{n}\sum_{l=1}^{m}\mu_{li}(q_l - q_{li}). \tag{6.14}$$

Before proceeding, we note without proof that the Lagrangian multiplier λ plays the same role and has the same range ($0 \leqslant \lambda < 1$), as it does in Section 6.1.[6]

Assuming strictly positive outputs ($x_i > 0$), and denoting marginal revenue in period i by $MR_i = \partial(x_i P_i(x))/\partial x_i$, the Kuhn–Tucker conditions[7] are:

$$(1-\lambda)MR_i = \eta_i, \qquad \text{for all } i; \tag{6.15}$$

$$\sum_{i=1}^{n}\mu_{li} \leqslant (1-\lambda s/r)\beta_l, \quad q_l\left(\sum_{i=1}^{n}\mu_{li} - \beta_l(1-\lambda s/r)\right) = 0, \qquad \text{for all } l; \tag{6.16}$$

$$\eta_i - \mu_{li} \leqslant (1-\lambda)b_l, \quad q_{li}(\eta_i - \mu_{li} - (1-\lambda)b_l) = 0, \qquad \text{for all } l,i; \tag{6.17}$$

$$\mu_{li} \geqslant 0, \quad \mu_{li}(q_l - q_{li}) = 0, \qquad \text{for all } l,i. \tag{6.18}$$

We wish to show that the above first-order conditions are equivalent to those of an unregulated profit-maximising monopolist who faces an artificial uniform proportional discount on all capacity purchases. In Section 6.1 this point is implicit. It turns out, however, that an explicit analysis of this characterisation lends considerable insight to the price and plant mix decisions of a regulated monopolist.

The indicated equivalence is obtained as follows. Since $(1-\lambda) > 0$, dividing (6.15)–(6.18) by $(1-\lambda)$ yields an equivalent set of first-order conditions, which we denote as (6.15′)–(6.18′). For future reference, we write these as:

$$MR_i = \hat{\eta}_i, \qquad \text{for all } i; \tag{6.15'}$$

$$\sum_{i=1}^{n} \hat{\mu}_{li} \leqslant \sigma(s)\beta_l, \ q_l(\sum_{i=1}^{n} \hat{\mu}_{li} - \sigma(s)\beta_l) = 0, \qquad \text{for all } l; \tag{6.16'}$$

$$\hat{\eta}_i - \hat{\mu}_{li} \leqslant b_l, \ q_{li}(\hat{\eta}_i - \hat{\mu}_{li} - b_l) = 0, \qquad \text{for all } l,i; \tag{6.17'}$$

$$\hat{\mu}_{li} \geqslant 0, \ \hat{\mu}_{li}(q_l - q_{li}) = 0, \qquad \text{for all } l,i; \tag{6.18'}$$

where the multipliers $\hat{\eta}_i$, $\hat{\mu}_{li}$ are just the corresponding η_i, μ_{li} in (6.15)–(6.18) divided by $1 - \lambda(s) > 0$, with $\lambda(s)$ the optimal Lagrange multiplier for the constrained optimisation problem (6.9)–(6.13), and where

$$\sigma(s) = (r - \lambda(s)s)/(r - \lambda(s)r). \tag{6.19}$$

The object of the above transformations is now at hand. Indeed, imitating the analysis of (6.9)–(6.18), it is straightforward to show that the conditions (6.15')–(6.18') are precisely the first-order conditions for the following unregulated profit-maximising problem:

$$\hat{\Pi}_R(s) = \sum_{i=1}^{n} x_i P_i(x) - \sum_{i=1}^{n} \sum_{l=1}^{m} b_l q_{li} - \sigma(s) \sum_{l=1}^{m} \beta_l q_l \tag{6.20}$$

subject to: (6.10), (6.11), (6.12).

From this analysis, we see that first-order conditions for the regulated problem (6.9)–(6.13) are equivalent to those for the unregulated problem (6.20), subject to (6.10)–(6.12). The only difference between (6.20) and (6.9) is that the per unit capacity costs in (6.20) (which are $\sigma(s)\beta_l$ for plant l) represent a uniform proportional discount of $1 - \sigma(s)$ off the capacity costs in (6.9). We note from (6.16') and (6.19) and the non-negativity of $\hat{\mu}_{li}$ and $1 - \lambda(s)$ that $\lambda(s)$ is non-negative so that $(r - \lambda(s)s)$ is also non-negative. This, together with $s > r$, implies from (6.19) that $0 < \sigma(s) \leqslant 1$, so that $1 - \sigma(s) \geqslant 0$ is, in fact, a discount.

From the above equivalence of (6.9)–(6.13) and (6.20), it is important to ascertain the effects of changes of s on $\sigma(s)$. Let s_m be the monopoly rate of return. When $s \geqslant s_m$, we would expect $\sigma(s_m) = 1$. This can be seen from (6.19). For $s \geqslant s_m$, $\lambda = 0$ implying $\sigma(s_m) = 1$. Moreover, for $s_m \geqslant s > r$ it can be shown that $d\sigma/ds > 0$, implying that as regulation is stiffened the imputed discount $1 - \sigma(s)$ on capital increases.[8]

The characterisation just derived of the regulated monopolist in terms of a behaviourally equivalent unregulated monpolist with different capacity costs makes the derivation of price and technology choice of the regulated monopolist a simple matter. First, we know that our behaviourally equivalent unregulated monopolist will (for its cost structure) minimise costs and set price by equating marginal revenue to marginal costs. Since the minimum cost solution for the diverse technology firm is completely known from earlier results,[9] the price and technology choices of the regulated monopolist will easily follow. Finally, by tracing the impact of the allowed rate of return s on $\sigma(s)$ and, thus on the costs of the behaviourally equivalent unregulated monopolist, we can characterise the behaviour of the regulated monopolist in response to the choice of the regulatory instrument s. To illustrate all of this, we now consider a special case in more detail.

An Example: The Two Plant, Two Period Case. The two-plant, two-period case may be specified along the lines of Crew and Kleindorfer (1971). Problem (6.20) becomes:

$$\text{Max } \hat{\Pi}R(s) = \sum_{i=1}^{2} x_i P_i(x) - \sum_{l=1}^{2}\sum_{i=1}^{2} b_l q_{li} - \sigma(s)\sum_{l=1}^{2} \beta_l q_l \tag{6.21}$$

subject to

$$x_i = q_{1i} + q_{2i}, \qquad i = 1,2 \tag{6.22}$$

$$q_l \geq q_{li}, \; i = 1,2, \; l = 1,2. \tag{6.23}$$

And the usual non-negativity constraints, $x_i, q_i, q_{li} \geq 0$.

The Kuhn–Tucker conditions for (6.21)–(6.23) are given by (6.15′)–(6.18′). Since these are the first-order conditions for an unregulated monopolist with a diverse technology (with capacity costs $\hat{\beta}_1 = \sigma(s)\beta_1$) their solution is the following as shown in Crew and Kleindorfer (1971) and discussed in Chapter 3:[10]

Case 1: Both plants 1 and 2 are used at optimum.

$$MR_1 = 2b_1 + \sigma(s)\beta_1 - (b_2 + \sigma(s)\beta_2), \tag{6.24}$$

$$MR_2 = b_2 + \sigma(s)\beta_2, \tag{6.25}$$

where MR_1 and MR_2 are respectively the off-peak and peak marginal revenues.[11] If (x_1, x_2) are the optimal outputs with $x_1 < x_2$, then the optimal supply pattern is given by:

$$(q_{11}, q_{21}, q_{12}, q_{22}, q_1, q_2) = (x_1, 0, x_1, x_2 - x_1, x_1, x_2 - x_1). \tag{6.26}$$

Case 2: Only Plant $l\varepsilon\{1,2\}$ is used at optimum.

$$MR_1 = b_l, \tag{6.24'}$$

$$MR_2 = b_l + \sigma(s)\beta_l, \tag{6.25'}$$

$$q_{li} = x_i, \; q_l = x_2; \; q_{ki} = q_k = 0, \qquad k \neq l. \tag{6.26'}$$

What distinguishes when each of the above cases will occur is the following inequality, which is developed from (3.26).

$$(\sigma(s)\beta_1 - \sigma(s)\beta_2)/2 < b_2 - b_1 < \sigma(s)\beta_1 - \sigma(s)\beta_2. \tag{6.27}$$

If (6.27) is satisfied, both plants are used. If the left inequality is violated, only plant 2 is used while if the right inequality fails only plant 1 is used. As we noted above, as s is decreased below the monopoly level, $\sigma(s)$ decreases. This affects not only the prices per (6.24)–(6.26) and (6.24')–(6.26'), but also the plant mix chosen as dictated by (6.27). We summarise these effects graphically in Figure 6.1, where the values of peak and off-peak marginal revenue at optimum are given as a function of $\sigma = \sigma(s)$. $QM \; \sigma(ds) = 1$, we have the unregulated case. Let us assume that for $\sigma = 1$, the left-hand inequality in (6.27) is violated, implying that only plant 2 is used and, from (6.24')–(6.26'), that marginal revenues at optimum are $MR_1 = b_2$, $MR_2 = b_2 + \beta_2$. The effect of progressively stiffening regulation, i.e., of decreasing s and therefore also $\sigma(s)$, is first to reduce the peak price with off-peak price unchanged, along the lines of Bailey (1972 and 1973). This continues until the rate of return is lowered sufficiently such that $\sigma = \sigma_2 = 2(b_1 - b_2)/(\beta_1 - \beta_2)$, where the effect of σ_2 in the inequality (6.27) is to make $\sigma_2(\beta_1 - \beta_2)$ just large enough to violate the left-hand inequality, implying that both plants would be used for $\sigma < \sigma_2$, with marginal revenues given in (6.24)–(6.26). As s and $\sigma(s)$ are further reduced, both prices are reduced with the peak price being reduced by more than the off-peak price. At $\sigma(s) = \sigma_1 = \sigma_2/2$, the right-hand inequality in (6.27) is just violated, implying that only plant 1 is used. From here on (6.24')–(6.26') imply that the off-peak price remains constant (with $MR_1 = b_1$) while peak price continues to fall, now at the rate implied by $MR_2 = b_1 + \sigma\beta_1$. Thus, the effect of stiffening regulation dramatically illustrates the analysis in Sheshinski (1971) (which we reconsider in Section 6.4 below) by showing that it is possible to reduce price but at the expense of increased X-inefficiency on the part of the firm. In the case of a diverse technology, the inefficiency is manifest. Stiffer regulation induces a shift to a more capital intensive higher b, lower β technology. In the case depicted in Figure 6.1, $\sigma_2 < 1$, stiffer regulation results in shifting entirely from plant 2 to plant 1, which should never be used on efficiency grounds.[12]

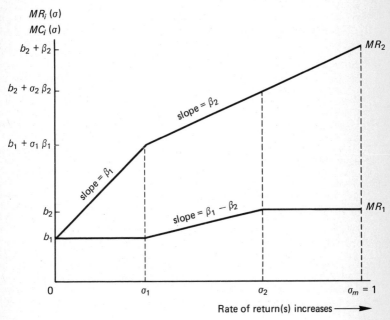

Figure 6.1

Also apparent from this analysis is the impact of regulation on output and the amounts of capacity of each type employed. From Figure 6.1 output is clearly non-decreasing in both periods as regulation is tightened. From (6.26) and (6.26'), we have

$$q_1 + q_2 = x_2, \tag{6.28}$$

$$q_1 = \begin{cases} 0 & \text{if } \sigma \geqslant \sigma_2 \\ x_1 & \text{if } \sigma_1 < \sigma < \sigma_2 \\ x_2 (> x_1) & \text{if } \sigma \leqslant \sigma_1. \end{cases} \tag{6.29}$$

Thus, since both x_1 and x_2 are non-decreasing in σ, we see that total capacity and total base-load capacity are non-decreasing as regulation is tightened.[13]

Our analysis, by providing a means of transforming the regulated problem into the same form as the unregulated problem, has enabled us to simplify the problem and highlight the effects of regulation under diverse technology. We have been able to show the effects of regulation on prices – peak price is always reduced, off-peak price may be reduced or remain unchanged. We have been able, in addition, to describe completely the effects of regulation on plant mix. Not only may regulation induce inefficient plants to be used but it may actually result in efficient plants not being used – a latter-day Gresham's Law, 'Bad plants drive out good plants' under regulation.

6.3 STOCHASTIC DEMAND AND RATE OF RETURN REGULATION

With stochastic demand basically the same effects are at work as in the deterministic case. Regulation distorts incentives with the effect that the firm behaves as if the price of capacity is lower than its actual price. However, the stochastic case is more complicated. We illustrate initially with a one plant case. For our basic framework we will retain our assumptions of Chapter 4 about additive independent stochastic demand. We assume expected profit maximisation; the regulated monopoly's problem is given by:

$$\text{Max } E\{\Pi(p,z,\tilde{u})\}, \tag{6.30}$$

subject to:

$$E\{\Pi(p,z,\tilde{u})\} \leqslant (s-\beta)z, \tag{6.31}$$

where $p \geqslant 0$, $z \geqslant 0$, $s - \beta > 0$, where s and β are as above, and the disturbance term $\tilde{u}$ is a bounded, continuous random variable, with components $\tilde{u}_i$ independent, with $E(\tilde{u}_i) = 0$. Thus there is some bounded interval $[u_{1i}, u_{2i}]$ such that $Pr\{\tilde{u}_i \varepsilon [u_{1i}, u_{2i}]\} = 1$. We define expected profits $E(\Pi)$ as follows:

$$E\{\Pi\} = E\{\sum_{i=1}^{2}(p_i - b)S_i(p_i, z, \tilde{u}_i) + r_i(D_i(p_i) + \tilde{u}_i - z) - \beta z\}, \tag{6.32}$$

where $S_i(p,z,\tilde{u}_i)=\min[D_i(p_i)+\tilde{u}_i,z]=$ actual sales and $r_i(D_i(p_i)+\tilde{u}_i-z)=$ rationing costs of excess demand are exactly as defined in Chapter 4.

With this framework it turns out that optimal behaviour under regulation may be to treat capacity as if it were a free good, thus inducing an Averch–Johnson effect with a vengeance. A more appropriate term might be 'gold plating', or, more exactly, gold plating on reliability, as we now show.[14] Let the maximum expected revenue obtainable when capacity is a free good be denoted by R^*. When capacity z is a free good the monopolist will set z high enough to ensure that demand is always less than z. Thus:

$$R^* = \text{Max } E \{\sum_{i=1}^{2} (p_i-b) [D_i(p_i)+\tilde{u}_i]\}. \tag{6.33}$$

or since $E\{u_i\}=0$, R^* reduces to the maximum obtainable deterministic revenue with capacity unconstrained:

$$R^* = \text{Max}_{p \geqslant b} \sum_{i=1}^{2} (p_i-b)D_i(p_i). \tag{6.34}$$

Letting p^* be the optional pricing solution to (6.34), we show below that if:

$$\frac{R^*}{s} \geqslant \text{Max}_{i\varepsilon\{1,2\}} [D_i(p_i^*)+u_{2i}], \tag{6.35}$$

then the regulated monopolist will set price equal to p^*, and $z^*=R^*/s$, thus achieving equality in the regulatory constraint. To establish the claim just made let $z^*=R^*/s$ and assume that optimal capacity z is less than z^*. Then:

$$E\{\Pi(p,z,\tilde{u})\} \leqslant (s-\beta)z < (s-\beta)z^* = E\{\Pi p^*,z^*,\tilde{u})\}, \tag{6.36}$$

where the first inequality holds since any optimal solution (p,z) must satisfy (6.31), the strict inequality follows from $(s-\beta)>0$, and the final equality holds by (6.35) and the definition of z^*. Thus, for any feasible price p,z cannot be optimal. Suppose, likewise, that z is greater than z^*. Then:

$$E\{\Pi(p,z,\tilde{u})\} = E\{R_0(p,z,\tilde{u})\} - \beta z < R^* - \beta z^* = E\{\Pi(p^*,z^*,\tilde{u})\}, \tag{6.37}$$

where R is net revenue and the inequality follows by definition of R^* as the maximum obtainable net revenue. We see again that z is non-optimal. Clearly z^* is the optimal capacity and, since (6.35) holds, p^* is feasible and also optimal in (6.30)–(6.32).

One implication is that the regulated monopolist may set his reliability level to unity, which we can see from (6.34) and the definition of u_{2i}.[15] Thus regulation may induce excessive investment in capacity to achieve very high reliability levels. Consider a numerical example utilising the demand functions (4.61)–(4.62) (i.e. $X_1(A) = 40 - P_1/7$ and $X_2(P_2) = 80 - 5P_2/7$) with $b = 5$ and $\beta = 10$ and $\mu_{1i} = -\gamma$, $u_{2i} = \gamma > 0$. We can easily show that (6.35) is satisfied for any s, β and γ satisfying $s/\beta < 7$ and $\gamma < 30$. For the case $s/\beta = 1.1$ and for any $\gamma < 30$ the solution to (6.30)–(6.32) is $p_1 = 142.5$, $p_2 = 58.5$ and $z = 431.4$. For this case, therefore, z^* is a massive five-fold multiple of the welfare-maximising optimal capacity. Thus Averch–Johnson effects, reliability and 'gold plating' all work in the same direction, i.e. towards excessive capacity. Rate-of-return regulation with stochastic demand provides the opportunity, in certain instances, for unrestrained gold plating in the name of reliability, as discussed in Crew and Kleindorfer (1978, 1979b). The tar baby appears to be thriving here. RoR regulation has induced excessive reliability, implying the apparent need to regulate further because of a distortion caused by regulation in the first place.

With the multiplant technology, the effect of regulation on capacity choice is more subtle. In the one plant case the effect takes place entirely through increasing the capacity. With multiple plant types it operates additionally on the mix of plant. More reliable or more capital intensive plants may be substituted for the efficient plant mix as regulation is stiffened. As this analysis applies primarily to electricity, we will examine this issue in detail in Chapter 8.

6.4 WELFARE IMPLICATIONS OF RATE OF RETURN REGULATION

The message of this chapter has been that, while regulation may be able to control the abuse of monopoly power, it does so at a price in input efficiency. Moreover, it was shown that, as regulation is tightened, the price in terms of this inefficiency increases. The welfare implications of increased regulation were examined by Bailey (1973) and Sheshinski (1971). We now indicate the effects of regulation using the traditional welfare measure of consumer and producer surplus. We express the social benefits arising from regulation when the allowed rate of return is s as:

$$W(s) = \int_0^{F(K(s),L(s))} P(y)dy - rK(s) - wL(s), \tag{6.38}$$

where $K(s)$ and $L(s)$ are the public utility's chosen capital and labour inputs when allowed rate of return s, so that $X(s) = F(K(s),L(s))$ is the resulting output level.

From (6.38) we see that:

$$\frac{dW}{ds} = P(X(s)) \left[F_K \frac{dK}{ds} + F_L \frac{dL}{ds} - r\frac{dK}{ds} - w\frac{dL}{ds} \right] \tag{6.39}$$

or, denoting $p = P(X(s))$:

$$\frac{dW}{ds} = (pF_K - r)\frac{dK}{ds} + (pF_L - w)\frac{dL}{ds}. \tag{6.40}$$

If $s = s_m$, the pure monopoly rate of return, then $\lambda = 0$ in (6.4) and (6.5) and we may rewrite these conditions as:

$$pF_K - r = -P'FF_K \tag{6.40a}$$

$$pF_L - w = -P'FF_L. \tag{6.40b}$$

Substituting (6.4a) and (6.5a) in (6.40) yields:

$$\frac{dW}{ds} = -P'F\left(F_K\frac{dK}{ds} + F_L\frac{dL}{ds}\right) < 0, \tag{6.41}$$

where the inequality follows from the fact that dK/ds and dL/ds are both negative when $r < s < s_m$ (Crew and Kleindorfer (1979a, p. 155)).

Thus the negative sign of dW/ds implies that if we reduce s from the monopoly return $s = s_m$, we increase the value of the social-welfare function. From this we see that some regulation is always desirable, unless marginal cost is zero.

To obtain the value of s for which W is maximised, we set (6.40) to zero, obtaining:

$$P\frac{dX}{ds} = \frac{dC}{ds}, \tag{6.42}$$

where $C(s) = rK(s) + wL(s) =$ total costs.

Thus cost increases as s decreases, because output increases and inefficiency increases with decreases in s. From (6.42) we can derive the following optimality condition in terms of p:

$$p = \frac{dC}{dX} \qquad\qquad (6.43)$$

Although (6.43) is similar to the standard welfare-optimality condition, it is not identical because dC/dX is higher as a result of the inefficient

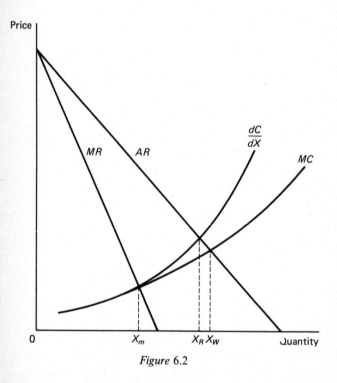

Figure 6.2

combination of inputs brought about by regulation. In terms of Figure 6.2 the effect of regulation is to cause a divergence of the (regulated) marginal-cost curve from the marginal cost of the pure monopolist. The different outputs of pure monopoly X_M, regulated monopoly X_R and welfare-maximising monopoly X_W are also shown. Thus for $r < s < s_m$ the value of s should be decreased until (6.43) is satisfied, to give optimum price and output as shown in Figure 6.2.[16]

While these results apply in the partial-equilibrium context, we

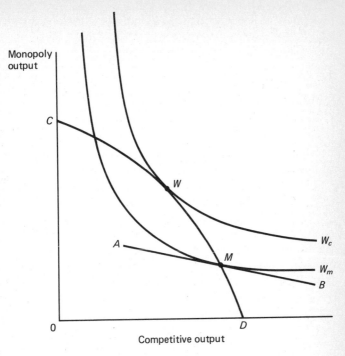

Figure 6.3

should note that regulation is not necessarily beneficial in the general equilibrium context. Figure 6.3 illustrates this for a two-sector model, one sector being a monopoly sector and the other a competitive sector. The effect of pure monopoly is to move the economy from the welfare optimum, point *W* on the transformation curve, to point *M*, the monopoly optimum. Point *M* is clearly on a lower social indifference curve (W_m).

If the regulation increases monopoly output, but only by using an inefficient combination of factors, the new transformation curve (or regulation possibility curve) diverges from the original one (*CD*) at *M* and offers lower levels of each output. However, as long as this curve is not below W_m, regulation is still beneficial because it offers the possibility of attaining a higher social indifference curve. Note that if regulation led to a point below the line *AB*, it would be particularly undesirable; leading to a price higher than the monopoly price.[17] While this, indeed, may be possible, as we will argue later, in the neoclassical framework employed in this chapter it is not considered. Regulation, in this framework, results in net gains because the neoclassical analysis does not examine issues of transactions costs and rent seeking that will be examined in the next and subsequent chapters.

6.5 PRICE STRUCTURE REGULATION: ALLOCATING FIXED COSTS

Averch–Johnson regulation is concerned primarily, as is RoR regulation in practice, with the regulation of the level of profits and pricing, rather than with the structure of prices. Price structure is important in theory and practice as is evidenced by the many regulations concerning price structure, e.g. those mandating certain forms of two-part and other tariff structures. The problem is particularly important in view of the large fixed costs facing utilities. The fact that many of these costs are common or joint implies that, as examined earlier, the economic allocation of fixed costs may be based upon complex formulae that are not readily amenable to translation into the kind of rules employed by accountants. This section is concerned with price structure regulation, in particular, with examining how accounting rules may diverge from the optimum implied by economic theory. The problems with joint and common cost allocation are also examined later in Part IV in the discussion of the individual industries. In this section we are concerned only with the problems of allocation of fixed costs ignoring the problem of jointness. This involves comparison of Ramsey prices with prices derived from various accounting rules for allocating fixed costs. We will now examine briefly some of the consequences of using accounting rules based upon the contributions of Braeutigam (1980) and Cole (1981).

The problem of accounting for fixed or common cost by means of fully distributed cost rules consists of recovering F in (6.44) across all products.

$$C(\mathbf{x}) = F + \sum_{i=1}^{n} C_i(x_i) \tag{6.44}$$

where $C(\mathbf{x})$ is total cost of producing $(x_1, \ldots, x_n)$ and $C_i(x_i)$ is the direct cost of product i. Let the contribution from each product i equal

$$Q_i(x_i) = R_i(x_i) - C_i(x_i) \tag{6.45}$$

where $R_i(x_i)$ is revenue from product i. A fully-distributed cost rule (FDC) requires that common costs, F, be allocated to each service such that F is fully recovered. Thus for price i a fraction f_i of F, will be allocated such that for all services

$$\sum_{i=1}^{n} f_i = 1 \qquad (6.46)$$

FDC pricing thus implies that

$$R_i(x_i) = f_i F + C_i(x_i) \qquad (6.47)$$

so that from (6.46) profits are zero. For example, when $C_i(X_i) = C_i X_i$, (2.16) implies that Ramsey pricing satisfies the FDC rule with

$$f_i = x_i \left(\frac{\mu}{\mu+1} \right) \frac{P_i(x_i)}{F\eta_i} \qquad (6.48)$$

where η is price elasticity of demand.

FDC rules commonly employed, as examined by Braeutigam, generally are of much simpler form such as share of the total output, with each output having equal weight, i.e.

$$f_i^0 = x_i / \sum_{j=1}^{n} x_j \qquad (6.49)$$

This and other rules, as Braeutigam shows, clearly give different results from the Ramsey rule. However, when demand characteristics are not well known regulators may be forced to resort to such measures. Is there any means of changing the FDC rules employed so that they can move closer to the Ramsey rule? Braeutigam shows that the rule

$$\frac{P_i - S_i C_i'(x_i)}{P_j - S_j C_i'(x_j)} = 1 \qquad (6.50)$$

with $S_i = C_i(x_i)/x_i C_i'(x_i)$ and $C_i' = $ marginal cost of x_i, will overprice (relative to Ramsey pricing) products with higher elasticities of demand. Thus by slightly lowering the prices with presumably higher demand elasticities and slightly raising those with lower elasticities it may be possible to move closer to economically efficient prices.

The problem of allocating fixed costs by accounting formulae is that in general it will not result in economically efficient pricing. The problem is important for a number of reasons. For one it may be the only feasible alternative for recovering fixed costs. For another where a regulated firm has both competitive and monopoly markets it has the incentive to overstate F so that as many of the costs as possible are allocated to the monopoly products. We will return to some of the implications of these issues in Parts IV and V.

6.6 PRODUCTIVITY AND INCENTIVE REGULATION

Under perfect information, the regulator could simply mandate efficient pricing and investment behaviour. However, under realistic assumptions on the costs of obtaining information, regulators will necessarily be considerably less informed than firms on such matters as technology, cost and demand conditions. Thus, a principal–agent problem under incomplete information arises, whereby the regulators must use procedures which employ relatively easily obtainable data (e.g. arising from audited acccounting records) to define incentives to induce firms to behave efficiently. Under RoR regulation, for example, the regulatory intervention is the commission process directed at determining a fair rate of return, together with a definition of the rate base and allowable expenses which make up the rate of return constraint. As we have seen, this form of regulation can provide incentives to improve welfare relative to unregulated monopoly, but it also provides incentives for allocative inefficiency. Results such as these have motivated a study of other modes of regulatory intervention directed at perhaps providing incentives for more efficient outcomes. The results to date have, however, not been encouraging. Rather it appears that the assumption of asymmetric information, so fundamental to the separation between regulators and regulated firms, has inherent in it unavoidable losses in welfare. The best we can hope for is a second-best solution, subject to these informational constraints. In spite of this, it is naturally an interesting issue to investigate alternative regulatory methods which may improve on some of the problems of RoR regulation or other inefficiency aspects of the monopoly problem.

We can classify recent research on alternative regulatory methods into two categories: those directed towards improving pricing efficiency and those directed towards X-efficiency. Under the former category are the proposals of Loeb and Magat (1979) and Vogelsang and Finsinger (1979), which are directed at inducing the regulated firm to price its ouput at marginal cost (Loeb–Magat) or Ramsey efficient prices (Vogelsang–Finsinger). In the latter category are the proposals of Sudit

(1979) and Crew, Kleindorfer and Sudit (1979) on productivity incentives. These incentives are designed to induce the regulated firm to invest in technology improvements and to engage in other cost reduction procedures, i.e. to reduce X-inefficiency. We consider first the ·Loeb–Magat and Vogelsang–Finsinger proposals, and a related proposal by Cross (1970), and then consider productivity regulation. A discussion of other recent research on regulating a monopolist under asymmetric information completes this section. Our purposes here will be primarily to describe these alternative regulatory proposals. A more detailed critique and comparison of their merits will be delayed until Chapter 7.

Loeb and Magat (1979) proposed a 'decentralized method of utility regulation' employing a system of taxes, subsidies and franchises aimed at promoting allocative and X-efficiency. What follows briefly summarises and extends their argument. In Figure 6.4 the regulator selects a price of $P_0 = AC$. The regulator would also inform the utility that if it lowered its price below P_0 that it would receive a lump sum subsidy equal to the consumer surplus for the difference between the two prices. This would provide the company with the incentive to move a price of $\hat{P} = mc$, to maximise its profits. Its profits would improve by the difference between CHP_0 and HGA. If $CHP_0 = HGA$, a zero profit solution would result. Thus Loeb and Magat argue that this method of regulation could lead to the efficient solution ($P = mc$), but only require the regulator to have knowledge of the piecewise linear demand curve through P_0, H, G and A. The subsidy required to achieve this is $P_0 GA\hat{P}$.

Vogelsang and Finsinger (1979) provide a regulatory rule which converges to economically efficient prices. Their approach employs an incentive type mechanism in the tradition of Cross (1970). Their iterative procedure converges to a set of prices which maximise consumer's surplus subject to a break-even profit constraint. Vogelsang and Finsinger assume that demand and cost functions do not change over time, and that the firm knows these functions, which are, like the demand functions, assumed to be continuous and well behaved. Their regulatory process requires that the regulator know costs, prices and quantities that the firm realised in the previous period. Thus at time j the regulator observes $x_j(p_j)$, $C(x_j)$, and $\Pi(p_j)$ where these are respectively output, total cost, and profit and p_j is price. For period $j+1$ the regulation defines the set of feasible or allowable prices by

$$R_j = \{ p \mid x_j p - C(x_j) \leqslant 0 \}. \tag{6.51}$$

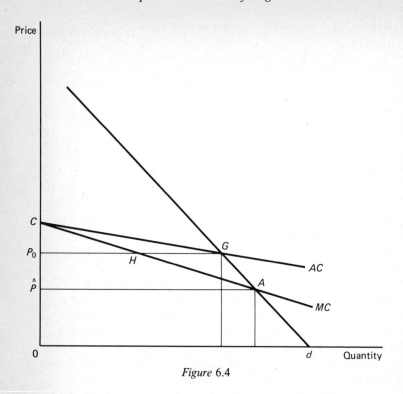

Figure 6.4

Thus if in period j the utility had made a profit the regulator would restrict prices in period $j + 1$ using (6.51), lowering the utility's maximal profits in that period. The utility would have an incentive to try to reduce its costs still further in an attempt to gain the benefit of the profits so generated until the next period. The Vogelsang–Finsinger approach to the regulated price is to have the regulator set, in effect, a Laspeyres price index and the firm would be allowed to choose whatever prices it wished within this constraint. Vogelsang-Finsinger show that if the firm myopically maximises profits subject to (6.51) then the resulting sequence of prices will converge to economically efficient (Ramsey) prices. Sappington (1980) has noted, however, that firms, faced with this form of regulation, may have incentives to engage in waste in early periods in order to relax the constraint in (6.51) on future price increases.

Cross (1970), like Vogelsang–Finsinger, does not incorporate a rate-of-return constraint into his pricing rule. His approach is to modify the existing average-cost pricing rule which he defines as $p = \gamma(AC)$ where γ

is a parameter set by the regulator. He assumes that it exceeds one, in line with the thinking that regulation fixes a price slightly in excess of the competitive level. He substitutes for the above rule the following incentive pricing rule:

$$p = \beta + \alpha(AC^*) \tag{6.52}$$

AC^* is the regulator's estimate of the firm's average total cost. β is a base below which price is not allowed to go. α is a 'sharing rate', less than one. Thus if AC^* is \$10, the regulator might set $\beta = 6$ and $\alpha = .4$ to give a price of \$10. If the firm introduces economies and it can get its cost down to \$9, it would face a price of \$9.60 retaining 60 cents of the cost saving within the firm. Both parties gain as a result of this cost reduction. The incentives are symmetric. If the firm became less efficient and let its costs rise to \$11 it would only receive \$10.40 under the formula.

Crew, Kleindorfer and Sudit (1979) and Sudit (1979), by building on recent developments in the area of productivity measurement, propose two schemes aimed at improving the incentives for productivity within a regulatory framework. Sudit's (1979) approach involves the commission in setting percentage rate increases, $\dot{p}/p$, that it will allow each year (where $\dot{p} = dp/dt$, the rate of price change). The percentage is derived from its forecast percentage increases in factor prices, $\dot{w}/w$, and an offset for productivity improvements, MPI. Productivity is measured by a Divisia index of total factor productivity. A company thus has an incentive to attempt to 'beat' the productivity gain attributed to it by the commission and thereby make additional profits. Periodically, the state of the company might be reviewed with a rate case where rates could be adjusted upward or downward to reflect differences between actual input prices and productivity and commission estimates.

Crew, Kleindorfer and Sudit (1979), attempt to place less responsibility on the commission for forecasting price increases and productivity offsets. The commission knows less about a company's costs and productivity than does the company. Crew, Kleindorfer and Sudit aimed to provide incentives for companies to reveal some of this information to the commission, thereby avoiding some of the problems that would arise from over- or under-estimates by the commission. The idea is to provide a reward for getting actual performance close to target while not providing any incentive to reduce performance below the maximum in the event that the company inadvertently under-forecasts its productivity growth.

Price increases $\dot{p}_j/p_j$ would be constrained by the following process:

$$\sum_{j=1}^{m} (\dot{p}_j/p_j)\beta_j = \sum_{i=1}^{n} (\dot{w}_i /w_i) a_i - \lambda B(MPI^*, T\dot{F}P/TFP) \qquad (6.53/6.54)$$

where a '·' represents the time derivative (d/dt), where $\dot{w}_i/w_i =$ input price increase for input i, $a_i = w_i x_i / \Sigma_{i=1}^{n} w_i x_i$; $x_i =$ quantity of input i, $y_j =$ quantity of output j, $\beta_j = p_j y_j / \Sigma_{j=1}^{m} p_j y_j$; where MPI^* is the target set by the firm, γ is a parameter and the 'bonus function' B is defined as

$$B\left(MPI^*, \frac{T\dot{F}P}{TFP}\right) = \begin{cases} \dfrac{T\dot{F}P}{TFP} + a\left(MPI^* - \dfrac{T\dot{F}P}{TFP}\right), \text{ when } MPI^* > \dfrac{T\dot{F}P}{TFP} \\[3mm] \dfrac{T\dot{F}P}{TFP} - b\left(MPI^* - \dfrac{T\dot{F}P}{TFP}\right), \text{ otherwise} \end{cases} \qquad (6.55)$$

and where $T\dot{F}P/TFP =$ growth rate in total factor productivity, and a, b are parameters satisfying $0 < a < 1$ and $b > 0$. The company's gain is defined as $CG = T\dot{F}P/TFP - \gamma B$. Using (6.54), we can write

$$CG = \begin{cases} \dfrac{T\dot{F}P}{TFP}(1 - \gamma(1-a)) - \gamma a MPI^*, \text{ if } MPI^* > \dfrac{T\dot{F}P}{TFP} \\[3mm] [1 - \gamma(1+b)]\dfrac{T\dot{F}P}{TFP} + \gamma b MPI^*, \text{ otherwise} \end{cases} \qquad (6.56)$$

From (6.55) we see that regardless of the level at which MPI^* is set $T\dot{F}P/TFP$ increases as long as $\gamma(1+b) < 1$. Thus (6.54) and (6.55) provide the appropriate incentives for productivity improvement. The firm will also reveal its best estimate of $T\dot{F}P/TFP = T^*$ since, for any fixed $T\dot{F}P/TFP = T^*$, CG is maximised at $MPI^* = T^*$.

The above proposals are directed at allocation and X-efficiency incentives and hint at the fundamental problem of regulation: Providing incentives to the regulated firm for efficient operation, subject to financial viability, by regulators who can only imperfectly observe the technology, demand and cost conditions of the firm. Recent research by Baron and Myerson (1982) and Sappington (1983) has addressed this issue explicitly in the framework of optimal Bayesian incentive compatible design problems. We briefly review here the Baron and Myerson framework.

Assume that the cost function of a monopolist is $C(q,m)$, where q is output and $m \in M$ is some unknown parameter. Suppose the regulator has some well-defined beliefs on the value of m in the form of a subjective probability distribution $F(m)$ over the possible values which one might assume. The regulator is concerned with the Ramsey problem of maximising consumer surplus

$$V(q) = \int_0^q P(x)dx, \tag{6.57}$$

subject to a break-even profit constraint

$$\Pi(q,m) = qP(q) - C(q,m) \geqslant 0, \tag{6.58}$$

where the inverse demand function $P(q)$ is assumed known by both the monopolist and the regulator.

Baron and Myerson assume the regulator has three regulatory instruments at his disposal. First, it can determine whether the firm will be allowed to go into business at all. Second, if the firm is allowed to go into business, the regulator can determine the price and output of the regulated firm. Third, the regulator can subsidise or tax the potential monopolist. The regulatory process is envisaged as follows. The regulator announces that, if the firm reveals its cost parameter m as being $\hat{m}$, then the firm will be paid a subsidy $s(\hat{m})$, (a tax extracted if $s(\hat{m}) < 0$), and then a lottery will be held with probability $r(\hat{m})$ that the firm will be allowed to go into business. If the firm is allowed to go into business, it is told (before the fact) that it will be held to prices and outputs $p(\hat{m})$, $q(\hat{m})$, depending on the revealed $\hat{m}$, and satisfying the demand equation $q(\hat{m}) = P(q(\hat{m}))$. The regulator's problem is to determine the function $r(m)$, $s(m)$ and $q(m)$ so as to maximise the expected value (over the regulator's subjective probability distribution F on m) of consumer surplus, subject to the profit constraint $\Pi(q(m),m) \geqslant 0$ and subject to the conditions of the indicated *ex ante* agreement with the monopolist – namely that after the revelation of m, the specified subsidy, lottery and price-output contract will be executed. Baron and Myerson first prove that it is no loss of generality to restrict attention to contracts (r,s,q) which induce the monopolist to truthfully reveal the parameter m. They also show, for special assumptions on the cost function, that the optimal contract (r,s,q) has the desirable feature that $r(m)$ is either 0 or 1 (i.e. the lottery is trivial) for all m, but this result is not general as Baron and Myerson also show by example, i.e. other specifications of the cost function lead to optimal contracts which entail non-degenerate lotteries (i.e. there is some probability at optimum that the monopolist will not be allowed to go into business).

The Baron and Myerson proposal has been generalised by Sappington (1983) to the multiproduct case and further extended by Baron and Besanko (1984). Although valuable as a theoretical benchmark, this proposal clearly suffers some fatal flaws as a practical regulatory proposal. Most importantly, it requires the regulator to have a publicly defendable 'subjective' probability function on potential cost conditions m. This appears an insurmountable barrier to any practical implementation of this proposal. Moreover, the just indicated problem of the non-degeneracy of the optimal entry probability $r(m)$ is not credible in practice if this contract is to regulate an on-going important public sector such as gas or electricity. This analysis does deal, however, with the fundamental regulatory problem of asymmetric information between regulators and regulated firms, an area of continuing importance for research.

6.7 CONCLUDING REMARKS

The models reviewed in this chapter have been in the neoclassical tradition in that:

1. unitary, rational actors (firms, consumers and regulators) are assumed with well-defined preferences (profits, surplus, and welfare);
2. transactions costs are not dealt with explicitly, either internal to the firm or between the regulator and the firm. In particular, production relationships are represented neoclassically and X-efficiency is not considered in any detail.

These assumptions allow a reasonable and parsimonious representation of the 'main effects' of regulation. Perhaps the most important conclusion from this analysis is that of Section 6.4, namely within the context of neoclassical assumptions, regulation can improve economic efficiency. However, these assumptions are arguably quite strong. In particular, the issues of rent seeking, transactions costs, and X-efficiency are sufficiently important that a more complete analysis of regulation is called for before concluding that one or another form of regulation is desirable. The following chapter therefore addresses these broader issues within the context of a comparative institutional assessment of various governance structures for monopoly regulation.

7 Alternative Governance Structures for Natural Monopoly

The previous chapters have primarily pursued a neoclassical framework for evaluating alternative approaches to regulating natural monopoly. For neoclassical economics, scale economies provide the basic justification for monopoly, with regulation a sometimes necessary evil to control monopoly's inherent allocative inefficiency. Neoclassical economics, however, says little about the variety of regulatory solutions devised for the natural monopoly problem. The new institutional economics, on the other hand, is concerned with questions such as the choice of one regulatory mode over another and the comparative efficiency of various hierarchical forms of organisation.[1] By utilising a comparative institutional assessment, the new institutional economics has a means, at least qualitatively, of evaluating the variety of regulatory solutions that exist. In this chapter we illustrate such a comparative institutional assessment for several alternative governance structures for natural monopolies.

Many alternative governance structures have been proposed for the natural monopoly problem. These run from unregulated monopoly to public enterprise, and several intermediate forms of public intervention in the management of the monopoly. The proponents of various governance structures have frequently failed to agree on a common basis for comparing their proposals with other competing alternatives. For example, Posner (1969) takes an anti-regulation stance, arguing that the deadweight losses of monopoly may be small against the potential benefits from dynamic and organisational efficiency gains which deregulation could bring. On the other hand, proponents of the new institutional economics, e.g. Williamson (1976) and Goldberg (1976), have tended to be kinder to regulation and argue their case by comparing alternative modes of governance on a broader set of dimensions, including the transactional costs of governance. One purpose of this chapter is to integrate the evaluation perspectives of these neoclassical and transactions cost comparisons of governance structures.

146

The chapter is divided as follows. Section 7.1 discusses efficiency and equity aspects of the natural monopoly problem, utilising both neoclassical and new institutional economic contributions. Section 7.2 describes alternative governance modes for monopolies. Section 7.3 performs a comparative institutional assessment, and Section 7.4 contains concluding remarks.

7.1 THE NEW INSTITUTIONAL ECONOMICS AND THE NATURAL MONOPOLY PROBLEM

The neoclassical view of the natural monopoly problem judges alternative governance structures against the benchmark of the Pareto criterion, usually complemented by the assumed feasibility of lump-sum transfers of income and the use of either Scitovsky–Kaldor–Hicks criteria or consumer and producer surplus welfare measures to characterise first-best solutions. Although there is nothing in the neoclassical theory to prevent more general approaches, as we have seen in previous chapters, the typical neoclassical framework for evaluating the natural monopoly problem has been a static model, with a fixed production function and with no consideration of distributional or organisational (i.e., X-) efficiency issues.

The new institutional economics takes a broader view and, at the same time, a more microscopic view of natural monopoly that includes the neoclassical approach. Historically, the neoclassical approach was first generalised by Williamson (1967) and Leibenstein (1966) to include organisational (or X-) efficiency considerations. Protected monopolies, it was argued, could not be expected to automatically choose the best available technology or organisational procedures. Thus, the effects of governance mode on such choices are clearly important. Building on these notions, Williamson advanced his framework of transactions cost analysis for comparative institutional assessment. According to this framework, a particular mode of economic organisation (e.g. an unregulated monopoly) is to be understood in terms of the collection of transactions it mediates and the costs surrounding these transactions. In the case of natural monopoly, these transactions include production transformation transactions, (production) firm-customer transactions (sales), firm-supplier transactions, (purchasing) and various other transactions depending on the governance mode employed. For example, in the rate-of-return regulated monopoly, discussed further below, a governance transaction would be the rate hearing to determine the allowable price increase for the monopoly's products. For the franchise bidding scheme of Demsetz (1968), a governance transaction would be the periodic bidding process (and possible turnover of assets to the winning bidder).

The point of the Williamson analysis is to define efficiency of a given governance mode in terms of minimisation of total transactions costs relative to total benefits. Such transactions costs arise, in part, because of the efforts required of boundedly rational economic agents in processing information and attenuating opportunism associated with transactions.[2] In early applications of this theory, Williamson (1975) analysed the question (mainly for intermediate product markets) as to whether a set of transactions would be better organised by a market (e.g. through contracts) or by a hierarchy (e.g. through vertical integration). The approach was extended by Crocker (1983) and Klein, Crawford and Alchian (1978). In a competitive setting, Williamson argues that this choice of organisational mode of governance would depend on which mode could perform the desired transactions at least cost. Williamson (1975 and 1984) has analysed in detail the characteristics of the underlying transactions which logically or historically favour one mode of governance over another. In particular, he argues that when transactions are recurrent, uncertain and involve substantial idiosyncratic (or transaction specific) investments, then there will be a relative advantage of unitary-hierarchical governance modes over market-mediated contractual modes. In these instances, a single hierarchy will tend to economise better on the costs of the desired transactions than would a contracting solution.

Governance structures for natural monopoly are likely to entail significant transactions costs, as Palay (1984) and others have argued. These may arise in a number of ways. We have already discussed allocative inefficiencies resulting from RoR regulation in the previous chapter. Such inefficiencies are one source of transaction costs. Another source of transactions costs is rent seeking. Rent seeking activities, as discussed in Chapter 5 and in Crew and Rowley (1986), generate significant potential for transactions costs. Lawyers take resources merely to resolve the problem of the distribution of the pie and therefore have an incentive to see distributional rules frequently changed so that they obtain additional work. Other transactions costs include resources spent by management in performing studies, the function of which is primarily to satisfy or convince the regulators. This takes resources from other activities which might have been used to improve productivity. Management becomes more representative of individuals whose ability is in satisfying the regulators and not performing say cost minimisation, (see Crew (1982)). Thus, X-inefficiencies from RoR regulation may induce two kinds of transaction costs, the direct and wholly visible kinds (like lawyers fees and regulator commission levies) and the indirect (like induced X-inefficiencies.) Empirically there is some support for high direct transactions costs, as we saw in Chapter 5.

It was the analysis of transactions costs, and in particular of transaction specific investments, which led Williamson (1976) and Goldberg (1976) to argue against the feasibility of franchise bidding and other deregulation options in certain natural monopoly sectors. As Goldberg (1976, p. 432) argues, 'The fact that a public utility (or natural monopoly) has to install long-lived, specialized capital equipment that has a very thin resale market', is a very important aspect of the natural monopoly problem. Applied to the franchise bidding problem, for example, the lack of credible market information on the value of future revenues/costs or the assets of the incumbent franchisee leads to significant opportunities for strategic behaviour and information problems in determining the value of the franchise for potential external bidders. Especially difficult would be the valuation of specific investments made in human capital to run the franchise. Similar problems have been raised by Joskow and Schmalensee (1984) in discussing the problems of deregulating the generation sector of electricity supply. The issue here is essentially that raised by Klein, Crawford and Alchian (1978), and analysed further by Kleindorfer and Knieps (1982), Williamson (1983) and Crew and Crocker (1985b) on the effects of transaction specific investment on efficient choice of governance mode. As Klein, Crawford and Alchian [1978, p. 298] explain, 'The crucial assumption ... is that, as assets become more specific and more appropriable quasi-rents are created (and therefore the possible gains from opportunistic behavior increase), the costs of contracting will generally increase more than the costs of vertical integration.' This transaction-specific investment along the import chain may be one explanation for the significant backward integration of most telecommunications and electricity systems. There are, of course, also transaction specific investments between utilities and final markets as illustrated in the following example.

The utility makes an investment in connecting a customer to the network. The amortised fixed cost of this investment is $400 a year and the current salvage value is $50 (yearly rental equivalent). The operating costs are $100 a year. The investment could not be used by any of the utility's other customers. Currently the utility is receiving $500 a year from its customer. The quasi-rent received by the utility is $350 a year, ($500–$100–$50), rental minus operating costs minus salvage value. The customer could cut his offer down to almost $150 a year it would still 'pay' the utility to supply him since he is getting a return over the scrap value of $50 a year.

The literature has discussed a number of ways of preventing appropriation of quasi-rents, including hostages (Williamson 1983), vertical integration (Klein, Crawford and Alchian 1978), franchising, contracting and regulation (Goldberg (1976) and Williamson (1976)). Because of the nature of most utilities' business, the use of hostages and vertical integration are not feasible for final markets.[3] Williamson (1976) and Goldberg (1976) argue that some form of administered contract (e.g. regulation) may be the most efficient governance mode to mediate the transactions between monopolies and their customers, and this is primarily because of the asset-specificity problem. The point is that in view of the high degree of asset specificity, both sides of the natural monopoly problem will see the benefits of expenditures to protect themselves. The appropriate mechanism to mediate the ensuing negotiation on the distribution of the quasi-rents arising from such assets may be some form of administered regulation.

Summarising the above, scale and scope economics are a first indicator of natural monopoly status. However, a protected monopoly can be expected to suffer various maladies in its pricing, output, technology development and organisational efficiency. Providing some incentives to combat these maladies leads to a study of alternative governance modes and their efficiency. The new institutional economics suggests that the analysis of such efficiency is best conducted at the level of the underlying transaction of the sector in question, and the manner in which the costs of these transactions are affected by alternative modes of governance. Transactions costs which may be affected by governance mode include the direct and indirect costs of operating the regulatory scheme, as well as costs arising from X-inefficiency, allocative (e.g. Averch–Johnson) effects and the like.

In addition to these efficiency issues, the new institutional economics also takes a broader view of market power than does neoclassical economics. It is concerned not only with the standard allocative inefficiency arguments of neoclassical economics, but also with equity aspects of natural monopoly. Various practices of monopoly may be considered unfair, and such practices may be the main objection to monopolies and the principal concern of regulation (Zajac 1982). Thus, perceived fairness is a further issue of importance in evaluating alternative governance modes.

7.2 DESCRIPTION OF ALTERNATIVE MODES OF GOVERNANCE

In this section we briefly describe the principal forms of governance employed to regulate natural monopoly. In the next section we will make qualitative comparisons of their relative efficiency. We distinguish between five basic forms:

Regulation
Public Enterprise
Franchise bidding
Contracting
Deregulation

These basic forms are then subdivided into various alternative regulatory structures which may be readily subsumed.

Regulation

Regulation as a solution to the natural monopoly problem, in particular RoR regulation as described in Chapters 5 and 6, involves some form of price control. The control is exercised, at least in the USA, by a politically-determined board or commission. Commissions fix prices and allow regulated utilities to present evidence to support their arguments that prices should be set differently. The hearing process employs the adversary process by which the company puts its case and one or more intervenors present a case to the contrary. The process, except for less stringent rules of evidence, is essentially the same process employed in the US courts of law.

Incentive regulation

Several suggestions have been proposed by economists that aim to be superior – from an allocative or X-efficiency point of view – to RoR regulation. We have described a number of these in Chapter 6. Of special interest here will be the incentive schemes proposed by Loeb and Magat (1979), Vogelsang and Finsinger (1979), and Crew, Kleindorfer and Sudit (1979).

Public enterprise

Public enterprise is a solution to the natural monopoly problem that is in widespread use. The basic idea is very simple. The government owns and manages the utility instead of it being in private hands. At least at first sight, public enterprise has several advantages. The cost savings arising from natural monopoly are automatically retained by society as a whole rather than being retained by the monopolist. Even if the public enterprise charged pure monopoly prices, the monopoly profits would be retained by the government the public enterprise being just another tax collector. The allocative inefficiency would continue, as taxes are a source of inefficiency anyway. However, pure monopoly behaviour is rarely advocated by the supporters of public enterprise. Rather public enterprise is typically envisaged as having the potential for maximising welfare. However, as we indicate below, it does not always work out that way.

Public enterprise takes a number of forms. In some countries, like the UK, it is the dominant form of organisation for natural monopoly, while in others, like the USA, alternative forms dominate. Public enterprise became the dominant form of organisation in the UK after the Second World War, when vast parts of British industry were taken over by the Government. The organisations created were called public corporations with management that was responsible to a Minister. Aside from responsibility to their Ministers, these corporations were not subject to regulation of any significance by other bodies. In the USA, the public enterprise takes the form of a federal, state or municipally owned entity. They vary considerably in size from the Tennessee Valley Authority (TVA) to small municipal electric companies which only distribute power and do not generate it.[4]

The actual objectives of public enterprise may not correspond closely to welfare maximisation, although in the case of the UK, the notion that public enterprise should operate 'in the public interest' figured highly in the founding statutes. On occasions, a welfare maximising approach was in evidence in 'Nationalised Industries' White Papers (HMSO 1967, 1978) recommending marginal cost pricing. In the USA the evidence of a welfare-maximising orientation by public enterprises appears to be weaker.[5] However, public enterprise in the USA has a strong tradition of being non-profit making behaviour like that of a pure monopolist unlikely.

Franchise bidding

Demsetz (1968) proposed franchise bidding as a means of dealing with the natural monopoly problems. The basic idea is to periodically publicly auction off the right to run the monopoly as a protected franchise. Bidders would be required to specify, say for the next period of five years, the prices they would charge for the monopoly's products. If for some bidder the discounted surplus associated with these prices is higher than for the present franchisee, the incumbent would be required to turn over the ownership of the franchise to the winning bidder. The incumbent would be compensated for the value of the transaction-specific assets by the winning bidder. Williamson (1976) has argued that there are significant transactions costs associated with this bidding-contracting process. To see why, let us consider the various types of franchise contracts relevant to natural monopoly: once-for-all contracts, incomplete long-term contracts, and recurrent short-term contracts. Once-for-all contracts are of two types: complete contingent claims contracts and incomplete contracts. The former would require that each potential franchisee specify the prices at which he is prepared to supply service, now and in the future, and even the price changes to be made if circumstances change in the future! Difficulties of writing, negotiating and enforcing complete contracts would seem to make them infeasible.

An alternative to a complete contract is an incomplete long-term contract. Here adjustments would be permitted for unanticipated developments. However, as this opens the door for opportunistic behaviour, penalty clauses may be included as part of the contract. Another possibility, which is used frequently in union contracts is arbitration as a means of dealing with events unforeseen by the contract.

Recurrent short-term contracts would apparently avoid some of the adjustment problems inherent in long-term contracts, since when each short-term contract is renewed, adjustments can be made. Adaptations thus do not have to be completely worked out in advance, or as Williamson (1976, p. 83) puts it, 'bridges are crossed one (or a few) at a time, as specific events occur'.

Deregulation

The final alternative which we will discuss as a solution to the natural monopoly problem is deregulation. The argument for deregulation rests on the notion that the gains from scale economies and price control are small in relation to the inefficiencies of regulation. Perhaps the strongest statement of the deregulation approach originated in Posner (1969, p. 643):

> the logical and empirical foundations of common carrier and public utility regulation are too shaky to support further extensions ... Non-extension offers the most substantial prospect for the eventual elimination of regulation ... (because) in the long run, there may be few natural monopolies, perhaps none, such is the pace of change in consumer taste and in technology in a dynamic economy.

A number of deregulatory alternatives are possible. We will consider unregulated monopoly, self-regulation and 'pseudo-competition'.

Unregulated monopoly would involve getting rid of the price regulatory apparatus in existence. For US airlines (admittedly not a natural monopoly) this involved abolition of the Civil Aeronautics Board, but not the safety regulations as enforced by the Federal Aviation Authority. In the case of utilities this would involve abolition of the regulatory commissions, although some regulation of safety, service standards and environment might continue. Along with this would go the abolition of the industries' exclusive franchises. There would be no legal prohibition against entry. There would be absolutely nothing legally to prevent two or more utilities supplying the same geographical area. According to the contestable market hypothesis of Baumol, Panzar and Willig (1982), when there are no sunk costs there would be no need for two firms actually to compete, merely the threat of entry would discourage the monopolist from raising his price above the cost-covering level. To the extent that the removal of the legal protection from potential rivals reduces entry barriers, the utility's ability to charge high prices is attenuated. Note, however, that this contestable market model has little applicability to the natural monopoly problem since sunk costs are typically significant in the traditional monopoly sectors.

Self-regulation is practised by the professions, e.g. medical, dental, and legal, with the state governments providing assistance with licensing and enforcement. Regulation by the professions, however, usually involves professional practices, the primary focus of utility regulation. On the surface, then, utility regulation has little in common with professional self-regulation. However, like the professions, the utilities are service oriented, and utilities may be able to design appropriate dispute resolution procedures that may be responsive to customer complaints, including presumably excessive or inappropriate rates. The potential for self-regulation would be increased if the state played an overseeing role. The companies should be aware that if the state deemed that inadequate due process was being given to customers, or that the self-regulators were not preventing monopoly exploitation, then the Commission could step in, fix rates and take other appropriate actions. The threat of this might place some discipline upon self-regulators.

Pseudo-competition perhaps best describes the situation currently existing in US telecommunications following the divestiture by AT&T of its operating companies. Here apparent competition and regulation exist simultaneously. Where a monopoly exists, presumably with first-mover advantages arising from sunk or idiosyncratic investment, some incentive by means of regulation or subsidy may be needed to promote entry. In telecommunications, AT&T Communications (ATCOM) tariffs are regulated interstate and intrastate. The tariffs of the other common carriers (OCCs) are regulated only by state regulators. The regulation of ATCOM fixes its rates preventing it from lowering them to compete with the OCCs. ATCOM pays higher access charges to local telephone companies than do OCCs. Thus the entrants receive a subsidy and protection by regulation from competition by the dominant firm, ATCOM, at least until equal access is achieved.

7.3 COMPARATIVE INSTITUTIONAL ASSESSMENT

Our comparative institutional assessment reflects 'the primitive state of comparative institutional analysis' noted by Williamson (1976, p. 75). The central issue we address is whether alternative regulatory modes differ systematically in efficiency and equity respects. First we propose a set of simple efficiency criteria, integrating those suggested by neoclassical and transactions cost approaches to the natural monopoly problems. Then we attempt rankings with respect to these criteria. Though the process is somewhat crude, it represents a starting point for subsequent, and perhaps more precise, quantitative comparisons.

Simple efficiency criteria

The first five criteria listed below are familiar in the traditional theory so we will not discuss them further. The remaining three, however, arise from the broader and deeper view of efficiency taken by the new institutional economics. The criteria are:

1. *Allocative efficiency*
2. *X-efficiency*
3. *Dynamic efficiency*
4. *Scale efficiency*
5. *Price control*
6. *Fairness.* Like price control 'fairness' constitutes an equity criterion. Price control involves fairness to the extent that it is considered unfair for a monopolist to exploit consumers. Fairness is much broader; it includes considerations of what is fair to the utility as well as the consumer. It involves consideration of issues of due process including notions such as 'dignity' discussed in Mashaw (1985) and Williamson (1984). It also involves participation, the right to a hearing, which is nicely summed up by the opening quote of Mashaw (1985).

> If you are a man who leads,
> Listen calmly to the speech of one who pleads;
> Don't stop him from purging his body
> Of that which he planned to tell.
> A man in distress wants to pour out his heart
> More than that his case be won.
> About him who stops a plea
> One says: "Why does he reject it?"
> Not all one pleads for can be granted,
> But a good hearing soothes the heart.
>
> The Instruction of Ptahhotep
> (Egyptian, 6th Dynasty, 2300–150 BC)

The notion of fairness then is an important element in the natural monopoly problem, as Zajac (1982) has emphasised.

7. *Transactions costs of governance.* As discussed above, there are likely to be high transactions costs associated with the operation of governance structures for natural monopoly. We therefore

consider transaction cost economy an important criterion for comparing various governance structures.

8. *Asset specificity.* Governance mode also affects the nature and magnitude of transactions specific investments undertaken by the utility and its customers. The efficiency of these investments is clearly an important element of the natural monopoly problem.

Efficiency ratings

Although a more complex rating system could be employed, little would be gained over a simple bivariate system by which we assign the value 1 to governance structure judged to be 'good' and 0 to those judged to be 'bad' on the performance attributes of interest. One alternative might involve weighting the various attributes according to their likely contribution to efficiency. However, in view of the potential complexities of relating such weighting schemes to an appropriate welfare measure, we report only simple zero/one weights. The rankings are shown in Table 7.1 which provides cross tabulations between governance structures and the eight efficiency attributes listed above.

We now proceed to provide our rationale for the assignments. Current RoR regulation does not score well because of poor performance in the traditional efficiency attributes. It is allocatively inefficient because it does not fully achieve the equality of price and average cost. On X-efficiency, RoR rates a zero because of Averch–Johnson effects, and other inefficient behaviour arguably induced by RoR regulation (see Williamson (1967), Crew and Kleindorfer (1979a) and Crew (1982)). Its performance on other attributes are what rescues it. It performs well on scale attributes, and also on the equity attributes of price control and fairness. On the fairness aspect, commissions provide opportunity for a hearing and have the teeth to make their decisions stick! On the transactions costs economy attributes, the key to the asset specificity problem is the protected franchise. As Goldberg (1976) and Williamson (1976) both argued, the franchise gives the utility the exclusive right to serve a territory and provides the utility with ample incentive to undertake the idiosyncratic investment needed to ensure service is provided. The commissions, moreover, provide the assurance to the consumers that they will not be subject to exploitation by the monopolist. However, whether the current form of RoR regulation (with entry protection) solves the asset-specificity problem at low cost is subject to question, hence our rating of 1*. Because there are very few

Table 7.1 Simple efficiency properties of alternative regulatory governance structures

Governance structure	Traditional efficiency attributes				Equity attributes		Transactions Cost issues	
	Allocative	X-Efficiency	Dynamic	Scale	Price Control	fairness	Transaction Cost economy	Asset specificity
RoR	0	0	0	1	1	1	1*	1
C-K-S[a]	1	1	1	1	1	0*	1	1
V-F,[b] Cross	1	1	1	1	1	1	0	1
L-M[c]	1	1	1	1	1	1	0	1
Public Enterprise	0	0	0	1	1	0*	1	1
FB	0	1	0	1	1	1	0	0
Self regulated	0	1	1	1	1	0	1	1
Unregulated	0	1	1	1	0	0	1	0
Ps Comp.	1	1	1	0	1	1	0	0

a Crew – Kleindorfer – Sudit
b Vogelsang – Finsinger
c Loeb – Magat

studies, (for example Gerwig (1962) and Crew and Kleindorfer (1985) on the transactions costs of operating the regulatory process, and because *a priori* transactions costs might be high or low in relation to alternatives, we give the rating of 1*, implying that there is considerable doubt in this rating. If our 1985 results for New Jersey water companies (see Chapter 5) have widespread application, then it is conceivable that there are considerable average transactions costs for small companies but low average transactions costs for very large companies. Scale effects may dominate, with the transactions costs of regulation apparently affecting costs in the same direction as natural monopoly.

The incentive based proposals of Loeb and Magat (1979), Vogelsang and Finsinger (1979), and Crew, Kleindorfer and Sudit (1979) perform well relative to RoR regulation. However, it should be noted that RoR regulation is a complete regulatory system, whereas the incentive based proposals discussed are not. Indeed, the implementation of any of these incentive proposals would require a commission-based hearing process, similar to RoR. Thus, one might more properly view the incentive proposals as taking the basic 'administered contract' framework of RoR regulation as given, with the focus of the commission hearings shifted from the determination of rate of return to setting and monitoring the parameters of the mechanims associated with the incentive-based proposal in question. With this proviso, we note, not surprisingly, that the incentive based proposals all score well on the traditional efficiency measures, since they are all designed to improve these inefficiencies in RoR regulation. However, Loeb–Magat and Vogelsang–Finsinger both score badly on transactions cost economy.

Loeb–Magat appears to involve transactions costs at least as high as current RoR regulation. As discussed in Chapter 6, the basic logic of the Loeb–Magat proposal is to provide an incentive, via taxes and subsidies, to induce the utility to maximise

$$\Pi(P,P_0) = \int_{P_0}^{P} D(P)dP + PD(P) - C(D(P))$$

where Π represents profits of the firm when it selects P as its price, where P_0 is the base price, $D(P)$ is the demand curve and $C(D)$ is the cost function. Maximising $\Pi(P,P_0)$ leads to $\hat{P} = \text{price} = \text{marginal cost}$ for any P_0. Note, however, that $\Pi(P,P_0) < 0$ is possible depending on P_0. The term $\int_{P_0}^{P} D(P)dP$ is the subsidy (if $P < P_0$) or tax (if $P > P_0$) paid/ collected by the regulator. It is true that given any initial P_o the Loeb– Magat scheme should result in the utility setting price, $\hat{P}$, equal to marginal cost. However, what happens when costs increase? The utility will want to increase price. If it increases price the regulator will reduce the subsidy and the company may make losses. This will result in a request – with subsequent debate and its resulting transactions cost – for an increase in the subsidy. The debate will concern the level of the new base level P_o sufficient to generate subsidies such that no losses are incurred. This is exactly the debate that occurs currently under RoR regulation. In addition there would be further debate over the demand curve which determines the slope, and therefore the size of the subsidy $\int_P^{P_0} D(p)dp$. The ensuing adversarial discussion on the shape of the demand curve is likely to be at least as costly a process as the current process for establishing the fair rate of return for a utility. Indeed, since demand studies are expensive and quite idiosyncratic to a franchise area, this process could well be considerably more expensive than the current rate of return testimony, which can use generic and publicly available data, e.g. from the stock market, and therefore a relatively few days of consultant and witness time.

Thus, Loeb–Magat is likely to score very badly on transactions cost economy, so badly as to exclude it perhaps from consideration as a viable scheme and certainly raising the question as to whether it indeed might be called a 'decentralised' scheme. In addition, as Sharkey (1979) has noted, to the extent that the Loeb–Magat proposal results in profits to the firm, rent-seeking will occur, dissipating the rents and resulting in increased deadweight loss.

Crew, Kleindorfer and Sudit on the other hand are concerned explicitly with transactions cost economy and do this by a procedure which aims to reduce considerably the frequency and extent of rate hearings. In terms of fairness, this is, arguably, given 0*. Fairness in the technical legal sense of due process is reduced because of less opportunity for a hearing. However, the process still remains, and the commission is envisaged as performing a different role, that of an auditor and monitor of performance.

Pseudo-competition scores badly on scale, transactions cost economy and asset specificity. However, where scale economies – the justification for natural monopoly – are not strong, the asset specificity problem may be less important.[6] However, against this, quality of service is likely to decline. So these two attributes may be less relevant for the competitive case. However, the transactions cost issue may be a problem. If managing competition involves more regulation, then high governance costs may result. For example, the efforts required to prevent the dominant US telecommunications firm ATCOM from engaging in anticompetitive behaviour may be rather high in transactions costs as Phillips (1982 and 1984) has argued. Similarly, there may exist significant costs of connecting several carriers, rather than one carrier to the network. Given the level of regulation, fairness, at least in the procedural sense, appears likely to score highly. In any event, we are dealing not with a hypothetical mode, but with something that is presently being tried with the Bell divestiture. From the comparative institutional assessment alone, it is difficult to predict the outcome. Advocates of competition will certainly stress the potential for dynamic efficiency in the competitive process, and will cite the improved choice and availability of cheap electronic telephone handsets which instantly became available on deregulating the market in terminal equipment.

Self regulation scores slightly better than RoR regulation. This is based upon the notion that without the problem of allowed rate of return and the Averch–Johnson effect, there is less tendency for X-inefficiency. Moreover, the companies, if they were able to improve efficiency, would have the potential to retain more of these gains than under RoR regulation. So self-regulation is likely to score better on both X-efficiency and dynamic efficiency. On price control, if the threat of intervention by the state is real, self-regulation may offer good performance. In terms of fairness, complaint resolution may be adequate under self-regulation but the availability of a formal indepen-dent process may mean that due process considerations are not given adequate weight. Transactions costs would presumably be reduced by the absence of the adversary process currently involved in commission hearings. Asset specificity would be resolved by protection of the right to serve and be served.

Public enterprise, franchise bidding, and unregulated monopoly all score very badly. Public enterprise does badly on all the traditional efficiencies but scale. Empirical evidence tends to support the notion that public enterprise does at least as badly as RoR regulated mono-poly.[7] In view of the zero ratings given to RoR regulation in the traditional efficiency measures, its zero ratings are also given to public enterprise. Like RoR regulation, public enterprise performs well on scale and asset specificity. Its absolute monopoly with its obligation to serve resolves the asset specificity problem in the same way as with RoR regulation. On price control, while there may be some doubt, due to the problem of X-efficiency and rent-seeking by managers and employees in public enterprise, it seems likely that the strong not-for-profit orientation of US public enterprises may have some tendency to control prices (see De Alessi (1974 and 1977) and Pescatrice and Trapani (1980). Public enterprise does well with transactions cost economy, because there is a tendency to equate government ownership of the enterprise with operation in the public interest. Hence public enterprises may avoid many of the costs needed to assume fairness, due process and the like. Our casual observations of the behaviour of municipal utilities in the US and British public corporations suggests that the results of this avoidance are less openness and fairness relative to RoR regulation; hence our rating of 0* for public enterprise.

Unregulated monopoly scores one on X-efficiency because of clear incentives for least-cost production. However, because of the potential for managerial discretion, along the lines of Williamson (1967) and Crew and Kleindorfer (1979c), as well as the original Leibenstein (1966) hypothesis, this rating is, as in the case of self-regulation, somewhat debatable. Performance on transactions costs economy is rated 1 because the costs of regulatory governance are, by definition, excluded here. This is debatable, however, to the extent that an unregulated monopoly would employ lobbying to ensure it maintained its monopoly. An unregulated monopoly gets 0 for asset specificity. With no protection of the right to be served, many consumers may not be served because of the size of the hostage required by the monopolist to assure that consumers do not appropriate quasi-rents generated by transaction specific investments.

Franchise bidding scores relatively badly. As Williamson (1976) indicates, franchise bidding scores poorly on transactions cost economy because of the high expenditure of transactions costs to administer the bidding process and turn over of assets. However, franchise bidding does well on fairness. The company and the governing body are, it would appear, in sufficiently frequent contact to ensure fairness prevails. Similarly, if the franchisee wishes to change the services, prices or the terms at which service is provided, he has to negotiate with the governing body. The process would typically be subject to public scrutiny, giving consumers the potential for comment. However, the process formally lacks the safeguards provided by the adversary process in RoR regulation. So while we give it a 1 we note that RoR regulation is likely to do better in this dimension. On the scale, it would also score 1 as a protected monopoly. On X-efficiency, it presumably avoids Averch–Johnson effects but it may be subject to other less specific aspects of X–inefficiency. On asset specificity, it does badly for reasons argued by Williamson (1976). Indeed, this is probably the 'Achilles heel' of franchise bidding. For example, if contracts are awarded on a short-term basis, the first-mover advantages conferred on incumbents either mean that others will be discouraged from bidding or if they are successful, costly transactions costs will result in determining the value of the incumbent's investment or the incumbent will price low with the intent of negotiating new terms after he has been awarded the new contract. Allocative efficiency is scored 0, because the result of franchise bidding will be to set price equal to average cost, as Telser (1969) has noted. Thus, price control scores 1 under franchise bidding.

7.4 DISCUSSION

Regarding our assignment in Section 3, we are unable to argue that 'most of the assignments are transparent or evident' Williamson (1980, p. 24). Because of the broader and more complex nature of the problem we consider, the results of our comparative institutional assessment are not as strong as those of Williamson (1980), Crew (1984) or Palay (1984). However, our analysis does show that it is possible to deal with broader and more complex problems and still derive applicable results. Indeed our analysis provides insights into the work of earlier writers and has some implications for policy.

Our analysis confirms and extends the work of Goldberg (1976) and Williamson (1976). They were highly critical of franchise bidding and provided a detailed analysis of its disadvantages as a governance structure for natural monopoly. When franchise bidding is compared with other governance structures, added weight is provided. It compares badly with all the other governance structures reviewed. In natural monopoly, because of the asset-specificity problem, franchise bidding appears to be no more promising than Williamson (1976) had argued.

The comparative institutional assessment gives us a pointer in the right direction. It gives a little more precision than was possible with the Williamson (1976) and Goldberg (1976) conclusions which argued that franchise bidding compared unfavourably with regulation but that they were not necessarily arguing for a particular form of regulation. Indeed their caution, before advocating RoR regulation, is well placed. While it performs somewhat better than franchise bidding, it does not score well. However, we can now be more definite in the direction we take. We have argued that public enterprise is unlikely to be a preferred alternative to RoR regulation. In addition, we can point to promising new developments that emphasise efficiency incentives through the regulatory process. All the proposals for incentive regulation compare very favourably with the alternatives.

We are now better able to evaluate the proposals for reform of regulation and natural monopoly governance structures now being considered in the USA and the UK. Concern with the existing institutional arrangements is well based to the extent that, in the UK, the concern is with public enterprise and, in the USA, the concern is with improving RoR regulation. In the USA there is a strong trend toward deregulation to suppress rent seeking and the vested interests which regulation creates. This is a powerful argument where abolition of regulation involves some other structure than natural monopoly. However, with natural monopoly, as our analysis has shown, the benefits in traditional efficiency terms may not be sufficient to justify the costs deregulation produces.[8] However, reforms in regulatory structures which consider the trade-offs between the various attributes provide considerable potential for improvement beyond the existing RoR structure. This is presumably a pointer as to how regulation might proceed.

In the UK, where public enterprise predominates, attempts to divest parts of public enterprise that are not a natural monopoly are well based. However, little change seems to be taking place in the natural monopoly public enterprises. Our analysis indicates that this is an area ripe for reform. Selected parts of the industries could be divested and operated by private enterprise subject to some form of incentive regulation. Both sectors could be carefully monitored by using performance measures, with incentives provided to get managers of public enterprise to attempt to match or exceed the performance of privately-owned utilities.

The analysis also throws light on recent reforms in telecommunications. In the UK, this involves divesting half of British Telecom's stock and the creation of a new competitor network, Mercury. In the US, the Bell divestiture is apparently more far-reaching, as discussed earlier. Our analysis points to some of the problems which will need to be addressed if these reforms are to succeed. The presence of significant scale economies (or subadditivity in long-distance telecommunications) is not the only issue of concern. The transactions costs and asset specificity problems are present for the system of managed competition now in operation after divestiture. Local telephone companies have problems of transactions specific investments, which the new structure may not solve as effectively as previously. The local companies now have no guarantee of their right to serve. Indeed they are currently being bypassed in the long-distance market as we discuss in Chapter 9. Hence they may not be prepared to make the investment as they did previously. They may require larger up-front payments to risk their exposure to up-front idiosyncratic investment. The consumer may still be adequately protected in making an up-front investment by the assurance that regulatory commissions will control prices as they do now. The net result may be inefficient, however, to the extent that scale economies prevail in connections and financing. If a telephone utility can reduce average connection costs as the volume of connections increase, a reduction in connections will reduce their benefits. Similarly, and more likely, the telephone industry may be better placed to finance the up-front investment than the majority of customers. By removing the right to serve, the company's incentive to do this is reduced. Connection charges are subject to regulatory approval and it may take regulators an excessive length of time to realise the changed willingness of the telephone companies to make the necessary up-front invest-ments. This may result in their failure to allow significantly higher connection charges and the result may be that local companies will fail to provide enough new lines in growing areas. These and other problems will remain under the pseudo-competitive organisation of telecommunications. Thus, pseudo-competition in telecommunications may not provide great advantages over the former RoR structure. The distribution of benefits and costs will be different, of course, but it is not clear that the substantial up-front costs of divestiture will be justified.

While we argue that comparative institutional assessment offers the promise of new insights, we would stress that our analysis has only touched the surface of this subject in the natural monopoly sector. One would expect considerably sharper conclusions to result from a similar study concentrating on individual industrial sectors. To this end, we turn attention in the next few chapters to specific industry studies in the natural monopoly sector.

Part IV

Regulated Industries

8 Electricity

The aim of this chapter is to examine the principles underlying the economics of electricity supply. In Section 8.1, we describe the institutional background of electricity supply. This includes an examination of interesting technical and economic factors and a short review of relevant historical developments in pricing that have taken place in the industry. Next, in Section 8.2, we assess the core of the theoretical developments of the previous chapters in determining an optimal pricing policy for electricity supply. In Section 8.3 we will discuss the effects of regulation in so far as they concern the traditional issues of pricing and investment as examined in the work of Averch and Johnson. Section 8.4 examines some of the current regulatory concerns for the industry, including recent policies to encourage alternative generation, the effects of environmental and nuclear regulation and the impact of deregulation movements. Our primary focus through this chapter will be on the US and the UK, with some concern also for international trends and innovations.

8.1 INSTITUTIONAL BACKGROUND

The electricity-supply industry was among the first high-technology industries and is of considerable importance in advanced economies because of its widespread uses as a source of light, motive power, heat and is also essential for certain electro-chemical processes. In short, electricity is a major industry of considerable interest and importance. From our point of view it is of further significance to the extent that its economic problems are amenable to analysis by the methodology discussed in the earlier chapters. We now propose to provide a condensed description of some economic and technical features of electricity supply.

To produce electricity in a form that is usable by the consumer requires three basic processes: generation, transmission and distribution. Generation is the process of converting other forms of energy into electricity. It is usually performed by power stations on a scale very large relative to the usage of individual customers. This large scale means that generation occurs in a centralised fashion, normally a considerable distance from consumer necessitating the other two processes of transmission and distribution. Transmission consists of sending the electricity generated at the power stations through wire at high voltage to substations where it is transformed down to low voltage ready for distribution through low-voltage lines to individual meters (consumers). The proportions of total costs attributable to these three activities are on the order of 65 per cent (generation), 10 per cent (transmission), and 25 per cent (distribution) for a typical utility, with capital costs making up roughly 40 per cent of total costs and the remaining 60 per cent accounted for by labour and energy (fuel) costs. The ownership structure of the three elements of the supply chain for electricity can vary considerably from complete vertical integration to separate ownership of each link in the chain.

We classify the methods for generating electricity as follows:

1. conventional thermal (i.e. coal, oil, gas);
2. nuclear;
3. gas turbine;
4. hydro-electric (including pumped storage);
5. other.

Under 'other' we include solar power, cogenerated power, wind, tides, diesel generation and geothermal power, to mention just a few. However, these sources are not very important, and it will be a number of years before they produce significant amounts of electricity. Co-generation, however is becoming increasingly important (see Crew and Crocker 1985b). For investment in the near future we consider only (1) and (2) above as most utilities (at least in the USA) perceive the risks with (2) as being too great. Most economical hydro-electric projects have probably already been undertaken, and this source can therefore be expected to produce only a relatively small amount of future power needs. As cogeneration is becoming increasingly important we will address its role in the industry separately below.

Thus, with a choice of plant types as described above, an electricity utility has to generate, transmit and distribute electricity. It aims to generate, transmit and distribute a given quantity of electricity at a minimum cost. In view of the fact that electricity is not economically storable and demand fluctuates periodically (and stochastically), generation faces the peak-load problem described in Part II. As we noted in Chapter 4, to meet demand at any moment at minimum cost requires that plants be operated in ascending order of running costs.

Thus as demand increases, plants of higher and higher running costs are brought into operation.

Plants are thus ranked according to marginal running costs (fuel plus costs of operating power-station auxiliaries like pumps and fuel-handling devices.)

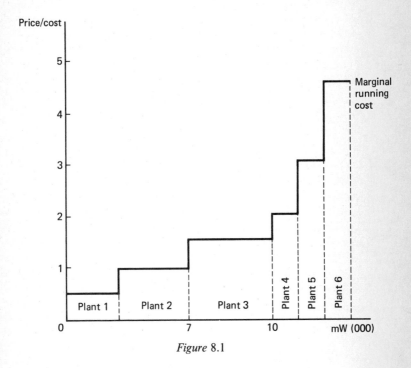

Figure 8.1

Figure 8.1 presents an example. When demand is 10,000 megawatts, plants 1–3 are operated. If demand increases slightly, plant 4 comes into operation. Clearly it is not cost-minimising to operate plant 5 for demands just under 10,000 megawatts. Similarly, if demand falls to 7000 megawatts, plant 3 would cease to operate. Thus at any moment plants are operated in ascending order of their running costs to achieve cost-minimisation. In practice there are a few complications which mean that this rule does not apply absolutely. Transmission costs can cause departures from the rule. Plant 2 may have lower running costs than plant 3 but if most of the demand at a particular moment in time is occurring close to plant 3 and many miles away from plant 2, the transmission costs might cause a departure from the regime. Maintenance outage as well as unforeseen plant outages, or transmission failures, can also cause a departure from the regime of Figure 8.1. Thus, for example, if there is a transmission failure between plant 1 and where the demand is occurring, the system has to depart from the plan. Such considerations are of some operating significance to engineers but do not raise fundamental problems for our analysis, and we will neglect them in the rest of this chapter.

The above short-run analysis underlies long-run decisions like the nature of the plant type to be installed for the replacement of existing plants or to expand the system. Such problems are solved typically by engineers and are known as system planning, and there exists a considerable literature on the subject. System planning is a problem in dynamic analysis, for demand may be growing over time, technology may be changing, and relative fuel costs may be changing. Moreover, the demand growth may not be a simple proportionate growth. For example, if a peak-load pricing tariff were generally adopted, we would expect off-peak demand to grow most rapidly and peak demand to decline or stabilise relative to off-peak demand. Thus detailed system planning is a function of the pricing policy, and optimally the two should be simultaneously determined. However, in practice system planning does not operate in this way as Turvey (1968b, p. 13) notes:

> Costs depend on the programme and help to determine tariffs, which in turn affect the growth of the load. To bring this interdependence into a formal analysis of optimizing the plant programme would not be helpful, however, since it is impossible to take account of it in practice, simultaneously determining future tariff levels and the plant programme.

As a result system planners and engineers have produced simplifying devices (or rules of thumb) which, while ignoring such problems, do provide an attempt to minimise long-run costs. The load curve is one such device; it plots demands in megawatts, say, over a given 24 hour period. In Figure 8.2a the daily load is plotted as a continuous curve. A load curve approximating very roughly a typical winter day in the UK is shown. A load curve for a typical summer day in the UK would be everywhere lower. (In the USA the situation would typically be somewhat reversed, with the increased load in the summer brought about by air conditioning.) The load-duration curve of Figure 8.2b measures how long a level of demand 'lasts' over the year. Thus peak demand obtains for only a few minutes a year, as shown by the steepness of the load-duration curve in Figure 8.2b. The load-duration curve is obtained by starting with the lowest value of demand on any day in the year. Since all demands were above this for the rest of the year, this demand was maintained for the whole year giving point A in Figure 8.2b. Similarly ranking demands in ascending order we are able to plot the whole load-duration curve AB. Thus at C load is maintained for about half the year.

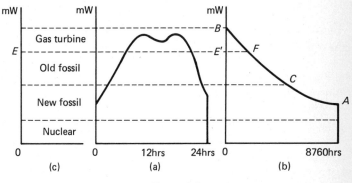

Figure 8.2

Let us now consider how the load and load-duration curves can be used in solving the short-run and long-run problem of cost minimisation. Imagine that we have four types of plant: nuclear, new fossil-fired, old fossil-fired and gas turbine. Nuclear plants have low running cost and high capacity costs (i.e. investment per megawatt). The new fossil-fuel plants are in between these limits with intermediate running costs and intermediate capacity costs. The new plant has lower running costs than the old because it is more efficient in its use of heat. If we rank these four types of plant in ascending order of fuel costs to the left in Figure 8.2c, we can then derive the operating regime of the plants. Thus on a typical winter day gas-turbine operation is given by the area above the horizontal line EF in Figure 8.2(a), and during the year such plants operate for a total of BEF plant hours, from Figure 8.2b. For the other types of plant similar areas may be examined to derive their annual operating hours.

It is clear (ignoring transmission costs) that Figure 8.2a–c provide a basis for short-run optimisation. If the plants are operated inversely to their marginal running costs, total running costs are minimised. Examination of Figure 8.2 reveals that this is indeed the case. Gas turbine operates for the shortest time and nuclear plants operate for the longest time. This short-run problem assumes, however, that capacity has been installed at quantities given by Figure 8.2c. The long-run problem, as to what are the optimal quantities of each type of capacity, is still as yet unanswered.

Before examining an approach to the solution of the long-run problem, we will first examine some of the interactions involved. Let us assume that we are considering replacing an old fossil-fired plant with a nuclear plant. In this case capacity costs are higher but there are substantial fuel savings while the nuclear plant is operating instead of the old plant. It is the magnitude of these over time that determines whether or not to install the nuclear plant. In particular the nuclear plant would be installed if the present value of the fuel cost savings exceeds the capital costs.

Looking at Figure 8.2a–c it is clear that the load-duration curve provides a basis for estimating the present value of cost savings. If the nuclear plant type is increased, then all other fossil-fuel plants will be 'pushed up' in the figure, causing them to operate for a shorter period (and the nuclear type to operate for an exactly corresponding longer period). The difference in the fuel costs for these periods are the fuel savings concerned. Thus Figure 8.2a–c provides a basis for least-cost operation in the short run; by providing a means for deriving the effect on running costs of different plant configurations, the figure also provides a basis for solving the long-run problem of the choice of cost-minimising plant mix for a given planned load profile. We return to this question below.

Implicit in the above discussion is the assumption that demand (and pricing policies) are fixed. This separation of system planning and pricing is typical of the industry, as well noted above. However, from the early days of electricity, the peak-load problem has been present and the need to provide an appropriate pricing policy recognised. The grandfather of electricity rate-making was the English engineer Dr John Hopkinson. In 1892, in his presidential address to the Junior Engineering Society, he argued that costs are determined by peak demand and that 'The ideal method of charge then is a fixed charge per quarter proportioned to the greatest rate of supply the consumer will ever take, and a charge by meter for the actual consumption.'[1] Maximum-demand tariffs, which were to become so popular in the industry over the years, were born. Their original intent was apparently to come to terms with the peak-load problem to the extent that they aimed to improve utilisation or load factor.

Hopkinson's basic approach has dominated the thinking on electricity rate-making. Indeed, developments in the UK and the USA until recently have been in the spirit of Hopkinson.[2] The approach, as it evolved, entailed separating costs into three categories:

1. consumer-related;
2. unit-related; and
3. demand-related.[3]

Prices were to be set so as to recover historical (accounting) costs over these three categories, with each of several customer classes paying its 'fair' share of the full costs. Let us now look at this proposal in more detail, starting with a description of the just-mentioned cost categories.

Consumer-related costs are those costs that are incurred no matter how large or how small the number of units consumed, for example billing, collection, connection and consumer service. Two-part and block tariffs would normally recover these costs in the fixed charge of the first block of the tariff.

Unit-related costs are those which vary directly with the number of units used. Such costs are mainly fuel, some a small part of distribution costs, and certain other works' costs of generation and transmission. Roughly they correspond to the b of our earlier analysis.

Demand-related costs are capacity related costs for generation, transmission and distribution vary with the speed and time with which users consume electricity. Roughly these costs correspond to the β of our earlier analysis.

Having divided up costs into these three categories, the rate analyst then divides the consumers into classes, the aim being that each class of consumer pays the total cost of supplying it, as defined in terms of the above categories. The idea behind this is an attempt to be fair to consumers as a class. The notion does not extend completely to individual consumers. An individual may pay more or less than the costs of supplying him, and this does not offend the notion of fairness applied in the industry.

Any procedure such as the above based on the allocation of full historical costs across customers will necessarily involve some averaging among individual consumers. In order for such a scheme to have any claim to logical consistency it would seem that the various consumer classes should each be reasonably homogeneous with regard to behaviour. One aspect of this is the time at which consumers make their maximum demand. Lewis (1941, p. 252), among others, has noted that all consumers do not make their maximum demands at the same time, so that the system-diversity factor, which is defined as the ratio of the sum of individual maxima to the system maximum, typically differs from unity. Homogeneous behaviour for a particular consumer group would mean that intra-group diversity is small compared with system diversity. Clearly the extent to which consumer groups can be homogeneously structured is crucial to the possibility of determining and stably allocating their fair share of full historical running and capacity costs to them.

In fact, experience has confirmed that stable consumer groups in terms of diversity and load factor can be determined.[4] The usual groupings are residential, commercial and industrial. Almost invariably residential consumers did not use enough to justify the maximum-demand-use metering used in industrial tariffs. Thus they were placed upon two-part or block tariffs while industrial consumers were charged according to maximum demand (Hopkinson) tariffs. The maximum demand tariff is roughly as discussed earlier, the charge per kW of maximum demand being adjusted downwards according to class diversity factors so as not to over-collect costs, an issue more fully examined in Section 8.3. For residential consumers the fixed charge collects the consumer related costs and the unit charge collects the unit and demand related costs. The unit costs are derived by taking the total of such costs for the system and dividing by total outputs. (This figure corresponds to the unit charge in a maximum demand tariff.) To the unit related charge is added the demand related charge in domestic tariffs. The demand related charge per unit is based upon the load factor of the group (in the UK about 40 per cent) and the diversity and is simply added to the unit related charge.[5] Two illustrative tariffs are given below in Table 8.1. Note for maximum demand tariff that the unit of energy consumption is the kW hour for any consumer, while maximum demand is expressed in terms of kilovolt-amperes (and not kW). This difference is necessary to take into account the technical matter, familiar to electrical engineers, of power factor.[6] The form of the tariffs in Table 8.1 is typical of tariffs that were commonly employed, at least until recently, in USA and UK utilities. The domestic tariff is sometimes in the form of a block tariff, for example the first 100 units at 13.44p and the remainder at 5.61p which gives identical revenue to the tariff in Table 8.1 provided the consumption is not less than 100 units. The original justification of such tariffs in

Table 8.1

Domestic (residential) tariff		
Quarterly standing charge	$ 7.78	
Charge per kilowatt-hour (kWh unit)	5.66 p	
Industrial maximum-demand tariff	*High voltage*	*Low voltage*
Monthly standing charge	£ 35.00	£ 13.50
Monthly service charge per kilovolt-ampere (kVa) with a minimum of 40 kVa		
Monthly demand per kilovolt-ampere (kVa)		
For each kVa of maximum demand – April through October	10 p	15 p
For each kVa of maximum demand – November	£ 4.55	£ 4.75
For each kVa of maximum demand – December through February	£ 6.30	£ 6.50
For each kVa of maximum demand – March	£ 2.00	£ 2.20
For the remainder		70 p
Unit charge		
For each kWh supplied	3.21 p	3.38 p
Free adjustment: for each penny by which the fuel cost per kWh differs from £ 45.00	0.00042 p	0.00044 p

Source: London Electricity Board (LEB), 'Domestic Tariff', April 1985; LEB, 'Tariff Industrial, Commercial and Miscellaneous Purposes', 1985.

preference to two-part tariffs was based on the fact that consumers whose usage was so small that they did not even use all the units in one high block would pay less than under a two-part tariff. Other tariffs, for example, time of day, are generally available in the UK. We do not illustrate these here.

For the most part, rate-making in the USA still conforms rather closely to the above approach, though, as we indicate later, there has been some recent movement towards marginal-cost pricing. The main exception to the above approach in the UK has been the Bulk Supply Tariff (BST), which is used by the Central Electricity Generating Board (CEGB) for the sale of electricity to the area boards. The CEGB, with trivial exceptions, sells only to area boards, which are responsible for dealing with the final consumer. The tariff has employed elements of time-of-day pricing since 1962. The 1962–3 BST, as explained in Meek (1963), departed from the traditional Hopkinson approach by fixing a total capacity charge and sharing this out between area boards according to their share of system-peak rather than individual maximum demands. It priced units according to the time of day: between 0700 hours and 2300 hours the unit charge was about one and a quarter times that charge made in the night hours. In addition, the tariff contained a fuel-cost adjustment factor which made provisions for increases (or decreases) in the unit rate if the price of coal changed from some pre-specified level.

In 1967 the CEGB introduced a major change in the tariff with three time-of-day unit charges and two capacity charges, one for peak capacity (about 10 per cent of system maximum demand) and one for 'basic' capacity. The peak-capacity charge was levied at a lower rate than the basic-capacity charge because of the fact the peak demands, as noted above, can be met at lower capacity costs by means of gas turbines. The procedure for measuring these charges, per kW, are to measure an area board's share of system maximum demand, to measure its share when system demand is about 90 per cent of system maximum demand, and to take the difference. This difference is expressed as a proportion of the sum of such differences for all area boards to give a board's peak capacity charge. Similarly the proportions are taken at the 90 per cent level to obtain the basic-capacity charge. While no exact equivalent to the CEGB exists in the USA, similar problems occur in various regional interchanges of power. These interchanges are federations of utilities which coordinate their bulk pricing and dispatching decisions in ways similar to the CEGB procedures.

In short, retail electricity tariffs in the UK and USA have traditionally been based upon principles apparently different from those outlined in Part II. Periodic variations in demand of the kind met in electricity supply would, according to the analysis of Part II, be priced by tariffs where the price varied according to the time of day, so-called time-of-day tariffs. Only within the last few years have such tariffs been offered as a matter of routine in the UK. In the USA they have been used only experimentally until recently but are now becoming more common in rate filings. While the use of time-of-day rates is nowhere as sophisticated or as widespread in the USA as in France, considerable strides have been made. This can be illustrated by Table 8.2 which is based upon Jersey Central Power and Light's 1984 tariff. In contrast, in France, Electricité de France (EDF) has approached the problem differently from the USA and the UK and has been responsible for innovations in time-of-day pricing and load-management devices. We will now comment briefly on some of these.

Table 8.2

Residential time-of-day rate				
Monthly fixed charge per customer			\$7.50 per month	
	Winter		*Summer*	
	Peak	*Off-peak*	*Peak*	*Off-peak*
All kWh consumed per month	13.2¢	6.4¢	17.45¢	6.4¢
Fuel adjustment charge (changed half-yearly)			0.7525¢	

Peak is 8.00am to 8.00pm weekdays
Off-peak is the rest of the time

Primary voltage (*large high voltage users*)		
Customer charge	\$125.00 per month	
	Winter	*Summer*
Demand charge per kW of maximum demand by customer *during peak hours*	\$9.01	\$10.01
	Peak	*Off-peak*
Energy charge	6.78¢	5.27¢
Fuel adjustment charge	0.7221¢	

Source: Jersey Central Power & Light's Tariffs, effective 1 May 1985.

French tariffs clearly departed from the pattern of Hopkinson rates common in the USA and the UK some years after the nationalisation of the industry in 1946, when the industry apparently had no less than 13,000 different tariffs.[7] In 1958 perhaps the most significant development in electricity pricing was the introduction of *le tarif vert* (the green tariff), which applied to high-voltage customers. Other consumers, making up the vast majority (over 99 per cent), are charged on the universal tariff, either with ('double tariff') or without ('simple tariff') a time-of-day rate.

The universal tariff has some novel features. The consumer must subscribe to a particular maximum kW load between 0.5 and 36 kW, for which he pays a fixed monthly charge. This subscribed demand is enforced by a circuit breaker, forcing the consumer to turn off some appliances and reset the breaker. The unit charge consists of two declining blocks.

Le tarif vert is rather complicated. As in the universal tariff, the consumer subscribes to a maximum demand. The kilowatt charge varies according to the voltage size of load (e.g. loads over 10,000 kW get a discount of 24 per cent) and according to where the maximum demand is at system peak. There are five energy charges, varying according to time of day and season. The energy charges do show a substantial differential between peak winter rate and lowest summer rate. Approximate rates for the most typical tariff (*tarif general*) in 1974 are given in Table 8.3, together with times in force. Variations also are incorporated into the tariff according to region, these can be substantial, reflecting factors such as the proximity of cheap hydro-electric power.

Table 8.3

	Winter			*Summer*	
	Peak 6¢	Full 3¢	Low 1¢	Full 2¢	Low 1¢
Time Periods	0700–0900 and 1700–1900 Nov–Feb	0600–2200 (except peak) Oct–Mar	2200–0600 (and Sundays)	0600–2200	2200–0600 (and Sundays)
Number of hours	408	2072	1864	2528	1888

The picture presented above of electricity supply contains some additional elements to those considered in the theory of Part II. Leaving aside inefficiencies caused by separation of cost minimisation (system planning) and pricing (rate-making), there is the perplexing feature in many tariffs that kW (demand) charges are present in addition to the normal two-part tariff charges of customer (fixed) and unit (kWh) charges. In the next two sections we consider optimal peak-load pricing for electricity and the relationship of such pricing to the noted kW (or demand) charges.

8.2 PEAK-LOAD PRICING AND ELECTRICITY PRICING

Wenders (1976) is probably the closest attempt at relating the theory of peak-load pricing to the pricing problem in electricity supply. In this section we review his results and compare them with our analysis of Part II. His approach is particularly interesting for its ability to combine system planner's tools like the load-duration curve in an analysis of peak-load pricing that very simply solves the problem of unequal-length periods.

He assumes three types of plant with annual (marginal) capacity costs per kW of β_1, β_2 and β_3. Wenders (1976, p. 233) defines 'marginal and average energy cost of producing a kW of electricity *for one year*', as b_1', b_2' *and* b_3'. These variables are of course not the same as our definition of b_i, which are defined over a period, e.g. \$/kWh. We will, however, at the moment proceed using Wenders' notation, leaving until later in the section the reconciliation of his results with ours.

Using a load-duration curve like the one used in Figure 8.2, Wenders first notes that optimal plant mix depends on the slope of the load-duration curve. In Figure 8.3 the year is divided into three periods which represent the following fractions of the year: $w_1 = t_1/t^*$, $w_2 = (t_2 - t_1)/t^*$, $w_3 = (t^* - t_2)/t^*$, where $t^* = 8760$ hours, where $Q_1 = q_1$, $Q_2 = q_1 + q_2$ and $Q_3 = q_1 + q_2 + q_3$, with q_1, q_2, q_3 the installed capacities of base, intermediate and peaking plant respectively.

If the firm has built q_1 units of base-load capacity and considers increasing q_1 by one unit, it has to consider the alternative of increasing intermediate capacity by one unit and can compare the (long-run) marginal costs of installing type 1 plants

$$MC_1 = \beta_1 + (t_2/t^*)b_1' \tag{8.1}$$

with one associated marginal cost of installing type 2 plant

$$MC_2 = \beta_2 + (t_2/t^*)b_2' \tag{8.2}$$

If $MC_1 < MC_2$, base load rather than intermediate capacity should be used and this would apply until $MC_1 = MC_2$, or:

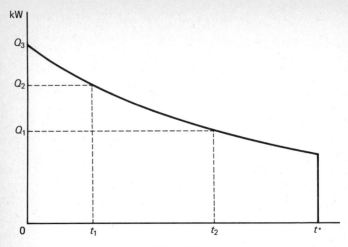

Figure 8.3

$$t_2/t^* = w_1 + w_2 = \frac{\beta_1 - \beta_2}{b_2' - b_1'} \ . \tag{8.3}$$

Similarly, intermediate capacity should be added until $MC_3 = MC_2$, or:

$$t_1/t^* = w_1 + w_2 = \frac{\beta_2 - \beta_1}{b_3' - b_2'} \ . \tag{8.4}$$

Finally, since $w_1 + w_2 + w_3 = 1$:

$$w_3 = 1 - \frac{\beta_1 - \beta_2}{b_2' - b_1'} \ . \tag{8.5}$$

We note from (8.3)–(8.5) that the optimal usage fractions w_1, w_2, w_3 depend only on the relative capital and running costs and not on the slope of the load-duration curve, though the *amounts installed of each kind of plant* depend on the shape of the load-duration curve.

The above analysis describes cost-minimising technology and system planning for a given load-duration curve (LDC). However, the LDC clearly depends on pricing policy. Let us therefore now consider the joint problem of welfare-optimal system planning and pricing. Using a simplified version of the load-duration curve of Figure 8.3 and the above analysis of marginal cost, Wenders places this joint problem in the context of the familiar welfare-maximising framework of Part II of this book. The simplified load-duration curve is shown in Figure 8.4. The demand periods are indicated by t'_1, t'_2 and t^*. Thus period 1 covers a fraction of one year given by $v_3 = t'_1/t^*$, $v_2 = (t'_2 - t'_1)/t^*$ and $v_1 = (t^* - t'_2)/t^*$. Period 3, the peak period, is serviced by q_1 of base capacity, q_2 of intermediate capacity and q_3 of peak capacity, period 2 by q_1 of base and q_2 of intermediate, and period 3 by q_1 of base capacity, as in Chapter 3.

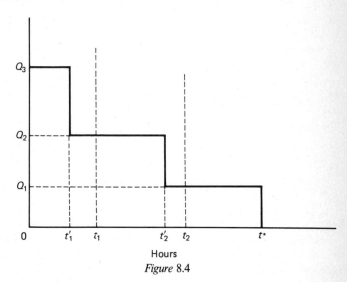

Hours

Figure 8.4

The dashed lines at t_1 and t_2 are the same as the t_1 and t_2 of Figure 8.3. Thus $v_3 < w_1$, $v_3 + v_2 < w_1 + w_2$. We can proceed to illustrate the optimal pricing policy using v_1, v_2, v_3 as weights in the social welfare function. With unequal length periods, the social welfare function W can be expressed as

$$W = \sum_{i=1}^{3} v_i \int_0^{x_i} P_i(y_i)\,dy_i - C_r - C_r, \qquad (8.6)$$

where the indicated quantities are:

v_i = unitless = fraction of year made up by pricing period i
x_i = kWh/year = 1 kWh continuous over the entire year
P_i = \$/kWh/year (so $\int_0^{x_i} Pi\,dy_i = \$$)
C_r = \$ = running cost and
C_c = \$ = capacity cost,

that is:

$$C_r = b'_1 q_1 + b'_2 (v_2 + v_3) q_2 + b'_3 v_3 q_3 \tag{8.7}$$

$$C_c = \beta_1 q_1 + \beta_2 q_2 + \beta_3 q_3. \tag{8.8}$$

Note that since P_i is the effective price of a kWh maintained over an entire year, $v_i P_i$ is the effective period for a kWh of demand maintained over the entire pricing period i.

Maximising W with respect to q_1, while noting that $x_3 = q_1 + q_2 + q_3$, $x_2 = q_1 + q_2$, $x_1 = q_1$, yields the following optimal prices for the situation depicted in Figure 8.4:

$$P'_3 = b'_3 + B_3 / \gamma_3 \tag{8.9}$$

$$P'_2 = \frac{(\gamma_2 + \gamma_3) b'_2 - \gamma_3 b'_3 + \beta_2 - \beta_3}{\gamma_2} \tag{8.10}$$

$$P'_1 = \frac{b'_1 - (\gamma_2 + \gamma_3) b'_2 + \beta_1 - \beta_2}{\gamma_1} \tag{8.11}$$

The above results are similar to those of Chapter 3, in that capacity costs are included in the off-peak periods. Indeed, the Wenders framework is readily transformed into our previous results if we recall our convention that marginal costs b and prices P are period based (e.g. \$/kWh) while in Wenders they are cycle based (e.g. \$/kW year). For example, if there are three equal-length periods ($v_1 = v_2 = v_3 = 1/3$), then $b'_i = 3 b_i$ and $P'_i = 3 P_i$. Thus, our notation of Chapter 3, results (8.9)–(8.11) become

$$P_3 = b_3 + \beta_3 \tag{8.12}$$

$$P_2 = 2 b_2 + \beta_2 - (b_3 + \beta_3) \tag{8.13}$$

$$P_3 = 3 b_1 + \beta_1 - (2 b_2 + \beta_2) \tag{8.14}$$

which is identical to the 3-period firm peak case (3.32)–(3.34). For unequal-length periods, one would have to go through the analysis of

Section 3.3 (while assuming 'flat' intra-pricing period demands) to obtain results compatible with Wenders' framework.

We may summarise the main points of Wenders' approach as follows:

A1: Decide on pricing periods (i.e., choose t_i' in Figure 8.4), such that the following assumption is justified;

A2: Assume 'flat' intra-pricing period demands as in Figure 8.4;

A3: Derive optimal capacities and prices (subject to A1–A2) by solving (8.6);

A4: Translate the LDC-based prices so obtained into time-of-day tariffs using the LDC/time translation procedure depicted in Figure 8.2.

Because A2 is a strong and restrictive assumption, the more general procedure of Section 3.3 is theoretically preferable to the Wenders framework. However, the transparency of systems planning issues in this simplified framework make it an intuitively useful aid to understanding electricity supply.

8.3 HOPKINSON AND OTHER DEMAND CHARGE TARIFFS[8]

As mentioned above, Hopkinson tariffs are almost universally used in electricity pricing, especially for commercial and industrial consumers. Under such a tariff, a customer pays not only per kWh electricity consumed, but also a 'demand charge' according to the maximum instantaneous demand (in kW) over the cycle in question (usually a month, a season, or a year). These commonly used tariffs are not representable in the standard marginal-cost pricing frameworks, where only a (possibly time-varying) per unit price (e.g. /kWh) is studied, but no maximum demand charge is levied. The purpose of this section is to analyse the efficiency of maximum demand charges relative to marginal-cost pricing as normally understood.

Let us begin by understanding what led Dr Hopkinson to suggest electricity tariffs with separate demand and energy charges. Nelson (1976) makes the point that when the Hopkinson tariffs were introduced in (1892), there was almost no diversity in demand – everyone's peak demand occurred at nightfall when they switched their lights on. Moreover, generating units were still quite small and distribution areas were limited. In particular, self-generation was a viable alternative. Under these conditions, the Hopkinson Tariffs, which collected all capacity (kW) costs through the demand charges and other costs through a per unit (kWh) energy charge, gave the appropriate marginal cost signals to consumers and allowed cost recovery and sustainable growth for the electricity industry. The key to the efficiency of these tariffs in the early days of electricity supply was the lack of scale economies in generation and distribution and the coincidence of each consumer's peak demand with the total supply system peak. This absence of consumer demand diversity implied that an additional unit of peak demand by any consumer would require a full additional unit of system capacity, so that separate pricing for capacity, in the form of demand charges, was appropriate.

Clearly, a great deal has changed since Hopkinson's time, especially with respect to scale economies and demand diversity. Yet Hopkinson tariffs and related accounting procedures have remained the basis of electricity rates to this day. It would do well to understand the reasons for their resilience. Aside from the usual pressures for stability which history imposes, we will argue that the Hopkinson tariff has both convenience and efficiency advantages over simpler per unit rate structures, which at least partially explain the staying power of demand charges in electricity tariffs.

As noted above, electricity rate-design calls for isolating costs (possibly by time-of-use) into three categories: customer costs, demand costs (capacity related costs – for generation, transmission, and distribution); and unit-related costs. The resulting costs are then allocated to specific consumer classes – typically residential, commercial, and industrial – on the basis of actual or expected consumption patterns of each class. Having allocated costs in each of these categories, rates for each class are designed to recover the costs apportioned to the class in each category. The easiest method of doing this is simply to levy a separate charge for each cost category as in the Hopkinson tariff. When historical accounting costs are used in defining these categories, a stable and understandable relationship is established between accounting costs, class apportioning procedures and rate structures. This is clearly a very desirable characteristic for rates when these are to be subjected to adversarial scrutiny, and it is likely to be one of the main reasons for the continuing popularity of such tariffs.

Beyond the above structural and administrative advantages, one may inquire whether demand charges are likely to be efficient. Economists have usually taken a negative view on this (see, e.g. Wenders and Taylor (1976)).

Electricity planners and public utility managers have been of a different mind, however. They argue the following advantages of separate demand and energy charges.

Efficient risk sharing

If the consumer faces an *ex ante* choice of what maximum demand to subscribe, utilities will gain important revealed preference information on worst-case conditions. Also, the consumer will bear a reasonable portion of the risk for exogenous events (e.g. the weather) affecting demand for electricity.

Avoiding needle-peaking

On the hot-hot day, there may exist a so-called needle peak, a peak within the peak period, under ordinary peak-load pricing. This has obvious negative effects on system reliability and capacity planning. The reason for such needle peaks under peak-load pricing without demand charges is that consumers do not have identical preferences for consumption over time and, in particular, within the peak period. Moreover, administrative constraints prevent defining large numbers of price schedules to deal in a first-best manner with different seasonal and daily preference patterns and their impact on system costs. Clearly, demand charges would suppress such needle-peaking.

Moving peaks

Information limitations on the part of rate designers and uncertainties on the structure of demand can prevent an accurate assessment of optimal peak-load prices. Indeed, such informational limitations can lead to a different peak period than that expected in response to a given peak-load tariff. One can, of course, readjust prices in response to this, but there are clearly limits on the ability to fine-tune pricing signals. The use of demand charges, it is argued, gives consumers more stable signals on capacity costs and allows them to adjust their own peak demand while paying a fair share of system capacity costs. Moreover, consumers adapt to environmental changes without undue variations in revenue and capacity requirements for the supplying utility.

We may sum up the above arguments roughly as follows. A number of practical difficulties prevent the precise implementation of marginal-cost pricing. Given that we will therefore be in a second-best world in any case, perhaps other tariff structures, e.g. Hopkinson tariffs, may be solid contenders.

Turning to the literature, relatively little has been done to clear up the contending views on the merits of demand charges and their relationship to marginal-cost pricing. Panzar and Sibley (1978) have established for the Brown and Johnson (1969) one-period model of public utility pricing under uncertainty that Hopkinson tariffs have the risk-sharing advantages described above. The problem with the Panzar–Sibley results is two-fold: first, their one-period model must per force neglect inter-temporal effects which are critical in electricity pricing. Second, they assume no demand diversity – everyone reacts to exogenous uncertainty in the same way and system peak is simply the sum of individual consumer peaks.

A related set of literature has dealt with interruptible tariffs. Under such a tariff, price reductions are offered consumers to induce them to allow the utility to curtail supply to these users at times of system peak demand. This is accomplished by activating a ripple control when excess demand occurs which limits usage of customers on interruptible rates to a pre-specified level. These tariffs are similar to Hopkinson tariffs, except that the limiting demand level is only imposed when system capacity is reached. The basic results of Marchand (1974) are that welfare and capacity utilisation improvements can be achieved using interruptible tariffs, depending on the magnitude of rationing inefficiencies in the absence of such tariffs. Again, the argument is an efficient risk-sharing argument.

While these results are suggestive, they do not provide a framework for comparative evaluation of marginal cost pricing and demand charges. The closest result from this comparative perspective are those of Finsinger and Kleindorfer (1981) on maximum demand pricing under conditions of certainty. We review the Finsinger–Kleindorfer model here.

Let $\mathbf{x} = (x_1, \ldots, x_n)$ denote the vector of quantities (of a non-storable good) supplied over a cycle consisting of n discrete periods of equal length. Prices are charged per unit per period (p_i) as well as per unit of maximum demand over the cycle (p_o). Thus, for the price vector $p = (p_0, p_1, \ldots, p_n)$, the bill for any consumer with demands $\mathbf{x} = (x_1, \ldots, x_n)$ is

$$E(\mathbf{x}, \mathbf{p}) = p_0 \operatorname{Max}\{x_1, \ldots, x_n\} + \sum_{i=1}^{n} p_i x_i. \tag{8.15}$$

Denote by T the (finite) set of consumers. We assume each consumer $\tau \in T$ has preferences representable by a twice continuously differentiable, separable utility function of the form $V(x,\tau) + m$, with $V(x,\tau)$ strictly concave in x, and where m, in money units, represents utility for all other goods in the economy. Thus if $M(\tau)$ is consumer τ's income, then the utility from consuming $\mathbf{x}$ is

$$u(\mathbf{x},\mathbf{p},m,\tau) = V(\mathbf{x},\tau) - E(\mathbf{x},\mathbf{p}) + M(\tau), \quad \tau \in T. \tag{8.16}$$

We denote the corresponding indirect utility demand functions by U and $\mathbf{x}(.,\tau)$ respectively, so that, suppressing the income argument,

$$U(\mathbf{p},\tau) = \text{Max}\{u(\mathbf{x},\mathbf{p},m,\tau) \mid \mathbf{x} \geq 0\} \tag{8.17}$$

with $\mathbf{x}(\mathbf{p},\tau)$ defined through $u(\mathbf{x}(p,\tau), \mathbf{p},m,\tau) = U(\mathbf{p},\tau)$. Total demand in period i will be denoted by

$$X_i(\mathbf{p}) = \sum_{\tau \in T} x_i(\mathbf{p},\tau). \tag{8.18}$$

Assuming positive quantities are consumed in each period, the solution to (8.17) is characterised by the following conditions:

$$\partial U(\mathbf{p},\tau)/\partial p_i = -x_i(\mathbf{p},\tau), \qquad i = 1, \ldots, n, \text{ (Roy's identity)}; \tag{8.19}$$

$$\frac{\partial Y(x,\tau)}{\partial x_i} = -U_i = p_i + \gamma_i(\tau), \qquad i = 1, \ldots, n; \tag{8.20}$$

$$\sum_{i=1}^{n} -\gamma_i(\tau) = p_0, \tag{8.21}$$

$$\gamma_i(\tau) \cdot [\text{Max}\{x_1(\mathbf{p},\tau), \ldots, x_n(\mathbf{p},\tau)\} - x_i(\mathbf{p},\tau)] = 0, \, i = 1, \ldots, n, \tag{8.22}$$

where $\gamma_i \geq 0$ is the Lagrange multiplier associated with the constraint that $x_i \leq \text{Max}[x_1, \ldots, x_n]$ in each period.

Our first result establishes that consumers would unanimously prefer to have demand charges reduced and assessed instead as unit charges per period. The rationale for this result is that by transferring such demand charges to unit charges per period, the worst that can happen is that these will be levied in the customer's peak period, which is where demand charges are levied anyway. (Proofs of all results are in the appendix to this chapter.)

Result 1: Let $\mathbf{p} = (p_0, p_1, \ldots, p_n)$ be any price vector with $p_0 > 0$. Then every consumer $\tau \in T$ is at least as well off under any price vector $\mathbf{p}'$ of the form

$$p_i = p_0 - d, \ p_i = p_i + a_i d, \qquad i = 1, \ldots, n$$

where $p_0 > d \geqslant 0$ and where the $\{a_i\}$ are arbitrary non-negative numbers summing to unity. In particular, if $d = p_0$, we see that all consumers prefer unit charges to demand charges.

To determine welfare optimal prices, we assume that a monopoly produces x using a proportional-cost technology. We denote by b the constant cost per unit of supplying the good in any period and by β the cost per unit of capacity. Denote by W the sum of consumers' and producers' surpluses. Given the quasi-linear form (8.16) of consumer utilities, W is easily obtained (see Section 2.2). Indeed, summing over consumers and assuming that capacity is set to exactly meet maximum demands, total welfare W may be expressed as

$$W(\mathbf{p}) = \sum_{\tau \in T} [U(\mathbf{p}, \tau) + \sum_{i=1}^{n} (p_i - b) x_i(p, \tau)$$

$$+ p_0 \operatorname{Max}\{x_i(\mathbf{p}, \tau), \ldots, x_n(\mathbf{p}, \tau)\}]$$

$$- \beta \operatorname{Max}\{X_1(\mathbf{p}), \ldots, X_n(\mathbf{p})\} . \qquad (8.24)$$

The first term in (8.24) represents consumers' surplus and the last three terms represent producers' surplus (i.e. profits). Using (8.15)–(8.19) we may simplify (8.24) as follows:

$$W(\mathbf{p}) = \sum_{\tau} V(\mathbf{x}(\mathbf{p}, \tau), \tau) - b \sum_{i=1}^{n} X_i(\mathbf{p}) - \beta \operatorname{Max}\{X_1(\mathbf{p}), \ldots X_n(\mathbf{p})\}. \quad (8.25)$$

The first term in (8.25) represents consumers' willingness to pay and the final terms represent the social costs of producing the goods over the n-period cycle.

Since at optimum capacity Q will be set to equal $\operatorname{Max}[X_1, \ldots, X_n]$, we can formulate the maximisation of $W(p)$ in (8.25) as follows:

$$\operatorname{Max} \sum_{\tau} [V(\mathbf{x}(\mathbf{p}, \tau), \tau) - b \sum_{i=1}^{n} x_i(p, \tau)] - \beta Q \qquad (8.26)$$

subject to:

$$\sum_{\tau} x_i(\mathbf{p}, \tau) = X_i(\mathbf{p}) \leqslant Q, \qquad i = 1, \ldots, n. \qquad (8.27)$$

Thus, the Kuhn–Tucker theorem yields the following first-order conditions for maximising W.

$$\frac{\partial W}{\partial p_i} = \sum_\tau \sum_{j=i} [V_j(x(\mathbf{p},\tau),\tau) - (b+\mu_j)] \frac{\partial x_i(\mathbf{p},\tau)}{\partial P_i} \tag{8.28}$$

$$\frac{\partial W}{\partial p_i} \leq 0, \ p_i \frac{\partial W}{\partial p_i} = 0, \qquad i = 0,1,\ldots,n; \tag{8.29}$$

$$\mu_i \geq 0, \ \mu_i(Q - X_i(p)) = 0, \quad i = 1,\ldots,n; \ \sum_{i=1}^{n} \mu_i = \beta; \tag{8.30}$$

where V_j in (8.28) is $\partial V/\partial x_j$ and μ_i is the multiplier associated with (8.27).

Our next result shows that when prices can be freely varied in each period, with no intra-period demand variation (i.e. the quantity x_i is consumed at a uniform rate in each period i) then maximum demand charges are inefficient and normal marginal cost pricing is welfare-optimal.

Result 2: A solution to maximising $W(\mathbf{p})$ in (8.25) is $p_0 = 0$ and $p_i = b + \mu_i$, $i = 1,\ldots,n$, where the μ_i are determined through (8.30). Thus, marginal-cost pricing is welfare-optimal when demand is flat in each pricing period.

The next two results may be viewed as a vindication of Hopkinson's original logic (and an extension of the corresponding Panzar–Sibley (1978) result for the deterministic, multiperiod case).

Result 3: Suppose that consumers all have their peak demands in the same period in response to prices $p_0 = \beta$ and $p_i = b$, $i = 1,\ldots,n$. Then, these (Hopkinson) prices are optimal.

Result 4: If all consumers have identical preferences, then the Hopkinson tariff $p_0 = \beta$ and $p_i = b$, $i \neq 0$, is optimal.

The above results show that simple Hopkinson tariffs can reproduce first-best results when there is no consumer diversity, at least not in the peak period. Of course, optimally structured peak-load pricing provides the first-best solution and therefore such tariffs could always (at best weakly) dominate Hopkinson tariffs. As we pointed out earlier, however, there are several informational and administrative impediments to designing and implementing optimal peak-load tariffs. Thus, peak-load tariffs designed subject to these impediments will be only second-best and a comparison of such tariffs with Hopkinson tariffs, which are also second-best, becomes a matter of interest. In this regard, the most demanding assumptions in our analysis thus far have been to assume no uncertainty and, further, that tariffs can be as complicated as we please, in the sense that n (the number of pricing periods) can be sufficiently large so that demands are homogeneous (or flat) within each pricing period. We leave the issue of uncertainty to future research (see Veall (1984) for a preliminary discussion).

Concerning demand variations, Finsinger and Kleindorfer (1981) report the results of a simulation study comparing Hopkinson and peak-load tariffs when there is consumer and demand diversity. Their results are based on the solutions to the following problems.

$$W_H = \underset{\mathbf{p} \in H}{\text{Max }} W(\mathbf{p}) \qquad W_p = \underset{\mathbf{p} \in P}{\text{Max }} W(\mathbf{p}), \qquad (8.31)$$

where

$$H = \{\mathbf{p} \in R^{n+1} \,|\, p_i = p_j, \text{ for all } i, j \in \{1, \ldots, n\} \} \qquad (8.32)$$

$$P = \{\mathbf{p} \in R^{n+1} \,|\, p_i = p' \in R_+, \, p_j = p'' \in R_+, \, i \in N', \, j \in N''\} \qquad (8.33)$$

where N', N'' are non-intersecting sets whose union equals $\{1, \ldots, n\}$.

The problem W_H solves for the best Hopkinson tariff from among the class of such tariffs having a uniform price per unit consumption across all periods. The problem W_p solves for the best peak-load tariff subject to the constraint that only two prices be used, p' prevails uniformly in the periods N' and p'' in the periods N''. We assume N', N'' are pre-specified. As long as $n > 2$, the above specification allows demand fluctuations within pricing periods. Note that both optimal solutions (to W_H and W_p) are second-best solutions when $n > 2$.

The results of the Finsinger–Kleindorfer simulation study confirm the hypothesis that when individual peaks differ significantly from the system peak (i.e. when consumer diversity is high), peak-load pricing is welfare superior to the Hopkinson tariffs considered here. The rationale for this is simple. As diversity increases, demand charges fall increasingly in system off-peak (but individual peak) periods. Thus, such demand charges cause significant departures from marginal-cost signals. Of course, when there is no consumer diversity, Hopkinson tariffs are welfare optimal (Results 3 and 4).

One would expect improvements if a modified Hopkinson tariff were used which levied demand charges only during an extended peak period, but not during clear system off-peak hours. Those consumers with individual peaks during the system off-peak periods would then not suffer needless welfare losses in the form of prices in excess of short-run marginal cost. Such modified Hopkinson tariffs are frequently seen in practice (see e.g. Tables 8.1, 8.2), but their theoretical study waits future research.

8.4 EFFECTS OF REGULATION ON PRICING AND INVESTMENT

In Chapter 6, we presented several models of monopoly regulation. None of these dealt specifically with quality issues. The issue of quality, in the form of reliability of service, is clearly central to electricity supply, and has received some attention in the literature. In this section, we discuss reliability in electricity supply and its relationship to rate-of-return regulation.[9]

Following the approach of Chapter 6, we develop a model of the profit-maximising rate-of-return regulated firm with both stochastic demand and supply considerations. We proceed in two stages. First we analyse a general model of pricing and reliability decisions by the rate-of-return regulated firm and show that, for any fixed rate of return, as the reliability of underlying technology improves, the expected profit-maximising monopolist has incentives to increase capital stock. We then analyse this further in a more detailed model and show how the optimal plant mix varies as rate of return and reliability of constituent technologies vary. This analysis shows that decreases in the allowed rate of return lead to a shift to more capital-intensive technologies, while increases in reliability of some particular technology lead to a more intensive use of the technology in question.

Disembodied reliability effects

We follow the framework introduced in Crew and Kleindorfer (1980). A regulated monopolist is assumed to use a technology described by the production function $F(K,L,a,u)$ with K a long-run factor (K is fixed before u is known) and L a short-run factor set after a random state of nature u has obtained, and where the parameter a is a reliability factor. Demand is described by $D(p,a,u)$ and the firm's output is given by $\text{Min}[D(p,a,u), F(K,L,a,u)]$. Letting $L(K,p,a,u)$ be the firm's optimal short-run response as a function of K, p and u, the profits of the firm are:

$$\Pi(p,K,a,u) = p \cdot \text{Min}[D(p,a,u), F(K,L(K,p,a,u)]$$
$$- w \, L(K,p,a,u) - rK, \qquad (8.34)$$

where w and r are factor prices for L and K.

The unregulated monopolist would strive to maximise the expected value of (8.34) by proper choice of (p,K). Rate-of-return regulation constrains this choice to satisfy certain *ex ante* and *ex post* requirements on realised rate-of-return on capital. There are many possible representations of such regulation under uncertainty.[10] We take a particularly simple model here, where the firm and the regulator agree that it is the expected rate of return which is constrained and, subject only to this *ex ante* constraint, the firm keeps all excess profits in the event of favourable *ex post* conditions. This leads to the following problem:

$$\underset{p,k}{\text{Max}} \; [R(p,K,a) - rK] \qquad (8.35)$$

subject to:

$$R(p,K,a) - rK \leqslant (s-r)K, \qquad (8.36)$$

where $s > r$ is the allowed rate of return and where the expected quasi-rents $R(p,K,a)$ are defined from equation (8.34) as

$$R(p,K,a) = E\{\Pi(p,K,a,\tilde{u})\} + rK \qquad (8.37)$$

so that equations (8.35) and (8.36) simply represent the problem of maximising expected profits subject to a restriction that the expected rate of return on capital, that is $R(p,K,a)/K$, not exceed the allowed rate.

Now there is nothing complicated about equations (8.35) and (8.36), since all stochastic elements have been *expected out*. Moreover, it is straightforward to derive the following first-order conditions for equations (8.35) and (8.36), where subscripts indicate partial derivatives:

$$R_p(1-\lambda) = 0 \qquad (8.38)$$

$$R_K - r = -\frac{\lambda(s-r)}{(1-\lambda)} \qquad (8.39)$$

where λ is the Lagrange multiplier for the constraint in equation (8.36), which, following the usual procedure (Bailey 1973), is easily shown to satisfy $0 \leqslant \lambda < 1$.

Now assume that s is fixed, the reliability parameter a varies, and p and K are adjusted to solve equations (8.38) and (8.39) with equation (8.36) holding as an equality. We may then take the total derivative in equation (8.36) to obtain

$$R_p \, dp/da + (R_K - s) \, dK/da + R_a = 0 \qquad (8.40)$$

from which, using equations (8.38) and (8.39) we have

$$dK/da = \frac{(1-\lambda)R_a}{(s-r)} . \qquad (8.41)$$

We now argue that it is reasonable to assume that $R_a > 0$. From equations (8.34) and (8.37), $R_a > 0$ would follow in particular if D_a, F_a and L_a are all positive, assumptions which each seem reasonable. Thus, assuming $R_a > 0$ imples from equation (8.41) and $\lambda < 1$ that $dK/da > 0$. As reliability increases, the optimal regulated capital stock also increases, essentially because increases in reliability imply expected quasi-rents, which would violate equation (8.36) unless capital stock were increased. Following the usual comparative static methods (Crew and Kleindorfer 1979a), it is possible to verify that $dK/ds < 0$. As the allowed rate of return is decreased, *ceteris paribus*, the regulated firm increases its capital stock. Indeed, proceeding as in Crew and Kleindorfer (1979a and 1980), one shows that the deterministic Averch–Johnson over-capitalisation effect carries over to the stochastic case.

The above results $dK/da > 0$, $dK/ds < 0$ are disembodied from plant mix considerations. That is, the increases in a analysed above have no direct relation to the choice of technology. In the next section we analyse a multiplant fixed-proportions model to understand the implications of reliability and technology choice in a regulated environment.

Technology choice and reliability

Let us now specify the problem of equations (8.35) and (8.36) in a more detailed fashion relative to technology. We will assume throughout that $D(p,a,u) = D(p,u)$, so that demand is not influenced by reliability. We assume throughout that $D_p(p,u) < 0$ and $D_u(p,u) > 0$ for all (p,u), where u is a random state of nature. Technology is assumed to be of the fixed-proportions type, two plant types available, whose (constant) per unit operating and capacity costs are given by b_j and B_j respectively, $j = 1,2$, where the following efficiency conditions are assumed to exclude dominated plant types:

$$0 < b_1 < b_2 \text{ and } B_1 > B_2 > 0 \tag{8.42}$$

Now let z_1 and z_2 be the amount of installed capacity of types 1 and 2 purchased by the firm. We assume that the amount of capacity actually available to the firm is then $q_j = a_j z_j$ where a_j represents the *availability factor* for plant type j. We will be using these deterministic availability factors as a surrogate for reliability, although such a simplifying assumption does not tell the whole story. Availability is deterministic to the extent that plant outage takes place because of a plant maintenance schedule (planned outage). However, unplanned outages may occur through equipment failure, so that, in practice, a_j would have a stochastic element.

In the short-run, it should be clear that minimum-cost operation is achieved when plants are scheduled for operation in increasing order of running costs b_j. Thus, if y_j is the output of plant type j, then if price is p,

$$y_1 = \text{Min}[q_1, D(p,u)]$$

$$y_2 = \text{Min}[D(p,u) - y_1, q_2] \tag{8.43}$$

where $(q_1, q_2) = (a_1 z_1, a_2 z_2)$ are the available capacities corresponding to the installed capacities (z_1, z_2). Total capacity available is $(q_1 + q_2)$ and total output is $\text{Min}[D(p,u),(q_1 + q_2)]$.

As in the previous model, we assume that the firm maximises the expected value of profit subject to the regulatory constraint that its expected profits do not exceed the rate of return on capital set by the regulatory commission. This may be written in the context of this model as follows:

$$\underset{p,q1,q2}{\text{Max}} \; E\{\Pi(p,q_1,q_2,u)\} = E\{p.\text{Min}[D(P,u),(q_1 + q_2)]$$

$$-\left(b_1 y_1 + b_2 y_2 + \frac{B_1}{a_1} q_1 + \frac{B_2}{a_2} q_2\right)\} \tag{8.44}$$

subject to

$$E\{\Pi(p,q_1,q_2,\tilde{u})\} \leqslant \frac{s-r}{r}\left(\frac{B_1}{a_1} q_1 + \frac{B_2}{a_2} q_2\right) \tag{8.45}$$

where the u_j are given by equation (8.24) and where $s > r$ is the allowed rate of return per dollar of invested capital. Note that we have substituted everywhere $z_j = q_j/a_j$ so that $[(B_1/a_1)q_1 + (B_2/a_2)q_2] = (B_1 z_1 + b_2 z_2)$ is just the total capital cost for the firm. We note from this that the effective-capacity costs for type-j plant are (B_j/a_j) per unit; note also that decreases in availability and reliability in our model have the same effect as increases in the per-unit capital cost of the respective techno-logy. Henceforth, we use the notation $\beta_j = B_j/a_j$ to denote effective per-unit capacity costs. With these notational conventions, we may rewrite equations (8.25) and (8.26) in the form of equations (8.16) and (8.17) as follows:

$$\text{Max } [R(p,q_1,q_2) - \sum_{j=1}^{2} \beta_j q_j] \tag{8.46}$$

Subject to

$$(p,q_1,q_2) \geqslant 0 \quad \text{and} \quad R(p,q_1,q_2) \leqslant \frac{s}{r} \sum_{j=1}^{2} \beta_j q_j \tag{8.47}$$

where the quasi-rents function R is defined here as

$$R(p,q_1,q_2) = E\{p.\text{Min}[D(p,u),(q_1+q_2)] - \sum_{j=1}^{2} b_j y_j\}. \tag{8.48}$$

Assuming $p > 0$ at optimum and denoting by $R_j = \partial R/\partial q_j$, $j = 1,2$, the Kuhn–Tucker conditions for equations (8.27) and (8.28) are

$$R_p(1-\lambda) = 0 \tag{8.49}$$

$$(1-\lambda)R_j + (\lambda s/r - 1)\beta_j \leqslant 0, \; q_j \geqslant 0 \tag{8.50}$$

$$q_j[(1-\lambda)R_j + (\lambda s/r - 1)\beta_j] = 0, \; \lambda \geqslant 0 \tag{8.51}$$

where λ is the multiplier associated with equation (8.47). As in the case of the deterministic Averch–Johnson problem in Bailey (1973), it can be shown that λ is in the range $0 \leqslant \lambda < 1$ for $s > r$. When $\lambda = 0$, equations (8.49) through (8.51) reduce to the first-order conditions associated with maximising equation (8.46) disregarding equation (8.47) that is, the unregulated case.

We now wish to show that the above first-order conditions are equivalent to those of an unregulated profit-maximising monopolist who faces an artificial, uniform proportional discount on all capacity purchases. The same point was made in Chapter 6 for the deterministic case, and it lends considerable insight into the capacity choices of the regulated monopolist.

The indicated equivalence is obtained from equations (8.49) through (8.51) as follows. Since $1-\lambda>0$, dividing equations (8.49) through (8.51) by $1-\lambda$ yields the following equivalent set of first-order conditions:

$$R_p=0 \tag{8.48'}$$

$$R_j-\delta(s)\beta_j\leqslant0 \tag{8.49'}$$

$$q_j\geqslant0,\ q_j[R_j-\delta(s)\beta_j]=0 \tag{8.50'}$$

where $\delta(s)$ is defined as

$$\delta(s)=\frac{r-\lambda(s)s}{r-\lambda(s)r} \tag{8.52}$$

with $\lambda(s)$ the optimal Lagrange multiplier for the constrained optimisation problem equations (8.49), (8.50) and (8.51).

The object of the above transformations is now at hand. Indeed, the reader may now readily verify that equations (8.49') through (8.51') are precisely the first-order conditions for the following unregulated profit-maximising problem:

$$\text{Max}[R(p,q_1,q_2)-\delta(s)\sum_{j=1}^{2}\beta_j q_j] \tag{8.53}$$

subject to $(p,q_1,q_2)\geqslant0$.

From this analysis, we see that the first-order conditions for the regulated problem (8.47) and (8.48) are equivalent to those for the unregulated problem (8.51). The only difference between equations (8.51) and (8.46) is that the per-unit capacity costs in equation (8.51) (which are $\delta(s)\beta_j$ for plant j) represent a uniform proportional discount of $1-\delta(s)$ off the capacity costs in equation (8.46). We note from equation (8.41) and (8.48) that $R_j>0$, $j=1,2$. Thus at optimum, equations (8.50) and (8.50') imply that $\delta(s)$ is nonnegative. This together with $s\geqslant1$, implies from equation (8.52) that $0\leqslant\delta(s)\leqslant1$. In fact, $1 - \delta(s) > 0$ is a discount – unless $\lambda(s) = 0$, the unregulated case, where $\delta(s) = 1$.

From the above equivalence of equation (8.46), (8.47) and (8.51), it is important to ascertain the effects of changes of s on $\delta(s)$. Let s_m be the monopoly rate of return. When $s > s_m$ we would expect $\delta(s) = 1$. This can be seen from equation (8.52). For $s > s_m$, $\lambda = 0$, implying $\delta(s) = 1$. Moreover, for $s_m > r$, it can be shown by methods analogous to those in Crew and Kleindorfer (1981) that $d\delta/ds > 0$, implying that as regulation is stiffened, the imputed discount $1 - \delta(s)$ on capital increases.

The characterisation just derived of the regulated monopolist in terms of a behaviourally equivalent unregulated monopolist with different capacity cost has several important consequences. First, suppose a utility management tells system planners to use a cost-of-capital figure uniformly discounted at the rate $\delta(s)$. Suppose they also tell system planners the demands and reliability levels for which they should plan, and that these levels, in fact, correspond to the optimal regulated solution. If system planners determine (q_1, q_2) so as to minimise expected costs subject to the stated reliability and demand constraints, then the optimal regulated capacity level (that is, the solution to equation (8.51)) would result. In this sense, cost minimisation is not antithetical to Averch–Johnson effects; it all depends on which costs are used.

The next feature of the above characterisation of interest is that it makes the derivation of price and technology choice of the regulated monopolist a simple matter. We know that our behaviourally equivalent unregulated monopolist will (for its cost structure) minimise costs and set price by equating expected marginal revenue to expected marginal costs. Since the minimum-cost solution for the diverse technology firm is completely known from earlier results,[11] the price and technology choices of the regulated monopolist easily follow. By tracing the impact of the allowed rate of return s on $\delta(s)$ and, thus, on the costs of the behaviourally equivalent unregulated monopolist, we can characterise the behaviour of the regulated monopolist in response to the choice of the regulatory instrument s. Finally, by noting the impact of changing the cost $\beta_j = B_j/a_j$ on the solution to equations (8.46) and (8.47), or equation (8.51), we also determine the effects of constituent technology reliability on overall system reliability at the regulated optimum.

To state our results we need the following definitions. *Cumulative capacity* through type-j plants is denoted Q_j, $j = 1, 2$. Thus, $Q_2 = q_1 + q_2$. *The reserve margin for type-j plants* is denoted by $M_j(p, Q_j)$ and is defined for each (p,Q_j), as the solution to $D[p,M_j(p,Q_j)]=Q_j$. Note that M_j is well-defined since $D_u>0$ is assumed.

Theorem:[12] The solution (p,q_1,q_2) to equations (8.27) and (8.28) satisfies the following comparative statics conditions whenever $r<s<s_m$, s_m being the monopoly rate of return:

$$\frac{dQ_i}{ds}<0,\ \frac{dM_i}{ds}<0,\ \frac{dz_i}{da_j}>0,\ j=1,2. \qquad (8.54)$$

Thus, we see the effects of tightening regulation are to shift plant mix towards more capital-intensive technologies and to increase reserve margins for both plant types. These effects are compounded with supply-side effects, in that as plants become more reliable their use is increased as long as s remains fixed. The rationale for the results on Q_j and M_j is the Averch–Johnson rationale, constructively interpreted in the present environment through the equivalence of equations (8.46), (8.47) and (8.51) and the noted fact that $d\delta/ds>0$ so that stiffening regulation increases the effective uniform discount on capital outlays for new plant. The rationale for the results on z_j is that given earlier. As plant availability factors increase, net expected revenue is increased and the effective price per unit of available capacity (B_j/a_j) is decreased. This leads directly to increases in z_j at optimum.

Some illustrative examples

In this section, we provide computational results to illustrate the above ideas. These utilised the following demand data:

$$D(p,\tilde{u})=100-p+\tilde{u} \qquad (8.55)$$

where $\tilde{u}$ is distributed normal $(0,\sigma)$, with σ the standard deviation of $\tilde{u}$. The cost data were as follows:

$$b_1=10,\ b_2=20,\ B_1=38,\ B_2=30. \qquad (8.56)$$

Two sets of availability data were run: $a_1=1.0$ and $a_1=0.95$. For all runs $a_2=1.0$ was assumed. These data led to $\beta_1=38$ for $a_1=1.0$ and $\beta_1=40$ for $a_1=0.95$.

Table 8.4 provides results for the case where the standard deviation σ of the (truncated) normal distribution for $\tilde{u}$ was 4. Table 8.5 provides the corresponding results for the case where $\sigma = 8$. For each of the listed cases, the problem of equation (8.51) was solved for various values of δ. We have computed the corresponding value of rate of returns implied for equations (8.44) and (8.45) by the optimal solution to equation (8.51), and this is listed under the column s in the tables. Thus, with $\sigma = 4$, the monopoly solution under perfect plant availability is the case $\delta = 1.0$ in the top half of Table 8.4; the implied rate of return on capital for this case was $s = 1.50$. The price was 71.98, $q_1 = 23.22$.

Table 8.4 Effects of changing the severity of regulation, $\tilde{u} \equiv N(0,4)$

δ	s	p	q_1	q_2	$q_1 - x$	$q_1 + q_2 - x$
		Results for $b_1 = 10$, $b_2 = 20$, $\beta_1 = 38$, $\beta_2 = 30$				
0.2	1.06	58.48	46.96	2.66	5.44	8.10
0.4	1.18	61.89	40.99	1.65	2.88	4.53
0.6	1.29	65.27	35.05	1.76	0.32	2.08
0.8	1.39	68.63	29.13	2.37	-2.24	0.13
1.0	1.50	71.98	23.22	3.24	-4.80	-1.56
		Results for $b_1 = 10$, $b_2 = 20$, $\beta_1 = 40$, $\beta_2 = 30$				
0.2	1.01	58.68	46.12	3.33	4.80	8.13
0.4	1.14	62.30	39.30	3.00	1.60	4.60
0.6	1.25	65.90	32.51	3.80	-1.60	2.20
0.8	1.35	69.48	25.72	5.10	-4.80	0.30
1.0	1.59	73.05	00.00	25.63	—	-1.33

For the demand function given in equation (8.36), M_1 and M_2 are simply given by total cumulative capacity Q_j minus the expected demand. For example, $M_2 = Q_2 - (100 - p)$. The last two columns in each table therefore tabulate the reserve margins for type-1 and type-2 capacity respectively.

From these tables, we see the results of the above theorem confirmed. In particular, note the shift toward more capital-intensive technology as s is lowered, implying that regulation is tightened. In the bottom parts of Tables 8.4 and 8.5, one may even note that the efficient (expected cost-minimisation) solution when $a_1 = 0.95$, calls for using only plants of type 2. However, as regulation is tightened, the uniform

Table 8.5   Effects of changing the severity of regulation, $\tilde{u} \equiv N(0,8)$

	Results for $b_1 = 10$, $b_2 = 20$, $\beta_1 = 38$, $\beta_2 = 30$					
δ	s	p	q_1	q_2	$q_1 - x$	$q_1 + q_2 - x$
0.2	1.16	58.64	44.08	1.34	2.72	4.06
0.4	1.28	62.25	39.19	0.85	1.44	2.29
0.6	1.38	65.84	34.32	0.93	0.16	1.09
0.8	1.49	69.44	29.44	1.27	-1.12	0.15
1.0	1.59	73.02	24.58	1.73	-2.40	-0.67

	Results for $b_1 = 10$, b_2, $\beta_1 = 40$, $\beta_2 = 30$					
δ	s	p	q_1	q_2	$q_1 - x$	$q_1 + q_2 - x$
0.2	1.11	58.84	43.56	1.68	2.40	4.08
0.4	1.22	62.66	38.14	1.53	0.80	2.33
0.6	1.33	66.46	32.74	1.95	-0.80	1.15
0.8	1.44	70.26	27.34	2.63	-2.40	0.23
1.0	1.71	74.06	00.00	25.38	—	0.56

discount on capital outlays implied by regulation induces the regulated firm to switch to an inefficient plant mix, now using (and increasingly so) plants of type 1 as regulation is tightened.

Note also that reserve margins are everywhere increasing as the allowed rate of return is decreased. Also, as expected, reserve margins are larger, *ceteris paribus*, when demand uncertainty is higher. Regulation, however, is not entirely without benefits, to the extent that price is reduced as regulation is stiffened. Thus the same dilemma exists under uncertainty as under certainty – it is possible to reduce price by regulation, but the price tag on this price reduction is the increased technological inefficiency resulting from the inefficiencies induced in the plant mix.

In Crew and Kleindorfer (1982, pp. 112–16) we tested the applicability of our hypothesis concerning the relationship between allowed rate of return and reserve margin. We will only report the conclusions of that test here. Our results using data from a sample of the 100 largest utilities showed no support for our hypothesised relationship that reserve margin varies inversely with the allowed rate of return. Rather, the main factors influencing the reserve margin seemed to be technological. This also does not support strong profit maximising behaviour on the part of utilities, but rather attention to engineering and technical standards that have long been the hallmark of the industry. In addition, during the period covered, 1965–78, the allowed rate of return typically exceeded the cost of capital. This may have had the effect of allowing utilities to give engineering standards prominence during this period.

8.5 THE TAR BABY EFFECT AT WORK IN ELECTRICITY REGULATION

The previous section indicates the inexorable tendency of regulation to expand its scope. This so-called tar baby effect (see McKie (1970)) is well illustrated in the reliability area: RoR regulation can be theoretically argued to induce excess reliability; therefore, reliability needs to be regulated as well as the firm's rate of return under RoR regulation.

The scope of regulation of electricity supply has increased in other areas as well. For example, regulators are increasingly concerned with the environment, with consequent impact on system planning for pollution control and siting decisions. Other developments and extensions of regulation include attempts by government to encourage alternative forms of generation. The ostensible objective in this area is the desire to promote energy conservation and perhaps competition. These developments have opened up further gaps that regulation has stepped in to fill. The tar baby effect is very much in evidence.

New regulatory concerns have been nowhere more in evidence than with nuclear power. A few years ago it seemed to be just another technology that apparently offered low cost power if it could be operated to satisfy base loads with a high capacity factor. However, with the upheaval caused by the Three Mile Island nuclear accident, fears about nuclear power have grown, and the federal Nuclear Regulatory Commission (NRC) has responded by very stringent safety regulations and supervision on both the construction and operation of nuclear power plants. This has resulted in construction delays for nuclear plants and reduction in the load factors of existing plants due to down time, with consequent cost increases. The problems presented to regulators have been considerable, and regulators are examining ways of easing the burden of bringing in new plants, because of their massive impact on rate base.[13]

The Pennsylvania and New Jersey Commissions have had to deal with the problems arising out of the Three Mile Island nuclear accident. The Three Mile Island complex is owned and operated by General Public Utilities (GPU) which does business (through three wholly-owned subsidiaries) in both New Jersey and Pennsylvania. The New Jersey Board of Public Utilities and Pennsylvania Public Utility

Commission removed the plant from the GPU's rate base, reducing and therefore R in equation (5.1) and thereby reducing the earnings that the company was allowed to make. This combined with the price that was required for replacement power from other utilities left GPU in a financial bind. Ultimately, the regulators allowed rate relief to enable the company to survive. The regulatory degrees of freedom, however, had been reduced by removal of the plant from the rate base. Adjustments then had to be made in the other variables in (5.1), principally 0 (operating expense) and s. These were forced up because of the financial markets perception of the higher risks when the plant was removed from the rate base. The net effect has not been determined. We cannot ascertain whether the increased return to compensate for risk exceeded what would have been demanded if the plant had remained in the rate base. In any event, these were unenviable and uncharted waters for regulators and companies. Given this, both seemed to steer through perhaps avoiding some of the worst reefs.

It is not clear, however, that the appropriate lessons have been learned. Nuclear power is now considered out of the question for most utilities because of fear and the attendant regulatory risks. Regulatory commissions still have not come to terms with the long-time horizons implied by nuclear power. The big increase in rate base and charges for capital recovery have led some regulatory commissions, for example New York, to consider some phase-in schemes that would imply a smaller impact on the consumer now and a larger impact later. This may be just putting off a potential problem. If nuclear power is as risky as it is apparently perceived, its future cash flows may be much less than forecast. In this event the value of the asset may decline rapidly. This would imply the need for high initial depreciation, which is just the opposite of what is being discussed. To the extent that the capital markets believe that such policies threaten capital recovery, a higher cost of capital will be demanded, which will flow through into higher rates through RoR regulation. Regulatory commissions still have a very short time horizon, and still have not come to terms with the problems some nuclear power projects may have brought to utilities they regulate. Instead of devising means of keeping nuclear plants out of rate base by all sorts of ingenious financing schemes, as described in Hyman (1983, pp. 141–42), which make the capital recovery much greater in the future, regulators should consider allowing utilities a return on plants under construction and not attempt to distort depreciation schedules so that these costs are to be recovered in the future. Such action would result in utilities being perceived by the market as less risky with a consequently lower cost of capital.

This extension of utility regulators' interest to include problems such as environment and energy conservation has led to attempts by regulators to encourage alternative forms of generation such as co-generation in competition with existing utility generation. This kind of competition has a number of features that arise from the fact that such competitors normally have to use the utility grid and therefore have either to sell to the utility or pay the utility a 'wheeling' charge for transmitting power across its lines. Because of the potential for monopoly power of this arrangement, regulators have intervened to promote cogeneration through the Public Utility Regulatory Policies Act 1978 (PURPA) and consequent policies by state regulatory commissions. We will now review some of the principal issues involved, with special reference to the regulatory problems that ensue.[14]

Cogeneration is a technology whereby electricity and heat are produced together, the heat being used to heat and cool buildings (by means of absorption chillers) or in some other process requiring heat. Cogeneration should be contrasted with central-station generation (the typical case) where electricity is generated and the heat produced is just disposed of by the cheapest means available, for example, into a lake or by means of a cooling tower.

Regulatory interest in developing cogeneration at first sight appears to be well-placed because it seems to offer the potential for energy conservation and competition. Indeed it appears to be a dominating technology: instead of having to dispose of the heat produced as a result of electricity generation, cogeneration makes it possible to put this heat to use, as a saleable product or input in a production process. Although, cogeneration has never been of much significance in the USA regulatory policy since 1978 has been directed at changing this.[15] A number of researchers, notably Joskow (1982), have challenged the wisdom of this approach.

Joskow's argument is that cogeneration costs may exceed the costs of producing electricity by central station and heat by a separate boiler, that is, cogeneration provides an example of joint production not having scope economies. Joint production may not display economies of scope for various technological reasons. However, there is more at issue than just the production cost functions as Teece (1980, p. 225) has argued: 'Economies of scope provide neither a necessary nor sufficient condition for cost savings to be achieved by merging specialized firms.' Crew and Crocker (1985b) examine this problem at length. In particular they show that because of problems of institutional arrangements, transaction-specific investments and the like, cogeneration may not be undertaken even when it passes the simple test devised by Joskow and may be undertaken even when it does not pass the test. Because of the cogeneration technology, the transaction-specific investments are somewhat complex. These investments include the production capital as well as facilities which have to be built to provide for the distribution of the heat. Similarly connections have to be made for the delivery of the electricity. All of these investments, which are illustrated in Figure

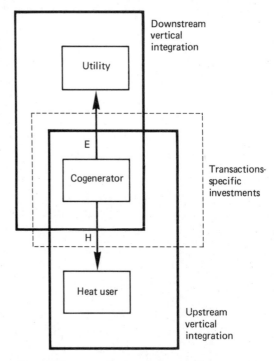

Figure 8.5   Transactions-specific investments and cogeneration

8.5, are transaction-specific in their nature. Where one party owns the cogeneration facility and supplies heat to a second party, there is a potential for 'hold-up'. The second party could, along the lines of Klein, Crawford and Alchian (1978), attempt to renege on the contract and pay a lower price thereby appropriating a larger share of the quasi-rents resulting from production. As heat facilities would have effectively zero value in an alternative use, the heat user could, after the transaction-specific investments are in place, force renegotiation and pay the cogenerator close to variable cost thereby appropriating the bulk of the quasi-rents. The cogenerator will also be subject to hold-up by the purchaser of electricity, so that independent ownership would be the result in the potential for hold up in both heat and electricity.

The solution to this problem proposed by Klein, Crawford and Alchian (1978) would be vertical integration, but even then if the facilities were owned by the electricity (heat) customers, hold-up would remain in the heat (electric) market. Another approach to the transactions-specific investment problem, which would involve partial vertical integration, is a joint venture, like those allowed under the Public Utility Regulatory Policy Act (PURPA) whereby an electric utility and a heat user become fifty-fifty partners in a cogeneration project. Although this might attenuate the hold-up problems in both markets problems, such as 'sweetheart' deals, still remain.[16]

One reason why the traditionally vertically integrated solutions may not work is that utilities have not been interested in using cogeneration to produce electricity, in cases where both the heat and the electricity were regulated. It would be entering a new (but related) business which was subject to RoR regulation just like its existing business. However, the new business of cogeneration would involve additional risks compared to its existing business of electricity generation. These would stem from the transactions-specific investments that would have to be made in the heat facilities. For example, a utility owning a cogeneration facility which sold heat to a plant requiring heat for its processes would be subject to hold-up and expropriation of the quasi-rents but not exactly along the lines of Klein, Crawford and Alchian (1978). In the case where electricity and heat are both regulated, the potential for hold-up is attenuated. The heat user cannot simply just threaten to drop out as in the Klein–Crawford–Alchian analysis, because it has the regulator to contend with. It still has to make this threat but it has to negotiate the price reduction through the regulator. This may reduce the effect of such threats because of the transactions costs of working through a powerful intermediary, the regulator. In view of these extra risks of the new business the utility would have little incentive to go into the business unless a higher allowed rate of return were offered by the regulator on the cogeneration project.

Allowing the sale of heat to be unregulated, however, raises additional problems with this type of governance structure: the utility may be induced to invest in inappropriate cogeneration technologies. Since the utility is partially sheltered from costs in electricity production by the rate of return regulation, the utility will choose to use a production process which produces heat efficiently and electricity less efficiently.

This is shown in Crew and Crocker (1985b), utilising a simple model in which a utility can invest in two types of cogeneration capital, K_1 and K_2. Each type produces both heat (H) and electricity (E), but K_1 produces electricity better than heat so that $\partial E/\partial K_1 > \partial E/\partial K_2 > 0$. Similarly, K_2 is more efficient in the production of heat: $\partial H/\partial K_2 > \partial H/\partial K_1 > 0$. When the utility chooses its capital mix for the cogeneration facility, we find that:

1. The Pareto optimal mix of capital consists of both K_1 and K_2;
2. a rate of return regulated utility which is exogenously precluded from selling heat invests only in the electricity intensive technology K_1 (which is the 'correct' choice under the circumstances, although the amount of investment is less than optimal); and
3. a rate-of-return regulated utility which is allowed to sell heat in an unregulated market invests entirely in the heat intensive capital K_2, producing electricity inefficiently (to the detriment of the electricity customers).

As a consequence, a utility which is allowed to sell heat in an unregulated market may distort its investment in an attempt to maximise the unregulated profits (by producing heat as cheaply as possible) while being protected (by rate-of-return regulation) from the increased costs incurred in the production of electricity. Although downstream vertical integration may eliminate the hold-up problem between the utility and the cogenerator, it causes inefficient investment in cogeneration facilities. This is an example of the tar baby effect: regulation of one aspect of a firm's business may induce distortions in other areas, which require regulation to correct.

Other solutions such as joint ventures still allow the same kind of distortions. In addition, the utility might undertake a sweetheart deal on the purchase of the electricity so as to obtain its share of the profits sheltered from regulation. One remedy for this might be more detailed regulation, leading again to a tar baby effect.

Other solutions like independent ownership of the cogeneration facilities would present other kinds of hold-up problems. For example, the utility might attempt to purchase the power at less than its value. This may be achievable because of the utility's monopoly power and the hold-up potential. Even where the cogenerator used the power generated in his own production processes he would be subject to hold up for back-up power.

It is because of such problems that actions by regulators, like

PURPA, were bound to run into difficulties. PURPA and state regulations promoting cogeneration have, in effect, made subsidies for cogeneration possible, and as a result created opportunities for rent seekers. The results are likely to be excessive amounts of cogeneration, the wrong mix of cogeneration technologies, excessive production by cogenerators when the power can be produced by the grid at lower cost, and increased regulatory problems of control, as utilities take advantage of the potential for sweetheart deals provided.[17] This may lead eventually to concern on the part of regulators that cogeneration joint ventures are being subsidised by the rate payers.[18]

The conclusions we draw from this are somewhat negative on the role of extending regulation. It seems that regulation begets additional regulation of increasingly questionable value. This is a particular problem where regulated industry interfaces directly with unregulated industry and where parts of a business are subject to regulation and parts are not. It seems that it is very difficult to have regulation and competition prevailing in the same industry. The fundamental question here is how to provide a hospitable environment for competitive entry, where efficient, without undermining the overall viability of the socially necessary electricity supply industry. Precisely the same problem is becoming increasingly important in the case of telecommunications to which we will now turn.

9 Telecommunications

Telecommunications has just been through the greatest corporate reorganisation in the history of US business. In view of the rate and extent of such changes we will have great difficulty in the course of one chapter in covering more than a few issues, let alone all of the current concerns. Accordingly our emphasis will be on what we judge to be the important underlying principles and selected problems of interest rather than attempting to provide a comprehensive discussion. Section 1 will present a brief background sketch of the development of the US telecommunications industry in its current form, including aspects of its technology. Section 2 will examine the institutional framework within which the pricing structure of the industry functions, including the role of peak-load pricing, as well as touching on contributions to such important issues as sustainability and cross subsidisation that have received considerable attention in the debate on the structure of the industry. Section 3 develops the background of Section 2 and provides a simple model of optimal pricing for a telephone operating company. Finally Section 4 will examine some of the major problems confronting the industry, especially the problems of regulation in an industry where competition is becoming increasingly significant.

9.1 BACKGROUND

Like electricity, telecommunications is a rather new industry that originated with the famous inventions of Alexander Graham Bell in 1876. Progress was rapid from there thanks to the organising genius of Theodore Vail who became manager of the Bell Telephone Company in 1878. He subsequently became President of the American Telephone and Telegraph Company in 1885, resigning in 1887. Vail returned to the industry in 1907 as President and brought about the structure of the industry that essentially survived until 1984. Out of Vail's efforts grew the largest company in the USA and a telephone system that was second to none in the world. Vail's company AT&T, after the consent decree of 1956, owned its Long Lines Department, eighteen wholly-owned Bell operating companies (BOCs), four majority-owned BOCs, Western Electric (the equipment manufacturing company), and Bell Laboratories. The 1956 consent decree prohibited AT&T or its subsidiaries from selling anything that was not tariffed (regulated). Arising out of the decree AT&T divested itself of its controlling interests in Bell Canada and Northern Electric Company, the equipment manufacturer. Until 1984 this organisation, the Bell System, provided over 80 per cent of the telephones in the USA and their customers originated more than 90 per cent of the calls made.

Because of a number of factors such as technological change, the pricing structure of the industry and a suit brought by the Justice Department in 1974, the Bell System was subject to numerous attacks culminating in the Divestiture by AT&T of the BOCs on 1 January 1984. A key issue in these developments was the cross-subsidisation of local service by long-distance service. The reasons for this had been primarily historical. Technological change had been more pronounced in long distance than it had been in local service. As a result, cost had fallen dramatically in real terms. Part of this cost reduction had resulted in a fall in the price of long-distance calls, but much of it had apparently been used to cross-subsidise local service.[1] In addition to pricing long distance above cost, long distance was – and still is – priced on the basis of a nationwide average based upon distance between points called. Thus, high density routes such as between New York and Chicago are priced at the same rate as sparse routes over the same distance. Modern microwave and other technological developments mean that there are scale economies in supplying high density routes. The effect of this structure of cross subsidy with prices priced above cost in some markets was to attract potential entrants, which the system resisted and which in part prompted the 1974 anti-trust suit and similar legal actions by competitors.[2] The entry of competitors into these highly profitable markets threatened the whole operation of the system. It brought forth the Bell system's counter-charge of cream-skinning as AT&T attempted to justify its position. Various efforts were made to reduce the impact of competition, including bulk rates to large customers through tariffs such as WATS (Wide Area Telephone Service) and private line services. However, the competition grew stronger and the anti-trust suit did not go away. Accordingly, on 8 January 1982 AT&T and the Justice Department agreed upon terms to settle the anti-trust suit with both agreeing to seek a modification of the 1956 consent decree. The settlement involved a radical restructuring of the industry and the greatest corporate divestiture of all time.

Under the terms of the resulting modified final judgement, Judge

Harold Greene approved the terms of the agreement reached. AT&T divested itself of the BOCs, which have now been reorganised into seven regional holding companies (ROCs). The regional companies are precluded from entering long-distance communications. Their territories are divided into 'local access and transport areas', (LATAs) within which they provide service. They are not allowed to provide service outside of these areas; such service is provided by long-distance carriers, principally AT&T. ROCs are allowed to retain the Yellow Pages and to market terminal equipment. Under the terms of Judge Greene's line-of-business order the ROCs are allowed to enter unregulated business ventures as long as the net revenues from these operations do not exceed 10 per cent of their total estimated net revenues.[3] AT&T retained ownership of its Western Electric, Bell Laboratories and Long Lines Department and long-distance facilities of divested BOCs to provide long-distance service, including international service,[4] AT&T is now free to enter unregulated businesses such as computers and information systems and is currently doing so. However, the bulk[5] of its business, long-distance telecommunications, remains currently regulated. How long this will be the case and the appropriate form of regulating a business which has both monopoly and competitive parts are controversial and open questions which we will discuss in detail below.

One of the most important consequence of the AT&T divestiture was the vertical disintegration of long-distance and local telephone service. To understand this, we briefly review the basic technological structure of the industry (see Figure 9.1). Local service, provided by the BOCs, consists, put in highly simplistic terms, of the cables between subscribers and the central office where calls can be switched between subscribers within a central office or be switched to trunks which connect different offices, or be switched to any of several long-distance carriers. The switching functions can be performed by all kinds of equipment, from the latest sophisticated digital equipment to some very old electro-mechanical equipment. When a call reaches a long-distance carrier, it is then transmitted (using cable, microwave or other means) to another local operating company or to another LATA within the same company. This local operating company then completes the call. Prior to divestiture this process was similar to what happened when a call originated in and terminated in the territories of non-Bell companies.

With reference to Figure 9.1, we can identify the following types of service or calls within the national network:

Local loop calls:	Two subscribers connected to the same central office (e.g. A calls B).
Intra-LATA calls:	Two subscribers in the same LATA, but connected to different Central Offices (e.g. A calls C).
Inter-LATA calls:	Two subscribers in different LATAs served by local companies and some long-distance carrier (e.g. A calls E). In this case, the long-distance (inter-LATA) portion of the call can be served by any of several competing carriers, not least AT&T.
Bypass lines:	Direct access to long-distance carriers, bypassing the local loop at one or both ends, can further complicate the above services.

Two key issues are associated with the current partially deregulated telecommunications environment in the USA: *first*, efficient pricing for the local network, including long-distance carrier access, to allow recovery of the large fixed costs associated with the local network; *second*, and related, the extent to which efficient prices are also sustainable or whether entry restrictions are required. These issues will be the primary concerns of this chapter.

9.2 SELECTED ISSUES IN THE PRICING OF TELECOMMUNICATIONS

In this and the next section we are going to be concerned primarily with the pricing problem of the regulated local telephone operating company. We will touch on the pricing policies of long-distance carriers, but, in view of the oligopolistic nature of this part of the industry, its potential and actual deregulation, and the fact that its pricing structure is, in part, a derivative of the pricing policy of local companies, the pricing of inter-LATA toll will not be our prime concern. Rather we concentrate on local access/usage. The local company has five main products: local access, local usage, intra-LATA toll, long distance (principally inter-LATA) access, and other services, some of which are regulated like time, while others are not, such as the Yellow Pages.

The pricing of telephone service is complicated by the joint costs (see Figure 9.1) arising among various services, especially between local and long distance. The price charged for local usage and access has generally been set at well below the 'stand-alone' cost of providing

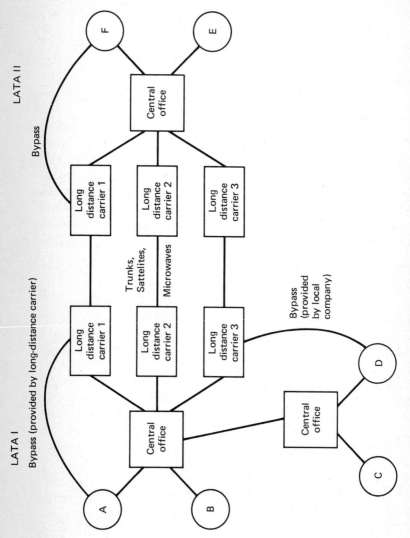

Figure 9.1 Simplified telecommunications networks

this service, a significant fraction of such costs being the fixed cost of the local network. Such a policy is certainly not in itself inefficient. As the local loop is used to complete both long distance and local calls, it is unlikely that all the fixed costs of this local network would economically be allocated to local calls. Indeed, using the arguments developed in Part I and Part II, Ramsey optimal joint product pricing would call for both local and long distance to pay, the share for each depending on demand. In the past there has been a tendency for long distance's share of the burden of the local loop's costs to grow. Currently there is concern among local telephone companies that if more of the cost of the local loop is not placed upon local service then the largest long-distance users will build their own, cheaper facilities and bypass the local companies' facilities, leaving an even bigger burden for the local users and the remaining long-distance users to bear. We return to this issue below as it is one of the major problems facing the industry today. However, our concern for the moment is with describing the pricing structure for local access and usage because this exacerbates this very problem.

The pricing of local service

Local service consists primarily of local access and usage. Local access is the ability to make and receive calls of any kind, local, or long distance. Local access is a complementary good in that without it it is impossible to make or receive calls.[6]

Other services make up local service such as directory assistance and various information services like time and jokes. We will not discuss these beyond arguing that, except for directory assistance, such services should be priced at what the traffic can bear. The companies should be free to use their own business judgement in setting such prices. We are going to be solely concerned with the pricing of local access and use. The majority of local calls are priced on a flat rate basis. In economic theory this is the club principle at work.[7] For a flat monthly fee, subscribers may make calls unrestricted as to volume and duration in a designated local area. This is identified by a list of NNX codes to which the subscriber may dial without any charge for usage. The flat monthly fee charged is determined by the regulators and may be a function of the number of telephones to which the subscriber has access in his local area. The use of the club principle as a pricing policy is not common. A pub charges for beer by the drink. Grocers charge for food by the quantity and type purchased. Traditionally economists have argued that efficient pricing calls for pricing of individual units at marginal cost, which cannot be achieved by a club. This is not to say that the club principle is always inefficient. For example, if demand were completely inelastic or if the transactions cost of metering required for unit charging were prohibitively costly or if marginal costs were zero, then the club principle would be optimal. Traditionally the demand for local service has been perceived as very inelastic, but not completely inelastic, the costs of metering have been high and at least short-run marginal costs have been close to zero. In such cases, then, it is possible that the benefits of measurement outweighed their costs, as explained in detail in Crew and Dansby (1982), so that telephone companies could argue the efficiency of flat-rate pricing. However, with the introduction of new electronic central office equipment the costs of measurement have fallen dramatically, making it efficient to replace flat-rate pricing with local measured service (LMS), i.e. pricing according to actual time patterns of use. However, LMS may be seen by subscribers as a rate increase in disguise. In addition, the popularity of flat-rate pricing (perhaps because it relieves the customer of the need to worry about his consumption) and the low price charged for local service has made it very difficult for telephone companies to obtain approval for LMS. This is in sharp contrast to European experience where measurement is more or less universal.

To provide a more formal basis for this discussion, consider the following simple model illustrating the comparison between LMS and flat-rate structures (see Crew and Dansby (1982) and Mitchell (1978)). Under flat rate the marginal price of incremental usage is zero and subscribers will consume OB in Figure 9.2. We now model the gains from LMS as the cost savings from producing the reduced output, i.e. DEBC. The losses from LMS are the metering costs, PFDG, plus the decrease in consumer's surplus, FCB, foregone as a result of the reduced consumption induced by raising the price of usage from O to P. Where measuring costs have been small the net benefit function would be expected to increase as a result of LMS provided elasticities were not too low. Table 9.1 gives a simple example to illustrate the effects on net benefits of employing LMS instead of flat rate. Based upon a range of figures for elasticity (η), marginal costs (mc) and metering costs (Mec) the net benefit of local measured service is computed for an 'average' customer. Following the approach of the industry we distinguish between minutes of use and 'set-up'.

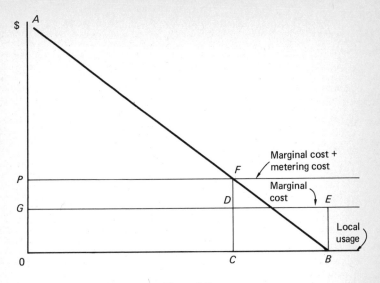

Figure 9.2

According to industry cost studies the marginal costs of setting up a call are higher than the marginal costs of continuing the call once the call has been set up. Thus we distinguish between marginal costs for the first minute, which include set-up costs, and the marginal costs for additional minutes. Likewise on the demand side additional minutes and set-ups are treated as two separate but complementary goods, because set-ups have to be purchased to allow the subscriber to purchase additional minutes of use. The demand for set-ups is similarly affected by the price of minutes of usage. Such interactions are ignored in the simple analysis of Table 9.1.

Other complexities ignored in Table 9.1 are peak load effects. As the peak determines the amount of capacity, the use of time-of-day rates would reduce what is known in the industry as 'the busy hour' and save additional costs. In this event the benefits of LMS would be increased, and a further effect would be that of improving utilisation at other times.[8] Plans for measured service call for peak-load pricing in varying degrees. Thus the figures in Table 9.1 are likely to be close to a lower bound on the efficiency gains from LMS.

Given the industry's claim that the stand-alone cost of providing

Table 9.1 Difference in net benefit for various elasticities and costs

	η	mc	meter cost	FR	LMS
Minutes	−0.1	$0.010	$0.000	679.4585	623.3437
Calls	−0.1	$0.020	$0.001	169.8646	147.8757
Net benefit					$0.280
	η	mc	meter cost	FR	LMS
Minutes	−0.2	$0.010	$0.000	679.2231	572.1134
Calls	−0.2	$0.020	$0.001	170.2385	129.0167
Net benefit					$0.538
	η	mc	meter cost	FR	LMS
Minutes	−0.2	$0.020	$0.000	679.2231	572.1134
Calls	−0.2	$0.040	$0.001	170.2385	129.0167
Net benefit					$2.022
	η	mc	meter cost	FR	LMS
Minutes	−0.01	$0.020	$0.000	421.7647	418.1281
Calls	−0.01	$0.040	$0.001	105.4411	103.9895
Net benefit					$0.069

local service is generally in the region of between $20 and $35 per line per month the gains from LMS as shown in Table 9.1 seem small by comparison. This arises for a number of reasons. Perhaps the most important of these is the way the industry allocates costs, which is as traffic-sensitive (TS) or non-traffic sensitive (NTS). The bulk of the costs of local service are considered non-traffic sensitive. The argument is that a subscriber requires a pair of wires that connect his equipment to the central office where switching of calls takes place. This wire pair (or to be precise the connection between the terminal equipment and the central office – known in the busines as the *customer loop* or *local loop*) is specific to the subscriber. Unlike the central office equipment, it cannot be used by other subscribers when he is not using it. It is customer-specific in nature. Unlike central office plant and trunks which connect central offices, this plant is, at least at first sight, not sensitive to increases in the volume of traffic. Hence, the industry argues that it is non-traffic sensitive and therefore is not included in the industry's definition and estimates of marginal costs. However, as we model below and as is also intuitively clear, as traffic increases consumers will demand more lines to ameliorate congestion in periods of high usage. This kind of congestion can only be reduced by adding further lines. These additional lines, and related switching costs, are clearly traffic sensitive. Thus, there is case for including some element of what the industry calls the NTS plant in long-run marginal cost.

Another reason for including most, if not all, of the local loop costs as part of the traffic-sensitive costs stems from the changing nature of technology. The local loop now may be something more complicated than just a dedicated pair of wires from the subscriber and the central office. The trend according to Carne (1984, p. 174) is 'to shorten loop lengths by moving switching closer to the customer'. Advances in digital technology which make possible the carrying on one line of more than one message simultaneously provides further arguments for treating a larger proportion of costs as traffic-sensitive, which would further increase the gains from introducing local measured service.

There may be other reasons for adopting LMS apart from strict efficiency gains. If the industry is becoming competitive, it needs the flexibility in its pricing that LMS offers. Because pricing on a club basis results in higher costs it may find itself at a disadvantage with competitors. Similarly it may find that revenues from its other services are reduced and it needs LMS to help it recover additional revenues. Alternatively it may decide that raising revenue through usage is preferable to raising the flat rate charge because the latter would presumably have a greater impact on the demand for access. Without a telephone – without access – you cannot make or receive any calls. The more people on the network the more valuable it is to be on the network.[9] Thus companies may wish to collect less from customers for accessing the network than for local usage so as to encourage maximum subscription to the network. Without LMS this option is not available to them.

The pricing of long distance

Long distance refers to all calls that are not local. These include calls between two LATAs (inter-LATA) and calls within a LATA (intra-LATA). The local companies are excluded from the former but, of course, do provide the vast majority of intra-LATA tolls. The inter-LATA carriers may enter this market, however, and if local companies continue the practice of pricing considerably in excess of marginal cost for such calls, such entry will certainly be attracted. However, the entry may not be universal. Many intra-LATA toll routes are low-density routes, and the entrant will only be interested in the high-density routes. Thus if prices are averaged, being a function only of distance, then entry will occur only on a selective basis with the entrants 'skimming the cream'. Where this is a problem companies will have to obtain relief from regulators to allow them to depart from average pricing and selectively lower rates on high-density routes. Alternatively some companies may seek regulatory sanctions to give them a monopoly on all intra-LATA toll calls. To do this, however, would be very much against the stated policy that the industry is to become more competitive. If technological change continues rapidly, it may be that the extent of scale economies enjoyed by the local companies will decline anyway. Moreover it might be increasingly difficult to enforce such restrictions, particularly if technological change makes the efficient scale of operations smaller.[10] The problem is one to which we will return in Section 3 where we discuss the difficulty of mixing regulation with a firm and an industry that are partially deregulated.

Toll calls are usually priced at a rate per minute for dialled calls, with operator services, such as person-to-person attracting a surcharge. Typically the first minute is charged at a higher rate than subsequent minutes presumably reflecting the extra costs of switching primarily to set up the call. The charges vary according to time of day. Most carriers on inter-LATA calls follow AT&T's (peak-load pricing) discount structure which allows a 40 per cent discount for calls between 5.00pm and 11.00pm except for Saturday. A 60 per cent discount is allowed between 11.00pm on a Friday and 5.00pm on a Saturday. The use of a discount structure of this kind is certainly in line with the discussion of Part II. However, we cannot say whether the discount structure is optimal, whether in fact the periods are appropriate or the discounts set at the appropriate percentages. Almost certainly the day period is appropriate if only one day period is to be used. It is conceivable that there should be a different rate, say, for morning than afternoon.[11] However, given our lack of information on this we are not in a position to argue for a change in this now. Competition may encourage competitors to experiment with different discount structures and this may be the best way of finding the optimum, although the recent tendency has been for other common carriers to converge to the AT&T time-of-day discount structure. The night rates may be too high at the moment. However, because of the price AT&T currently has to pay for access there may be little that it can do about this, as we now discuss.

Pricing of access to long-distance companies

When an inter-LATA call is made it uses facilities belonging to local companies to complete the call.[12] The local companies are compensated for the use of these from two sources, from their customers and from the long-distance carriers. Their customers pay Customer Access Line Charges (CALC). This is a charge per line of $1 a month in the case of residence and single-line users, and between $4 and $6 a month in the case of multi-line business users. The long distance carrier also compensates the local company for the use of these facilities. Currently AT&T pays a different rate from the rate paid by other carriers, the reason being that the access provided is different in each case, as we discuss below. Where both are provided with 'equal access', both would pay the same rate.

Let us look at an example where AT&T is used to make a call between Newark, NJ and San Francisco. AT&T pays around 9 cents for the use of the local carrier's facilities to take the call to the 'point of presence', AT&T's switch. It also pays around 9 cents for the use of the other local company's facilities when it completes the call in San Francisco. If the call is not completed it still would have to pay a reduced charge for one minute of use because it used the facilities of the local company in originating the call.[13] This rate per minute is considerably in excess of what local companies get per minute of use for local service even where LMS is in operation. It also does not vary according to time of day, placing a floor on the discounts AT&T might be able to offer for calls made at night.

The rate paid by other carriers is considerably less than that paid by AT&T. They also have different, and inferior, access arrangements. Their access is provided by means of lines which they rent from the local company. Their subscribers have to call an access number and then they can use their carrier's network. These lines are rented on a flat-rate basis with no charge being made to the long-distance carrier for minutes of use. Given assumed average monthly usage of 9000 minutes per line the price paid per minute is 3.3 cents at the originating end of the call and somewhat more than this at the terminating end of the call.[14]

The current system with different price structures for AT&T and other carriers is scheduled to change, when equal access is available. This would give all long-distance carriers the same access as AT&T is currently enjoying. However, competition is likely to mean that this system cannot survive, because this charge of about 18 cents per minute is in excess of cost, as evidenced by actual bypass already and a growing potential for further bypass. Moreover part of these charges are ear-marked to subsidise rural telecommunications implying further evidence of price above cost. In view of the existence of prices above costs, competition will drive carriers to find alternatives to bypass the local companies. Where a carrier can obtain local access by building his own access facility from say a large customer to his switch at lower cost than the amount charged by the local company, it will be in his interest to do so or else a competitor may come in and offer service to his customer at more attractive rates. Alternatively he may rent a private line from the local company, at lower rates. In the first instance the local company has completely lost the business, while in the second instance he has lost part of the revenue.

There are other consequences of the kind of bypass that takes place. In the case of bypass where the local company's facilities are still used, the effect is that the local company gets less. This is evidence of possible over-pricing currently and continued cross-subsidisation by long distance of local. The other kind of bypass, where the local company's facilities are displaced by ones built by the long-distance carrier, has other problems. The costs of providing access this way may exceed the local company's cost of providing access. The problem is that the local company is regulated and has to make charges based upon the tariff for access. If this is set too high, the long-distance carrier may be encouraged to bypass even though his costs exceed those of the local company. There are a number of reasons for believing that this might be the case, principally depreciation and capital recovery policies under RoR regulation.

Traditionally regulated utilities have recovered their capital by means of depreciation schedules that have very long lives. As long as technology changed slowly, the fact that the facilities could be made to last for a long time with relatively low maintenance costs meant that this policy did not present major problems. However, because of technological change the economic life of certain facilities, particularly central-office switching, has declined substantially. The depreciation schedules have not kept up with this and, as a result, there is a large amount of capital that is unrecovered. Assets are valued on the books of companies far in excess of their actual value. The difference between the actual value and the value shown on the books is called the 'depreciation reserve deficiency'. Were this just a book-keeping matter there would not be a major problem. In a competitive industry then this would not be a problem. However, because the industry is regulated the reserve deficiency is a major problem because the value of the plant on the books actually determines the rates under RoR regulation.

Let us briefly examine how the reserve deficiency might encourage uneconomic bypass under regulation. Recalling equation (5.1) we note that the company's revenue and therefore its prices are based upon the book value of its rate base less accrued depreciation. If the accrued depreciation is less than the economic or real depreciation then the rate base and therefore the rates will be higher. However, competitors will base their decisions on their own actual cost. This will be unaffected by the inadequate past capital recovery since they are building from new. It may be lower than the figure used by the regulated firm because the latter includes unrecovered depreciation. Thus the local companies could be bypassed not because their real costs were excessive but because of the effects of regulation. Resolving this problem would require either that the local companies write off some of the reserve deficiency or that they be permitted to recover capital more quickly before competitive entry increases. The argument for this proposal is based upon equity. The reserve deficiency was built up during a period when the company's monopoly looked assured by the regulatory process, and the problem of slow capital recovery did not seem a major one. When the rules were changed the depreciation schedules were not changed accordingly. On efficiency grounds the argument in favour would be that this would be what would efficiently happen if the local companies were unregulated.

The issues of sustainability and cross-subsidy arise with regard to bypass. Many have argued that the current price structure for inter-exchange access is not sustainable, and hence entry (bypass) will result. Where bypass takes place the local telephone company will find that it has to spread its fixed costs over smaller customer and output base. The result will be a rise in the rate for local service. If the bypass is uneconomic, long-distance rates will fall by less, maybe considerably less, than the local rates increase. The challenge, and from the point of view of economic theory it may not be the major challenge, is to design rates for inter-exchange access that do not encourage uneconomic bypass. The real challenge may be to convince regulators to implement policies that allow the regulated BOCs the flexibility to adopt efficient pricing policies. We will now outline the main road signs to efficient pricing.

Currently there is an incentive to bypass the local telephone companies because long-distance carriers can provide access to some of their customers at lower cost than the rates being charged to them. There seems to be little doubt that if there is bypass the losses of revenue to the local companies will far exceed the long-run cost savings that the companies will achieve as a result of being able to redesign their networks for less traffic. Indeed, as we argued in the previous section, the prices paid for access, at least by AT&T, far exceed the costs of providing the service. Competitive bypass will drive down access charges to marginal cost. Price will be based upon the local company's estimate of the costs to the long-distance carrier of providing access directly, or from an alternative source. For the company this estimate may be a ceiling on the price that it can charge the carriers. The carrier may prefer to provide its own facilities to the extent that it considers the ownership and direct control of them an advantage. There is also a transaction-specific investment problem. Once the carrier has installed its own facilities its short-run marginal costs, which are below its long-run marginal cost, become the price which the local carrier must charge to be competitive. In addition there may be some instances when the long-distance carrier can bypass at very low cost in which case bypass would be efficient and the local operating company would be better off allowing bypass rather than trying to compete. In general whether a local company should prevent bypass depends on the net revenue effect on the company of the bypass and considerations of the effect of the complementary nature of access and usage.[15] For the issue of competitive bypass it is a matter of employing the burden test (Zajac 1978) to determine how the company responds. The burden test is a test for cross subsidy. It aims at answering the question, 'Is the company better off as a result of no longer providing a service?' If the answer is yes then the argument is that the service was a burden on the rest of the ratepayers and therefore was being cross-subsidised by other services. The test might apply to bypass by taking the company's estimate of the price needed to prevent bypass and using this to provide the estimate of the revenue for this service. If the service were discontinued, then this would be the revenue loss. If this exceeded the long-run incremental costs of not providing this service on the local company's network, then bypass would be uneconomic and the local company should prevent bypass by pricing at a level, if necessary, down to a long-run incremental cost.

How the company would price for access by long-distance carriers depends on whether transactions-specific investments are involved or not. It would normally be in the company's interest not to use transaction-specific investments because of the risks of hold-up. Normally the service will be supplied by using facilities that are used to supply other carriers, local customers, and intra-LATA toll customers. In this event the prices should reflect the peak load characteristics and would therefore incorporate time-of-day discounts. This would encourage improved utilisation of the network and would encourage the long-distance carriers to offer even bigger off-peak discounts.

Such changes would mean that local service would cost more. This would be mitigated partially by introducing LMS. However, a major problem would still remain of recovering additional revenue. Moreover the local service would still be regulated and would still offer, at least in large sections of a company's territory, more potential for monopoly power than that offered by long-distance access. Other problems that remain would be how regulators might be able to subsidise local access and rural telecommunications. Here the solution may be to have competitive prices but by general taxation subsidise rural service. The problem with this would be the usual allocative and transaction cost inefficiencies of taxation. These inefficiencies would clearly have to be compared to those of the present system of cross-subsidies.

9.3 A SIMPLE PRICING MODEL FOR A LOCAL REGULATED TELEPHONE OPERATING COMPANY

The optimal pricing policy for a local telephone company would draw on the rules for Ramsey optimal pricing developed in Part I and peak load pricing developed in Part II. The appropriate model is the multiproduct pricing problem with peak loads. The products would be access lines, local usage, toll and inter-LATA access. However, to keep our model simple we are only going to be concerned with the problem of pricing two product – local access and usage – and we are not going to deal with peak-load pricing aspects. Thus we make the simplifying assumption that the company is selling only two (complementary) products, access and usage. In addition, we assume that there exists only one class of customers, multi-line users. We are ignoring the problem of small users, i.e. users of a single line, or a very small number of lines, such as residential and small business consumers. Our attention is confined to the problem of large users such as

business, universities, hospitals, etc. We discuss the generalisation of
this model to peak loads and small consumers below.

Our model is a variant of the preference based model of welfare-
optimal pricing presented in Chapter 2. We seek prices for the joint
good, call-minutes (local measured service) and lines (access). To
simplify the presentation, we assume that all consumers (t ∈ T) have
identical preferences of the form

$$U(x_1, x_2, m) = v(x_1, x_2 - x_1) + m, \tag{9.1}$$

where m is a numeraire commodity, x_1 represents minutes of calls
(made or received) in a typical period (e.g. a day) and x_2 represents the
number of access lines (expressed in 24×60 minutes) purchased by
the consumer. We assume that both x_1 and x_2 are continuous
variables. This corresponds to a business consumer where x_2 is large
enough to be treated as a continuous variable.

The interpretation of $v(x_1, x_2 - x_1)$ in 9.1 is the following. The
consumer values both calls x_1 and lack congestion $x_2 - x_1$. We assume
the following conditions on the partial derivatives of v:

$$v_1 > 0, \ v_2 > 0, \ v_{11} < 0, \ v_{22} < 0, \ v_{12} > 0, \ v_{11}v_{22} - v_{12}^2 > 0. \tag{9.2}$$

In particular, v is concave and $v_{12} > 0$ implies that calls and lack of
congestion are complementary goods.

We can convert the above preference representation into that of
equation (2.17) by defining (for each identical consumer t ∈ T)

$$V(\mathbf{x}, t) = v(x_1, x_2 - x_1). \tag{9.3}$$

Note that V inherits the concavity of v. Given $\mathbf{P} = (P_1, P_2)$, the
consumer choice problem is

$$\underset{x_1 \leqslant x_2}{\text{Max}} \ [V(\mathbf{x}, t) - \mathbf{Px}], \qquad t \in T \tag{9.4}$$

which we assume has an interior solution $0 < x_1 < x_2$. (Given (9.2), an
interior solution obtains if $v(z, 0) = v(0, z) = 0$ for all $z \in R$, a reasonable
assumption.) This leads to demand functions $\mathbf{x}(\mathbf{P})$ satisfying from (9.3)

$$v_1(x_1, x_2 - x_1) - v_2(x_1, x_2 - x_1) = P_1; \quad v_2(x_1, x_2 - x_1) = P_2 \tag{9.5}$$

$$\frac{\partial x_1}{\partial P_1} = \frac{v_{22}}{\Gamma}; \ \frac{\partial x_1}{\partial P_2} = \frac{\partial x_2}{\partial P_1} = \frac{v_{22} - v_{12}}{\Gamma}; \ \frac{\partial x_2}{\partial P_2} = \frac{v_{11} - 2v_{12} + v_{22}}{\Gamma},$$

(9.6)

all of which are negative since $\Gamma = v_{11}v_{22} - v_{12}^2 > 0$ by (9.2).

Now denote the cost of service by $C(X)$ where $X(p) = Nx(p)$, N being the number of consumers. Applying the results of Chapter 2 (see especially equation (2.26)) it follows that $P_1 - C_1$ has the opposite sign of

$$\eta_{22} - \frac{R_2}{R_1}\eta_{21} = \left(\frac{P_2}{X_2}\frac{\partial X_2}{\partial P_2} - \frac{P_2 X_2}{P_1 X_1}\frac{P_1}{X_2}\frac{\partial X_2}{\partial P_1}\right) =$$

$$\left(\frac{P_2}{X_2}\frac{\partial X_2}{\partial P_2} - \frac{X_2}{X_1}\frac{\partial X_2}{\partial P_1}\right)$$

(9.7)

From (9.6) we can rewrite (9.7) as

$$\eta_{22} - \frac{R_2}{R_1}\eta_{21} = \frac{P_2}{X_2\Gamma}\left[(v_{11} - v_{12}) + \left(1 - \frac{X_2}{X_1}\right)(v_{22} - v_{12})\right]$$

(9.8)

where we have abbreviated $v_{ij}(x_1, x_2 - x_1) = v_{ij}$. From this and (9.2), $P_1 < C_1$ (i.e. $\eta_{22} > \frac{R_2}{R_1}\eta_{21}$) if X_2/X_1 is sufficiently large. Similarly, $P_2 - C_2$ has the opposite sign of

$$\eta_{11} - \frac{R_1}{R_2}\eta_{12} = \left(\frac{P_1}{X_1\Gamma}\left[v_{22}\left(1 - \frac{X_1}{X_2}\right) + v_{12}\frac{X_1}{X_2}\right]\right),$$

(9.9)

which, from (9.2), shows that $p < C_2$ if $x_1/x_2 = X_1/X_2$ is sufficiently large. Solving (9.8) and (9.9) for the values r_1 and r_2 of X_1/X_2 at which (9.3) and (9.9) equal zero, we obtain the qualitative behaviour shown in Figure 9.3 below for the optimal price margins. We note that the cross-over points r_1, r_1 satisfy $r_1 < r_2$ since

$$r_1 = \frac{v_{22} - v_{12}}{v_{22} - 2v_{12} + v_{12}}$$

(9.10)

$$r_2 = \frac{v_{22}}{v_{22} - v_{12}}$$

(9.11)

and therefore (since the denominators of (9.10)–(9.11) are both negative), $r_2 - r_1$ has the sign of $v_{11}v_{22} - v_{12}^2 > 0$ (by (9.2)). Thus, $r_1 < r_2$ as shown in Figure 9.3.

Of course, Figure 9.3 leaves open the question, under what circumstances will X_1/X_2 lie in the three regions of interest:

$B_1: [0, r_1):$ $P_1 < C_1,\ P_2 > C_2,$

$B_2: (r_1, r_2]:$ $P_1 \geqslant C_1,\ P_2 \geqslant C_2,$

$B_3: [r_2, 1]:$ $P_1 > C_1,\ P_2 < C_2.$

We do not pursue this in detail here, but simply remark that manipulation of (9.10)–(9.11) shows that B_1 obtains when

$$\frac{X_2 - X_1}{X_1} = \frac{x_2 - x_1}{x_1} > \frac{v_{11} - v_{12}}{v_{22} - v_{12}} > \frac{v_{12}}{-v_{22}} \tag{9.12}$$

and B_2 obtains when

$$\frac{X_2 - X_1}{X_1} = \frac{x_2 - x_1}{x_1} > \frac{v_{12}}{-v_{22}} \tag{9.13}$$

and otherwise B_3 obtains.

Example: A simple example illustrates the above points. Suppose $v(x,y)$ in (9.1) is specified as

$$v(x,y) = \sqrt{x}\,[1 + \log(1 + y)], \tag{9.14}$$

so that $x = x_1$, and $y = x_2 - x_1$. Then v is concave, increasing with $v_{12} > 0$ as desired. Assume that the number of consumers $N = 1000$ and that the cost function $C(X) = C_1 X_1 + C_2 X_2 + F$. Then, it can be verified from the above that the following are Ramsey optimal solutions for the parameters specified (where k is the Ramsey number of (2.26)).

As can be seen from Table 9.2, when the cost of access is high relative to usage cost, access should be priced below marginal cost. As access cost decreases relative to usage, both goods should be priced above marginal cost. (If access were cheap enough, usage could presumably be priced below marginal cost.) This is in line with the intuition embodied in the pricing practices of King Gillette and Theodore Vail.

In Chapter 2 we showed that Ramsey-optimal prices could be below marginal cost in the case of complementary products. Similarly here, we have shown by means of a more microscopic examination of

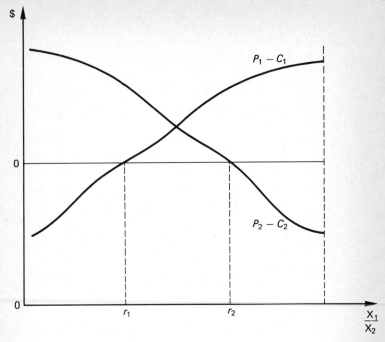

Figure 9.3

Table 9.2   Illustrative Ramsey solutions

	Parameters			Ramsey solution values			
C_1	C_2	F	k	P_1	P_2	X_1	X_2
0.140	0.626	10	0.091	0.176	0.612	0.667	1.00
1.045	0.331	10	0.033	1.049	0.333	1.00	3.00

the underlying preferences, taking into account the congestion that can arise because of the relationship between access and usage, that access may, indeed, be optimally priced below marginal cost. While we have only analysed the case of large customers (where x_2 could be taken to be a continuous variable), the case of smaller customers (with indivisible demands for lines) should continue to correspond to the case of high access cost relative to usage cost, i.e. the case where access would be priced below marginal cost.

When peak loads are incorporated into the model, the peak and the shoulder around it would drive the demand for access. Thus, in a more complete model which included access and time-of-day pricing, the above results suggest that access might well be priced below marginal cost. Some products, for example, those supplied at the peak, would be priced above marginal cost, while others, such as off-peak offerings, would be priced at or below marginal cost. We are not concerned with the development of such a model here. Our main point is already clear; Ramsey rules for local telephone pricing may involve non-trivial departures from marginal cost.

9.4 PROBLEMS OF REGULATING TELECOMMUNICATIONS WITH PARTIAL DEREGULATION

It is clear from the discussion of Sections 1 and 2 that many of the problems facing the telecommunications industry arise from the simultaneous interaction of competition and regulation of the industry. In this section we will review the issue of regulation where some parts of the firm are unregulated or deregulated and other parts, the bulk of the business, are regulated. The problem occurs at two levels. AT&T is regulated while its long-distance competitors are not. The Regional Operating Companies are completely regulated although they do have the Yellow Pages and sales of terminal equipment and a waiver by Judge Greene to enter unregulated business on a limited scale. The unregulated parts of the regulated companies will almost certainly grow. This process will be encouraged by the uncertainties currently inherent in the regulatory structure of the industry. The companies do not know whether regulation will be modified and extended to deal with some of their problems or whether it will be removed. Moreover they do not know what form such regulation will take. Given the additional degrees of freedom provided by the potential to enter deregulated ventures, and the added benefits of diversification, it is likely that entry into unregulated fields will be attractive. However, entry by regulated firms into unregulated business presents regulators with fundamental problems as we now discuss.

The argument for continued regulation of AT&T is based upon the notion that without regulation, AT&T, because of its huge size and its first-mover advantages, would be able to crush fledgling competitors. This and the reduced rates for access are intended to give the competition a breathing space while they grow. The danger with this policy is that it may continue for a long time because the competition is unwilling or unable to face head-on competition from AT&T until AT&T's share of the market has fallen drastically. Phillips (1982) has argued that this kind of managed competition may become a permanent regulatory feature. If when regulation were relaxed AT&T really did turn out to have massive scale economies relative to the other companies and competed very hard, the other companies might scream for regulation as a means of attenuating the power of the dominant firm. If such demands for regulation were successful then the divestiture would not have brought the promised advantages of competition. Indeed it might have created a new and excessive regulatory apparatus and some of the benefits of natural monopoly may have been lost. While there are risks in such a policy, we would argue that an immediate and definite timetable be enacted into law much in the way it was done with the airlines and the Civil Aeronautics Board whereby regulation is abolished at a certain date in the future following a fixed transition process, lasting say, three years. During the transition period, AT&T would experience steadily reducing regulation. For example, the first year may be considered the last year of the current system. In the second year AT&T might be allowed freedom to change its prices in real terms by 5 per cent. In the third year it might be allowed to make changes of no more than 10 per cent. If it wished to make changes, either increases or decreases, above these levels it would be required to seek regulatory approval.

The situation with the ROCs and the role of regulation is more complex. Establishing a schedule for immediate deregulation is not likely to be feasible in this sector, however, because of the undoubted monopoly power still possessed by local operating companies in certain areas of their business, particularly in the area of residential service the area considered to be the main constituency for state regulatory bodies. In addition, these companies face a severe deficiency in their depreciation reserves. This is something that requires regulatory attention in the absence of immediate deregulation.[16] One approach might be to allow companies relief immediately so that they can write off a significant portion of the reserve deficiency and use an incentive based regulation scheme, such as C-K-S earlier, to set prices for an experimental five-year period. From the regulator's point of view some means of preventing the local user from being gouged is the foremost issue. Given this we will continue our remarks to some of the problems of regulating what are essentially partially deregulated firms.

In Chapter 8 we discussed some of the problems of regulating electric utilities where they were involved in ownership of non-regulated cogeneration companies. Here, as explained in Crew and Crocker (1985), distortions in capital investment, in the nature of the technology employed, may affect the regulated firm with unregulated cogeneration interests. In the case of local telephone companies the problem of technology distortions may also arise but the main concern may be with other issues. A major concern of Judge Greene in his line-of-business opinion was that the ROCs might use their regulated business to enable them to undertake predatory pricing by cross subsidising competitive ventures from their regulated business. He raised the problem of allocation of common costs. This is a major potential regulatory problem. The regulated firm would have an incentive to undertake sweetheart deals with its unregulated subsidiaries. The deals might take the form of supplying the regulated subsidiaries with inputs produced by the regulated part at below cost, or they might involve the regulated operation purchasing services from the unregulated subsidiary at above cost or both. The opportunities might be considerable.

Combining regulated and unregulated business activities under the regulatory umbrella may also have deleterious effects on pricing in the monopoly sector. To see how this might happen, let us consider a simple model. Assume that the bypass market is unregulated and the telephone company competes in this market by setting up private lines. This activity competes with the telephone company's other inter-exchange carrier access service. We wish to understand the effects of using the combined capital if both market activities (private lines and carrier access) were used to define the rate base of a rate-of-return regulated company. This discussion extends the discussion of Averch–Johnson (1962, pp. 1057–59).

Let $X(p_1,p_2)$ and $Y(p_1,p_2)$ be demand for carrier access and private lines, with respective prices p_1 and p_2. If RoR regulation is applied across both markets, the company would face the following problem (see, e.g. the Averch–Johnson formulation section 6.1)

$$\text{Max } \pi(p_1,p_2,K_1,K_2) = (p_1 - b_1)X(p_1,p_2) + (p_2 - b_2)Y(p_1,p_2) - rK \tag{9.15}$$

$$\text{S.t. } \pi(p_1,p_2, K_1, K_2) \leqslant (s-r)K \tag{9.16}$$

$$h(X(p_1,p_2) + Y(p_1,p_2)) \leqslant K, \tag{9.17}$$

where we have assumed a proportional cost technology with variable costs b_1, b_2 respectively, capital cost r, and where we have scaled the outputs X and Y so that h represents the per unit capital cost for both outputs, i.e. $K_1 = hX$, $K_2 = hY$. Since at optimum (9.17) will hold as an equality, we can eliminate $K = h(X + Y)$ from (9.15)–(9.17) to obtain the equivalent formulation

$$\text{Max } \pi(p_1,p_2) = (p_1 - b_1 - hr)X + (p_2 - b_2 - hr)Y \tag{9.18}$$

subject to

$$\pi(p_1,p_2) \leqslant h(s - r)\left[(X(p_1,p_2) + Y(p_1,p_2))\right] \tag{9.19}$$

Suppose that the private line market (Y) is purely competitive in the sense that the competition can sell all it wishes at the competitive price $p_2^c = b_2 + hr$. Then, the optimal solution to the above problem is to set output $Y = Y^c$ at a level sufficient to ensure that (9.16) is satisfied at the monopoly price p_1^m i.e.

$$(p_1^m - b_1 - hr)X^m + (p_2 - b_2 - hr)Y^c = (p_1^m - b_1 - hr)X^m = (s - r)h(X^m + Y^c) \tag{9.20}$$

i.e. $Y^c = (p_1^m - b_1 - hs)X^m/h(s - r)$, where $X^m = x(p_1^m, p_2^c)$. The reason (p_1^m, p_2^c) solves (9.18)–(9.19) is that the company can make, at best, zero profits in the Y market and, at best, monopoly profits in the X market. The solution (p_1^m, p_2^c) achieves this best of all possible worlds for the company. Note that since X and Y are substitutes (i.e., $Y_1 > 0$, $X_2 > 0$), setting the monopoly price in the X market will increase demand in the Y market. The key assumption here is that at prices (p_1^m, p_2^c) the company can sell enough in the Y market to justify (9.20).

When imperfect competition prevails in the Y market, as examined in Crew and Crocker (1985), the company faces more complicated tradeoffs between profit-seeking in the Y market and relaxation of the rate-of-return constraint. The major advantage of this model is the opportunity provided by regulation to earn monopoly profits in the monopoly market through inflating the rate base by selling in the competitive market. The obvious solution to this is to force divestiture on the part of the business supplying the competitive sector. We are not, however, advocating such divestiture as a policy recommendation for several reasons. Most importantly, such divestiture could take place through regulatory process as opposed to an anti-trust suit. The rich rent-seeking opportunities in regulation suggest that the potential losses from implementing such a policy might not be worth the gains. In particular, such a process would involve examining how competitive the bypass market really is, as well as the magnitude of joint-cost economies between the two markets. In the end, divestiture, even if desirable, might not result from this adversarial process.

9.4 CONCLUDING REMARKS

In the absence of divestiture of the competitive business, regulators face a dilemma. They can either apply an unmodified RoR regulation to both market activities with possible monopoly results as in the above model. Or they can attempt to apply differential rates-of-return constraints to each of the markets. This latter approach appears at first glance to be straightforward if rates of return in the arguably competitive sector could be easily estimated. However, issues of joint cost allocation and other difficulties would probably make this a fertile area for rent seekers. Thus, this second alternative of more refined regulation could be just another instance of the regulatory tar baby enticing us into a transactions-cost rich briar patch.

Given the problems of regulating a partially deregulated firm, Judge Greene's opinion imposing limits on the entry of ROCs into unregulated business may be prudent. If the local companies are to remain regulated, there seem to be some powerful arguments for not mixing regulated and unregulated ventures. A radical solution would be to simply deregulate local companies (with the usual transition period). Of course, this would be countered by arguments for regulation to preserve scale economies.[17] These arguments, however, relying as they must on either engineering cost analyses or econometric results, do not take into account the other deleterious effects of monopoly and regulation, such as X-inefficiency and rent seeking. These latter have the potential for totally eating the benefits arising from scale economies.

The companies themselves need to decide which way they want to go. Do they really want to abandon regulation because the potential gains from the process are small compared to the benefits obtainable from unregulated oligopoly markets, or are the potential benefits to them from having both regulated and unregulated parts greater? Similarly legislators and regulators need to decide on the direction they wish to take. We return to this discussion of the feasibility of deregulation for utilities in Chapter 12.

10 Gas

Gas in the USA is supplied primarily from wells connected to pipelines which transport the gas to the 'city gate' of the local distribution companies, who then supply gas to the retail customer whether residential, commercial or industrial. Other arrangements may exist, such as direct supply to a large customer by the pipeline, bypassing the local distribution company. The process has been subjected to varying degrees of regulation over the years. In this chapter we will examine some of the economic consequences of the regulation of the industry as well as review some of the considerations concerning the nature of efficient pricing in the industry. Section 1 will be concerned with some of the institutional and regulatory background. Section 2 will be concerned with pricing and regulatory problems including the economics of some contractual relationships. In Section 3, as with the other industries examined, the effect of partial deregulation and the impact of competition will be examined, including a concluding discussion of whether further deregulation of the industry is feasible.

10.1 INSTITUTIONAL BACKGROUND

Natural gas is not one gas but a series of hydrocarbons, such as methane, ethane, propane, butane, hexane, heptane and octane. Gas may also be artificially manufactured by gas companies or may be a byproduct of oil production or refining. In 1982 gas accounted for 18.4 quadrillion Btus of total energy consumption of 70.8.[1] Most of the gas was sold to industrial customers. Gas is formed from the decay of organic matter and collects in underground traps, called natural gas fields. Natural gas and oil producers explore for, produce, and sell the gas to customers, primarily transmission companies, who then transport it and sell it to the gas distribution companies. Major gas producing areas are Texas, Louisiana, Oklahoma, Appalachia, Alaska, Mexico and Canada, and in addition, exploration is taking place off the continental shelf. The major consumers of gas are located at some distance from these production areas. It is the role of the gas pipelines to transport the gas across the vast distances between the producers and the consumers.

The industry possesses most of the features of natural monopolies which we have reviewed earlier, such as large transaction-specific investments, low variable costs, and scale economies. There appear to be few economies of scope in the industry, at least judging by the lack of a significant vertically integrated structure. Most gas pipeline companies buy their gas directly from producers, with only a small proportion of their gas coming from their own production subsidiaries. Thus the pipelines buy the gas from the gas producers and then resell it to customers, most of which are unaffiliated distribution companies. Pipelines are in the business of selling a bundling of gas and transportation services, although recently the issue has arisen as to whether they should take on common carrier status, which would require that they transport gas owned by others.

The gas industry has been subject to extensive regulation at three levels, beginning with the producers, extending to pipelines, and finally to retail sales by distribution companies. Well-head prices of natural gas sold in interstate commerce have been regulated at the federal level since 1954.[2] Interstate pipelines have been controlled under the Natural Gas Act of 1938, which regulated interstate rates for natural gas pipelines, including the sale of gas to and by these pipelines. This was expressly federal regulation and was confined to purely interstate commerce. Intrastate pipelines were subject to state regulation, and distribution companies are subject to RoR regulation by state public utility commissions.

With the Natural Gas Policy Act of 1978 (NGPA), the extensive regulation of well-head prices was drastically changed. Prior to 1978, the Federal Power Commission (FPC) attempted to regulate well-head prices for geographic areas. In response to the regulation a system of two-tiered gas prices developed with intrastate gas, which was not subject to Federal regulation, being priced much higher than interstate gas causing allocative distortions. NGPA attempted to address this problem by establishing ceiling prices for gas according to various categories. The most important distinction was that between 'old gas' (gas dedicated to interstate commerce before NGPA) and 'new gas'. Old gas would continue to be subject to price ceilings. However, new gas effective 1 January 1985 would not be subject to price ceilings. In the interim the price ceilings for new gas were gradually raised. NGPA allowed for an immediate decontrol of a special category of gas called 'high cost' gas and a phased decontrol of new gas removing all controls on new gas by 1 January 1985. Old gas continued subject to control but this amount declines as old wells are depleted.

Regulation of interstate pipelines is based on the principle of RoR regulation described earlier and also employ 'two-part' tariffs. Rates are based upon a demand charge and a commodity charge, which are different from maximum demand tariffs employed in industrial electric rates. The demand charge is a subscribed demand charge. The customer subscribes for a certain maximum level of consumption per period, for example, expressed in million cubic feet per day. The amount for which the customer subscribes is the maximum amount that the pipeline is obliged to supply for the term of the agreement. The customer also pays a commodity charge based upon the quantity actually consumed in the course of the month. Bills are rendered on monthly basis and demand charges are levied on a monthly basis. Thus, a pipeline customer's monthly unit price is minimised if its consumption is constant per month at the level of the maximum allowed per month according to the demand charge.

The pipelines typically buy the gas from producers and then resell it to distributors; normally the pipelines do not transport independently owned gas. Since gas was extensively price-regulated at the well-head before NGPA, the advantages of purchasing gas directly from the producer and then negotiating its carriage by a pipeline were normally not very great, at least in the case of gas sold in interstate markets which was subject to regulation by the Federal Power Commission. However, because intrastate gas was unregulated, a n-tiered system of prices had developed with consequent and growing shortages in the interstate market. During the period since 1978 some pipelines, when faced with gas shortages, purchased some gas under contract with very high take-or-pay obligations and therefore effectively at very high prices when demand declined.[3] As the pipelines sale prices for gas were based upon their average acquisition cost some of the pipelines felt justified in paying very high prices so that they would safeguard their supply. However, with the decline in oil prices, gas prices rose by less than the amount allowed under the phased decontrol. As gas demand declined by 1981 pipelines with large 'take-or-pay' obligations cut back on their purchases of low-cost gas with low take obligations and bought the expensive gas, as the cheapest way of resolving their take-or-pay obligations. Thus pipelines that had purchased expensive gas or had entered long-term contracts for gas that provided for escalation whose prices were now in excess of the market price found that they had spare capacity. In addition in some instances where 'take-or-pay' provisions existed in their contracts they also found that they were required to pay for gas which they did not use.

The industry then has to overcome a legacy of past regulatory actions and is in the midst of certain changes, some of which are in the direction of increased interface with competitive markets. For example, as well-head prices are deregulated there may be opportunities of consumers to deal with the producers directly and then have a pipeline transport the gas. As pipelines are not required to be common carriers, the issue of mandatory carriage has arisen. Competition is also occurring between gas pipelines and gas distributors as large customer to bypass the distribution grid and connect with the pipeline directly.

10.2 PRICING AND REGULATORY ISSUES

Gas, like electricity and the telephone system, has a peak-load problem in both transmission and distribution. The problem arises because of the fact that transportation capacity is limited by the size of the pipelines or distribution pipes. Even though storage possibilities, within the limits of drainage constraints, exist a peak-load problem still remains as outlined in Crew and Kleindorfer (1979a, pp.54–7), which derives the following for a two-plant case, which might correspond to the case where the company gets its gas from the pipeline at a cost of $\beta_1 + b_1$, or produces it by a gas manufacturing process, $\beta_2 + b_2$. If pipeline gas is stored and sold in the next period it has a storage cost of c. In Chapter 3, we showed the optimal prices in a two-period model, without storage, are given by (10.1).

$$p_1 = 2b_1 + \beta_1 - (b_2 + \beta_2), \quad p_2 = b_2 + \beta_2 \qquad (10.1)$$

$$p_1 = b_1 + (\beta_1 - c)/2, \qquad p_2 = b_1 + (\beta_1 + c)/2 \qquad (10.2)$$

where (10.2) holds if storage is used, i.e., if $c < 2b_2 + 2\beta_2 - (2b_1 + \beta_1)$, and (10.1) holds otherwise, if it is cheaper to manufacture the gas. In practice, gas manufacturing is not used except in rather few instances where peak demand is unusually high, in which case it is used to supplement storage.

Another means employed by gas utilities to deal with their peak demands is the interruptible tariff. In return for lower year-round rates certain large customers choose to restrict their consumption during periods of peak winter demands at the utility's request. Typically such customers have an alternative fuel available such as oil, which is presumably cheaper to store than gas. Such tariffs are being offered to cogenerators by some gas companies because cogeneration plants are typically dual-fuelled. Some of the economic theory of interruptible tariffs has been examined by Hamlen and Jen (1983). Interruptible rates are efficient to the extent that it is cheaper for the customer to provide oil storage and dual-firing rather then the pipeline or distributor providing storage or peak production capacity. The companies have an incentive to set rates that are consistent with (10.1)–(10.2) plus some insurance premium to enhance supply reliability made necessary because of the stochastic nature of demand.

Although economic efficiency considerations may indicate that some form of peak-load pricing should be used, very little use is made of peak-load pricing in either the distribution or transmission parts of the industry. Mostly gas is sold by means of block or two-part tariffs by distribution companies. Transmission companies use the simple subscribed demand tariffs described earlier. There seems to be little beyond interruptible tariffs in an attempt to shave peak demands. Given the seasonal nature of demand, it may seem surprising that seasonal rates are not employed. However, when we take a closer look at the nature of the contracts employed in the industry it is not surprising that little peak-load or seasonal pricing is employed.

As mentioned previously, most pipeline rates to distributors have a demand charge and a commodity charge. If the demand charge were set to cover the fixed costs of the pipeline it may correspond to efficient pricing in the sense that Hopkinson rates (described in Chapter 8) do so when there is no diversity of demand. To the extent that each distributor's peak occurs at approximately the same time as the other distributors who are customers of the pipeline because all of their demands are related to temperature, keeping the individual distributor's peak down will keep the pipeline peak down. Thus charging all the fixed costs onto maximum or subscribed demand will create the incentive to reduce the peak. However, pipeline contracts may load some of the fixed cost onto the commodity charge. This will attenuate the incentive of the distributor to offer seasonal or off-peak discounts.

In some instances this is combined with a mimumum bill provision, for example Central Illinois Power and Light Co (CILCO).[4]

Minimum bill contracts are not necessarily the same as take-or-pay contracts in their effect. They are restricted between a pipeline and its customers and may in part arise as pipelines seek to reduce their own exposure arising from take-or-pay obligations. They can take various forms. For example, in the Panhandle case the minimum bill provisions depend on the classification of buyer. Panhandle had two classes of service: General Service and Limited Service. General Service buyers are required to obtain all their requirements from Panhandle. Their minimum bill is only the demand charge. On the other hand Limited Service buyers face a minimum bill of the demand charge plus 75 per cent of the contract demand times the commodity charge. Thus Panhandle's customer CILCO would be effectively precluded from purchasing (cheaper) gas from an alternative supplier to the extent that it would end up paying a higher price to Panhandle for less gas. This would apply particularly when CILCO's demand was low in relation to its subscribed demand.[5]

While minimum bills *per se* may not work against peak-load pricing in retail gas markets, they do when a company has a large minimum bill obligation. In this instance the distribution company is concerned with selling as much gas as it can and may not be overly concerned with shaving the peak. Moreover the extent to which capacity charges are placed in the commodity charge, rather than demand charge, further reduces the incentive to incorporate peak-load pricing. In addition to the minimum bill provision Panhandle tariffs, as approved by the FPC, incorporated a provision where fixed costs were included in the commodity charge which could be as high as 75 per cent (under the 'United formula' used in the Panhandle tariff). Thus to the extent that capacity costs are included in the commodity charge the potential for peak-load pricing is reduced because the company has limited potential to charge lower prices in the off-peak periods because its own marginal acquisition cost is low.

While the subscribed demand and other tariffs used in the gas industry are similar to tariffs used in electricity and water the gas industry does have one type of tariff, the take-or-pay contract, which seems to be peculiar only to the gas industry. Take-or-pay contracts are used in the industry between well-head producers and pipelines. The pipeline agrees to pay a certain sum, y for x units of gas. If the pipeline takes less than x units it still has to pay y for whatever amount of gas it takes. If, however, it buys more than x units it pays for the additional supplies at a unit price specified in the contract. Thus if a pipeline at its existing prices has a demand for less than x units of gas its marginal cost of supplying any increase in demand is zero. The take-or-pay contract apparently gives it an incentive to try to broker marginal quantities of gas at low prices.[6]

Masten and Crocker (1985) have made a careful study of an economic explanation for take-or-pay contracts. One argument is that well-head price regulation, producers required 'generous' take-or-pay provisions to enable them, at least partially, to circumvent the impact of price regulation. However, as Masten and Crocker point out, take-or-pay contracts existed long before price regulation. Indeed, they argue that other features of the industry provide the driving force for the existence of take-or-pay contracts in the following way. It is not possible for a natural gas producer to appropriate fully his reserves of gas since a neighbour could drill a well and drain gas away from the field. In addition, gas may drain away from some fields once the wells have been drilled. Thus a producer has an incentive to sell his gas as quickly as possible. A customer who does not take as much gas as expected thus leaves the producer with a commodity that may decline in storage. In such a situation it seems appropriate for a producer to try to protect the value of his investment by entering into a take-or-pay contract.

Masten and Crocker's main argument concerns the role of take-or-pay contracts in efficient resource allocation. Their argument is that such contracts are long term and therefore must be incomplete. As the number and complexity of the provisions for contingent claims in a contract increases, it becomes increasingly difficult for courts to adjudicate between the two parties and insure performance. To avoid this problem contracts are written which employ unilateral options instead of contingent claims provisions. This is the way to understand take-or-pay contracts. In view of the costly nature to the producer of a failure by the buyer to take the amount of gas agreed the take-or-pay provision provides a penalty for such failure to take delivery. The penalty, moreover, provides incentives for economic efficiency. Let us assume that the gas has a value to the pipeline of v. If the price that the pipeline has to pay for the gas is y, in the absence of a take-or-pay provision, it would breach the contract whenever $v < y$. If the value to the producer is s – what the producer can obtain from other buyers, or the resource value of leaving the gas in the ground – then breach will result in an efficient allocation of resources if $v < s$, because in this case the gas would go to a user who valued it higher than the pipeline breaching the contract. However, if $y > v > s$ buyers will find it profitable to breach the contract even though it is inefficient to do so, because this would result in gas not being routed to its highest valued use. Inefficient breach can be eliminated by assessing a penalty $d = y - s$ paid by the buyer in the event of breach. Given such a penalty the buyer would breach the contract only when it is socially efficient for him to do so. This can be represented as a 'take' percentage by dividing by y. Thus the take-or-pay provision would have the effect of discouraging this kind of 'inefficient' breach of contract. Moreover, it would avoid the costly adjudicatory apparatus of the court to determine whether or not various complex contingencies had been satisfied. Masten and Crocker then argue that take-or-pay contracts were employed because of the incentives that they created and because they were transactions cost minimising.[7] However, to the extent that price regulation causes distortions in incentives, it is not surprising that it had an effect on take-or-pay contracts. In addition to the properties analysed by Masten and Crocker, it is clear that take-or-pay contracts become attractive as a means of circumventing price control, by increasing the take percentage. This has caused a legacy of distortions now faced by the industry following partial well-head price deregulation.

10.3 IMPLICATIONS FOR REGULATION OF COMPETITION IN THE GAS INDUSTRY

As with the other industries, there is a movement in the gas industry toward deregulation and expansion into competitive markets. The well-head price of natural gas, at least in the case of new gas, has now been deregulated. Changes are also taking place in the transmission and distribution parts of the industry. Along with the desire to reduce regulation has come the entry of regulated companies into competitive and unregulated markets. The availability of spot gas supplies and the continued existence of long-term contracts, many of which are at high prices, has led to the formation of new businesses to take advantage of the opportunities created.

With the availability of unregulated gas supplies, both contract and spot, there has developed an increased demand for 'carriage'. Carriage is simply the transporting by the pipeline of the gas from the well-head to the buyer. The buyer may be an end user, a broker, or a gas distribution company wishing to take advantage of some favourably priced gas. This kind of arrangement is different from typical industry practice described in Section 2 which involves the pipeline purchasing the gas directly from the well head and then reselling it bundled with the transportation to the end user or distribution company.[8] There has been a concern that perhaps pipelines might not be willing to perform carriage in cases where the buyer went directly to the well-head, often displacing the pipeline's own sales of gas. If a policy of competitive markets in well-head gas is to be established, it is important that potential buyers are not kept out of the market because of pipeline refusal to transport because it competes with the pipelines' own gas. One solution might be to require pipelines to be common carriers in addition to their traditional duty of gas sales. Another, more radical, solution might be for the pipelines to divest their ownership of gas and be only common carriers. In either case this would not appear to reduce the amount of regulation of pipelines required. For such reason regulators are considering whether it is necessary to introduce rules for mandatory carriage that would require pipelines to carry gas under certain circumstances.[9]

The problem of carriage has arisen in part because of the changes brought about by the partial deregulation of NGPA. This has created new opportunities not just for pipelines but also for gas distribution companies. As with the other industries gas distribution companies also have opportunities to enter competitive markets and also face a bypass problem. Large industrial customers may find it cheaper to obtain their gas from pipelines directly rather than from the distribution company, thereby bypassing the distribution company. Alternatively the gas distribution company may set up a separate subsidiary, as in the case of NUI,[10] which has Energy Marketing Exchange (EME), which acts as a gas broker locating spot gas, and arranging transportation for large industrial customers. Rate Counsel in New Jersey opposes this kind of arrangement on the grounds that it takes away sales from NUI's utility, Elizabethtown Gas, and also reduces that amount of gross receipts and franchise tax collected because sales independent of the utility do not attract the tax. Here both the New Jersey Gross Receipts and Franchise Tax and competition from the pipelines and oil pose a bypass problem which gas utilities cannot ignore. The taxes make it very hard for gas utilities to compete. In any event the net effect is similar for the other ratepayers. Bypass will occur and any prudent utility is going to take steps not to be the loser as a result. As the New Jersey Rate Counsel's concerns indicate there are clearly problems when competition and regulation interface. What Rate Counsel or other intervenors can do about these problems as the issue with NUI indicates, is not simple.

Holding companies do propose new regulatory problems where competition and regulation are mixed together, as Crew and Crocker (1985) have discussed. In the case of a holding company, there may be an incentive to relegate the most expensive gas to the distribution company and its relatively captive customers, while routing the least expensive gas to the competitive bypass market through its subsidiary.[11] In this event a vicious circle would be created. As the price to the regulated customers increased so more of the larger ones would find it worthwhile to bypass the distribution company.

Rate Counsel and other such public intervenors may have good reason to be concerned about the effects of such developments. It is difficult to see how they can be avoided. Gas holding company managements are usually well qualified to perform such functions as EME. To prevent them from getting into the business would not prevent the problem. If the business is profitable, and in the New Jersey case, it is presumably made so by the tax treatment if nothing else, then other companies will enter and the utility will lose the business. The holding company in this case is a device for holding on to some of the benefits and adjusting to the tax situation. However, it is also a device for bringing about subsidies from the regulated to the unregulated business.[12] Here an intervenor has a concern from both efficiency and equity grounds. As we noted in the previous chapters and as analysed by Crew and Crocker (1985a) effective regulation is ellusive in such circumstances.

Given the potential for entry into competitive and unregulated ventures that appears to exist in the gas industry it is clear that there are going to be continued problems of regulating this industry effectively.[13] This raises the question of whether it is worth continuing to try to regulate. The captive customers for gas are probably not as captive as those for electricity and water. Residential customers use gas for heating, cooking and water heating. There is competition in the long run for these uses from electricity, oil and wood. Given this and the costs imposed by operating the regulatory process the alternative of complete deregulation may be attractive. We will defer discussion of this until the concluding chapter.

11 Water Supply

Unlike telecommunications and electricity, where the industry is dominated by large companies, water is supplied by many small companies both regulated and municipals. In some instances small companies have been consolidated into larger groups such as American and General Water Works. Most of the companies are small and even the industry leaders such as Hackensack Water and Elizabethtown Water are small by the standards of Bell telephone operating companies and electric companies like PSE&G. Despite the relatively small scale of some of the companies, the industry faces problems similar to those faced by the giants in electricity and telecommunications. Moreover, some of the changes, including technology, affecting those industries are beginning to have an impact on water utilities.

In this chapter we review some of the important problems facing the water industry. In Section 1 we briefly examine the nature of the industry and examine how its structure and technology affect is pricing policy. Section 2 examines the practical aspects of implementing efficient pricing policy. Section 3 examines some of the regulatory problems of the industry including those arising from small size of company, environmental problems and the need to assure water quality, as well as the pervasive issue of regulation of a firm with unregulated parts. Finally, Section 4 presents conclusions and implications for the direction of the industry and regulation.

11.1 BACKGROUND TO NATURE OF TECHNOLOGY AND EFFECTS ON PRICING

The technology of water supply involves collecting water in a reservoir, either above or below ground, transporting it to a treatment plant and then distributing it to customers. Thus, like electricity supply, a water utility has the three functions of generation, transmission and distribution. Transmission may be important in linking various watersheds together so that in the event of shortage in one watershed the water can be transported from another having sufficient water. Transmission can also be used to handle peak demands. After purification in the treatment plant, the costs of distribution are significant.

The costs of distribution are highly dependent on the distance from the treatment plant. In addition to the capital costs of providing transmission, there are the costs of maintaining the pipes and mains and the additional costs of pumping. Each gallon delivered to a distant location has an additional pumping cost compared to the costs at a closer location. These considerations are regarded as significant, at least by some in the industry. For example, Schlenger (1983) has proposed for large water companies that prices be varied according to distance from the treatment facility. Thus customers in a distant pumping district would pay more than customers in a closer district. This 'zonal pricing' policy could have an impact on optimal location of large customers. A large user of water may find a closer location more attractive than a distant one, whereas currently the location decision is unaffected and customers close to the plant would subsidise such a distant large user. It should be noted, however, that zonal pricing raises issues of equity, administrative expense and consumer acceptance which have made it an infrequently used practice.

Another concern about pricing arises from the stochastic nature of demand and supply of water. For simplicity we will just consider stochastic supply.[1] The company faces a stochastic supply for water, because the amount of water in the reservoir depends on weather. Broad average weather patterns are established over the years, but within these there can be considerable fluctuations. It would be far too costly for a company to build enough capacity to take into account every possible shortage of supply. So it is inevitable that at constant prices a company will find itself short of water on occasions. One solution to this problem, based upon the results in Part II, would require that the pricing policy be allowed to vary according to weather conditions. In times of shortage, price would be raised and in times of abundance price would be lowered. It is obvious that straightforward application of the methods of Part II would show this policy to be Pareto superior to uniform pricing. How is it then that such pricing is hardly used and uniform pricing is the standard for the industry? The main reason for the nearly universal use of uniform pricing is that, at least until recently, the metering costs of flexible non-uniform pricing were prohibitive.[2] Recently, however, because of innovations in metering technology this has changed and there may now exist the potential to introduce more efficient pricing policies in water.[3] Thus, a discussion regarding the structure of an optimal pricing policy for water supply is appropriate.

The problem facing a water company is not how to maintain a

constant level of water in the reservoir year round but how to have the maximum amount in the reservoir immediately prior to the dry season or period when demand is ahead of supply. From experience, the company is able to estimate how much it should have in its reservoirs at each time of the year. These levels are plotted and are referred to in the industry as the 'rule curve'. If the water level is equal to or exceeds the level on the rule curve, then the company does nothing. If the level is less than the level on the rule curve, then the company attempts to reduce demand by moral suasion and exhortation in the form of advertising, or it initiates rationing if it perceives the situation as particularly serious. However, in view of the transactions costs and problems associated with rationing, the likelihood is that the company will not resort to rationing until the situation of shortage is serious and by then drastic measures are often required. Contrast this with a situation where if the company were able to employ flexible pricing it would change its prices each time, say each month, it up-dated its forecast. If water level were below the rule curve, the company would raise price. If it were above, the company might lower price. This policy would have considerable advantages over the present uniform pricing policy which results in customers restricting consumption in times when supplies are abundant and all the disadvantages of rationing in times of drought.

To illustrate how a flexible pricing policy along these lines might operate we now examine a computer simulation of a flexible pricing policy of the sort just described. Such a simulation model is readily usable, even for small companies, in evaluating alternative pricing policies. We note in passing that analytical results for water pricing are largely unavailable given the complexity of such policies under stochastic supply conditions.

11.2 PRICING POLICY FOR STOCHASTIC SUPPLY CONDITIONS[4]

The problem of optimal pricing for water was examined by Riley and Scherer (1979), who provided the essentials of the solution under deterministic conditions. Hence, we restate the problem only in an abbreviated form. The regulated water company is assumed to maximise profits subject to a regulatory constraint and the following capacity and mass-balance constraints.[5]

1. Maximum flow to customers cannot exceed maximum capacity.
2. Amount of water stored cannot exceed storage capacity.
3. Amount of water in storage must be non-negative.
4. Inflow equals amount added to storage plus amount consumed plus amount spilled over the dam.

Figure 11–1a (based on Riley and Scherer's Figure 1) shows inflow and demand at a uniform price over time. The solid line, designated 'optimal supply', shows the amount that the company should supply at Riley and Scherer's optimal prices, which would vary continuously over time; prices would be raised to prevent a drawdown of the reservoir before demand peaks. Figure 11–2b shows the price that the company would charge based upon the constraint that prices can only be changed in discrete increments and at discrete intervals. Thus in intervals (t_1, t_2) price is raised so that more water can be stored. During (t_2, t_4) peak price is charged and demand is met by the rationing effect of the higher price and by drawing on storage. Under this seasonal pricing policy only s is drawn instead of S under uniform pricing. In interval $[t_4, t_6]$ price is lowered and storage falls before eventually rising at t_6, starting the cycle again. Thus prices that are raised for summer and lowered in the fall would tend to be optimal for the seasonal pattern employed here.

To take account of the fact that inflow and demand are both stochastic variables subject primarily to variations in the weather, we propose a pricing policy which differs from Riley and Scherer's in that it attempts by means of a simple iterative procedure to take into account stochastic variations in supply and demand.[6] To illustrate the decision-making problem faced by a water utility the approach adopted will discuss two simple iterative schemes which incorporate the main feature of an optimal policy.[7]

Suppose a water utility with automatic metering for all of its customers reads and bills monthly and is permitted to change its prices every month. If the company wished to make a price change in the next month, it would be required to include a notice in its current monthly bill as well as advertise the change in newspapers, as approved by the regulator. To use price as a device for rationing would require that monthly price changes be made promptly. It would, therefore, be necessary that the company wishing to make a price change be permitted to short-cut the traditional regulatory process for rate increases. This fundamental change would, in turn, require further basic changes in regulation to make the policy acceptable and to

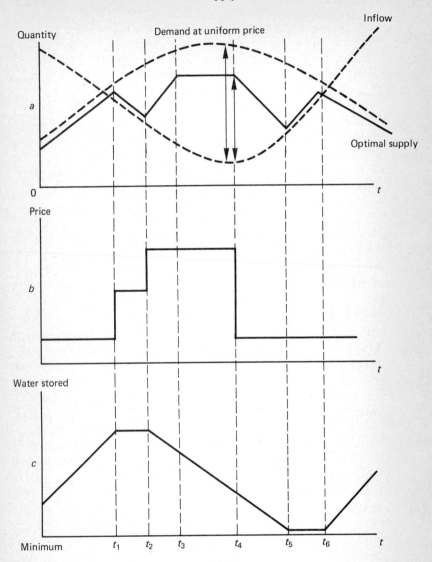

Inflow

Quantity

Demand at uniform price

a

0   Optimal supply

Price

b

Water stored

c

Minimum t_1 t_2 t_3 t_4 t_5 t_6 *t*

Figure 11.1   Optimal fluctuations in price, supply and storage

continue to allow the regulator to have effective control over the monopoly power of the company. These changes are an integral part of the proposal. The company and its regulators would first agree to an optimal storage schedule $\bar{w}$ in monthly increments after the pattern of Figure 11–2c. This would be the target it would plan to achieve; it approximates what is known in the water business as the 'rule curve'. This rule curve would be reviewed periodically as long-term demand increases. In addition, the company would construct a price schedule $p(x)$ to relate price in each period to water level at the beginning of that period. At the end of each period, whether actual water level w were equal to target $\bar{w}$ would depend on consumption in the period, x, and actual rainfall r. If, at the end of each period, actual water level w was equal to target level $\bar{w}$, then price $p(x)$ would be charged. If w exceeded w, then the price would be lowered to $p(x)$ using the price schedule set by the regulator, where x is the output that equates w and $\bar{w}$. Similarly, if w were less than $\bar{w}$, the price would be raised. Since the schedule $p(x)$ would be approved by the regulator, the company would not be required to seek regulatory approval to make any changes consistent with the schedule. It would, however, be required to seek regulatory approval for changes in the schedule. The company would thus have to decide whether or not to change price in any period in accordance with the schedule. Presumably, if the difference between w and $\bar{w}$ were small, no change would be made.

Two policies derived from this proposal are illustrated. Assume that seasonally varying demands are represented by demand functions of the form $x = ap^{-2}$, where 'a' varies by month over the year, as shown in Tables 11.2 and 11.3. (Definitions of variables used are given in Table 11.1.) Table 11.2 represents a *myopic price adjustment policy* which changes price in the next period immediately if $w \neq \bar{w}$. Actual output x is thus equalised with target output $\bar{x}$ by means of price adjustments in each period. The prices are calculated from the schedule and are restricted to be between 40 cents and $12 per unit of water, where 40 cents is the short-run marginal cost, and $12 is the upper limit allowed by the regulator. The results can be compared to the situation where price is uniform over all periods. As illustrated in Table 11.3, uniform prices result in lower profits, M, but slightly higher welfare, $TR + S - TC$. However, this provides massive departures from the rule curve as illustrated by $w/\bar{w}$.

An *alternative seasonal pricing policy* changes price in the next period only when actual stored water w differs from target amount stored $\bar{w}$ by more than 10 per cent. Here it is envisioned that the regulator would

Table 11.1   Definition of variables used

SRMC	Short-run marginal cost
SRTC	Short-run total cost per month
TR	Total revenue
$W-\text{bar}=\bar{w}$	Target water level in reservoir
R	Rainfall
$R-\text{Bar}=\bar{r}$	Target rainfall for month
W	Amount of water actually stored in reservoir
$X-\text{Bar}=\bar{x}$	Target output
$X=R+W_t-W_{t-1}$	Actual output = Rainfall plus amount stored at end of period less amount stored at the end of the previous period
P	Price
a	Demand parameter
M	Difference between total revenue and total cost
S	Consumer's surplus
FC	Fixed costs
STC	Total short-run costs
RR	Revenue requirements
Welfare	Sum of $S + M$ over all periods
Profit	Sum of $TR-STC-FC$ over all periods

allow three rates; a winter rate of 50 cents, a spring rate of $5.00, and a summer rate of $9.00, with the company having the right to raise rates by up to 33.33 per cent in the summer, up to 100 per cent in the spring, and up to 500 per cent in the winter, and to lower rates by 66.66 per cent in the summer, 50 per cent in the spring, and 20 per cent in the winter. The result of this policy is shown in Table 11.4.

The company in Tables 11.2 and 11.4 makes substantial profits, *M*. The profits result because of the low demand elasticity assumed and because demand exceeds capacity, resulting in high market clearing prices. This might be caused by a one-time drought or it may be due to inadequate capacity. The large profits produced by the rationing of capacity with prices would present a problem that would not arise with the uniform pricing policy illustrated in Table 11.3. (In this case the company makes only minor profits above its revenue requirements.) This problem might be handled by placing profits in escrow, subject to the supervision of the regulator. The company could apply to the regulator for escrowed funds when its rate of return fell below the allowed return or when it had capacity expansions to finance, the amount taken out of escrow being used to reduce the company's financing requirement. However, the opportunities for mischief with such escrowed funds are manifest.

The three cases in Tables 11.2 to 11.4 have various efficiency/equity characteristics. At least at first sight, in terms of the familiar definition of economic efficiency,[8] the uniform pricing policy of Table 11.3 appears superior. This is because it involves almost no excess profit ($M = 4.3$). However, if the water level drops to about a third of its target, in terms of the rule curve used by water utilities and their regulators, it is off by grossly unacceptable levels; rationing would have to be introduced before the situation became this drastic. This would result in a failure of the company to earn its revenue requirements. It would also result in significant transactions costs as well as shortage costs borne by consumers. Thus, because of the fact that the $TR + R - TC$ in Tables 11.2–11.4a fails to take into account the effects (shortage and rationing costs) of stochastic demand, it will provide a significant over-estimate of the net benefits in the case of uniform prices. By contrast, the pricing policies of Tables 11.2 and 11.4 permit the company to stay much closer to its target water storage. However, the company makes considerable profits in both cases and considerably in excess of the profits in the uniform case in Table 11.3. The scheme of Table 11.4 is probably the best overall, because it has fewer adjustments in prices than the myopic rule, provides higher net benefits (because it avoids rationing) than uniform pricing, but requires raising prices to politically unacceptable levels. Clearly a flexible pricing policy with upper limits on prices would be the appropriate compromise solution between price rationing and non-price rationing. This mirrors similar trade-offs discussed in Chapter 4.

The cases shown in Tables 11.2–11.4 do not take into account expansion of capacity, the desirability of which would be signalled by excess profits and shortage of capacity as in Tables 11.2 and 11.4. Tables 11.2a to 11.4a compare the investment increments that would be required approximately to optimise in accordance with the respective pricing rules of Tables 11.2 to 11.4. The capacity expansion problem is approached by a number of simple rules. Capacity is increased by a small amount, say 3 per cent, until $w/\bar{w}$ is close to or exceeds 100 per cent in all cases. Profit is then examined, and price and capacity are adjusted to bring profit and $w/\bar{w}$ in line with targets. If profit is positive price is lowered. If this results in $w/\bar{w}$ dropping below 100 per cent, capacity is increased until profit approaches zero. A zero profit solution is thus reached by successive iterations in price and capacity. In the case of Table 11.4a the situation is more complex. When $w/\bar{w}$ is close to 100 per cent, price is raised by the percentage of the deficit plus 20 per cent. Then $w/\bar{w}$ and M are examined. If, after the changes, M is still negative, prices are raised by successively smaller increments until the target is approached. Capacity may also be raised or lowered by successively smaller increments to get closer to target.

The seasonal pricing policy shown in Table 11.4a is the best policy with respect to maximising net benefits and maintaining reservoir storage according to the rule curve (that is, $w/\bar{w}$ of at least 100 per cent). Table 11.2a, the myopic pricing policy, fares worst of the three in terms of both consumers' surplus and total revenue. Even uniform pricing, Table 11.3a, does better. This may seem surprising because uniform pricing does not use capacity efficiently. However, the uniform pricing policy results in break-even, while the myopic pricing policy results in high profits (large M). The myopic policy fails to take into account the known seasonality of demand and makes adjustments as if nothing were known about demand and supply in the next period. It tends to over-compensate for shortages and surpluses, taking no account of what is likely to happen in the next period. Its other problem is that it is not allowed to operate without restriction, because there is a cap on prices of $12. If price were allowed to adjust to the proper rationing level, this would mean charging $32, over double the amount. Total capacity would, however, be reduced, and performance on the rule curve would be, of course, improved somewhat. Total benefits (total revenue plus consumer surplus) are actually less than with the uniform pricing case. The myopic pricing policy, in addition, involves frequent price changes, presenting problems of consumer acceptability. A final major problem is the failure to keep close to target revenue requirements. Indeed, substantial excess profits are produced in each case, creating severe regulatory problems. This alone would make the myopic pricing policy unacceptable. The policies of Tables 11.4 and 11.4a would therefore be preferred.

The problem of excess profits would arise under the policy of Tables 11.4 and 11.4a when investment was required and/or especially dry weather occurred. These profits would require the regulator's attention and could be handled in one of several ways. These might include having the regulator pay the escrow to customers, not in proportion to their bills, or to company shareholders for a corresponding reduction in rate base. Both of these proposals clearly raise issues of transactions cost, of course, and a more complete comparative institutional assessment (as in Chapter 7) would be required before making any recommendations here.

From an efficiency point of view, the policy has advantages over the current policy. Under current policy, excess capacity may be built to

Table 11.2 Simulated prices under a myopic decision rule

	Jan	Feb	Mar	Apr	May	Jun	Jul	Aug	Sep	Oct	Nov	Dec
RR	$443	$443	$443	$443	$443	$443	$443	$443	$443	$443	$443	$443
SRMC	$0.40	$0.40	$0.40	$0.40	$0.40	$0.40	$0.40	$0.40	$0.40	$0.40	$0.40	$0.40
TR	$319	$53	$58	$97	$820	$1,049	$1,291	$1,460	$1,168	$183	$78	$68
W-BAR	350	410	450	470	440	350	280	210	160	100	180	250
R-BAR	150	160	150	140	120	70	80	80	100	110	190	200
R	160	200	200	80	60	40	20	40	70	120	170	200
X-BAR	87	135	153	140	90	100	110	100	88	131	120	110
$R + W_i - (W_i - 1) = X$	75	132	144	140	90	100	110	122	97	131	120	110
P	$4.26	$0.40	$0.40	$0.69	$9.11	$10.49	$11.73	$12.00	$12.00	$1.39	$0.65	$0.62
W	385	453	470	410	380	320	230	148	121	110	160	250
OVERFLOW	0	0	39	0	0	0	0	0	0	0	0	0
a	0	110	120	130	140	160	180	200	160	140	110	100
W LESS W-BAR	35	43	20	−60	−60	−30	−50	−62	−39	10	−20	0
M	−124	−390	−385	−346	377	606	848	1018	726	−260	−365	−374
TR+S	$3,007	$4,957	$7,666	$11,435	$16,395	$32,101	$57,997	$98,400	$32,071	$16,554	$4,951	$3,069
SRTC	$30	$53	$58	$56	$36	$0	$44	$49	$39	$52	$48	$44
FC	$4,762											
WELFARE	$283,294											
PROFIT	$1,331											
R/R-BAR%	106.67%	125.00%	133.33%	57.14%	50.00%	28.57%	50.00%	50.00%	70.00%	109.09%	89.47%	100.00%
R-R-BAR	10	40	50	−60	−60	−30	−50	−40	−30	10	−20	0
W/W-BAR	110.05%	110.50%	104.44%	87.23%	86.36%	91.43%	82.14%	70.63%	75.62%	88.89%	100.00%	100.00%

Table 11.2a Simulated capacity expansion under a myopic decision rule

	Jan	Feb	Mar	Apr	May	Jun	Jul	Aug	Sep	Oct	Nov	Dec
SRMC	$492	$492	$492	$492	$492	$492	$492	$492	$492	$492	$492	$492
	$0.40	$0.40	$0.40	$0.40	$0.40	$0.40	$0.40	$0.40	$0.40	$0.40	$0.40	$0.40
TR	$158	$53	$58	$88	$743	$951	$1170	$1324	$1059	$166	$70	$62
W-BAR	350	410	450	470	440	350	280	210	160	100	180	250
R-BAR	168.225	179.44	168.225	157.01	134.58	78.505	78.505	89.72	112.15	123.365	213.085	224.3
R	179.44	224.3	224.3	89.72	67.29	44.86	22.43	44.86	78.505	134.58	190.655	224.3
X-BAR	87	135	153	140	90	100	110	100	88	131	120	110
$R \times W_t - (W_t - 1) = X$	89	132	144	143	92	102	113	125	100	134	123	113
P	$1.77	$0.40	$0.40	$0.61	$8.06	$9.27	$10.38	$10.61	$10.61	$1.23	$0.57	$0.55
W	390	482	527	473	448	391	300	221	199	200	267	379
OVERFLOW 0	0	0	0	0	0	0	0	0	0	0	0	0
a	100	110	120	130	140	160	180	200	160	140	110	100
W LESS W-BAR	40	72	77	3	8	41	20	11	39	100	87	129
M	-334	-439	-434	-404	251	458	678	831	567	-326	-422	-430
TR+S	$3047	$4957	$7666	$11438	$16414	$32126	$58028	$98435	$32099	$16558	$4953	$3071
SRTC	$36	$53	$58	$57	$37	$41	$45	$50	$40	$54	$49	$45
FC	$5341											
WELFARE	$282885											
PROFIT	($5)											
R/R-BAR%	106.67%	125.00%	133.33%	57.14%	50.00%	57.14%	28.57%	50.00%	70.00%	109.09%	89.47%	100.00%
R − R-Bar	11	45	56	-67	-67	-34	-56	-45	-34	11	-22	0
W/W-BAR	111.51%	117.67%	117.13%	100.71%	101.91%	111.65%	107.31%	105.06%	124.61%	199.72%	148.55%	151.58%

Table 11.3 Simulated uniform prices

	Jan	Feb	Mar	Apr	May	Jun	Jul	Aug	Sep	Oct	Nov	Dec
RR	$438	$438	$438	$438	$438	$438	$438	$438	$438	$438	$438	$438
SRMC	$0.40	$0.40	$0.40	$0.40	$0.40	$0.40	$0.40	$0.40	$0.40	$0.40	$0.40	$0.40
TR	$319	$351	$383	$414	$446	$510	$574	$638	$510	$446	$351	$319
W-BAR	350	410	450	470	440	350	280	210	160	100	180	250
R-BAR	150	160	150	140	120	70	70	80	100	110	190	200
R	160	200	200	80	60	40	20	40	70	120	170	200
X-BAR	87	135	170	140	133	128	118	83	44	64	79	107
$R+W_t-(W_t-1)=X$	75	82	90	97	105	120	135	150	120	105	82	75
P	$4.26	$4.26	$4.26	$4.26	$4.26	$4.26	$4.26	$4.26	$4.26	$4.26	$4.26	$4.26
W	385	470	470	453	408	328	213	104	54	69	157	282
OVERFLOW	0	33	110	0	0	0	0	0	0	0	0	0
a	100	110	120	130	140	160	180	200	160	140	110	100
W LESS W-BAR	35	60	20	−17	−32	−22	−67	−106	−106	−31	−23	32
M	($119)	($87)	($55)	($24)	$8	$72	$136	$200	$72	$8	($87(	($119)
TR×S	$3007	$4883	$7584	$11356	$16488	$32236	$58177	$98606	$32236	$16488	$4883	$3007
SRTC	$30	$33	$36	$39	$42	$48	$54	$60	$48	$42	$33	$30
FC	$4762											
WELFARE	$283694											
PROFIT	$4											
R/R-BAR%	106.67%	125.00%	133.33%	50.00%	50.00%	57.14%	28.57%	50.00%	70.00%	109.09%	89.47%	100.00%
R−R-BAR	10	40	50	−60	−60	−30	−50	−40	−30	10	20	0
W/W-BAR	110.05%	114.63%	104.44%	96.32%	92.71%	93.77%	76.25%	49.44%	33.80%	69.31%	87.21%	112.86%

Table 11.3a   Simulated capacity expansion with uniform prices

	Jan	Feb	Mar	Apr	May	Jun	Jul	Aug	Sep	Oct	Nov	Dec
SMRC	$488	$488	$488	$488	$488	$488	$488	$488	$488	$488	$488	$488
	$0.40	$0.40	$0.40	$0.40	$0.40	$0.40	$0.40	$0.40	$0.40	$0.40	$0.40	$0.40
TR	$354	$390	$425	$461	$496	$567	$638	$708	$567	$496	$390	$354
W-BAR	350	410	450	470	440	350	280	210	160	100	180	250
R-BAR	169.125	180.4	169.125	157.85	135.3	78.925	78.925	90.2	112.75	124.025	214.225	225.5
R	180.4	225.5	225.5	90.2	67.65	45.1	22.55	45.1	78.925	135.3	191.675	225.5
X-BAR	87	135	170	140	133	128	118	83	44	64	79	107
$R + W_t - (W_{t-1}) = X$	73	87	95	95	102	117	131	146	117	102	80	73
P	$4.86	$4.86	$4.86	$4.86	$4.86	$4.86	$4.86	$4.86	$4.86	$4.86	$4.86	$4.86
W	408	530	530	525	491	419	311	210	172	206	317	470
OVERFLOW	0	12	127	0	0	0	0	0	0	0	0	0
a	100	110	120	130	140	160	180	200	160	140	110	100
W LESS W-BAR	58	120	80	55	51	69	31	0	12	106	137	220
M	($133)	($98)	($62)	($27)	$8	$79	$150	$221	$79	$8	($98)	($133)
TR+S	$2998	$4873	$7574	$11345	$16476	$32222	$58161	$98588	$32222	$16476	$4873	$2998
SRTC	$29	$32	$35	$38	$41	$47	$52	$58	$47	$41	$32	$29
FC	$5369											
WELFARE	$282954											
PROFIT	($5)											
R/R-BAR%	106.67%	125.00%	133.33%	57.14%	50.00%	57.14%	28.57%	50.00%	70.00%	109.09%	89.47%	100.00%
R−R-BAR	11	45	56	−68	−68	−34	−56	−45	−34	11	−23	0
W/W-BAR	116.43%	129.25%	117.76%	111.78%	111.58%	119.84%	111.00%	100.05%	107.76%	205.66%	176.20%	187.91%

Table 11.4 Simulated seasonal prices

	Jan	Feb	Mar	Apr	May	Jun	Jul	Aug	Sep	Oct	Nov	Dec
RR	$442	$442	$442	$442	$442	$442	$442	$442	$442	$442	$442	$442
SRMC	$0.40	$0.40	$0.40	$0.40	$0.40	$0.40	$0.40	$0.40	$0.40	$0.40	$0.40	$0.40
TR	$319	$53	$58	$471	$507	$580	$1,044	$1,460	$1,168	$140	$63	$100
W-BAR	350	410	450	470	440	350	280	210	160	100	180	250
R-BAR	150	160	150	140	120	70	70	80	100	110	190	200
R	160	200	200	80	60	40	20	40	70	120	170	200
X-BAR	87	135	153	140	136	134	128	112	101	143	123	107
$R+W_t-(W_t-1)=X$	75	132	144	94	101	116	116	122	97	140	126	100
P	$4.26	$0.40	$0.40	$5.00	$5.00	$5.00	$9.00	$12.00	$12.00	$1.00	$0.50	$1.00
W	385	453	470	456	414	338	242	161	133	113	157	257
OVERFLOW	0	0	39	0	0	0	0	0	0	0	0	0
a	100	110	120	130	140	160	180	200	160	140	110	100
W LESS W-BAR	35	43	20	−14	−26	−12	−38	−49	−27	13	−23	7
M	($123)	($389)	($385)	$29	$65	$138	$602	$1,018	$726	($302)	($379)	($342)
$TR+S$	$3007	$4957	$7666	$11342	$16473	$32219	$58059	$98400	$32071	$16565	$4955	$3061
SRTC	$30	$53	$58	$38	$41	$46	$46	$49	$39	$56	$51	$40
FC	$4762											
WELFARE	$283467											
PROFIT	$655											
R/R-BAR%	106.67%	125.00%	133.33%	57.14%	50.00%	57.14%	28.57%	50.00%	70.00%	109.09%	89.47%	100.00%
$R-R$-BAR	10	40	50	−60	−60	−30	−50	−40	−30	10	−20	0
W/W-BAR	110.05%	110.50%	104.44%	96.97%	94.16%	96.67%	86.55%	76.51%	83.34%	113.34%	87.21%	102.79%

Table 11.4a   Simulated capacity expansion under seasonal pricing

	Jan	Feb	Mar	Apr	May	Jun	Jul	Aug	Sep	Oct	Nov	Dec
SRMC	$471	$471	$471	$471	$471	$471	$471	$471	$471	$471	$471	$471
	$0.40	$0.40	$0.40	$0.40	$0.40	$0.40	$0.40	$0.40	$0.40	$0.40	$0.40	$0.40
TR	$64	$70	$77	$524	$564	$645	$1,161	$1,290	$1,032	$89	$70	$64
W-BAR	350	410	450	470	440	350	280	210	160	100	180	250
R-BAR	160.5	171.2	160.5	149.8	128.4	74.9	74.9	85.6	107	117.7	203.3	214
R	171.2	214	214	85.6	64.2	42.8	21.4	42.8	74.9	128.4	181.9	214
X-BAR	87	135	153	140	136	134	128	112	101	143	123	107
$R+W_t-(W_t-1)=X$	112	123	134	92	99	113	113	125	100	157	123	112
P	$0.57	$0.57	$0.57	$5.71	$5.71	$5.71	$10.28	$10.28	$10.28	$0.57	$0.57	$0.57
W	359	450	503	497	462	392	300	218	192	164	223	325
OVERFLOW	0	0	0	0	0	0	0	0	0	0	0	0
a	100	110	120	130	140	160	180	200	160	140	110	100
W LESS W-BAR	9	40	53	27	22	42	20	8	32	64	43	75
M	($407)	($401)	($395)	$53	$93	$174	$690	$819	$561	($382)	($401)	($407)
TR+S	$3070	$4953	$7661	$11329	$16458	$32202	$58030	$98443	$32105	$16577	$4953	$3070
SRTC	$45	$49	$54	$37	$40	$45	$45	$50	$40	$63	$49	$45
FC	$5095											
WELFARE	$283196											
PROFIT	($5)											
R/R-BAR%	106.67%	125.00%	133.33%	57.14%	50.00%	57.14%	28.57%	50.00%	70.00%	109.09%	89.47%	100.00%
R – R-BAR	11	43	54	–64	–64	–32	–54	–43	–32	11	–21	0
W/W-BAR	102.67%	109.83%	111.76%	105.69%	105.03%	112.01%	107.32%	103.71%	120.19%	164.11%	123.87%	130.05%

meet a 50-year drought, because that drought can only be dealt with by means of rationing and an inflexible pricing policy. Flexible pricing provides a more efficient means of matching supply to demand. If supply is short, price can help ration it. If price cannot be changed, the only way to prevent long-term shortages is to plan to build extra capacity. Thus, flexible pricing (with price rationing) may mean that less capacity is required than in the case of uniform pricing (with quantity rationing).

11.3 REGULATORY PROBLEMS

Water utilities face rate-of-return regulation and environmental regulation. Both types of regulation have a rather severe impact on the many small companies in the industry. In view of the fact that water companies are supplying potable water it is not suprising that water companies are subject to environmental regulation. It is important that customers should receive water that is free of bacterial and other contaminants. Therefore regulation is employed to achieve certain quality standards. However, as the problem of contamination increases with the discovery and use of more hazardous substances, the problems for regulators and water companies increase. Regulations may be imposed that have prohibitively high compliance costs for small water companies and in many instances may involve problems that they do not in reality face. Regulation in such instances may either result in prohibitively costly service or non-compliance with the regulation. Compliance may be difficult to enforce in the case of small companies since fines will provide little deterrent in the absence of any significant assets. Moreover, to insist on enforcing the regulations fully might result in service being terminated.

Small companies face a number of problems in the area of rate-of-return regulation. There are many fixed costs associated with rate cases that do not vary with the amount of the filing. Small companies thus face proportionately much higher costs than large companies as a result of rate filings. As shown in Crew and Kleindorfer (1985), they file less frequently, presumably because of the relatively higher costs and lack of specialised expertise to deal with regulatory authorities. Their liquidity and ability to provide adequate service are thus undermined by their problems in obtaining timely rate relief. In view of their infrequent use of the regulatory process, they have little if any familiarity and expertise in the process and are likely to find that rate relief, when granted, is inadequate.

In view of the long lives of the capital equipment employed in water supply, it may take many years of inadequate returns before small water systems show serious deterioration. When this does happen, however, it may be very expensive to restore adequate service. The current regulatory policy of requiring small companies to file case materials similar to large companies gives scant recognition to the transactions costs facing small water companies and the major problems that are accumulating as a result of these costs.

11.4 IMPLICATIONS

Like the other utilities, water is facing a number of interesting problems. The problems of larger companies are not unlike some of the problems of the electric and telephone utilities: They want to enter unregulated business. For example, automatic meter reading might be owned and operated by a separate unregulated subsidiary of a water company, by a joint venture between a telephone company and a water company, or by a joint venture involving ownership with an entirely unregulated business. This would create similar regulatory problems to those discussed earlier where a regulated company also operates unregulated businesses.

At the other extreme are the problems of the small companies whose size places them at a disadvantage when dealing with regulation. The problems of small companies can be handled in a number of ways. One possibility may be municipal takeover; this may be inevitable if the capital is allowed to deteriorate indefinitely. Another possibility, which may prevent municipal takeover, is to make regulation more responsive to the needs of small companies. This may involve the use of simple methods involving automatic adjustments in rates, thereby avoiding heavy regulatory transactions costs of rate hearings. If this is coordinated with environmental regulation to ensure minimum service quality, then the decay of small water companies may be halted. A further alternative is the takeover of small companies by larger groups. However, this type of restructuring has already taken place with the water holding companies, some of which hold properties nationwide. Unfortunately many of the properties which might benefit from takeover are very unattractive and too small to warrant consideration for takeover by water utility holding companies. Even with their expertise in dealing with regulators, the holding companies would see little prospect of return from such properties. Thus, of these alternatives, the prospect of regulatory reform looks the most promising for small companies. Regulators need to develop streamlined methods of regulating small water utilities.

While innovations in technology such as automatic metering make efficient rates for water feasible, it is clear from the simulations and suggestive discussion of this chapter that there is plenty of scope for future research into clarifying optimal pricing and investment policies. Researchers now have an incentive to develop optimal pricing policies in the knowledge that major technical barriers to implementation no longer exist. Institutional barriers, including regulatory opposition, however, do exist to hinder the implementation of efficient rates. Regulators may object to giving the discretion to companies to implement non-traditional pricing schemes, such as those examined in Section 3. They need to become more aware of the advantages that improved economic efficiency would provide by way of reduced investment and enhanced ability to deal with drought conditions. Companies need to overcome their reluctance to consider such policies as well. The industry then is not short of regulatory challenges.

12 Implications for Future Research and Policy

Our primary concern in this book has been with recent advances in the economics of public utility regulation. In this chapter we will briefly restate the main lines that these advances have taken and discuss what we believe to be the most promising avenues for future research and some of the implications for regulatory policy.

12.1 PRICING

Since the publication of Crew and Kleindorfer (1979a) there has been some growth in the application of efficient pricing principles to utilities. Peak-load pricing has grown in its use in electric utilities, although it is by no means widespread. Time-of-day pricing has been in use in long-distance telecommunications for several years. However, little progress has been made in the extension of usage pricing to local telephone, let alone peak-load pricing. Similarly, in terms of access pricing, there has been little progress with time-of-day pricing and gross inefficiencies still remain. In gas there have been major steps toward efficient pricing with the 1978 Act deregulating new gas at the well-head. This has opened the door, however, to other inefficiencies, at least in the transition period during which some natural gas is still regulated. Different institutional structures may have to be created to deal with the new situation. For example, should gas pipelines be designated common carriers, and if so, what pricing policies might be employed to deal with peak demand, firm supplies and interruptible supplies?

In applied microeconomic theory, Ramsey pricing has maintained its central position as a benchmark for optimal pricing. Its role in decreasing cost industries and industries that have subadditive cost structures has received considerable attention. It has been extended to include complications like demand complementarity, which can lead to economically efficient prices below marginal cost in certain instances. While Ramsey pricing is not obviously widespread in its use, the problems of sustainability and efficient break-even pricing faced by industries such as telecommunications suggest that the extended

Ramsey pricing paradigm will continue to be a fundamental framework for understanding and evaluating regulatory institutions.

New technology makes more sophisticated pricing systems feasible that were not so previously. For example, as digital equipment makes the cost of measuring local calls inexpensive, pricing of local usage will become feasible, and the gains from peak-load pricing and economically efficient pricing can be achieved. While the major problems for efficient pricing may have been solved conceptually, the actual design of new pricing systems for local telephone companies that are constrained welfare maximising is non-trivial, e.g. because of informational and sustainability issues, to say nothing of efficient regulatory policy. Similarly with the advances that are taking place in the remote metering of water and gas more efficient pricing for these industries may not be far away.

12.2 THE NEW INSTITUTIONAL ECONOMICS

Developments in the new institutional economics have focused on the implications of bounded rationality and opportunism on the net efficiency, including transactions costs, of alternative governance structures. Such an approach is particularly relevant to comparative institutional assessments of regulatory governance structures for natural monopoly, since significant (internal and external) transactions costs may be caused by regulation. The new institutional economics leads to a deeper understanding of several issues hitherto addressed in the neoclassical framework. However, the crude and incomplete estimates of regulatory transactions costs presently available are inadequate for determining the welfare consequences of current regulatory structures, let alone characteristics of various alternative governance modes. Finding ways of measuring regulatory transactions costs is therefore an important item on the research agenda if the new institutional economics is to have practical application to the design of optimal regulatory governance structures for natural monopoly.

Other developments of interest here include understanding and measuring transactions costs in a broad sense. For instance, how does regulation affect the internal operation of the firm? To what extent is the firm changing its internal organisation and operation to satisfy demands of regulators rather than considerations of efficiency? If this is significant, then the costs of regulation are much higher than previously envisioned. Determining appropriate, testable theory in this regard remains a significant research problem.

12.3 RENT SEEKING

The theory of rent seeking was developed in the public choice literature. It seems to be particularly promising as an approach for evaluating certain aspects of regulation of natural monopolies. Rent seeking focuses on the opportunities for gains that are artificially created when natural monopolies are regulated, or when changes are made in the regulatory process which (threaten to) create or destroy rents. It explains several aspects of regulation which are not so explained by traditional economic theories such as the capture theory. For example, it provides a ready explanation for deregulation moves on the part of regulated industries, as well as the failure of regulated firms to make super-normal returns, which may be completely dissipated by rent seeking.

While rent seeking offers appealing insights into the theory of regulation, as in the case of transaction costs, it is very important to be able to measure its effects. For example, are rents taken primarily by insiders, employees of the firm and the regulatory commissions, or by outsiders such as regulatory attorneys, lobbyists and the like? Are most of the rents dissipated up front or are they consumed in an on-going process needed to legitimate and administer the monopoly? Almost nothing is known of the significance and magnitudes of the quantities involved. Moreover, as with transactions costs, many of the effects of rent seeking are hidden. Indeed, there may be incentives for rent seekers, in an attempt to preserve their rents, to ensure that their gains from rent seeking are hidden.

12.4 CONTESTABLE MARKETS AND SUSTAINABLE INDUSTRY STRUCTURES

Recent developments in industrial economics have propounded the notion that the restrictive assumption of large numbers required for competitive markets may not be needed as long as a market is contestable. Actual firms competing in a market may not be needed as long as there are not major barriers to entry in terms of sunk costs. This implies the existence of potential entrants who will enter the market if the (single) supplier attempts to charge prices that result in more than a competitive return. Deregulation of airline carriers has lent some support to the contestability theories where capital is mobile. However, in the case of utilities capital is not mobile. Indeed, in the language of the new institutional economics, it is highly transaction-specific. This limits considerably the role of contestable market theories to the regulation of natural monopoly. Instead it focuses interest on the related question of when investments in such transactions-specific assets can be undertaken by rational investors (i.e. when such investments can earn normal returns). This sustainability question is compounded with pricing, quality of service and regulatory governance issues, which we have reviewed for the telephone, gas and electric industries. Clearly, much research remains to be done here in clarifying the conditions under which controlled entry promotes efficiency and a viable infrastructure for the public utility sector.

12.5 INTERFACE OF REGULATED AND UNREGULATED BUSINESSES

The deregulation movement has not just brought entry to traditional utility markets, it has also increased interest by utilities of entering unregulated markets themselves. This has created significant problems in regulating the interface between their traditional regulated industries and their new non-regulated businesses. The interface presents a number of problems, not least the problem of subsidy of the unregulated or competitive business venture controlled by the regulated parent utility. As more utilities move into competitive lines regulatory control may be more difficult to achieve, and distortions in efficiency may occur, as new means are devised to avoid regulation.

Theories of the regulated firm in unregulated markets need to be developed further. In addition, the design of regulatory mechanisms for such firms which satisfy reasonable efficiency criteria including transactions-cost efficiency remains a further fruitful area for research.

12.6 OTHER POTENTIAL AREAS FOR DEVELOPMENT

The issues discussed above are likely to have additional ramifications for policy and future research. For example, with the current moves to deregulate utilities, anti-trust policy may take on a new role. It may in some instances replace regulation. If AT&T Communications does finally succeed in getting rid of existing regulation of its long-distance business, by federal and state regulators, anti-trust may enter the picture as a means of preventing abuse of market power by AT&T Communications, the dominant carrier. Similarly to the extent that predatory pricing by subsidiaries of regulated monopolies is perceived as a threat, anti-trust may face new challenges.

Concerning regulation itself, new research and policy directions are clearly visible. These come foremost from new perspectives on incentives and transactions costs arising out of recent advances in the new institutional economics and the theory of rent seeking. Regulatory institutions cannot ignore the welfare implications of rent seeking and transactions costs. They may have to trade-off some abuse of market power to avoid some of the welfare losses induced by transactions costs and rent seeking. Approaches to regulation using automatic rate adjustments with incentives for efficiency may provide the appropriate tradeoff between X-inefficiency and regulatory transactions costs. New regulatory schemes that rely less on the formal due process safeguards of the current system of quasi-judicial regulation may offer further promise of efficiency gains in regulated industries, provided that the market power trade-off is not excessive. The challenges for the theory and practice of regulation of natural monopoly have never been greater.

Notes

1 Background

1. The interested reader is referred to Faulhaber (1975), Panzar (1980) and Phillips (1980) for discussions of the problems of economies of scope and sustainability. We also address these issues in Chapter 2.
2. Panzar and Willig (1981) provide a more rigorous definition of this and also show that economies of scope exist if and only if the cost function in respect of the input shared by each output is subadditive. We will pursue economies of scale and scope more rigorously in the next chapter.
3. We are concerned with what is known as the problem of governance choice. Governance means the set of transactions needed to perform a certain task or tasks. In the case of natural monopoly the choice of governance mode concerns the choice between the various ways of controlling the natural monopoly.
4. The early version of the theory, as developed by Leibenstein (1966), concentrated particularly on production costs differences. It was for the new institutional economics to provide the added precision made possible by the introduction of transactions costs.

2 Efficiency and Equity Aspects

1. See Arrow and Scitovsky (1969) and Mishan (1971) for an introduction to this literature.
2. We will usually distinguish the variable of integration (y in (2.2)) from the variable limits of integration (x in (2.2)).
3. This definition and related analysis are due to Hotelling (1932). See also Pressman (1970) for a more recent discussion.
4. The reader not interested in the technical details need not be concerned with the nature of line integrals. For the reader wishing to pursue this, the appendix to Chapter 2 of Crew and Kleindorfer (1979) gives an explanation. Other explanations may be found in Pressman (1970).
5. When the budget constraint has to be met exactly the following looser conditions can be applied in place of (2.6)–(2.7). For all i,j,k:

$$p_k\left(\frac{\partial P_i}{\partial q_j}-\frac{\partial P_j}{\partial q_i}\right)+p_i\left(\frac{\partial P_j}{\partial q_k}-\frac{\partial P_k}{\partial q_i}\right)+p_j\left(\frac{\partial P_k}{\partial q_i}-\frac{\partial P_i}{\partial q_k}\right)=0.$$

When all income elasticities are equal across goods and individuals these latter conditions are easily shown to hold whether budgets are fixed or not.

6. See Samuelson (1947), Little (1957) and Silberberg (1978).

7. Willig (1976) provides bounds within which consumer surplus approximates Hicksian compensating and equivalent variations.

8. See Comanor and Leibenstein (1969) and Crew (1975) for a development of these issues.

9. The importance of this issue might be noted by reference to the 'early' literature, for example Coase (1946), Farrell (1958), Henderson (1948), Hotelling (1938), Ruggles (1949), Tyndall (1951) and Wiseman (1957). For some recent restatements, see Drèze (1964), Marchand (1973), Feldstein (1972), Ng and Weisser (1974).

10. Let $C(x)$ represent total costs at output level x. Let $AC(x)$ denote average costs $C(x)/x$ and let $MC(x)$ denote marginal cost $dC(x)/dx$. The reader can easily verify that $dAC(x)/dx = [MC(x) - AC(x)]/x$, so that, for any positive output level x, if $dAC(x)/dx < 0$ then $MC(x) < AC(x)$. It can also be verified that if $MC(x)$ is everywhere decreasing (concave costs), then assuming $C(x) \geqslant 0$, $MC(x) < AC(x)$. Thus either decreasing marginal or average costs leads to the result that marginal cost will be less than average cost. There are reasons other than scale economies that can cause observed average costs to exceed marginal costs. Feldstein (1972, p. 183–4) states: 'Although there are now several econometric studies showing approximately constant returns to scale in the production of electricity, the very substantial distribution costs imply that long-run marginal cost is much less than long run average costs.' This is possibly true, but such differences could arise from the fact that an inefficient pricing policy is employed with the effect that capacity is not utilised to the full. As will become apparent in the next and subsequent chapters, such under-utilisation could mean that $LRAC$ (defined as $LRTC$ divided by total output) is greater than $LRMC$, ignoring distribution costs.

11. This argument about least distortion applies only to the case of increasing returns. When decreasing returns obtain, a symmetric argument could be applied with a maximum profit constraint replacing (2.22). But such a case could also be handled by setting $p_i = MC_i$ and employing a lump-sum tax to absorb surpluses without introducing allocative inefficiencies.

12. Other forms of these conditions also exist in the literature, e.g. Rohlfs (1979):

$$\left[\frac{P_i - C_i}{P_i} \right] \zeta_i = \left[\frac{P_j - C_j}{P_j} \right] \zeta_j, \qquad \text{for all } i,j \qquad (*)$$

where $\zeta_i = 1/[\Sigma_j (R_j/R_i) \varphi_{ji}]$, where $\varphi_{ji} = (\partial P_j(X_1, \ldots, X_n)/\partial X_i)(X_i/P_j)$, with $P(X)$ the inverse demand function (i.e. $P(X(\mathbf{p})) = \mathbf{p}$). Rohlfs calls φ_{ji} 'flexibility' of price j with respect to product i and ζ_i the super-elasticity of product i. The reader should note however, that $\varphi_{ji} \neq 1/\eta_{ij}$ since $\partial P_j(X_1, \ldots, X_n)/\partial X_i \neq 1/(\partial X_i(P_1, \ldots, P_n)/\partial P_j))$ and the interpretation of ζ_i and therefore also of (*) is difficult. Indeed, φ_{ji} need not even have the same sign as η_{ij} (see Nguyen and MacGregor-Reid (1977)).

13.   It is interesting to relate (2.35) and (2.36) to the scope economics of Chapter 1. Assuming (2.35)–(2.36) hold for a cost function $C(x,y)$ for two products (x,y) we have

$$C(x,y) = C((x,0)+(0,y)) = C(0.5(2x,0)+0.5(0,2y))$$

$$\leqslant 0.5C(2x,0)+0.5C(0,2y) < C(x,0)+C(0,y),$$

so that (2.35) and (2.36) together imply that joint production is always more efficient than independent production.

14.   This is related to Faulhaber and Levinson's (1981) notion of anonymous equity. If prices can be found satisfying anonymous equity, then no consumer group can be attracted away by an entrant attempting to fill the demands of that consumer group. We also note in passing that Postlewaite and Panzar (1984) provide a preliminary analysis of sustainability of nonlinear prices, and their results are not encouraging for the existence of sustainable nonlinear price schedules.

15.   Baumol, Bailey and Willig (p. 405) state the following: In an intertemporal setting, 'unsustainability can come closer to being the rule than the exception'.

16.   The notion has something in common with Okun's notion that fairness is so important in some cases that allocation cannot be entrusted to the market.

17.   Governance is usually used to mean the 'governance of contractual relations' (Williamson 1979, pp. 223–4) which is 'the institutional framework in which contracts are initiated, negotiated, motivated, adapted, enforced and terminated' (Palay 1984, p. 265).

18.   Moreover as finding the efficient solution is by no means trivial, the simplification provided by using (2.1) offers considerable benefits.

3   Deterministic Models of Peak-load Pricing

1.   The reader wishing to explore this theory in detail should consult Crew and Kleindorfer (1979a).

2.   If we were to start Figure 3.3 at the origin, we would have to replace β, β' and β'' with $b+\beta$, $2b+\beta'$ and $3b+\beta''$.

3.   See, for example, Hotelling (1932), Drèze (1964) and Nelson (1964).

4.   We use the term 'plant' throughout this book to refer to the various types of capacity available. It is hoped that this will not detract from interpreting the results in areas where 'plant' is not the usual designation of capital equipment (e.g. in transportation).

5.   See Turvey (1969) for a discussion of the determination of b_1, β_1. for b_1 this is a straightforward allocation of operating costs once units have been fixed. For β_1 this consists essentially of pro-rating the annuitised cost of building and maintaining the plant over its useful life. Thus, if the basic cycle is one year and the life of a plant of size 100 is 50 years,

then β would equal 1/100th of the annuity sufficient to maintain and replace the given plant after 50 years.

6. Of course, when cost minimisation cannot be assumed, for example under regulation of a profit-maximising firm (as in Chapter 6), then the various problem specifications lead to different possibilities for describing departures from cost-minimising behaviour. Note that economies of scale can be treated via the cost-function formulation (3.1).

7. Rigorous proofs to establish (3.19)–(3.20) as necessary conditions for using both plant types are given in Crew Kleindorfer (1979a).

8. More generally, multipart tariffs are specified through break-points $0 = \bar{x} < \bar{x}_1 < \ldots < \bar{x}_k$ and prices p_{1i}, p_{2i}, where marginal unit x in $\bar{x}_{j-1} \leqslant x < x_j$ is sold at price p_{ji} in period i. The two-part tariff in the text is obtained by specifying p_{1i} so that $p_{1i} \bar{x}_1 = F$ and letting $\bar{x}_1$ approach zero.

4 Stochastic Models of Peak-load Pricing

1. In general it can be established for the deterministic case that excess demand is optimal only when demand varies within pricing periods. Even here, however, one would expect that the zero excess-demand condition (imposed in the previous chapters) is a close approximation to reality, especially when demand uncertainty is low (see Crew and Kleindorfer (1979a, p. 52).

2. The reader can easily verify this solution from (3.10)–(3.13) for the case of $m = n = 1$.

3. The analysis of this section was developed originally in Crew and Kleindorfer (1976). Copyright © 1976, The American Telephone and Telegraph Company, reprinted with permission from the *Bell Journal of Economics*.

4. See Carlton (1977) and Rees (1980) for further discussion on this point.

5. On pp. 69–77 we also discuss the multiplicative form $D(p,\tilde{v}) = v\tilde{X}(p)$, with $E(\tilde{v}) = 1$. It should be noted that equation (4.1) and the non-negativity of x imply that $\tilde{u}$ should actually depend on p. In equations (4.26) and (4.27) we show that $b_1 \leqslant p_i \leqslant b_1 + \beta_1$ for all i. Thus (4.1) need only be a good approximation of demand in this range.

6. Given the regularity conditions above (see (4.2)), one condition which assures the existence of $\bar{W}$ is that $\tilde{u}$ have a compact range, i.e. there is some closed and bounded set $\Omega^c R^n$ such that $Pr\{\tilde{u} \ \varepsilon \ \Omega\} = 1$.

7. Strictly speaking, these are first-order conditions. It can be shown, however, that these conditions are also sufficient (see Crew and Kleindorfer 1979, p. 92).

8. When taking expected values with respect to a random variable, say $\tilde{u}$, we use the notation $\int u dF(u)$, where $F(u)$ is the cumulative distribution function of $\tilde{u}$. The reader who wishes may substitute $dF(u) = f(u)du$ everywhere, where $f(u)$ is the density function of $\tilde{u}$.

9. If rationing costs are strictly monotonic i.e. $r_i'(y) > 0$ when $y > 0$), then $F_i(z - X_i(p_i)) > 0$ is certainly satisfied since $F_i(z - X_i(p_i)) = 0$ implies $F_i(Q_l - X_i(p_i)) = 0$, for all $l = 1, \ldots, m$. Moreover, $F_i(z - X_i(p_i)) = 0$,

implies $E\{r_i'(X_i(p_i)+u_i-z)\}>0$. From (5.11) these two conditions would violate $\partial \bar{W}/\partial p_i=0$, which is a necessary condition (except in the uninteresting case $p_i=0$).

10. This contrasts with the recent results by Carlton (1977), to which we return in Section 4.3. Carlton finds that price may exceed $b_1+\beta_1$ if rationing is sufficiently inefficient (e.g. if rationing is random).

11. Alternatively, the reader may think of the following analysis as being restricted to the peak period, where all off-peak periods are such that demand is less than optimal capacity with probability 1, with the consequence see (4.17) for $m=1$) that price $=b$ in off-peak periods. See Crew and Kleindorfer (1978) and Sherman and Visscher (1978) for a discussion of the multiperiod case.

12. This statement assumes that (4.11)–(4.12) (or their equivalents, (4.35)–(4.36)) are sufficient for optimality.

13. See Billingsley (1968, p. 24) for a proof of this; assuming that $\tilde{u}\rightarrow0$ means convergence in distribution to a random variable having a degenerate distribution centered at the origin.

14. See also the more extended discussion of these issues in Crew and Kleindorfer (1978).

15. These costs could well be borne by the producer, even if they are just surplus losses. For example, for a utility employing a two-part tariff, the utility might agree to pay (by reducing entry fees) those consumers who will be cut off in the event of excess demand (see also Dansby (1977) in this regard).

16. For a more detailed discussion, see Sherman and Visscher (1978).

17. See also note 15 in this regard.

18. The reader will note that any price between 0 and 15 would be optimal. However, in line with our assumption we are disregarding any 'optimal' prices which do not at least recover operating expenses.

5 Origin and Operation of Regulation in the USA

1. *Munn* v. *Illinois*, 94 US 113 (1877).
2. *Sinking Fund Cases*, 99 US 700, 747 (1878).
3. *Budd* v. *New York*, 143 US 517 (1892)
4. *Nebbia* v. *New York*, 291 US 502 (1934), p. 531.
5. See *Federal Power Commission* v. *Hope Natural Gas Co.*, 320 US 591 (1944) and also Phillips (1984)
6. See *Hope Natural Gas Co.*, *op cit.*, p. 603.
7. *Market Street Railway Co* v. *Railroad Commission of California*, 324 US 548, 567 (1945).
8. For a detailed examination of the philosophical aspects of such issues see Nozick (1974)
9. Posner (1974, p. 335). He states the theory very clearly although he is putting it forward as a straw man to knock down with his own theory. See Bonbright (1961) for an illustration of the public interest theory.
10. For a description of how the electric companies worked to obtain regulated status see Anderson (1980, 4–16) in Wilson (1980).

11. The hold-up problem may not be exactly along the lines of Klein, Crawford and Alchian (1978) but may arise from the effects of franchise bidding. For a further discussion, see Chapter 7.

12. If some of the rent seekers earn rents, the area $ACGB$ is reduced somewhat by the amount of such rents.

13. Although the total welfare function (5.3) is only defined for $\eta > 1$, welfare *comparisons* for (P,G) pairs when $\eta \leqslant 1$ are still justified provided the demand function is of the assumed constant elasticity form over the relevant range of prices compared.

14. This is not a matter of universal agreement. For example Phillips (1982 and 1985) has argued that the telecommunications industry will be subject to more regulation rather than less under the current structure as weaker competitors strive to protect their positions. Phillips' notion is similar to the economic theories concerning the demand for cartel management.

6   Models of Monopoly Regulation

1. A list of some major contributions is: Bailey (1973), Baumol and Klevorick (1970), El Hodiri and Takayama (1973), Kafoglis (1969), Takayama (1969), Westfield (1965), Zajac (1970 and 1972).

2. It is possible to show that $0 < \lambda < 1$ if (6.2) is binding, as Baumol and Klevorick (1970), Bailey (1973), and Takayama (1969) have done.

3. For a formal proof of this, see Baumol and Klevorick (1970).

4. This section is based on Crew and Kleindorfer (1981).

5. The regulatory constraint appears at first unfamiliar when compared with the one plant constraint $\pi \leqslant (s - \beta)q_l$. It can be derived straightforwardly from the basic form of the multiplant constraint $\pi \leqslant (s-r)\Sigma h_l q_l$. A slight rearrangement using $rh_l = \beta_l$ yields equation (6.13).

6. The fact that $\lambda < 1$, for example, follows directly from (6.16) below and $\mu_{1l} \geqslant 0$ since this implies $1 - \lambda s/r \geqslant 0$, that is $\lambda \leqslant r/s < 1$.

7. In view of the convex set formed by the constraints, the Kuhn–Tucker conditions are both necessary and sufficient if the profit function is concave and differentiable, which we henceforth assume.

8. For the proof of $d\sigma/ds > 0$ see Crew and Kleindorfer (1981).

9. See Chapter 3. These results are stated in the context of a welfare-maximising firm, but structurally there is no problem applying the results here where price and output are determined by equating marginal revenue instead of price to marginal cost.

10. Refer to note 8.

11. We assume a firm peak case here, where $x_2 > x_1$ at the prices implied by (6.24)–(6.25).

12. The reader can verify that if $\sigma_2 > 1$, then only the first two regions of Figure 6.1 apply, while if $\sigma_1 > 1$, only the first region in Figure 6.1 applies. Only in the last case will proper choices on types of technology be made by the regulated monopolist for all levels of the allowed rate of

return s. Of course, in all cases the price distortions of the monopolist will continue, as evident from Figure 6.1.

13. As is shown in Crew and Kleindorfer (1981) it follows that $d\sigma/ds > 0$ and that $d(\Sigma\beta_l q_l)/ds < 0$. This is the classic Averch–Johnson result that outlay on capital increases as the allowed rate of return is lowered. One advantage of our approach is that it looks deeper into the diverse technology problem integrating plant mix and pricing consequences of regulation.

14. We regard gold plating as synonymous with rate-base padding. This is probably not the usual use of the term. For example, Zajac (1972, p. 311) notes: 'In the past, rate base padding allegations have generally been of two forms: (1) that regulated firms "gold plate", i.e., use unnecessarily expensive materials and designs or (2) that they maintain excessive spare capacity.' Our analysis will be concerned with the second of these components of rate-base padding.

15. We can see this by noting that $u_{2i} = \text{Max } \tilde{u}_i$, by definition, implying from (6.35) and $z^* = R^*/s$ that demand cannot exceed capacity.

16. Bailey (1973, p. 107) criticises Sheshinski (1971) on the grounds that 'he neglected ... to point out the possibility that the solution $s = r$ may be optimal; instead he left the reader with the impression that an interior $s(s > r)$ will always maximise social welfare'. However, her criticism seems to rely on resolving the indeterminacy that results when $s = r$ by assuming that 'the regulated firm operates efficiently when $s = r$'. Klevorick (1971) also discussed several possibilities for the firm when $s = r$. However, to assume at $s = r$ that the firm will become efficient surely serves only to add a *deus ex machina* to the regulator's inadequate tool-box. We have not dealt with, and at this stage will not deal with, the issue of when $s = r$ is welfare optimal.

17. For an introduction to the use of general equilibrium in the analysis of regulation, see Bailey (1973, pp. 107–9) and Peles and Stein (1976, pp. 287–9).

7 Alternative Governance Structures for Natural Monopoly

1. Williamson (1976, p. 73) highlighted the problem as follows: 'Merely to show that regulation is flawed, however, does not establish that regulation is an inferior mode of organizing economic activity ... (thus) before regulation is supplanted there is an obligation to assess the properties of the proposed alternative.'

2. This approach differs considerably from the neoclassical approach. The latter has the notion of economic man who is self-seeking and rational with apparently unbounded capabilities in this area. The new institutional economics sees man as being rational but only within the limits placed upon him by his ability to process information. It, however, views man as pursuing his own self-interest and doing so with guile – opportunism. Thus transaction costs are minimised to the extent that bounded rationality is economised and opportunism attenuated.

3. The majority of a utility's customers are final consumers – households –

making vertical integration infeasible for them. The product is supplied
so extensively, to almost every business, that takeover of business by a
utility is not feasible. Although rare in practice, backward integration by
a customer of a utility might be feasible where the customer was big and
a large proportion of its costs derived from inputs purchased from the
utility.

4. In Europe public enterprise is the dominant governance structure for
   natural monopoly, and in France, for example, Electricité de France is
   known for being perhaps the most innovative of all natural monopolies,
   at least in its application of efficient pricing.

5. De Alessi (1974 and 1977) shows that public enterprise rate structures
   were less complex, innovative, and marginal-cost based than in regulated
   electric companies.

6. Evans and Heckman (1984) reject the hypothesis that the Bell system's
   cost function was subadditive for the output levels produced between
   1958–77, casting doubt on the importance of scale or natural monopoly
   and lending some weight to the competitive view.

7. Feigenbaum and Teeples (1983) showed no difference in the costs of
   public and private water utilities. Pescatrice and Trapani (1980) show
   that publicly owned untilities have significantly lower costs than
   privately owned utilities. Meyer (1975) gets mixed results. Moore (1970),
   Wallace and Junk (1970) Crain and Zardkoohi (1978), and De Allessi
   (1974) show higher costs for publicly-owned than for privately-owned
   utilities. In other industries Blankart's (1980) survey shows usually
   inferior performance by public enterprise.

8. To the extent that rent-seeking still occurs in the course of and after
   deregulation monopoly rents may be eaten up, along the lines of Crew
   and Rowley (1986).

8 Electricity

1. This is cited by Lewis (1941) from Hopkinson's *Original Papers*. For a
   survey of later developments of Hopkinson's approach, see Schiller
   (1945a and 1945b) and *Electric Utility Rate Design Study* (1977).

2. On the Continent, however, the situation has been totally different, the
   time-of-day tariffs of *Electricité de France* presenting a different approach. We will discuss this briefly later on in this chapter. For details
   see Acton, Manning and Mitchell (1978).

3. In the USA these are usually called 'customer', 'energy' and 'demand'.

4. Load factor is a means of measuring the extent to which capacity is
   utilised. Thus system load factor is the ratio, expressed as a percentage of
   (a) the units of electricity supplied through the system in a year to, (b) the
   number which would have been supplied if maximum demand had been
   maintained for all 8760 hours of the year.

5. The calculation turns out to be a fairly routine one in view of the
   experience that the load factor of domestic consumers is not very
   sensitive to the size of the consumer's total consumption. For more
   details, see Crew (1966), De Salvia (1969) and Ineson (1963).

6. See Ineson (1963) for a brief explanation.

7. This monstrous figure is taken from *Electric Utility Rate Design Study* (1977).

8. This section is based upon Finsinger and Kleindorfer (1981).

9. This section is based upon Crew and Kleindorfer (1982).

10. These various forms are distinguished not only according to the decision process of the firm, but also according to how often the firm may violate its rate-of-return constraint and what happens to excess revenues when it does. These matters are examined in detail in Crew and Kleindorfer (1980).

11. Crew and Kleindorfer (1976) provide results characterising minimum expected-cost operation and technology choice in the optimal welfare context. These results can be extended to develop, in simple terms, the effect of regulation on prices in a profit-maximising context, substituting marginal revenue (MR) for price in these earlier derivations. Using Crew and Kleindorfer (1976, pp. 213–16), $MR = \Sigma_j \, \gamma_j b_j$ where γ_j is the probability that plant j will be the last plant used conditional upon sufficient capacity being available to meet demand. Depending upon the value of $\delta(s)$, the plants forming the convex technological frontier, that is, those satisfying

$$\frac{\delta(s)(\beta_j - \beta_j + 1)}{b_{j+1} - b_j} < \frac{\delta(s)(\beta_{j-1} - \beta_j)}{b_j - b_{j-1}} < 1$$

will vary, with the least capital-intensive plants being eliminated as $\delta(s)$ is reduced. The actual amount of each plant used will depend upon the following relation

$$\delta(s)(\beta_j - \beta_{j+1}) = (b_{j+1} - b_j) Pr \left[D(p, \tilde{u}) \geqslant \sum_j q_j \right]$$

Thus, the conditional probabilities γ_j will depend upon the amount of each plant type used with a consequent reduction in MR and thus also price s is reduced.

12. For a formal proof of this theorem see Crew and Kleindorfer (1981). We provide here only an intuitive explanation of these results.

13. There are a number of troubled plants like Long Island Lighting Company's Shoreham plant and Public Service New Hampshire's Seabrook plant. Delays have led to massive cost overruns for these plants. They are now estimated to have a capital cost of $4000 per kW in the case of Shoreham and capital cost of $2800 in the case of Seabrook. This translates into a cost per kWh of 18 cents and 12 cents respectively. These figures are based upon estimates cited by Itteilag and Pavle (1985).

14. The arguments here are based upon Crew and Crocker (1985), which contains detailed development and proofs of the principal results.

15. It is apparently succeeding. Recently the Department of Energy has raised its projections cogeneration capacity to 47,435 MW by the end

of the century. In 1980 there were 8087 MW of capacity (see *Cogeneration Report*, 18 January 1985, p. 1.)

16. A sweetheart deal occurs when an apparently arms-length transaction is used to mask a surreptitious and more comfortable deal

17. *Cogeneration Report*, 18 January 1985, p. 6 cites John Eustis as indicating that there are plans to soften the avoided-cost standard, so that full avoided cost may not be paid. Eustis is also quoted as holding the opinion that utilities will attempt to obtain relaxation of the 50 per cent ownership rule.

18. The subsidies provided by ratepayers have the effect of raising costs for ratepayers in a number of ways. They may, depending on the tariff even result in actual energy waste compared to the case where the electricity is produced by the grid. For example, in the case of the Trenton District Energy Company, the times that the steam will have to be dumped correspond to the times when PSE&G's demand is lowest – spring and autumn, and night and early morning. At other times some displacement will occur because diesel's running costs compare very unfavourably with those of base-load and intermediate plant. Using PJM's energy cost figures for 1983 if TDEC dumped steam for the whole of the off-peak period the extra energy wasted is estimated to be valued at $389,835. This figure varies inversely with the amount of steam dumped. Crew and Crocker (1985b) estimate that PSE&F's customers would pay $1.21 million in excess of what it would have cost PSE&G to buy the power from PJM or produce it itself. This works out at $101.21 per kW capacity. Thus while the project may have some saving to society in terms of total energy used a price is extracted from PSE&G's ratepayers. This provides support for our argument that institutional arrangements need to be devised that allow benefits, such as energy savings, without the use of a subsidy.

9 Telecommuncations

1. In Chapter 2 we argued that pricing a complentary good below marginal cost may be Ramsey optimal under certain circumstances. Less formally, Phillips (1985) has argued that this policy may have been based upon sound economic principles and not just been the result of chance developments in technology:

> old Theodore Vail was motivated in pricing decisions much as was King C. Gillette. People would not use the telephone (safety razor blade) unless they owned a telephone (razor). Pricing an access good at less than full cost – perhaps even less than marginal cost – makes sense if through that process there are more compensating increments to net revenue from a related, complementary good.

(1985 p. 8; see also Phillips and Roberts, 1985.)

2. For example Microwave Communications, Inc. (Docket No 16509–

19), 18 FCC 2d 953 (1969), and Specialized Common Carriers (Docket No 18920), 29 FCC 2d 870 [1971].

3. See Opinion Misc. No. 82–0025, 26 July 1984.

4. The divested operating companies accounted for about three-quarters of the total of AT&T according to Arthur D. Little, *Analysis of Telecommunications Industry Restructuring 3* (September 1977).

5. According to Carne (1984, p. 21) in 1984 $37 billion out of a total of $56.6 billion derives from domestic and overseas long distance.

6. Other utilities have similar, but simpler, problems of pricing access. You cannot buy gas unless you are connected to the gas main. However, you can only use the gas main to get gas. If you could use the same pipe to get gas and water then the same problem as that of local and long distance would arise.

7. A 'club' is an organisation which provides a service to its members, the price of which is a flat fee allowing unlimited consumption of the club's service over a given period.

8. According to the principles of Part II the prices would need to be set in such a way that shifting peaks were accounted for.

9. This is known as the access externality. It is obviously difficult to quantify. Squire (1973) has argued that there are not only access externalities but call externalities. These arise from the fact that when a call is made one party, the recipient of the call in most cases, receives a benefit for which he does not pay. Such effects may result in departures from marginal cost. However, as long as local service was cheap there was little reason to be concerned about the access or the call externality.

10. If this is indeed the impact of technological change the effect of regulation would be to preserve the monopoly position and to reduce the rate of technological change.

11. British Telecom, for example, has three rates operating – two day rates and one rate for evening, night and weekend. Traffic patterns will determine whether this is justified in the USA.

12. Long-distance carriers could also provide intra-LATA toll calls utilising the local company's facilities at both ends and just using its own facilities within the LATA to transmit the call. The bulk of this discussion, however, will concern inter-LATA access.

13. Part of the payment is taken by the National Exchange Carriers Association (NECA) and pooled for distribution among carriers according to their obligations to serve sparsely-populated areas. In this example New Jersey Bell would be a net contributor to the pool and Pacific Telephone a net recipient.

14. The minutes of usage are not normally measured by the local companies. The rate of $300 per line is based upon the assumption that usage averages 9000 minutes. The long-distance carriers therefore have an incentive to improve utilisation of their lines. At the terminating end of the call the carrier may have to pay a toll charge if the call terminates outside the local calling area.

15. We will argue in the next section that the profit maximising firm under

Averch–Johnson regulation will under plausible assumptions find it in its interests to prevent bypass.

16. If this sector were to be deregulated immediately, companies would drastically raise their local rates. They may, however, not report higher profits as they would probably use the extra revenue to write off some of the capital in the depreciation reserve.

17. Sharkey (1982, pp. 189–213), writing prior to Divestiture assembled a number of powerful arguments, using principally engineering cost analyses, to show that departure from the monopoly would result in duplication of facilities, and therefore presumably higher costs.

10 Gas

1. US Energy Information Administration (EIA), *Monthly Energy Review*, May 1983.
2. *Philips Petroleum Com.* v. *Wisconsin*, 374 US 672 (1954).
3. A take-or-pay contract obliges a pipeline to pay for a certain amount of gas at a specified price whether it takes it or not. Thus a pipeline, with a take-or-pay contract one and a contract without take-pay-provisions at lower prices than the other will find it cheaper not to buy from the cheaper producer taking the minimum of gas from him and pay for the maximum of gas up to the take obligation from the more expensive producer. This raises the price paid for gas and creates perverse incentives by leaving the cheaper gas unused. Take an example where a pipeline has two contracts, one with 'take' obligations of x, and a unit price of ap ($a > 1$), and the other with a unit price of p but no 'take' obligations. If the customer's requirements are say only $1.5x$ his costs will be minimised at $apx + .5px$. However, in the absence of a take-or-pay obligation his costs would have only been $(1.5)px$ since he would have used only the cheaper gas.
4. In *Central Illinois Light Co.* v. *Panhandle Eastern Pipe Co.*, FERC Docket No. RP82–105–000, some of the fixed charges were built into the commodity charge, as well as a minimum bill.
5. In view of the transaction-specific investments made by the pipeline this kind of contract may be seen as an attempt, in the absence of vertical integration along the lines of Klein, Crawford and Alchian (1978) to prevent hold-up by the gas distributor and thereby avoid expropriation of its quasi-rents. While it may succeed in this regard it does impose other inefficiencies.
6. Recently there has been an expansion by traditional utilities into gas brokering as we will see in Section 3. The extent that this arises from the desire to enter unregulated business or from the availability of surplus gas on take-or-pay contracts is not clear.
7. They support their argument by means of some empirical work. They showed both the effects of price regulation and the efficient breach properties at work, both being significant. The effect of price regulation they calculated at the mean values of the independent variables, to increase the predicted take obligation from 79 per cent to 85 per cent.

8. Historically this has been the arrangement that has prevailed. Originally the pipelines may have been the only buyers of the gas in the absence of developed markets. Regulation in the form of the 1938 Act which required pipelines to have reserves and the well-head price control also contributed to this. The effect now is for pipelines to own most of the gas. As a result they may look unfavourably on a policy that mandated them to carry gas that displaced the gas they owned particularly if take-or-pay obligations are involved.

9. FERC has issued a 'Notice of Proposed Rulemaking' in this regard.

10. See *Sunday Star Ledger*, 9 June 1985. NUI through EME is attempting to adjust to the new opportunities created by the deregulation of gas prices at the well-head. If they did not do this someone else would, so Elizabethtown Gas would likely lose the business anyway.

11. This problem is akin to that raised by Crew and Crocker (1985) with regard to cogeneration where the regulated customers end up with the higher priced capital.

12. For details see in Crew and Crocker (1985a) for several ways including transfer prices and subsidised inputs that the partially regulated firm may use to exploit its regulated monopoly position.

13. We have not indicated all the possibilities available to gas companies. In encouraging cogeneration PURPA also made available opportunities to gas companies both as partners in cogeneration projects and as suppliers to them.

11 Water Supply

1. It really is more complex than this. For example dry weather means not only that supply is down but also the demand increases for sprinkling and crop irrigation. Thus demand is related directly with the stochastic supply. We will, however, ignore such considerations.

2. This is not to say that attempts have not been made to introduce innovative rates that attempted to take into account at least the seasonal nature of water supply. For the Spring Valley Water Company the New York Public Service Commission approved a seasonal rate, with rates increasing in the summer months. Unfortunately, as it proved impossible to read all meters on or close to the start of the new rate period, estimates had to be made which attenuated the effects of the seasonal pricing policy.

3. The innovation we have in mind is a system of automatic meter reading which is performed over the telephone lines. Instead of reading meters by means of walking meter readers, this would all be performed automatically over the telephone. A computer would call the customer's number and would read the meter. This would be done in the dead of night to minimise busies and to improve utilisation of telephone company plant. For all the customers of a company it could be accomplished over a very short period making it possible for the company to change rates frequently in response to supply conditions.

4. The material which follows is based largely on Crew and Schlenger (1985).

5. All of these conditions refer to the amount of water consumed per period.
6. Riley and Scherer do not treat these as stochastic variables.
7. The procedure is highly simplified, ignoring problems of capacity of treatment, confining itself entirely to a balance between optimal storage and demand.
8. Net benefits = total benefits–total costs = total revenues + consumer's surplus – total costs. To the extent that this measure fails to take into account the costs of shortages, induced by stochastic variations in demand and supply, it is an inadequate measure of short-run benefits. In the long run, maximising net benefits will result in the familiar zero profit result if constant returns prevail. However, in the event of short-run capacity shortages, excess profits may be earned when net benefits are maximised. In this case, because the regulator is concerned with controlling prices, it is assumed that a price will not be set high enough to ration capacity. Hence, the only way water can be conserved and excess profits avoided is by rationing.
9. Of course, for each of the three regimes studied, we have only determined that one price and capacity configuration approximately zero profits. It would clearly be of interest to determine the entire set of price-capacity pairs yielding zero profits, so that welfare and supply reliability could be optimised subject to a break-even constraint, along the lines of Crew and Kleindorfer (1979a and 1980).

Appendix

DERIVATION OF FIRST-ORDER CONDITIONS
(CHAPTER 4)

We derive the first derivatives of the expected welfare function $\bar{W}$ equation (4.10) of Section 4.2. We shall assume that $\bar{W}$ is sufficiently regular to allow interchanging the expectation and differentiation operators. This being so, we have from (4.1) and the chain rule:

$$\frac{\partial}{\partial p_i}\left(\sum_{i=1}^{n} \int_0^{S_i(p_i,u_i,z)} P_i(z_i - u_i)dx_i \right)$$

$$= P_i(S_i(p_i,u_i,z) - u_i)\frac{\partial}{\partial p_i}S_i(p_i,u_i,z)$$

$$= \begin{cases} p_i X'_i(p) & \text{if } u_i < z - X_i(p_i) \\ \\ 0 & \text{if } u_i > z - X_i(p_i), \end{cases} \tag{4.1A}$$

where $'$ denotes differentiation and S_i is as defied in (4.8), and $P_i = X_i^{-1}$, so that $P_i(X_i(p_i)) = p_i$. Thus, after interchanging expectation and differentiation, (4.1A) yields:

$$\frac{\partial}{\partial p_i}\left(E\left\{ \sum_{i=1}^{n} \int_0^{S_i(p_i,\tilde{u}_i,z)} P_i(x_i - \tilde{u}_i)dx_i \right\} \right)$$

$$= \sum_{i=1}^{n} p_i X'_i(p_i)F_i(z - X_i(p_i)). \tag{4.2A}$$

From (4.5) and (4.3) plant l will be used in period i precisely when

$$Q_{l-1} - X_i(p_i) \leqslant \tilde{u}_i \leqslant Q_l - X_i(p_i),$$

so that:

$$E\{b_l q_{li}(D_i(p_i,u_i),\mathbf{q})\} = b_l \int_{Q_{l-1}-X_i(p_i)}^{Q_l - X_i(p_i)} (D_i(p_i,\tilde{u}_i) - Q_{l-1})dF_i(u_i). \tag{4.3A}$$

From (4.42) an interchange of expectation and differentiation yields:

$$\frac{\partial}{\partial p_i} E\{b_l q_{li}(D_i(p_i,\tilde{u}_i),\mathbf{q})\}$$

$$= b_i \int_{Q_{l-1}-X_i(p_i)}^{Q_l-X_i(p_i)} \frac{\partial}{\partial p_i} (D_i(p_i,u_i) - Q_{l-1}) dF_i(u_i)$$

$$= b_i X_i'(p_i)(F_i(Q_l - X_i(p_i)) - F_i(Q_{l-1} - X_i(p_i)))]. \tag{4.4A}$$

Similarly:

$$\frac{\partial}{\partial p_i} E\{r_i(X_i(p_i) + \tilde{u} - z) = X_i'(p_i)E\{r'_i(X_i') + \tilde{u}_i - z)\}. \tag{4.5A}$$

Combining (4.A2), (4.A4) and (4.A5) with (4.10), we obtain (4.11).

Proceeding to the derivation of $\partial \bar{W}/\partial q_k$, we recall that $z = q_1 + \ldots + q_m$ so that:

$$\frac{\partial}{\partial q_k}\left(\sum_{i=1}^n \int_0^{S_i(p_i,u_i,z)} P_i(x_i - \tilde{u}_i)dx_i\right)$$

$$= \begin{cases} 0 & \text{if } u_i < z - X_i(p_i) \\ P_i(z - u_i) & \text{if } u_i > z - X_i(p_i) \end{cases} \tag{4.6A}$$

so that, interchanging expectation and differentiation:

$$\frac{\partial}{\partial q_k}\left(E\{\sum_{i=1}^n \int^{S_i(p_i,u_i,z)} P_i(x_i - u_i)dx_i\}\right)$$

$$= \sum_{i=1}^n \int_{z-X_i(p_i)}^{\infty} P_i(z - u_i)dF_i(u_i). \tag{4.7A}$$

Also, (4.A3) implies:

$$\frac{\partial}{\partial q_k}\left(E\left\{\sum_{i=1}^n \sum_{l=1}^m b_l q_{li}(D_i(p_i,\tilde{u}_i),\mathbf{q})\right\}\right)$$

$$- b_k[1 - F_i(Q_k - X_i(p_i))] + \sum_{l=k+1}^m b_i[F_i(Q_l - X_i(p_i)) -$$

$$- F_i(Q_{l-1} - X_i(p_i))]. \tag{4.8A}$$

Finally, interchanging expectation and differentiation:

$$\frac{\partial}{\partial q_k}(E\{r_i(X_i(p_i) + \tilde{u}_i - z)\}) = E\{r'_i(X_i(p_i) + \tilde{u}_i - z)\}, \tag{4.9A}$$

so that (4.10) and (4.A7)–(4.A9) yield (4.12), as desired.

PROOF OF RESULTS FROM SECTION 8.3 (CHAPTER 8)

Proof of Result 1: Fix any $\tau \in T$. First note from (8.15) that, for any p, p' as given above, $E(x, p')$ will be no greater than $E(x,p)$ for any $x \geqslant 0$. Thus, by revealed preference, we have

$$U(p', \tau) = V(x(p', \tau), \tau) - E(x(p, \tau),p') + m(\tau)$$

$$\geqslant V(x(p, \tau), \tau) - E(x(p, \tau),p') + m(\tau)$$

$$\geqslant V(x(p, \tau), \tau) - E(x(p, \tau),p) + m(\tau) = U(p,\tau).$$

We see that every consumer would just as soon face prices p' as p.

Proof of Result 2: The reader may check directly that the asserted solution satisfies the necessary condition (8.28)–(8.30) by noting from (8.20)–(8.22) that $p_0 = 0$ implies $V_i = p_i$ for all i. From this and (8.28), $\partial W/\partial p_i = 0$ for all i. Thus, the necessary conditions are satisfied by marginal-cost pricing. Concerning sufficiency, it can be verified following the proof of Result 1 that $\partial W/\partial p_0 \leqslant 0$ whenever (8.28)–(8.30) are satisfied and $p_0 > 0$.

Proof of Result 3: Assume that all consumers have a firm peak in some period i in the sense that $x_i(p,\tau) > x_j(p,\tau)$ for $j \neq i$ and for all τ. Then, from (8.19)–(8.22), the prices given will yield $\gamma_i(\tau) = p_0 = \beta$ and $\gamma_i(\tau) = 0$ for $j \neq i$. Thus, setting $\mu_i = \beta$ and $\mu_j = 0$ for $j \neq i$, the first-order conditions (8.28)–(8.30) will hold, since $V_i = p_i + \gamma_i(\tau) = b + \mu_i$ will obtain in all periods.

Proof of Result 4: Since consumers are identical, for any price vector the set of periods at which the system peak is achieved coincide with the set of periods at which each consumer's maximum demand is achieved. Thus, considering the price vector $\mathbf{p}$ given by $p_0 = \beta$ and $xp_i = b$, $i \neq 0$, we can define (for an arbitrary consumer τ, the quantities $\mu_i(\tau) = \gamma_i(\tau)$ and $p_i = b + \mu_i$, $i = 1, \ldots, n$. It is easy to check that the marginal cost) price vector $\mathbf{p}' = (0, p_1, \ldots, p_n)$ solves (8.28)–(8.30) and induces the same allocation as the assumed Hopkinson tariff p. Thus, p is optimal (as is also p', of course).

References

ACTON, J. P., MANNING, W. G., Jr and MITCHELL, B. M. (1978), *Peak Load Pricing: European Lessons for US Energy Policy* (Cambridge, Mass., Ballinger Publishing Co.)

AKERLOF, G. A., (1970) 'The Market for "Lemons": Qualitative Uncertainty and the Market Mechanism', *Quarterly Journal of Economics*, 84, August, pp. 488–500.

ALCHIAN, A. A. and DEMSETZ, H. (1972), 'Production, Information Costs, and Economic Organization', *American Economic Review*, 62, 5, December, pp. 777–95.

ANDERSON, D. G. (1980) 'State Regulation of Utilities', in Wilson J. Q. (ed.)

ARROW, K. J. (1971) *Essays in the Theory of Risk Bearing* (Chicago, Markham).

ARROW, K. J. and SCITOVSKY, T. (1969) *Readings in Welfare Economics*, (Homewood, Irwin).

AVERCH, H. and JOHNSON, L. L. (1962) 'Behavior of the Firm Under Regulatory Constraint', *American Economic Review*, 52, December, pp. 1052–69.

AXELROD, R. (1984) *The Evolution of Cooperation* (New York, Basic Books).

AXELROD, R. and HAMILTON, W. D. (1981) 'The Evolution of Co-operation', *Science*, 211, pp. 1390–96.

BAILEY, E. E. (1972) 'Peak Load Pricing under Regulatory Constraint', *Journal of Political Economy*, 80, July/August, pp. 662–79.

BAILEY, E. E. (1973) *Economic Theory of Regulatory Constraint* (Lexington Books, D.C. Heath).

BAILEY, E. E. and WHITE, L. J. (1974), 'Reversals in Peak and Off-Peak Prices', *Bell Journal of Economics*, 5, 1, Spring, pp. 75–92.

BARON, D. P. and BESANKO, D. (1984) 'Regulation, Asymmetric Information and Auditing', *Rand Journal of Economics*, 15, Winter, pp. 447–70.

BARON, D. P. and MYERSON, R. (1982) 'Regulating a Monopolist with Unknown Costs', *Econometrica*, 50, pp. 911–30.

BAUMOL, W. J. (1977) 'On the Proper Tests for Natural Monopoly in a Multiproduct Industry', *American Economic Review*, 67, 5, December, pp. 809–22.

BAUMOL, W. J., BAILEY, E. E. and WILLIG, R. D. (1977) 'Weak Invisible Hand Theorems on the Sustainability of Natural Monopoly', *American Economic Review*, 67, pp. 350–65.

BAUMOL, W. J. and BRADFORD, D. (1970), 'Optimal Departures from Marginal Cost Pricing', *American Economic Review*, 60, June, pp. 265–83.

BAUMOL, W. J. and KLEVORICK, A. K. (1970) 'Input Choices and Rate of Return Regulation: An Overview of the Discussion', *Bell Journal of Economics*, 1, Autumn, 162–90.

BAUMOL, W. J., PANZAR, J. C. and WILLIG, R. D. (1982) 'Weak Invisible Hand Theorems on the Sustainability of Prices in a Multiproduct Monopoly', *American Economic Review*, 67, June, pp. 350–65.

BAUMOL, W. J., PANZAR, J. C. and WILLIG, R. D. (1984) *Contestable Markets and the Theory of Industrial Structure* (New York, Harcourt, Brace and Jovanovich).

BILLINGSLEY, P. (1968) *Convergence of Probability Measures* (New York, NY, Wiley).

BLANKART, C. B. (1980) 'Bureaucratic Problems in Public Choice', in Roskamp, K. W. (ed.), *Public Choice and Public Finance* (Cujas Publications, Paris).

BOITEUX, M. (1949) 'La tarification des demandes en point: application de la theorie de la vente au cout marginal', *Revue Generale de l'electricite*, 58, August, pp. 321–40; translated as 'Peak Load Pricing', *Journal of Business*, 33, April 1960, pp. 157–79.

BOITEUX, M. (1956) 'Sur la gestion des monopoles publics astrients a l'equilibre budgetaire', *Econometrica*, 24, January, pp. 22–40; translated as 'On the Management of Public Monopolies Subject to Budgetary Constraints', *Journal of Economic Theory*, 3, 3, September 1971, pp. 219–40.

BONBRIGHT, J. C. (1961) *Principles of Public Utility Rates* (New York, NY, Columbia University Press).

BÖS, D. (1986) *Public Enterprise Economics* (North-Holland, Amsterdam).

BÖS, D., TILLMANN, G., and ZIMMERMANN, H. G. (1983) 'Bureaucratic Public Enterprises', Discussion Papers, University of Bonn, West Germany.

BOYES, W. J. (1976) 'An Emperical Examination of the Averch–Johnson Effect', *Economic Inquiry*, 14, March, pp. 25–35.

BRAEUTIGAM, R. R. (1980) 'An Analysis of Fully Distributed Cost Pricing in Regulated Industries', *Bell Journal of Economics*, 11, Spring, pp. 182–96

BROWN, B., JR. and JOHNSON, M. B. (1969) 'Public Utility Pricing and Output under Risk', *American Economic Review*, 59, March, pp. 119–29.

BUCHANAN, J. M., TOLLISON, R. D. and TULLOCK, G. (eds) (1980) *Toward a Theory of the Rent-Seeking Society* (Texas A&M Press, College Station, Texas).

CARLTON, D. W. (1977) 'Peak Load Pricing with Stochastic Demands', *American Economic Review*, 67, 5, December, pp. 1006–10.

CARNE, E. BRYAN (1984) *Modern Telecommunication* (New York, Plenum Press).

CHAMBERLAIN, J. (1984) 'Municipal Goverment: Past, Present and Future', *The New Review*, 61, June.

CHAO, H. (1983) 'Peak Local Pricing and Capacity Planning with Demand and Supply Uncertainty,' *Bell Journal of Economics*, 14, Spring, 179–90.

COASE, R. (1937) 'The Nature of the Firm', *Economica*, 13, pp. 386–405.

COASE, R. (1946) 'The Marginal Cost Controversy', *Economica*, 13, August, pp. 169–82.

COLE, L. P. (1981) 'A Note on Fully Distributed Cost Prices', *Bell Journal of Economics*, 12, Spring, pp. 329–34.

COMANOR, W. and LEIBENSTEIN, H. (1969) 'Allocative Efficiency, X-Efficiency and the Measurement of Welfare Losses,' *Economica*, 36, August 1969, pp. 304–9.

COMMONS, J. (1934) *Institutional Economics* (Madison, Wis., University of Wisconsin Press).

COURVILLE, L. (1974) 'Regulation and Efficiency in the electric Utility Industry', *Bell Journal of Economics*, 5, Spring, pp. 53–74.

CRAIN, W. M. and ZARDKOOHI, A. (1978) 'A Test of the Property-Rights Theory of the Firm: Water Utilities in the United States', *Journal of Law and Economics*, 21, October, pp. 395–408.

CREW, M. A. (1966) 'Pennine Electricity Board', in Kempner and Wills (1966); also reprinted in Turvey (1968a).

CREW, M. A. (1975) *Theory of the Firm* (London, Longmans).

CREW, M. A. (ed.) (1979) *Problems in Public Utility Economics and Regulation* (Lexington Books, Lexington).

CREW, M. A. (ed.) (1980) *Issues in Public Utility Economics and Regulation* (Lexington Books, Lexington).

CREW, M. A. (ed.) (1982) *Regulatory Reform and Public Utilities* (Lexington, Mass., Lexington Books.)

CREW, M. A., (1984) 'Royalty Contracts: an Efficient Form of Contracting?', *Southern Economic Journal*, 50, January, pp. 724–33.

CREW, M. A. (ed.) (1985) *Analysing the Impact of Regulatory Change* (Lexington, Lexington Books).

CREW, M. A. and CROCKER, K. J. (1985a) 'Regulating the Partially Deregulated Firm' (Unpublished).

CREW, M. A. and CROCKER, K. J. (1985b) 'Vertically Integrated Governance Structures and Optimal Institutional Arrangements for Cogeneration', *Journal of Institutional and Theoretical Economics*, December.

CREW, M. A. and DANSBY, R. E. (1982) 'A Cost Benefit Analysis of Local Measured Service', in CREW (ed.) 1982.

CREW, M. A. and KLEINDORFER, P. R. (1971) 'Marshall and Turvey on Peak Loads or Joint Product Pricing', *Journal of Political Economy*, 79, 6, November/December, pp. 1369–77.

CREW, M. A. and KLEINDORFER, P. R. (1975a) 'On Off-Peak Pricing: An Alternative Technological Solution', *Kyklos*, 28, 1, pp. 80–93.

CREW, M. A. and KLEINDORFER, P. R. (1975b) 'Optimal Plant Mix in Peak Load Pricing', *Scottish Journal of Political Economy*, 22, 3, November, pp. 277–91.

CREW, M. A. and KLEINDORFER, P. R. (1976) 'Peak Load Pricing with a Diverse Technology', *Bell Journal of Economics*, 7, Spring, pp. 207–31.

CREW, M. A. and KLEINDORFER, P. R. (1978) 'Reliability and Public Utility Pricing', *American Economic Review*, 68, March, pp. 31–40.

CREW, M. A. and KLEINDORFER, P. R. (1979a) *Public Utility Economics* (London, Macmillan).

CREW, M. A. and KLEINDORFER, P. R. (1979b) 'Some Elementary Considerations of Reliability and Regulation', in CREW (ed.) 1979.

CREW, M. A. and KLEINDORFER, P. R. (1979c) 'Managerial Discretion and Public Utility Regulation', *Southern Economic Journal*, 45, January 1979b. pp. 696–709.

CREW, M. A. and KLEINDORFER, P. R. (1980) 'Public Utility Regulation and Reliability with Applications to Public Utilities', in CREW (ed.) (1980).

CREW, M. A. and KLEINDORFER, P. R. (1981) 'Regulation and Diverse Technology and the Peak Load Problem', *Southern Economic Journal*, 48, October, pp. 335–43.

CREW, M. A. and KLEINDORFER, P. R. (1982) 'Electricity Pricing and Plant Mix under Supply and Demand Uncertainty', in CREW (ed.) (1982).

CREW, M. A. and KLEINDORFER, P. R. (1985) 'Governance Costs of Rate-of-Return Regulation', *Journal of Institutional and Theoretical Economics* 141, March, pp. 104–23.

CREW, M. A., KLEINDORFER, P. R. and SUDIT, E. F. (1979) 'Incentives for Efficiency in the Nationalised Industries: Beyond the 1978 White Paper', *The Journal of Industrial Affairs*, 7, Autumn, pp. 11–15.

CREW, M. A. and ROWLEY, C. K. (1986) 'Regulation as an Instrument for Industrial Policy', *Journal of Institutional and Theoretical Economics* (forthcoming).

CREW, M. A. and SCHLENGER, D. L. (1985) 'Opportunities for Regulation and Rate Design of Innovative Metering Technology in Water Utilities', in CREW (ed.) (1985).

CROCKER, K. J. (1983) 'Vertical Integration and the Strategic Use of Private Information', *Bell Journal of Economics*, 14, Spring, pp. 236–48.

CROSS, J. G. (1970) 'Incentive Pricing and Utility Regulation', *Quarterly Journal of Economics*, 84, May, pp. 236–253.

DANSBY, R. E. (1975) 'Peak Load Pricing with Time Varying Demands', Bell Laboratories, Holmdel, New Jersey, 1975.

DANSBY, R. E. (1977) 'Multi-Period Pricing with Stochastic Demand', Bell Laboratories Economic Discussion Paper No 111, October.

DAVIS, O. A. and WHINSTON, A. B. (1965) 'Welfare Economics and the Theory of Second Best', *Review of Economic Studies*, 32, January, pp. 1–14.

DE ALESSI, L. (1974) 'An Economic Analysis of Government Ownership and Regulation: Theory and the Evidence from the Electric Power Industry', *Public Choice*, 19, Fall, pp. 526–538.

DE ALESSI, L. (1977) 'Ownership and Peak Load Pricing in the Electric Power Industry', *Quarterly Review of Economics and Business*, 17, Winter, pp. 7–26.

DE SALVIA, D. N. (1969) 'An application of Peak Load Pricing', *Journal of Business*, 42, 4, October, pp. 458–76.

DEMSETZ, H. (1968) 'Why Regulate Utilities', *Journal of Law and Economics*, 11, April, pp. 55–65.

Domestic Tariffs Experiment (1974) (London, Electricity Council).

DRÈZE, J. (1964) 'Some Postwar Contributions of French Economists to Theory and Public Policy, with Special Emphasis on Problems of Resource Allocation', *American Economic Review*, 54 supplement, June, pp. 1–64.

DUPUIT, J. (1844) 'De la Mesure de l'Utilité des Travaux publics', *Annales des Ponts et Chaussées*, 8; reprinted in Arrow and Scitovsky (1969).

EL HODIRI, M. and TAKAYAMA, A. (1973) 'Behavior of the Firm under Regulatory Constraint: Clarifications', *American Economic Review*, 63, March, pp. 235–37.

Electric Utility Rate Design Study (1977) 'Analysis of Electric Pricing in France and Great Britain', Topic 1.2, 25 January. Electric Power Research Institute, Palo Alto, California.

EVANS, D. S. and HECKMAN, J. J. (1984) 'A Test for Subadditivity of the Cost Function With and Application to the Bell System', *American Economic Review*, 74, September, pp. 615–23.

FARRELL, M. J. (1958) 'In Defense of Public Utility Price Theory', *Oxford Economic Papers*, 10, February, pp. 109–23.

FAULHABER, G. R. (1975) 'Cross-Subsidization: Pricing in Public Enterprises', *American Economic Review*, 65:5, December, pp. 966–77.

FAULHABER, G. R. and LEVINSON, S. (1981) 'Subsidy Free Prices and Anonymous Equity', *American Economic Review*, 71, December, pp. 1083–91.

FEIGENBAUM, S. and TEEPLES, R. (1983) 'Public Versus Private Water Delivery: A Hedonic Cost Approach', *Review of Economics and Statistics*, 65, November, pp. 672–78.

FELDSTEIN, M. S. (1972) 'Equity and Efficiency in Public Pricing', *Quarterly Journal of Economics*, 86, May, pp. 175–87.

FINSINGER, J. and KLEINDORFER, P. R. (1981), 'Demand Charges and Electricity Tariffs', Working Paper, Department of Decision Sciences, University of Pennsylvania, Philadelphia, Pennsylvania.

GERWIG, R. W. (1962) 'Natural Gas Production: a Study of Costs Regulation', *Journal of Law and Economics*, 5, October, pp. 69–92.

GLAESER, M. G. (1957) *Public Utilities and American Capitalism* (New York, NY, The Macmillan Company).

GOLDBERG, V. P. (1976) 'Regulation and Administered Contracts', *Bell Journal of Economics*, 7, Autumn, pp. 426–48.

HAMLEN, W. A. JR. and JEN, R. (1983) 'An Alternative Model of Interruptible Service Pricing and Rationing', *Southern Economic Journal*, 49:4, April, pp. 1108–21.

HAYAK, F. (1945) 'The Use of Knowledge in Society', *American Economic Review*, 35, September, pp. 519–30.

HAYASHI, P. M. and TRAPANI, J. M. (1976) 'Rate-of-Return Regulation and the Firm's Equilibrium Capital–Labor Ratio: Further Empirical Evidence of the Averch–Johnson Hypothesis', *Southern Economic Journal*, 42, January, pp. 384–98.

HENDERSON, A. M. (1948) 'Price and Profits in State Enterprise', *Review of Economic Studies*, 16, pp. 13–24.

HENDERSON, J. M. and QUANDT, R. E. (1971) *Microeconomic Theory* (New York, NY, McGraw-Hill).

HIRSHLEIFER, J. (1958) 'Peak Loads and Efficient Pricing: Comment', *Quarterly Journal of Economics*, 72, August, pp. 451–62.

HOTELLING, H. (1932) 'Edgeworth's Taxation Paradox and the Nature of

Demand and Supply Functions', *Journal of Political Economy*, 40, 5, October, pp. 577–616.

HOTELLING, H. (1935), 'Demand Function with Limited Budgets', *Econometrica*, 3, January, pp. 66–78.

HOTELLING, H. (1938) 'The General Welfare in Relation to Problems of Taxation and of Railway and Utility Rates', *Econometrica*, 6, July, pp. 242–69.

HYMAN, L. S. (1983) Americas Electric Utilities: Past, Present and Future, Arlington, VA., *Public Utilities Reports*, 1983.

INESON, J. L. (1963) 'Fixing Electricity Tariffs', *Electrical Power Engineer*, June–August, pp. 1–11.

ITTEILAG, R. and PAVLE, J. (1985) 'Impact of Nuclear Plants' Anticipated Costs on Future Prices', *Gas Energy Review*, 13, January, pp. 11–15.

JOSKOW, P. L. (1982a) 'Industrial Cogeneration and Electricity Production in the US.' in CREW (ed.) (1982) Lexington Books.

JOSKOW, P. L. (1982b) 'The Simple Economics of Industrial Cogeneration', *The Energy Journal*, 3, pp. 1–22.

JOSKOW, P. L. and SCHMALENSEE, R. (1984) *Markets for Power* (Cambridge, Mass., MIT Press).

KAFUGLIS, M. Z. (1969), 'Output of the Restrained Firm,' *American Economic Review*, 59, pp. 553–7.

KAHN, A. E. (1970) *The Economics of Regulation: Vol. 1* (New York, NY, Wiley).

KAHN, A. E. (1971) *The Economics of Regulation: Vol. 2* (New York, NY, Wiley).

KEMPNER, T. and WILLS, G. (1966) *Bradford Exercises in Management* (London, Nelson).

KLEIN, B., CRAWFORD, R. G. and ALCHIAN, A. A. (1978) 'Vertical Integration, Appropriable Rents, and the Competitive Contracting Process', *Journal of Law and Economics*, 21, October, pp. 297–326.

KLEINDORFER, P. R. and GLOVER, K. (1973) 'Linear Convex Stochastic Optimal Control with Application in Production Planning', *IEEE Transactions on Automatic Control*, 18, 1, February, pp. 56–9.

KLEINDORFER, P. R. and KNIEPS, G. (1982) 'Vertical Integration and Transactions-Specific Sunk Costs', *European Economic Review*, 19, pp. 71–87.

KLEVORICK, A. K. (1971) 'The "Optimal" Fair Rate of Return', *Bell Journal of Economics*, 2 (Spring), pp. 122–53.

LANCASTER, K. (1979) 'The Problem of Second Best in Relation to Electricity Pricing', *Electric Utility Rate Design Study*, 7, August.

LEIBENSTEIN, H. (1966) 'Allocative Efficiency versus X-Efficiency', *American Economic Review*, 56, June, pp. 392–415.

LELAND, H. A. and MEYER, R. A. (1976) ' Monopoly Pricing Structures with Imperfect Discrimination', *Bell Journal of Economics*, 7, Autumn, pp. 449–62.

LEWIS, W. A. (1941) 'The Two-Part Tariff', *Economica*, 8, August, pp. 249–70.

LINDSAY, C. M. (1976) 'A Theory of Government Enterprise', *Journal of Political Economy*, October, pp. 1061–77.

LIPSEY, R. E. and LANCASTER, K. M. (1956) 'The General Theory of Second Best', *Review of Economic Studies*, 24, 1, pp. 11–32.

LITTLE, I. M. D. (1957) *Critique of Welfare Economics* (Oxford, Oxford University Press).

LOEB, M. and MAGAT, W. A. (1979) 'A Decentralised Method for Utility Regulation', *Journal of Law and Economics*, 22, October, pp. 58–73.

MARCHAND, M. G. (1973) 'The Economic Principles of Telephone Rates Under Budgetary Constraint', *Review of Economic Studies*, 40, October, pp. 507–15.

MARCHAND, M. G. (1974) 'Pricing Power Supplied on an Interruptible Basis', *European Economic Review*, 5, pp. 263–74.

MARINO, A. (1978) 'Peak-load Pricing in a Neoclassical Technology with Bounds on Variable Input Utilization', *Bell Journal of Economics*, 9, Spring, pp. 249–59.

MARSHALL, A. (1890) *Principles of Economics* (London, Macmillan).

MASTEN, S. E. and CROCKER, K. J. (1985) 'Efficient Adaption in Take-or-Pay Contracts: Take-or-Pay Provisions for Natural Gas', *American Economic Review*, 75, December, pp 1083–93.

MASHAW, J. (1985) *Appropriate, Competent and Dignified: Due Process Ideals for an Administrative State* (Yale University Press, New Haven).

McCORMICK, R. E., SHUGART, W. F. and TOLLISON, R. D. (1984) 'The Disinterest in Deregulation', *American Economic Review*, 74, December, pp. 1075–79.

McKIE, J. W. (1970) 'Regulation and the Free Market: the Problem of Boundaries', *Bell Journal of Economics*, 1, Spring, pp. 6–26.

MEEK, R. L. (1963) 'The Bulk Supply Tariff for Electricity', *Oxford Economic Papers*, 15, July, pp. 107–23.

MEYER, R. A. (1975a) 'Monopoly Pricing and Capacity Choice Under Uncertainty', *American Economic Review*, 65, June, pp. 426–37.

MEYER, R. A. (1975b) 'Publicly Owned Versus Privately Owned Utilities: A Policy Choice', *Review of Economics and Statistics*, 57, November, pp. 391–99.

MISHAN, E. J. (1971) *Cost-Benefit Analysis* (London, Allen and Unwin).

MISHAN, E. J. (1981) *An Introduction to Normative Economics* (New York, NY, Oxford University Press).

MITCHELL, B. M. (1978) 'Optimal Pricing for Local Telephone Service', *American Economic Review*, 68, September, pp. 517–37.

MITCHELL, B. M. and KLEINDORFER, P. R. (eds) (1980) *Regulated Industries and Public Enterprise* (Lexington, Massachusetts, Lexington Books).

MOORE, J. G. (1970) 'The Effectiveness of Regulation of Electricity Prices', *Southern Economic Journal*, 36, July, pp. 365–75.

Nationalised Industries: a Review of Economic and Financial Objectives, Cmnd 3437, White Paper, HMSO, London, 1967.

Nationalised Industries, The, Cmnd 7131, White Paper, HMSO, London, 1978.

NELSON, J. R. (1964), *Marginal Cost Pricing in Practice*, (Englewood Cliffs, NJ, Prentice-Hall).

NELSON, J. R. (1976) 'Marginal Cost Pricing' in H. Trebing (ed.), *Essays on*

Public Utility Pricing and Regulation (East Lansing, Mich., Michigan University Press).

NG, T. K. and WEISSER, M. (1974) 'Optimal Pricing with a Balanced Budget Constraint – the Case of the Two-Part Tariff', *Review of Economic Studies*, 41, July, pp. 337–45.

NGUYEN, D. T. and MACGREGOR-REID, G. J. (1977) 'Interdependent Demands, Regulatory Constraint and Peak-Load Pricing', *Journal of Industrial Economics*, 25, June, pp. 275–93.

NISKANEN, W. A. (1971) *Bureaucracy and Representative Government* (New York, NY, Aldine-Atherton).

NISKANEN, W. A. (1973) *Bureaucracy, Servant or Master?* (London, Institute of Economic Affairs).

NOZICK, R. (1974) *Anarchy, State and Utopia* (New York, NY, Basic Books).

OI, W. Y. (1971) 'A Disneyland Dilemma: Two-Part Tariffs for a Mickey Mouse Monopoly', *Quarterly Journal of Economics*, 85, 1, February, pp. 77–96.

OKUN, A. M. (1975) *Equality and Efficiency: the Big Tradeoffs* (Washington DC, Brookings Institution).

OWEN, B. M. and BRAEUTIGAM, R. (1978) *The Regulation Game: Strategic Uses of the Administrative Process* (Cambridge, Mass.: Ballinger).

PALAY, T. A. (1984) 'Comparative Institutional Economics: the Governance of Rail Freight Contracting', *Journal of Law and Economics*, 13, June, pp. 265–88.

PANZAR, J. C. (1976) 'A Neoclassical Approach to Peak Load Pricing', *Bell Journal of Economics*, 7, Autumn, pp. 521–30.

PANZAR, J. C. (1980) 'Sustainability, Efficiency and Vertical Integration', in MITCHELL, B. M., and KLEINDORFER, P. R. (eds) (1980) *Regulated Industries and Public Enterprise* (Lexington, Lexington Books).

PANZAR, J. C. and SIBLEY, D. S. (1978) 'Public Utility Pricing Under Risk', *American Economic Review*, 6871, December, pp. 888–95.

PANZAR, J. C. and WILLIG, R. D. (1977) 'Free Entry and the Sustainability of Natural Monopoly', *Bell Journal of Economics*, 8, Spring, pp. 1–22.

PANZAR, J. C. and WILLIG, R. D. (1981) 'Economies of Scope', *American Economic Review*, 71, May, pp. 268–72.

PELES, T. C. and STEIN, J. L. (1976) 'The Effect of Rate of Return Regulation is Highly Sensitive to the Nature of Uncertainty', *American Economic Review*, 66, June, pp. 278–89.

PELTZMAN, S. (1976) 'Toward a More General Theory of Regulation', *Journal of Law and Economics*, 19, August, pp. 211–40.

PESCATRICE, D. R. and TRAPANI, J. M. (1980) 'The Performance and Objectives of Public and Private Utilities Operating in the United States', *Journal of Public Economics*, 13, pp. 259–76.

PETERSON, H. C. (1975) 'An Emperical Test of Regulatory Effects', *Bell Journal of Economics*, 6, Spring, pp. 111–26.

PHILLIPS, A. (1980) 'Ramsey Pricing and Sustainability with Interdependent Demand', in MITCHELL, B. M. and KLEINDORFER, P. R. (eds)

(1980) *Regulated Industries and Public Enterprise* (Lexington, Mass., Lexington Books).

PHILLIPS, A. (1982) 'The Impossibility of Competition in Telecommunications', in CREW (ed.) (1982).

PHILLIPS A. (1985) 'The Re-integration of Telecommunications: An Interim View', in CREW (ed.) (1984).

PHILLIPS, A. and ROBERTS, G. L. (1985) 'Borrowing from Peter to Pay Paul: More on Departures from Marginal Cost', in FISHER, F. M. (ed.) *Antitrust and Regulation: Essays in Honor of John McGowan* (Cambridge, Mass., MIT Press).

PHILLIPS, C. F., JR. (1984) *The Regulation of Public Utilities*, Public Utility Reports, (Arlington, Virginia).

POSNER, R. A. (1969) 'Natural Monopoly and its Regulation', *Stanford Law Review*, 21, February, pp. 548–643.

POSNER, R. A. (1974) 'Theories of Economic Regulation', *Bell Journal of Economics*, 5, Autumn, pp. 335–58.

POSNER, R. A. (1975) 'The Social Costs of Monopoly Regulation', *Journal of Political Economy*, 83, August, pp. 807–27.

POSTLEWAITE, A. W. and PANZAR, J. C. (1984) 'Sustainable Outlay Schedules', Discussion Paper no. 172, C.S.O.I., University of Pennsylvania.

PRESSMAN, I. (1970) 'A Mathematical Formulation of the Peak Load Pricing Problem', *Bell Journal of Economics*, 1, Autumn, pp. 304–26.

RAMSEY, F. P. (1927) 'A Contribution to the Theory of Taxation', *Economic Journal*, 37, March, pp. 47–61.

RAWLS, J. (1971) *A Theory of Justice* (Cambridge, Mass., Harvard University Press).

RAWLS, J. (1974a) 'Some Reasons for the Minimax Criterion', *American Economic Review*, 64, May, pp. 341–45.

RAWLS, J. (1974b) 'Reply', *Quarterly Journal of Economics*, November, pp. 633–55.

REES, R. (1974) 'A Reconsideration of the Expense Preference Theory of the Firm', *Econometrica*, 41, August, pp. 295–307.

REES, R. A. (1980) 'Consumer Choice and Nonprice Rationing in Public Utility Pricing', in MITCHELL, B. M. and KLEINDORFER, P. R. (eds) (1980) *Regulated Industries and Public Enterprise* (Lexington, Mass., Lexington Books).

RILEY, J. G. and SCHERER, C. R. (1979) 'Optimal Water Pricing and Storage With Cyclical Supply and Demand', *Water Resources Research*, 15, April, pp. 233–39.

ROHLFS, G. (1979) 'Economically Efficient Bell System Prices', *Bell Laboratories Discussion Paper* No. 138.

ROSKAMP, K. W. (ed.) (1980) *Public Choice and Public Finance* (Cujas Publications, Paris).

RUGGLES, N. (1949) 'The Welfare Basis of the Marginal Cost Pricing Principle', *Review of Economic Studies*, 17, pp. 29–46.

SAMUELSON, P. A. (1947) *Foundations of Economic Analysis* (Cambridge, Mass., Harvard University Press).

SAMUELSON, P. A. (1954) 'The Pure Theory of Public Expenditure', *The Review of Economics and Statistics*, 36, November, pp. 387–89.

SAPPINGTON, D. (1980) 'Strategic Firm Behavior under a Dynamic Adjustment Prcess', *Bell Journal of Economics*, 11, Spring, pp. 360–72.

SAPPINGTON, D. (1983) 'Optimal Regulation of a Multiproduct Monopoly with Unknown Technological Capabilities', *Bell Journal of Economics*, 14, Autumn, pp. 453–63.

SCHERER, F. M. (1970) *Market Structure and Economic Performance* (Chicago, Ill., Rand McNally).

SCHILLER, P. (1945a) *Technical Report R/7106: Methods of Allocating to Classes of Consumers or Load the Demand Related Portion of the Standing Costs of Electricity Supply* (London, British Electrical and Allied Industries).

SCHILLER, P. (1945b) *Technical Report K/T109: An Improved Method for Allocating the Demand Related Portion of the Standing Cost of Electricity Supply* (London, British Electrical and Allied Industries).

SCHLENGER, D. L. (1983) 'Developing Water Utility Costs Estimates incorporating Spacial Factors', *Proceedings of Symposium on Cost Estimates for Water Supply Policy Studies* (Vicksberg, Miss., Environmental Laboratory, US Army Engineers Waterways Experimental Station).

SCHMALENSEE, R. (1971) *The Control of Natural Monopoly* (Lexington, Mass., Lexington Books).

SCHMALENSEE, R. (1979) *The Control of Natural Monopolies* (Lexington, Mass., Lexington Books).

SHARKEY, W. W. (1979) 'A Decentralized Method for Utility Regulation: a Comment', *Journal of Law and Economics*, 22, October, pp. 74–5.

SHARKEY, W. W. (1982) *The Theory of Natural Monopoly* (New York, Cambridge University Press).

SHERMAN, R. (1974) *The Economics of Industry* (Boston, Mass., Little Brown).

SHERMAN, R. (1977) 'Financial Aspects of Rate of Return Regulation', *Southern Economic Journal*, 44, 2, October, pp. 240–48.

SHERMAN, R. and VISSCHER, M. L. (1978) 'Second Best Pricing with Stochastic Demand', *American Economic Review*, 68, 1, March, pp. 41–53.

SHESHINSKI, E. (1971) 'Welfare Aspects of a Regulatory Constraint: Note', *American Economic Review*, 61, March, pp. 175–78.

SILBERBERG, E. (1978) *The Structure of Economics: a Mathematical Analysis* (New York, McGraw-Hill).

SIMON, H. A. (1961) *Administrative Behavior* (New York, Macmillan).

SMITHSON, C. W. (1978) 'The Degree of Regulation and the Monopoly Firm, Further Empirical Evidence', *Southern Economic Journal*, 44, 3, January, pp. 568–80.

SPANN, R. M. (1974) 'Rate of Return Regulation and Efficiency in Production: An Empirical Test of the Averch–Johnson Thesis', *Bell Journal of Economics*, 5, Spring, pp. 38–52.

SQUIRE, L. (1973) 'Some Aspects of Optimal Pricing for Telecommunications', *Bell Journal of Economics*, 4, Autumn, pp. 515–25.

STEINER, P. O. (1957) 'Peak Loads and Efficiency Pricing', *Quarterly Journal of Economics*, 71, November, pp. 585–610.

STIGLER, G. J. (1971) 'The Economic Theory of Regulation', *Bell Journal of Economics*, 2, Spring, pp. 3–21.

SUDIT, E. F. (1979) 'Automatic Rate Adjustment Based on Total Factor Productivity in Public Utility Regulation', in CREW (ed.) (1979).

TAKAYAMA, A. (1969) 'Behavior of the Firm under Regulatory Constraint', *American Economic Review*, 59, June, pp. 255–60.

TEECE, D. J. (1980) 'Economies of Scope and the Scope of the Enterprise', *Journal of Economic Behavior and Organization*, 1, pp. 223–47.

TELSER, L. G. (1969) 'On the Regulation of Industry: a Note', *Journal of Political Economy*, 79, November/December, pp. 937–52.

TELSON, M. (1975) 'The Economics of Alternative Levels of Reliability for Electric Power Generation Systems', *Bell Journal of Economics*, 6, Autumn, pp. 679–94.

TULLOCK, G. (1967) 'The Welfare Costs of Tariffs, Monopolies, and Theft', *Western Economic Journal*, 5, June, pp. 224–32.

TULLOCK, G. (1975) 'The Transitional Gains Trap', *Bell Journal of Economics*, 6, Autumn, pp. 671–678.

TURVEY, R. (ed.) (1968a) *Public Enterprise* (Harmondsworth, Penguin).

TURVEY, R. (1968b) *Optimal Pricing and Investment in Electricity Supply: An Essay in Applied Welfare Economics* (London, Allen and Unwin).

TURVEY, R. (1969) 'Marginal Cost', *Economic Journal*, 79, June, pp. 282–99.

TURVEY, R. (1970) 'Peak Load Pricing Under Risk: Comment', *American Economic Review*, 60, June.

TURVEY, R. (1971) *Economic Analysis and Public Enterprise* (London, Allen and Unwin).

TYNDALL, D. G. (1951) 'The Relative Merits of Amerage Cost Pricing, Marginal Cost Pricing and Price Discrimination', *Quarterly Journal of Economics*, 56, August, pp. 342–72.

VEALL, M. R. (1983) 'Industrial Electricity Demand and the Hopkinson Rate: an Application of the Extreme Value Distribution', *Bell Journal of Economics*, 14, Autumn, pp. 427–40.

VISSCHER, M. L. (1973) 'Welfare-Maximising Price and Output with Stochastic Demand: Comment', *American Economic Review*, 63, March, pp. 224–29.

VOGELSANG, I. and FINSINGER, J. (1979) 'A Regulatory Adjustment Process for Optimal Pricing by Multiproduct Monopoly Firms', *Bell Journal of Economics*, 10, Spring, pp. 157–71.

WALLACE, R. L. and JUNK, P. E. (1970) 'Economic Inefficiency of Small Municipal Electric Generating Systems', *Land Economics*, 46, November, pp. 98–104.

WENDERS, J. T. (1976) 'Peak Load Pricing in the Electricity Industry', *Bell Journal of Economics*, 7 Spring, pp. 232–41.

WENDERS, J. T. and TAYLOR, L. D. (1976) 'Experiments in Seasonal-Time-of-Day Pricing of Electricity to Residential Users', *Bell Journal of Economics*, 7, Autumn, pp. 531–52.

WESTFIELD, F. M. (1965) 'Conspiracy and Regulation', *American Economic Review*, 55, June, pp. 424–43.

WILLIAMSON, O. E. (1964) *The Economics of Discretionary Behavior: Managerial Objectives in a Theory of the Firm* (Englewood Cliffs, NJ, Prentice-Hall).

WILLIAMSON, O. E. (1966) 'Peak Load Pricing and Optimal Capacity under Contraints', *American Economic Review*, 56, September, pp. 810–27.

WILLIAMSON, O. E. (1967) *The Economics of Discretionary Behavior: Managerial Incentives in the Theory of the Firm* (Chicago, Ill., Markham).

WILLIAMSON, O. E. (1968) 'Economies as an Antitrust Defense: the Welfare Tradeoffs', *American Economic Review*, 58, March, pp. 18–36.

WILLIAMSON, O. E., (1970) *Corporate Control and Business Behavior* (Englewood Cliffs, NJ, Prentice-Hall).

WILLIAMSON, O. E. (1975) *Markets and Hierarchies: Analysis and Antitrust Implications* (New York, NY, Free Press).

WILLIAMSON, O. E. (1976) 'Franchise Bidding for Natural Monopolies – in General and with Respect to CATV', *Bell Journal of Economics*, 7, Spring, pp. 73–104.

WILLIAMSON, O. E. (1979) 'Transactions Cost Economics: the Governance of Contractual Relations', *Journal of Law and Economies*, 22, October, pp. 233–61.

WILLIAMSON, O. E. (1980) 'The Organization of Work: a Comparative Institutional Assessment', *Journal of Economic Behavior and Organization*, 1, pp. 5–38.

WILLIAMSON, O. E. (1983) 'Credible Commitments: Using Hostages to Support Exchange', *American Economic Review*, 75, September, pp. 519–40.

WILLIAMSON, O. E. (1984) 'The Economies of Governance: Framework and Implications', *Journal of Institutional and Theoretical Economics*, 140, March, pp. 195–223.

WILLIG, R. D. (1976) 'Consumer's Surplus Without Apology', *American Economic Review*, 66, 4, September, pp. 589–97.

WILSON, J. Q. (1980) *The Politics of Regulation* (New York, Basic Books).

WISEMAN, J. (1957) 'The Theory of Public Utility Price: An Empty Box', *Oxford Economic Papers*, 9, February, pp. 56–74.

ZAJAC, E. E. (1970) 'A Geometric Treatment of the Averch–Johnson Behavior of the Firm Model', *American Economic Review*, 60, March, pp. 117–25.

ZAJAC, E. E. (1972) 'A Note on "Gold Plating" or "Rate Base Padding" ', *Bell Journal of Economics*, 3, Spring, pp. 311–15.

ZAJAC, E. E. (1978) *Fairness or Efficiency?* (Cambridge, Mass. Ballinger).

ZAJAC, E. E. (1982) 'Toward a Theory of Perceived Economic Justice in Regulation', Bell Laboratories Economic Discussion Paper No. 2335, January.

Index

Acton, J. P.   275
Akerlof, G. A.   28
Alchian, A.   29
  electricity   207
  gas   279
  regulation   148, 149–50, 273
allocative efficiency, 156, 158
alternative governance structures for
  natural monopoly   29–30,
  146–65
  comparative institutional
    assessment   155–63, 165
  description of   151–5
  new institutional
    economics   147–51
Anderson, D. G.   272
anti-trust policy   264–5
Arrow, K.   28, 268
asset specificity   157, 158
Averch, H. and Johnson, L. L.
  electricity   169, 195, 197, 200, 232
  regulation   120–4, 131–2, 150,
    157, 161–2
Axelrod, R.   113, 117

Bailey, E. E.   2, 24, 270
  electricity   195
  peak-load pricing models   53
  regulation   128, 132, 274
Baron, D. P.   142–4
Baumol, W. J.   4, 17, 22, 24, 26, 270
  regulation   154, 270, 273
Bell, A. G. and Bell
  Telephone   164, 210–11
benefit, net   7, 10
  see also sustainability
Besanko, D.   144
Billingsley, P.   272
Blankart, C. B.   275
Boiteux, M.   17, 33–7, 56
Bonbright, J. C.   272
Bös, D.   29, 111
bounded rationality   29
Bradford, D.   17
Bradley, Justice   97

Braeutigam, R.   107–8, 136–7
break-even pricing   16, 17–22
Brown, B. Jr and Johnson, M.
  B.   168
  peak-load pricing models   56–7,
    61, 64, 71–2, 74, 79, 82–3, 87
Buchanan, J. M.   101
Budd v. New York   97
bureaucracies and
  regulation   107–11

cable television   3, 4
capture theories of regulation   105,
  106–7
Carlton, D. W.   57, 73–5, 271, 272
Carne, E. B.   219, 277
Chamberlain, J.   95
Chao, H.   39
Coase, R.   28, 269
cogenerated power (electricity and
  heat)   170, 205–7, 232
Cole, L. P.   136
Comanor, W.   269
Commons, J.   28
comparative institutional
  assessment   155–63, 165
  efficiency ratings   157–63
  simple efficiency criteria   156–7
competition   263
  pseudo-   155, 160–1, 165
consumer
  -related electricity costs   175, 186
  types of   176, 235
costs   49
  electricity   170–5, 186, 205
  fixed, allocating   136–8
  proportional to excess
    demand   70–3
  rationing: and reliability
    constraints   79–80; in
    stochastic models   59–61
  telecommunications   213–19,
    222–3
  water   245–7
  see also pricing; transaction

Crain, W. M. 275
Crawford, R. G. 207, 279
  regulation 148, 149–50, 206
Crew, M. A. 9, 261, 268, 269
  efficiency and equity 12
  electricity 170, 193, 195, 199,
      202, 205, 208, 216, 233
  gas 238, 243–4, 280
  peak-load pricing models 33, 39,
      44–5, 57, 65, 69, 216, 281–2
  regulation: natural
      monopoly 148–9, 152,
      157–9, 160, 162, 163, 203–8,
      280–4; peak-load
      problem 127–8, 130, 217,
      238; productivity and
      incentive 139, 141;
      rate-of-return 113–17, 132–3
  telecommunications 216, 232–3
  water 256
Crocker, K. J. 148, 149
  electricity 170, 205, 208, 276, 277
  gas 240–2, 243–4, 280
  telecommunications 232–3
Cross, J. G. 139, 140–1
cross-subsidy 23, 223

Dansby, R. E. 39, 49, 216
Davis, O. A. 14
De Alessi, L. 161, 275
De Salvia, D. N. 275
demand
  charges *see* tariffs
  for electricity 172, 174–6, 185–6,
      192
  excess 57: costs proportional
      to 70–3
  stochastic 56–8: models of 58–9
  and supply, water 248–51
  time-varying 48–51
  see also peak-load
Demsetz, H. 3, 29, 148, 153
deregulated/unregulated
  gas 237, 242, 243–4
  governance structure 154–5
  heat sales 207–8, 232
  interface with regulated
      businesses 230–4
  regulation and, interface with 279

  structure 158, 161–2
  telecommunications 230–4
  transport 279
  see also regulation
deterministic models of peak-load
      pricing 33–55
  profit maximisation and
      second-best results 52–5
  technology, diverse: multi-period
      pricing 41–8; problems
      of 37–41
  time-varying demand and
      unequal-length
      periods 48–51
deterministic solutions and
      stochastic models 81–2
disembodied reliability
      effects 193–5
distribution
  of electricity 169
  of gas 236–8
  of water 245–6
Douglas, Justice 98
Drèze, J. 56, 270
Dupuit, J. 10
dynamic efficiency 156, 158

economic justice 27, 100
  see also equity
economics, new institutional 28–30,
      147–51, 264–5
economies of scale or scope 3, 5–6
  and electricity 205
  and regulation 93–4, 118, 150
efficiency 8, 14–15, 28, 30
  criteria, simple 156–7
  ratings 157–63
  technology in stochastic
      models 65–7
  see also regulation
El Hodiri, M. 273
electricity 3, 4, 169–209
  Hopkinson and other
      tariffs 185–93
  institutional background 169–81
  peak-load pricing 174, 181–5
  pricing and investment 193–203,
      261
  tar baby effect 203–9

energy *see* power
equity 96–103, 119
  in natural monopoly
    regulation 7, 8–9, 10, 26–8,
      30
Eustis, J. 277
Evans, D. S. 275

fairness 156, 158
  see also equity
Farrell, M. J. 14, 269
Faulhaber, G. R. 6, 270
Feigenbaum, S. 275
Feldstein, M. S. 269
Finsinger, J.
  electricity 188, 192, 276
  regulation 138–9, 152, 158–9
first-order conditions, derivation
  of 282–4
fixed costs, allocating 136–8
fossil fuel
  for electricity generation 170,
    173–4
  see also gas
France 33
  electricity tariffs 179–80
franchise bidding 3, 149, 153, 158,
  161, 162–3
frequency of transactions 30
future research and policy
    implications 263–7
  contestable markets and
    sustainable structures 265–6
  new institutional
    economics 264–5
  potential development
    areas 266–7
  pricing 263–4
  regulated and unregulated
    interface 230–4
  rent seeking 265

gas 3, 4, 235–44
  competition regulation 242–4
  electricity generated from 170,
    173
  institutional background 235–8
  pricing and regulation 236–7,
    238–42, 263–4

generation/production
  of electricity 169–71
  of gas 235–7
  of water 245
Gillette, King A. 228, 277
Glaeser, M. G. 96
Goldberg, V. P. 107, 118, 146,
  149–50, 157, 163
governance structures *see*
    alternative governance, *etc.*
Greene, Judge H. 211–12, 230, 232,
  234

Hamilton, W. D. 117
Hamlen, W. A. Jr 239
Hayak, F. 28
heat generation *see* cogenerated
Henderson, J. M. 269
Hirshleifer, J. 33
holding companies and gas 243–4
Hope case 97–8, 100
Hopkinson, J. and electricity
    tariffs 174–6, 178, 185–6, 188,
      191–3, 239, 275
Hotelling, H. 10, 13, 38, 268, 269,
  270
hydro-electricity 170
Hyman, L. S. 204

incentives 99, 108–11
  regulation 138–44, 151–2
inefficiencies in regulation 101–19
Ineson, J. L. 275–6
institutional economics, new 28–30,
  147–51, 264–6
interruptible tariffs 188, 238–9
investment
  electricity *see* pricing, electricity
  transaction-specificity of 29–30,
    107, 149–50, 206: *see also*
    transaction costs

Jen, R. 239
Johnson, L. L. *see* Averch and
    Johnson
Johnson, M. B. *see* Brown and
    Johnson
Joskow, P. L. 149, 205, 206
Junk, P. E. 275

'just price'   27–8
    see also equity
justice, economic   27, 100
    see also equity

Kafoglis, M. Z.   273
Kahn, A. E.   26
Klein, B.   207
    regulation   148, 149–50
Kleindorfer, P. R.   9, 149
    efficiency and equity   12
    electricity   170, 188, 192, 195,
        199, 202, 208
    gas   238
    peak-load pricing models   *see*
        under Crew
    regulation: natural
        monopoly   149, 152, 157–9,
        160, 162; peak-load
        problem   127–8, 130;
        productivity and
        incentive   139, 141;
        rate-of-return   113–17, 132–3
    water   256, 279
Klevorick, A. K.   273, 274
Knieps, G.   149
Kuhn–Tucker theorem and
    conditions   41, 47, 52, 127,
    191, 197

Lancaster, K. M.   14–15, 17
Leibenstein, H.   8, 15, 147, 162, 268
Leland, H. A.   54
Levinson, C. H.   270
Lewis, W. A.   176
Lindsay, C. M.   107
Lipsey, R. E.   14, 17
Little, I. M. D.   269
load-duration curve,
    electricity   172–4, 181
local telecommunications   *see under*
    pricing, telecommunications
Loeb, M.   138–9, 152, 160
long-distance
    telecommunications   *see under*
    pricing, telecommunications

McCormick, R. E.   112

MacGregor-Reid, G. J.   269
McKie, J. W.   203
Magat, W. A., regulation   138–9,
    152, 160
Manning, W. G. Jr   275
Marchand, M. G.   188
marginal-cost pricing   13–14, 15,
    188
Marino, A.   41
Marshall, A.   10, 11
Mashaw, J.   111, 156
Masten, S. E.   240–2
maximisation, profit   52–5
Meek, R. L.   178
Meyer, R. A.   55, 57, 79, 275
milk, sale of   97
Mishan, E. J.   13, 268
Mitchell, B. M.   216, 275
monopoly, natural   *see* alternative
    governance; natural monopoly
monopoly regulations, models
    of   120–45
    Averch–Johnson result   121–4,
        131
    peak-load problem   124–30
    price structure: fixed costs
        allocation   136–8
    productivity and incentive
        regulation   138–44
    rate of return: and stochastic
        demand   130–2; and welfare
        implications   132–6
monopoly regulations (USA),
    origins of   93–105
Moore, J. G.   275
multi-period pricing   *see under*
    technology, diverse
multiproduct utilities   4, 5, 6, 7, 22
Munn v. *Illinois*   96–7
Myerson, R.   142–4

natural monopoly   3
    defining   4–7
    in equity regulation   7, 8–9, 10,
        26–8, 30
    second-best problem and   13–22
    sustainability of   5–7, 10, 22–6
    see also alternative governance;
        monopoly

'natural price' 96
Nebbia v. *New York* 97
needle-peaking, avoiding 187
Nelson, J. R. 185, 270
  neo-classical models 146–7
  see also monopoly regulations,
    models
  net benefit 7, 10
  see also sustainability
New Jersey water problem 103–4,
    113, 118, 159
new institutional economics 28–30,
    147–51, 264–5
Ng, T. K. 54, 269
Nguyen, D. T. 269
Niskanen, W. A. 107, 111
Nozick, R. 270
nuclear power 170, 173–4, 203–4

Oi, W. Y. 22, 54
Okun, A. M. 27, 29
opportunities 29
optimal
  capacity in stochastic
    models 65–7
  plant mix 44–5
  practice 45–8
optimality conditions in stochastic
    models 62–5
Owen, B. M. 107–8

Palay, T. A. 148, 163, 270
Panzar, J. C. 23, 26, 268
  electricity 188
  peak-load pricing models 39, 41
  regulation 154
peak-load
  pricing in electricity
    industry 174, 181–5: *see
    also* deterministic models;
    stochastic models
  problems: gas 238–40; and
    regulation 124–30;
    telecommunications 217
  see also demand
peaks in electricity demand 187–93
Peles, T. C. 274
Peltzman, S. 106

Pescatrice, D. R. 161, 275
Phillips, A. 20, 26, 268
  electricity 275
  regulation 161
  telecommunications 231
Phillips, C. F. Jr 100
pipelines *see* transmission, gas
plant mix, optimal 44–5
policy implications *see* future
    research
Posner, R. A. regulation 105–6,
    107, 146, 154, 272
Postlewaite, A. W. 270
power supplies *see* electricity; gas;
    nuclear
practice, optimal 45–8
Pressman, I. 13, 38, 39, 52
price
  control 156, 158
  'just' 27–8
pricing
  break-even 16, 17–22
  electricity 193–203, 275–7:
    disembodied reliability
    effects 193–5;
    examples 200–3;
    peak-load 174, 181–5;
    technology choice and
    reliability 195–200
  future research and policy
    implications 261–2
  gas industry 236–7, 238–42
  marginal-cost 13–14, 15, 188
  regulation, allocating fixed
    costs 136–8
  second best 77–9
  telecommunications 211, 213–25:
    local service 211, 212,
    215–19; long distance 211,
    212, 219–25, 278
  under uncertainty, stochastic
    models of 58–70
  water supply 246: technology
    and 245–7
  see also costs
principal–agent model 108–11
prisoner's dilemma model 116, 117
'private-interest' theories of
    regulation 105–6

production
  costs, stochastic models of 59
  see also costs: generation
productivity regulation 138–44
profits
  maximisation 52–5
  rationing and reliability 70–80
pseudo-competition 155, 160–1,
  165
public enterprise 152–3, 158, 161
public utilities *see* industries;
  peak-load; pricing; regulation;
  welfare economic foundations
public-interest theories of
  regulation 105

quality issues and electricity 193
quasi-rents 150

Ramsey, F. P. and pricing 17–20,
  26, 99, 120, 136–40, 215, 225,
  228–30, 264–70
random rationing 73–7
rate of return regulation
  efficiency 157–60
  electricity 193–5, 203
  stochastic demand and 130–2
  in USA 16–17, 98–9, 103,
    111–18
  and water 260
  welfare implications 132–6
rationality, bounded 29
rationing
  costs in stochastic models 59–61
  reliability and profits 70–80
Rawls, J. 27
Rees, R. 269
regulation 7, 9, 151
  electricity: pricing and
    investment 193–203; tar
    baby effect 203–9
  gas industry 236:
    competition 242–4; pricing
    and 236–7, 238–42
  interface with unregulated
    businesses
  natural monopoly, equity
    aspects 7, 8–9, 10, 26–8, 30

telecommunications 230–4: local
  company and 225–30
water supply 260–1
see also deregulated; public
  utilities reliability
electricity: disembodied
  effects 193–5; technology
  choice and 195–200
  rationing and profits 70–80
rents, quasi- 150
rent-seeking 101–8, 112, 118–19,
  265
reserve deficiency in
  telecommunications 222–3
reserve margin and electricity 202
rights *see* justice
Riley, J. G. 247–8
risk-sharing and electricity
  industry 187
Roberts, G. L. 20
Rowley, C. K. 148

salt, sale of 101
Samuelson, P. A. 28
Sappington, D. 140, 144
scale *see* economies of scale
scale efficiency 156, 158
Scherer, C. R. 247–8
Scherer, F. M. 14
Schlenger, D. L. 246
Schmalensee, R. 26, 149
Scitovsky, T. 268
Scitovsky–Kaldor–Hicks
  criteria 147
scope *see* economies of scale
second best
  and natural monopoly 13–22
  pricing 77–9
  results and profit
    maximisation 52–5
self-regulation 158, 161
Sharkey, W. W. 160, 279
Sherman, R. 14, 78
Sheshinski, E. 128, 132–3
Shughart, W. F. 112
Sibley, D. S. 188
Silberberg, E. 269
Simon, H. A. 29

single-product utilities   4, 5–6
  see also gas; water
social welfare function   11–13
  in stochastic models   58, 61–2
specificity, asset   157, 158
Squire, L.   278
status quo, concern for   100
Stein, J. L.   274
Steiner, P. O.   33–7, 56
stochastic demand and rate of return
  regulation   130–2
stochastic models of peak-load
  pricing   56–89
  demand problems   56–8
  numerical illustrations   80–6
  of pricing under
    uncertainty   58–70
  rationing, reliability and
    profits   70–80
stochastic supply conditions and
  water pricing   246
subadditivity   4, 6
subsidisation, cross-   23
Sudit, E. F.   139, 141, 152, 158–9,
  160
supply and demand
  for water   248–51
  see also peak-load
sustainability   223
  of natural monopoly   5–7, 10,
    22–6
system planning in electricity
  industry   172, 174

Takayama, A.   273
take-or-pay contract and gas   240–2
tarif vert   180–1
tariffs
  electricity   172, 176–93:
    regulation and   193–203
  gas   240–1
  see also pricing
Taylor, L. D.   186
technology
  change: and
    telecommunications   211,
    222; and water   245
  choice and reliability in electricity
    industry   195–200

diverse, and multi-period
  pricing   41–8: optimal plant
    mix   44–5; optimal
    practice   45–8; problems
    of   37–42
  efficient, in stochastic
    models   65–7
  water supply and   245–7
Teece, D. J.   5, 205
Teeples, R.   275
telecommunications   3, 4, 210–34
  background   210–13
  deregulation   163
  model for local regulated
    company   225–30
  pricing   211, 213–25
  pseudo-competition   158, 164
  regulation   94–5, 119: with
    partial deregulation   230–4
Telser, L. G.   163
thermal electricity generation   *see*
  fossil fuel
Three Mile Island nuclear
  accident   203
Tillmann, G.   111
time-varying demand and
  unequal-length periods   48–51
TIT-FOR-TAT   117
Tollison, R. D.   101, 112
transaction costs   8
  analysis   147–50
  of governance   156–60
  of regulation   111–18
transactions   28–30
  frequency of   30
transaction-specific
  investment   29–30, 107,
    149–50, 206
  see also transaction costs
transmission
  of electricity   169, 171–2
  of gas   235–9, 242–3
  of water   145
transport
  deregulated   154, 264
  regulated   111, 119
Trapani, J. M.   161, 275
Tullock, G.   95–6, 101, 103, 112,
  119

Turvey, R. 57, 172, 270
Tyndall, D. G. 269

uncertainty, pricing under 58–70
unequal-length periods and
    time-varying demand 48–51
unit-related electricity costs 175,
    186
United Kingdom
    electricity supply 172, 174–5,
        176–8
    'just price' concept 27
    public enterprises in 152, 162,
        164
    public ownership, arguments
        for 95
    transport 111
United States
    deregulation 154–5, 164
    electricity supply 170, 175,
        176–7, 178, 203–7
    'fair price' concept 28
    regulation, origin and operation
        93–119, 151–3, 161:
        monopoly 93–105;
        operation and incentives
        theories 108–11; origins and
        purpose theories 105–8; rate
        of return 16–17, 98–9, 103,
        111–18
    see also gas; telecommunications;
        water
unregulated *see* deregulated

Vail, T. 28, 94–5
Veall, M. R. 192
vertical disintegration in
    telecommunications 212
vertical integration in
    electricity 207
Visscher, M. L. 57, 73–4, 78, 272
Vogelsang, I. 138–9, 152, 158–9

Wallace, R. L. 275
waste treatment 3
water supply 245–62
    implications 261–2
    New Jersey problem 103–4, 113,
        118, 159

pricing policy for stochastic
    supply 246, 247–60
regulation problems 254–5
technology and effects on
    pricing 245–7
weather and water supply 246–7
Weisser, M. 54
welfare economic foundations
    background 3–9
    efficiency equity aspects 10–30:
        in natural monopoly 26–8;
        new institutional economics
        28–30; second best and
        natural monopoly
        problem 13–22; social
        welfare function 11–13;
        sustainability of natural
        monopoly 22–6;
        implications of rate of return
        regulation 132–6
    optimal break-even pricing 16,
        17–22
Wenders, J. T. 181, 183–6
Westfield, F. M. 273
Whinston, A. B. 14
White, L. J. 53–4
Williamson, O. E. 2
    new institutional economics 28–30
    peak–load pricing models 33, 56
    regulation 8, 272: natural
        monopoly 26, 93, 104,
        146–57 *passim*, 162–3;
        operation and
        incentives 111
Willig, R. D.
    deregulation 154
    efficiency and equity 13, 19, 22,
        24, 26, 268
Wilson, J. Q. 272
Wiseman, J. 269

X-efficiency 8, 15, 28, 99, 138, 156,
    157, 158

Zajac, E. E. 10, 26–7, 224
    regulation 100, 108, 150, 156, 273
Zardkoohi, A. 275
Zimmermann, H. G. 111
'zonal pricing' policy and
    water 246